THE POLITICS OF PRINCIPLE

Under its first chief justice, Arthur Chaskalson, the South African Constitutional Court built an unrivalled reputation in the comparative constitutional law community for technically accomplished and morally enlightened decision-making. At the same time, the Court proved remarkably effective in asserting its institutional role in post-apartheid politics. While each of these accomplishments is noteworthy in its own right, the Court's simultaneous success in legal and political terms demands separate investigation. Drawing on and synthesising various insights from judicial politics and legal theory, this study offers an interdisciplinary explanation for the Chaskalson Court's achievement. Rather than a purely political strategy of the kind modelled by rational choice theorists, the study argues, the Court's achievement is attributable to a series of adjudicative strategies in different areas of law. In combination, these strategies allowed the Court to satisfy institutional norms of public reason-giving while at the same time avoiding political attack.

THEUNIS ROUX is Professor of Law at the University of New South Wales, Sydney, Australia. He is a former Secretary-General of the International Association of Constitutional Law (IACL) and the Founding Director of the South African Institute for Advanced Constitutional, Public, Human Rights and International Law (SAIFAC).

CAMBRIDGE STUDIES IN CONSTITUTIONAL LAW

The aim of this series is to produce leading monographs in constitutional law. All areas of constitutional law and public law fall within the ambit of the series, including human rights and civil liberties law, administrative law, as well as constitutional theory and the history of constitutional law. A wide variety of scholarly approaches is encouraged, with the governing criterion being simply that the work is of interest to an international audience. Thus, works concerned with only one jurisdiction will be included in the series as appropriate, while, at the same time, the series will include works which are explicitly comparative or theoretical – or both. The series editors likewise welcome proposals that work at the intersection of constitutional and international law, or that seek to bridge the gaps between civil law systems, the US, and the common law jurisdictions of the Commonwealth.

Series Editors
David Dyzenhaus
Professor of Law and Philosophy,
University of Toronto, Canada
Adam Tomkins
John Millar Professor of Public Law,
University of Glasgow, UK

Editorial Advisory Board
T. R. S. Allan,
Cambridge, UK
Damian Chalmers,
LSE, UK
Sujit Choudhry,
Toronto, Canada
Monica Claes,
Maastricht, Netherlands
David Cole,
Georgetown, USA
K. D. Ewing,
King's College London, UK
David Feldman,
Cambridge, UK
Cora Hoexter, Witwatersrand,
South Africa
Christoph Moellers,
Goettingen, Germany
Adrienne Stone,
Melbourne, Australia
Adrian Vermeule,
Harvard, USA

THE POLITICS OF PRINCIPLE

The First South African Constitutional Court, 1995–2005

THEUNIS ROUX

CAMBRIDGE
UNIVERSITY PRESS

CAMBRIDGE UNIVERSITY PRESS
Cambridge, New York, Melbourne, Madrid, Cape Town,
Singapore, São Paulo, Delhi, Mexico City

Cambridge University Press
The Edinburgh Building, Cambridge CB2 8RU, UK

Published in the United States of America by Cambridge University Press, New York

www.cambridge.org
Information on this title: www.cambridge.org/9781107013643

© Theunis Roux 2013

First published 2013

Printed and bound in the United Kingdom by the MPG Books Group

A catalogue record for this publication is available from the British Library

Library of Congress Cataloguing in Publication data
Roux, Theunis.
The politics of principle : the first South African Constitutional Court,
1995–2005 / Theunis Roux.
pages cm. – (Cambridge studies in constitutional law ; 6)
Includes bibliographical references.
ISBN 978-1-107-01364-3 (Hardback) – ISBN 978-1-107-61906-7 (Paperback)
1. South Africa. Constitutional Court–History.   2. Constitutional courts–South
Africa–History.   3. Constitutional law–South Africa.   4. South Africa–Politics
and government–History.   I. Title.
KTL2620.R68 2013
347.68′035–dc23
2012036779

ISBN 978-1-107-01364-3 Hardback
ISBN 978-1-107-61906-7 Paperback

For my father,
who taught me how to paint

CONTENTS

ix

ACKNOWLEDGEMENTS

My interest in the politics of judicial review was sparked in 2002 by an invitation to attend a workshop in Bergen, Norway, organised by the Chr. Michelsen Institute. Our host, Siri Gloppen, had gathered together a remarkable group of (then still relatively) young researchers, all with an interest in constitutional courts in new democracies. Up to that point, as a University of Cape Town LLB graduate and Cambridge PhD, I had only ever heard academic lawyers talk about courts, in those reverential tones they use even when delivering the harshest of criticisms. So you can imagine the thrill of listening to the keynote speaker, Martin Shapiro, casually dismiss (not by frontal assault but in passing) the legalist model of judging. I can still picture Professor Shapiro – in physical appearance and destructive effect not unlike Marlon Brando in *The Godfather* – dispatching the latest theorist/family member to fail to understand the rules, the *real* rules, that determine how things work. On the long plane journey back to South Africa I read Siri's PhD thesis and was again struck by the very different way political scientists view courts, and in particular by their focus on the policy outcome of judicial decisions. I was intrigued, but at the same time not entirely convinced, by this new scholarly discourse, and determined to find some way of reconciling the two perspectives that made sense to me.

My first attempt was published in the anthology of papers emerging from the Bergen workshop,[1] and I realise now to my horror that I have spent the last ten years rewriting that piece, developing the argument each time but not deviating fundamentally from my initial insight: that law and politics are best conceived as interacting social systems, each with its own distinctive characteristics and inner logic, but open to influence by the other. For most of those ten years, I was living in South Africa, working first at the Centre for Applied Legal Studies (CALS) and

[1] Siri Gloppen, Robero Gargarella and Elin Skaar (eds.), *Democratization and the Judiciary: The Accountability Function of Courts in New Democracies* (London: Frank Cass, 2002).

then at the South African Institute for Advanced Constitutional, Public, Human Rights and International Law (SAIFAC). SAIFAC was the brainchild of Laurie Ackermann, the Chaskalson Court's leading comparativist and someone with a far-sighted vision for the role of public-law scholarship in the promotion of democracy, not just in South Africa, but on the African continent as a whole. In my four years as Director of SAIFAC, Laurie became a mentor and a friend, and I will be forever grateful to him for giving me the opportunity to assist in making his vision a reality. Laurie and I see the interaction between law and politics very differently, and I fear that he will not like everything in this book, but he is the sort of person who forgives good-faith mistakes and I hope he will do so again in this instance.

During my time at CALS and SAIFAC, I was part of a close-knit community of legal academics whose efforts to support South Africa's constitutional democracy are insufficiently recognised, both by foreign commentators on the Constitutional Court and by some of the judges themselves. One of the central players in this community is Stu Woolman, now the Elizabeth Bradley Chair of Ethics, Governance and Sustainable Development at Wits Business School. Stu's tireless work in editing the leading academic commentary on the Court's case law, *Constitutional Law of South Africa* – much of which he has written himself – gave me the space to indulge my parochial concerns, confident in the knowledge that Stu and his team would leave no judicial sentence unglossed. Stu has also recently completed his own book, *The Selfless Constitution*, and I advise anyone planning on reading this book to go there first before coming back to the work of a mere mortal.

The intellectual stimulation of working in a young constitutional democracy is matched in almost equal measure by the dangers of living in what are by definition uncertain times. In my case, this correlation was borne out in 2008, when three armed men broke into my family's home in Johannesburg, tied up my wife and two young daughters, and ransacked the property, stealing many precious but financially valueless items that had been collected on our travels around the globe. The most painful loss, apart from my children's innocence, was an oil painting given to me by my father, and subsequently re-created by him, at the age of 82, as his contribution to our healing process. It is this painting that adorns the front cover of this book. The tree is a Namaqua fig or 'melkerhout', which has the capacity to grow in the most barren of conditions, seemingly out of pure rock. I have inherited none of my father's artistic skill, but what I know about how to represent the world by leaving some things out, I have learned from him.

The invasion of our home accelerated an already-planned move to Australia, where I was fortunate to be offered a position at the University of New South Wales. UNSW Law Faculty is renowned for its commitment to social justice and its unusually collegiate atmosphere, and in neither respect has its reputation proved unfounded. What I did not anticipate, however, was the Faculty's generosity in allowing me to devote the first three-and-a-half years of my new position to writing what amounts to a lament for the country I left behind. I would like to thank David Dixon, the Dean of the Law Faculty, for his faith in me, and also Brendan Edgeworth, who was Head of School for most of the time during which the book was written, for his consistent support.

One colleague at the Faculty, in particular, has made the transition to life in Australia less painful, and that is Martin Krygier. Martin, as all who meet him quickly appreciate, is that most unfashionable and therefore perennially inspiring of people: a scholar and public intellectual whose mind and academic sensibility were fashioned before the time of key performance indicators and comparative benchmarking. Without Martin's friendship and counsel this book would not have been written. In addition to everything else, Martin, and his wife Julie Hamblin, generously allowed me the use of their rural retreat in Bucketty, north of Sydney, where two of the chapters of this book were written. Martin may not have been able to curb all of my enthusiasms, but whatever is of value in this book I owe to him.

At the end of my first year in Australia, in November 2009, Adrienne Stone invited me to participate in a colloquium at which I presented a very crude version of Chapters 1 and 2. Her colleague at Melbourne Law School, Cheryl Saunders, whom I had gotten to know through the International Association of Constitutional Law (IACL), had earlier been instrumental in convincing UNSW to take a chance on me. I have seen far less of Cheryl in Australia than I did in South Africa, which says much about her peripatetic lifestyle and my contrastingly hermitic one. I regret particularly having to withdraw almost completely from the community of scholars I got to know and admire at the IACL. I hope that the publication of this book will provide some explanation.

In April 2011, I was granted funding by UNSW to take a draft of the first three chapters on a North American road tour. I would like to thank the following people who graciously arranged for me to present seminars at their institutions: Stephen Ellmann at New York Law School, Frank Michelman at Harvard Law School, Wil Waluchow at McMaster University, Sujit Choudhry, who was then still at Toronto Law School, and Tom Ginsburg and Rosalind Dixon at Chicago Law School. I am delighted that Rosalind has since returned to UNSW, her alma mater, to work. She has already raised my game (and forced me to think more quickly on my feet), for which I am grateful.

As this project neared its end in January 2012 and my writing energies were beginning to flag, I was fortunate to secure a two-month fellowship at the Stellenbosch Institute for Advanced Study (STIAS). When I began the fellowship, the book still seemed like an insurmountable hurdle. By its end, I felt that I was in the home straight. I thank André van der Walt for facilitating this opportunity and Hendrik Geyer for hosting me. While in Stellenbosch, Sandy Liebenberg arranged a seminar for me with her postgraduate students that I found stimulating and helpful. On my way back to Australia in February 2012, I presented a draft of Chapter 4 at Wits Law School, hosted by Jonathan Klaaren, and of Chapter 5 at SAIFAC, hosted by my successor as Director, David Bilchitz. Independently of these seminars, I was also fortunate to receive detailed comments on Chapters 4 and 5 from Roger Southall and Martin Chanock respectively.

Rosalind Dixon and Martin Krygier opened their homes for one last discussion of the full manuscript in July 2012. I thank Rosalind, Martin, Andy Durbach, Beth Goldblatt and Ben Golder for taking the time to read and comment on the book on that occasion. They have saved me much (but, I fear, not all) embarrassment. In addition to reading the manuscript and providing helpful advice, my research assistant, Rob Woods, compiled the Bibliography and Table of cases with care and attention. I will eventually forgive him for writing a precociously brilliant LLB research paper in which he applied the conceptual framework developed in this book to explain the Australian High Court's reluctance to enter the rights arena.

Finally, to Stephen and Anthony, whose friendship I deeply cherish, thank you for understanding the reasons behind my physical absence. We will grow old together, but not just yet.

Much of Chapter 6 was previously published in Theunis Roux, 'The Constitutional Value System and Social Values in South Africa' in András Sajó and Renáta Uitz (eds.), *Constitutional Topography: Values and Constitutions* (The Hague: Eleven International Publishing, 2010). One paragraph from Chapter 8 appeared in Theunis Roux, 'The Arbitrariness Vortex: Constitutional Property Law after *FNB*' in Stu Woolman and Michael Bishop (eds.), *Constitutional Conversations* (Pretoria University Press, 2008).

~

Introduction

On 11 October 1996, two and a half years after the end of apartheid, South Africa adopted a Constitution[1] that gave the eleven judges of that country's Constitutional Court the power to strike down any 'law or conduct' they found to be inconsistent with the new supreme law.[2] The circumstances leading up to this constitutional-design choice have been analysed from several different perspectives: by historians interested in the internal dynamics of the constitution-making process,[3] by transitional justice scholars interested in South Africa's attempt to deal with its authoritarian past,[4] and by comparative politics scholars interested in the causes and nature of South Africa's turn to liberal constitutionalism.[5] What has not been so extensively studied, however, is how it came about that a court that was given such a politically awkward and morally contested mandate – one that several mature democracies have been reluctant to give to their courts – was able to carry it out it so successfully. This book aims to fill that gap. In formal terms it is devoted to assessing the performance of the South African Constitutional Court in the first

[1] Constitution of the Republic of South Africa, 1996 ('the 1996 Constitution').

[2] 1996 Constitution, s 2.

[3] See Hassen Ebrahim, *The Soul of a Nation: Constitution-Making in South Africa* (Cape Town: Oxford University Press, 1998); Richard Spitz with Matthew Chaskalson, *The Politics of Transition: A Hidden History of South Africa's Negotiated Settlement* (Oxford: Hart Publishing, 2000).

[4] See, for example, Richard A. Wilson, *The Politics of Truth and Reconciliation in South Africa: Legitimizing the Post-Apartheid State* (Cambridge University Press, 2001).

[5] The two leading accounts of the lessons to be drawn from the South African experience are Heinz Klug, *Constituting Democracy: Law, Globalism and South Africa's Political Reconstruction* (Cambridge University Press, 2000) and Jens Meierhenrich, *The Legacies of Law: Long-Run Consequences of Legal Development in South Africa, 1652–2000* (Cambridge University Press, 2008). South Africa is one of four countries considered in Ran Hirschl, *Towards Juristocracy: The Origins and Consequences of the New Constitutionalism* (Cambridge, MA: Harvard University Press, 2004). There is also a short, but insightful, comparative treatment of South Africa in Tom Ginsburg, *Judicial Review in New Democracies: Constitutional Courts in Asian Cases* (Cambridge University Press, 2003) 55–7.

decade of its existence, from the establishment of the Court under the interim Constitution[6] on 14 February 1995 to the retirement of its first chief justice, Arthur Chaskalson, on 31 May 2005.[7] This time in the life of the Court is thought by many to have been exceptional. Of all the constitutional courts that were established after the end of the Cold War, only the Hungarian Constitutional Court under President László Sólyom comes close to it.[8] The period in question includes such celebrated decisions as *S v. Makwanyane*,[9] on the constitutionality of the death penalty, and the Court's two major social rights decisions, *Grootboom*[10] and *Treatment Action Campaign*.[11] Through these and other decisions, the Court built an unrivalled reputation in the comparative constitutional law community for technically accomplished and morally enlightened decision-making.[12] The judges were fêted on the

---

[6] Constitution of the Republic of South Africa, 1993 ('the interim Constitution'). Following Penelope Andrews and Stephen Ellmann (eds.), *The Post-Apartheid Constitutions: Perspectives on South Africa's Basic Law* (Johannesburg: Witwatersrand University Press, 2001), the 1996 Constitution and the interim Constitution will be collectively referred to as 'the post-apartheid Constitutions'.

[7] Arthur Chaskalson was appointed President of the Court under the interim Constitution in June 1994, but the Court was formally opened by President Nelson Mandela only on 14 February 1995, and heard its first case (*S v. Makwanyane and Another* 1995 (3) SA 391 (CC), 1995 (6) BCLR 665 (CC)) on that day. Its first judgment, *S v. Zuma and Others* 1995 (2) SA 642 (CC), 1995 (4) BCLR 401 (SA)), was delivered on 5 April 1995. Chaskalson's title was changed to that of Chief Justice in November 2001. For simplicity's sake, this book refers throughout to 'Justice Chaskalson'.

[8] Other highly regarded constitutional courts to emerge after the end of the Cold War include the Polish, Israeli, South Korean and Colombian Constitutional Courts. On the record of the Hungarian Constitutional Court, see András Sajó, 'Reading the Invisible Constitution: Judicial Review in Hungary' (1995) 15 *Oxford Journal of Legal Studies* 253; Herman Schwartz, *The Struggle for Constitutional Justice in Post-Communist Europe* (University of Chicago Press, 2000) 75–108; László Sólyom and Georg Brunner (eds.), *Constitutional Judiciary in a New Democracy: The Hungarian Constitutional Court* (Ann Arbor, MI: University of Michigan Press, 2000); Gábor Halmai, 'The Hungarian Approach to Constitutional Review: The End of Activism? The First Decade of the Hungarian Constitutional Court' in Wojciech Sadurski (ed.), *Constitutional Justice, East and West: Democratic Legitimacy and Constitutional Courts in Post-Communist Europe in a Comparative Perspective* (The Hague: Kluwer Law International, 2002) 189–211.

[9] Above, note 7.

[10] *Government of the Republic of South Africa and Others v. Grootboom and Others* 2001 (1) SA 46 (CC), 2000 (11) BCLR 1169 (CC).

[11] *Minister of Health and Others v. Treatment Action Campaign and Others (No 2)* 2002 (5) SA 721 (CC), 2002 (10) BCLR 1033 (CC).

[12] The term 'comparative constitutional law community' will be made to do a lot of work in this study and thus it is worth defining up front. It is used here to mean the transnational community of legal academics, judges and practising lawyers interested in comparing the

international speaking circuit, their decisions cited by fellow judges in new and old democracies, and their jurisprudence written about and analysed in almost universally approving terms by legal academics. At the same time, the Court made remarkable strides in asserting its institutional role in South African politics. What began as a necessary device for the enforcement of a multiparty political pact had, by the time of Justice Chaskalson's departure from office, become a powerful political institution in its own right.

Such a degree of success was not inevitable and therefore demands explanation. In setting itself this task, this study begins by articulating more precisely what the criteria for assessing the performance of a constitutional court should be. Two main sets of criteria are explored: legal and political. These criteria suggest themselves because they capture the common-sense understanding of the Chaskalson Court's achievement. On the one hand, the Court was held in high regard by lawyers – its decisions described as 'extraordinary',[13] 'influential',[14] 'impressive',[15] and generally as having contributed to international understanding of the way a modern liberal-democratic constitution like the South African ought to be interpreted. On the other hand, the Court handed down a number of decisions in politically controversial cases, all of which were enforced, and none of which triggered a debilitating attack on the Court.

If this common-sense understanding of the Chaskalson Court's achievement is correct, the explanation for its success must lie, first, in providing a conceptually rich account of what it means to say that a constitutional court has been successful in legal and political terms and, secondly, in exploring how it came about that the Chaskalson Court was able to achieve success on these two fronts *at the same time*. What is remarkable about the Court's achievement, in other words, is not just that it handed down some very fine decisions, or that it managed to stay out of political trouble, but that it did each of these things without compromising its ability to do the other. The two phenomena, significant

way constitutional courts in different parts of the world go about their work with a view to understanding the general patterns, dynamics, argumentative tropes, constraints and transformative possibilities of this form of judicial practice.

[13] Cass R. Sunstein, *Designing Democracy: What Constitutions Do* (New York, NY: Oxford University Press, 2001).

[14] Ronald Dworkin, 'Response to Overseas Commentators' (2003) 1 *International Journal of Constitutional Law* 651, 651.

[15] Mark S. Kende, 'The Fifth Anniversary of the South African Constitutional Court: In Defense of Judicial Pragmatism' (2002) 26 *Vermont Law Review* 753, 766.

enough in themselves, require an overarching explanation that satisfac-
torily accounts for their co-existence.

Chapter 1 draws on two bodies of literature in an initial attempt to
answer this question: the relatively self-contained field of judicial politics
and the broader and more permeable field of liberal legal theory. The first
body of literature consists mainly of accounts of judicial behaviour in the
United States, but also of some accounts of the performance of constitutional courts in new democracies. Of the three main approaches in this
field, the so-called strategic approach and the historical-institutionalist
approach are the ones most obviously relevant to this study. According to
the first, constitutional judges are politically constrained actors who must
sometimes forgo their policy preferences in order to take account of the
capacity of other political actors to frustrate their decisions. From this
perspective, what constitutional judges need to do is to calibrate their
decisions to the policy preferences of these other political actors. In this
way, constitutional judges can ensure that their decisions are enforced
and that their court's institutional legitimacy is gradually enhanced. On
the historical-institutionalist approach, by contrast, a constitutional
court's success is associated with its capacity to differentiate itself as a
legal actor. Only in this way may a court assert and defend its constitutionally assigned veto role in national politics.

When these two approaches are applied to South Africa, it is clear that
the political dimension of the Chaskalson Court's achievement must be
understood in quite specific terms. As studies by James Gibson and
others have shown,[16] the Court never built much institutional legitimacy
(in the sense of 'diffuse public support'), and thus the kind of success that
the strategic approach posits for a well-functioning constitutional court
eluded it. Nevertheless, measured by its capacity to decide politically
controversial cases and have its decisions enforced, the Court was very
effective. Indeed, the interesting thing about the Chaskalson Court is that
it was able to play its constitutionally assigned veto role from the very
outset, and that it continued to play this role without ever building much
institutional legitimacy.

---

[16] See James L. Gibson and Gregory A. Caldeira, 'Defenders of Democracy? Legitimacy,
Popular Acceptance, and the South African Constitutional Court' (2003) 65 *Journal of
Politics* 1; James L. Gibson, 'The Evolving Legitimacy of the South African Constitutional
Court' in François Du Bois and Antje Du Bois-Pedain (eds.), *Justice and Reconciliation in
Post-Apartheid South Africa* (Cambridge University Press, 2008) 229.

The legal dimension of the Court's achievement must likewise be carefully defined. Although the performance of constitutional courts in legal terms inevitably depends on an evaluation of the Court's decision-making record, the Chaskalson Court's reputation in the comparative constitutional law community is a broader phenomenon than can be captured by any particular normative theory of judicial review. Rather than adopting one of the available theories, therefore, this study develops its own account of the Court's legal-professional reputation. According to this account, the Court's success in legal terms consisted in its ability to satisfy certain widely shared criteria associated with the liberal-legalist ideal of adjudication according to law. Since this aspect of the Court's achievement required it to eschew both ideological and result-oriented decision-making, its simultaneous success in legal and political terms is indeed intriguing and worthy of explanation. In particular, what is remarkable about the Court's achievement is the way in which it was able to give a principled account of the post-apartheid Constitutions without triggering a debilitating attack on its independence. Explaining this achievement requires an interdisciplinary approach that synthesises the insights and methods of judicial politics and liberal legal theory.

Chapter 2 takes the first step in this direction by developing a conceptual framework for assessing the performance of constitutional courts in interdisciplinary law/politics terms. The prerequisite for any such framework, the chapter argues, is a mediating concept that will enable us to examine how constitutional courts manage the sometimes contradictory legal and political influences impacting on them ('the law/politics tension'). Though not ideal in all respects, the best candidate for such a concept is the notion of constraint, which is used by both liberal legal theorists and judicial politics scholars to refer to a particular type of influence on judicial behaviour, disregard for which entails a loss in legal or political terms. Following the discussion in Chapter 1, the constraining influence of law is said to consist in a court's need, on pain of triggering a loss in legal legitimacy, to give principled answers to the questions it is asked to decide. The constraining influence of politics, in turn, is said to consist in the capacity and inclination of major political actors to thwart a court's commitment to principled decision-making by undermining its institutional independence.

By conceiving of the legal and political influences on constitutional adjudication as interacting forms of constraint in this way, it is possible to see how a court's response to one set of constraints may affect its ability to respond to the other. It is also possible to see that the precise interaction between the legal and political constraints impacting on a court will depend on the relative strength of these constraints. Chapter 2 represents this idea in the form of a two-dimensional matrix, the four sectors of which correspond to four ideal types. The first of the four sectors thus represents the typical court in a mature constitutional democracy, which is insulated from political attack by a well-established political culture of respect for judicial independence, but which is at the same time constrained by a strong legal-professional attachment to the ideal of adjudication according to law. The other three sectors of the matrix and their corresponding ideal types are: the court in a new or recently redesigned constitutional democracy, where the legal profession maintains a strong attachment to the ideal of adjudication according to law, but where there is at the same time a weak political culture of respect for judicial independence; the court in a new or fragile constitutional democracy, with no political tradition of respect for judicial independence, and a weakly developed legal-professional attachment to the ideal of adjudication according to law; and the court in a new or fragile constitutional democracy, with no political tradition of respect for judicial independence and a weakly developed legal-professional attachment to the ideal of adjudication according to law, but where fortuitous political circumstances insulate the court from political attack.

When viewed in this way, the performance of a constitutional court may be seen to depend on (a) its position on the matrix at Time T_1 (the start of the analysis marked, say, by the appointment of a new chief justice) and (b) its capacity to manage the legal and political constraints impacting on it from Time T_1 to Time T_2 (the chief justice's retirement). Although factors beyond the court's control will undoubtedly affect its performance, there is reason to think that a constitutional court may be able, not only to manage the law/politics tension from within its particular sector of the matrix, but also to alter its position. In this sense, a successful constitutional court may be thought of as a court that is able to exploit aspects of its political and institutional environment to maintain its position in, or manoeuvre itself towards, the normatively preferred sector of the matrix.

Chapter 3 sets out the methodology used to operationalise this conceptual framework. Mapping the Chaskalson Court's starting position on the matrix at the commencement of its work, the chapter argues, requires a qualitative assessment of various factors, including both the impact of colonialism and apartheid on the development of South African legal-professional culture and the nature and extent of the new democratic

Government's commitment to judicial independence. This broad-brush analysis then needs to be complemented by an analysis of the legal and political constraints impacting on the Court in particular cases. By moving from the general to the particular in this way, any provisional conclusions arrived at after the first stage of the analysis may be tested and refined during the second stage.

Chapters 4 and 5 comprise the first part of this two-stage project. Chapter 4 explores the political context for judicial review from 1995 to 2005, breaking this period up into the Mandela-led racial reconciliation era and the ensuing period of technocratic centralism under President Thabo Mbeki. The nature of the African National Congress's commitment to judicial independence changed during this time, the chapter argues, from a commitment that was initially based on its strategic interest in the Court's capacity to consolidate the transition to democracy to one based on the Court's role in legitimating the ANC's social transformation project. As that project began to falter, and as the moderate wing of the ANC that had supported the constitutional settlement began to lose control of the party, the Court became increasingly exposed to political attack. By the time of Justice Chaskalson's retirement, the fragility of the ANC's support for the Court that was later to surface in the leadership battle between Mbeki and his successor as President, Jacob Zuma, was already apparent.

Turning to the legal constraints impacting on the Court, Chapter 5 assesses a range of factors relevant to the changing nature of South African legal-professional culture's attachment to the ideal of adjudication according to law, including the impact of colonialism and apartheid on the dominant mode of legal reasoning, the necessary and contingent changes to that dominant mode triggered by the adoption of the post-apartheid Constitutions, and the Chaskalson Court judges' legal-professional socialisation. In combination, the chapter argues, these factors suggest that the members of the Chaskalson Court shared a strong judicial ethic of decision-making according to law. At the same time, the transition to a system of rights-based judicial review meant that the Court had to adapt South Africa's fairly formalist mode of legal reasoning to the more substantive methods required to give effect to the post-apartheid Constitutions. This situation was both advantageous and disadvantageous to the Court. On the one hand, giving effect to the post-apartheid Constitutions' textual commitment to substantive legal reasoning provided the Court with clear opportunities to develop flexible, context-sensitive review standards. On the other, the Court could not entirely abandon, at least not immediately, South

African legal-professional culture's attachment to reasoning according to authoritative rules. Understanding the way the Court mediated these competing concerns forms a key part of the overall explanation for its achievement.

In light of these considerations, the conclusion drawn at the end of Chapter 5 is that, for most of the period covered in this study, the Chaskalson Court was relatively strongly constrained by both law and politics. Although initially quite well insulated from the effects of its low public support by the ANC's commitment to judicial independence, the Court became progressively more exposed to political attack as Chaskalson's term as Chief Justice progressed, certainly when compared to courts in mature constitutional democracies. At the same time, a shared judicial ethic of decision-making according to law, supported by a strong legal-professional attachment to the separation of law and politics, exerted a powerful influence on the Court: there was a real sense in which case outcomes, though not absolutely determined by law, needed to be justified by principled reasons that were both internally consistent and also faithful to the text and moral commitments of the post-apartheid Constitutions. The fact that the Court was doubly constrained in this way explains why there was such a degree of international interest in its work and also why the Court's apparent success in negotiating the competing legal and political constraints impacting on it was met with such acclaim.

The remaining chapters examine the Court's decision-making record. Drawing on the earlier theoretical discussion, these chapters deploy the notion of an 'adjudicative strategy' as the main heuristic device for understanding what the Court did. As used here, the term refers to the Court's development of a series of doctrines that responded, on the one hand, to the relatively strong pressure exerted by South African legal-professional culture to decide cases in a principled way and, on the other, to the need to avoid a debilitating attack on its independence.

Chapter 6 begins the analysis by exploring the Chaskalson Court's approach in three cases in which the post-apartheid Constitutions' moral values ran counter to positive morality: *S v. Makwanyane*[17] (on the constitutionality of the death penalty), *Bhe*[18] (on the compatibility of the customary law principle of male primogeniture with the right to

---

[17] 1995 (3) SA 391 (CC), 1995 (6) BCLR 665 (CC).

[18] *Bhe v. Magistrate Khayelitsha; Shibi v. Sithole; South African Human Rights Commission v. President of the RSA* 2005 (1) SA 563 (CC), 2005 (1) BCLR 1 (CC).

equality), and *Fourie*[19] (on same-sex marriage). In all of these cases, the Court was faced with the same basic difficulty: how to enforce the Constitution's moral values against countervailing social values without alienating a significant section of the South African population. On the one hand, close examination of the politics of these cases reveals that this difficulty was not as intractable as it first appeared. Given the ANC's political dominance, the Court was able to exploit differences between the party leadership and the ANC's mass political support base to hand down legally plausible and, in some cases, highly persuasive decisions. On the other hand, the cases illustrate the Court's sensitivity to the long-run consequences of the divergence between the post-apartheid Constitutions' moral vision and positive morality, and therefore to the need to persuade the South African public of the appropriateness of its decisions. The Court attempted to do this, the chapter argues, through a distinctive adjudicative strategy that saw it vindicating the Constitution's moral values, not through an appeal to the framers' intentions, or to an overarching political theory, but by depicting the post-apartheid Constitutions' moral values as the embodiment of South Africans' higher moral aspirations.

Chapter 7, on the Court's social rights jurisprudence, is in many ways the pivotal chapter in the book since it is this aspect of the Court's record that is most contested in the legal-academic literature. By framing the central question as being about the Court's capacity to manage the competing demands of law and politics, the chapter takes issue with those scholars who argue that the Court should have given greater normative content to social rights. Such arguments – while reminding us of what was lost as a matter of principle in cases like *Grootboom*[20] and *Treatment Action Campaign*[21] – do not present a realistic picture of the political constraints under which the Court operated. When those constraints are taken into account, the adoption of the reasonableness review standard emerges as a largely successful strategy on the part of the Court to assert an institutionally sustainable role for itself.

---

[19] *Minister of Home Affairs and Another* v. *Fourie and Another* 2006 (1) SA 524 (CC), 2006 (3) BCLR 355 (CC).
[20] *Government of the Republic of South Africa* v. *Grootboom* 2001 (1) SA 46 (CC), 2000 (11) BCLR 1169 (CC).
[21] *Minister of Health and Others* v. *Treatment Action Campaign and Others (2)* 2002 (5) SA 721 (CC), 2002 (10) BCLR 1075 (CC).

Chapter 8 makes roughly the same argument in relation to the Chaskalson Court's property rights decisions. The leading case in this respect is *First National Bank*,[22] in which the Court announced a flexible, context-sensitive review standard for alleged violations of the constitutional property clause. Indeed, the *First National Bank* case is the paradigmatic example of the way the Court was able to devise a review standard that minimised the risk of its being confronted at some later date with an irreconcilable choice between fidelity to law and the need to safeguard itself from political attack. In another case, *Modderklip*,[23] the Court can be seen to have shifted the doctrinal basis for the decision from property rights, on which the Supreme Court of Appeal's decision had been based, to the right of access to court. Since the order handed down in this case remained essentially unchanged, it is reasonable to suppose that the Chaskalson Court did this to avoid laying down an awkward doctrinal rule that might have restricted its room for manoeuvre in later cases.

The Chaskalson Court's political rights jurisprudence is perhaps the most disappointing aspect of its record, in the sense that it failed to work out a convincing institutional role for itself. Its decision in the *United Democratic Movement* case, for example,[24] has been widely criticised for relying on a thin conception of democracy inadequate to the task of ensuring that the ANC did not abuse its dominant position in South African politics. Chapter 9 largely endorses this critique, and argues that the Court's rather deferential review standard in this case, as well as the *New National Party* case,[25] misconstrued the contribution a robust political rights jurisprudence might have made to the Court's long-term institutional independence.

Chapter 10 deals with three cross-cutting issues – the Court's separation of powers doctrine, its decisions on access and jurisdiction, and purely rhetorical strategies. The first two issues are important in the

---

[22] *First National Bank of SA t/a Wesbank* v. *Commissioner for the South African Revenue Services and Another; First National Bank of SA t/a Wesbank* v. *Minister of Finance* 2002 (4) SA 768 (CC), 2002 (7) BCLR 702 (CC).

[23] *President of the RSA and Another* v. *Modderklip Boerdery (Pty) Ltd* 2005 (5) SA 3 (CC), 2005 (8) BCLR 786 (CC).

[24] *United Democratic Movement* v. *President of the Republic of South Africa and Others (African Christian Democratic Party and Others Intervening; Institute for Democracy and Another as* Amici Curiae*) (No 1)* 2003 (1) SA 488 (CC), 2002 (11) BCLR 1179 (CC).

[25] *New National Party of South Africa* v. *Government of the Republic of South Africa and Others* 1999 (3) SA 191 (CC), 1999 (5) BCLR 489 (CC).

following way: Had the Court's separation of powers doctrine been determinate, in the sense that its decisions to defer to the political branches could all have been explained as a consistent application of this doctrine, this study's reliance on the notion of 'adjudicative strategy' would have been greatly undermined. As it turns out, close examination of this aspect of the Court's case law reveals two mutually incompatible versions of its separation of powers doctrine: a version in which the enforcement of a clearly articulated constitutional right is always justified, however much such enforcement requires the Court to intrude into the political branches' sphere of operation, and a version in which the fact that the enforcement of a right requires the Court to intrude into the political branches' sphere of operation becomes a reason to lower the review standard in respect of the right. Far from undermining the argument about the Court's approach to the interpretation of its mandate, this conclusion suggests that its separation of powers doctrine was an integral part of it. Likewise, the Court's jurisprudence on access and jurisdiction illustrates how it was able to control the flow of cases through its docket and ensure that the politics of each case was apparent by the time it came to decide it.

The last part of Chapter 10 focuses on the purely rhetorical strategies deployed by the Court to manage its relationship with the political branches. In *Treatment Action Campaign*,[26] for example, the Court was careful to praise the Government's anti-retroviral programme before finding constitutional fault with it. In other cases, doctrinally redundant passages may be seen to have played an important part in the Court's evocation of the spirit of the post-apartheid Constitutions. As with its decisions on positive morality and property rights, the Court's strategy in these cases appears to have been to articulate a particular moral sensibility rather than to develop a philosophically rigorous account of the constitutional value system.

The Conclusion returns to the conceptual framework developed in Chapter 2 to summarise the way the Chaskalson Court negotiated the law/politics tension to avoid political attack. The book then fast-forwards to the present and reflects on whether the changed political context in which the Court now finds itself requires adjustment to some of its established doctrines.

---

[26] *Minister of Health and Others* v. *Treatment Action Campaign and Others (2)* 2002 (5) SA 721 (CC), 2002 (10) BCLR 1075 (CC).

PART I

Problematic, Theory, Methodology

The Chaskalson Court's achievement

There is something quite intriguing, the Introduction to this study has argued, about the way the Chaskalson Court responded to its mandate under the post-apartheid Constitutions. Not only did the Court build a strong legal-professional reputation. It was also remarkably effective in asserting its institutional role in South African politics. Explaining this achievement requires a particular kind of interdisciplinary study, one that synthesises the conceptual frameworks and methods of judicial politics and liberal legal theory.

The purpose of this chapter is to examine this claim more closely: to clarify the nature of the Court's success in legal and political terms and to show why its achievement might be best explained by means of an interdisciplinary study of the sort proposed. To do this, we will need to give a positive answer to three questions: (1) Do judicial politics scholars and liberal legal theorists really conceive of the success of constitutional courts in significantly different terms? (2) If they do, was the Chaskalson Court indeed successful according to the criteria applied by each field? (3) If it was, is there something about this combined achievement that neither field on its own can adequately explain?

The first section sets out the three main approaches currently being pursued in judicial politics and discusses their suitability, on the one hand, to interdisciplinary research and, on the other, to application outside the United States. The second section draws out the criteria that the three judicial politics approaches use to assess the performance of constitutional courts. Although there has been some work on this topic already, the discussion clarifies several points that are only implicit in the literature. The third section examines the main features of the Chaskalson Court's performance in political terms and finds that it was indeed successful according to criteria that judicial politics scholars regard as significant. While the Court never built much institutional legitimacy, it was able to decide a range of politically controversial cases and have these decisions enforced. It was also able to act as a forum for public impact litigation and for contestation over the design of South Africa's electoral system. All of these aspects of its record suggest that it was able effectively to assert its veto role in South African politics without compromising its institutional independence.

Given the extent of disagreement in normative constitutional theory over the criteria for assessing the performance of constitutional courts, the second half of the chapter takes a slightly different tack. It begins by analysing comments made by four prominent American legal theorists on the Chaskalson Court's record, two of them liberal legalists and the other two members of the Critical Legal School. Despite their different normative commitments, the chapter argues, there is a surprising degree of overlap between the standards applied by these theorists when assessing the Court's record. All four theorists thus appreciated the technical skill with which the Court went about answering the questions put to it. They also were impressed by the Court's capacity to give morally persuasive reasons for its decisions, particularly in relation to socio-economic rights. What separates the four is disagreement over the Court's tendency to present its decisions as legally constrained, with one of the critical legal theorists strongly decrying this rhetorical posture and the two liberal legalists appreciating the Court's capacity to justify its institutional role in this way, especially given the awkwardness of its mandate. If these views are representative, the chapter argues, the Chaskalson Court's reputation in the comparative constitutional law community must have had something to do with the technical quality and moral persuasiveness of its decision-making record, together with its ability to satisfy certain shared criteria associated with the liberal-legalist ideal of adjudication according to law.

The rest of the chapter proceeds on this basis, working its way from a discussion of the common elements of the Dworkinian and legal positivist conceptions of this ideal to an account of the shared criteria likely informing the Court's reputation: (1) the adoption of an adjudicatory style appropriate to the enforcement of a rights-based constitution; (2) the elaboration, either on a case-by-case basis or by means of a more fully developed political theory, of a morally persuasive account of the content of constitutional rights and the review standards according to which they should be enforced; and (3) the articulation of a defensible understanding of the Court's institutional function within the separation of powers.

These criteria, the final section argues, are not unrelated to the criteria applied by judicial politics scholars: the Chaskalson Court's ability to assert its veto role in South African politics was thus crucially dependent on its capacity to develop a principled understanding of its mandate. The demands made on constitutional judges by the two sets of criteria are nevertheless in tension. In politically controversial cases, liberal legalists insist, constitutional judges' duty to do justice according to law means that they must disregard the likely institutional consequences of their decision. For judicial politics scholars, on the other hand, such cases are precisely when constitutional judges need to think about the impact of their decision on their court's capacity to perform its institutional role. Given this tension, there *is* something worth investigating about the Chaskalson Court's achievement, and moreover something that an interdisciplinary study of the kind proposed here is best able to explore.

1.1   Judicial politics: a brief introduction

The field of judicial politics,[1] like political science generally, is dominated by scholars working in and on the United States. There has, however, been a long tradition of using methods and models first developed by American scholars to study courts in other countries.[2] After 1989, and the third wave of democratisation, increasing attention has been paid to the role of courts in Latin America, Asia and Eastern Europe.[3] In this comparative form, the main preoccupations of the field have been the political foundations of judicial independence and the role of courts in the consolidation of democracy and the

---

[1] The field is also known as 'public law' or 'law and courts'. For a full intellectual history, see Nancy Maveety, 'The Study of Judicial Behavior and the Discipline of Political Science' in Nancy Maveety (ed.), *The Pioneers of Judicial Behavior* (Ann Arbor, MI: University of Michigan Press, 2003) 1.

[2] See C. Neal Tate, 'The Literature of Comparative Judicial Politics: A 118 Year Survey' (2002) 12(2) *Law & Courts* 3 and (2002) 12(3) *Law & Courts* 3 (updated version available at http://sitemason.vanderbilt.edu/site/d5YnT2/home); Alec Stone Sweet, *Governing with Judges: Constitutional Politics in Europe* (Oxford University Press, 2000); John Ferejohn, Frances Rosenbluth and Charles Shipan, 'Comparative Judicial Politics' in Charles Boix and Susan C. Stokes (eds.), *The Oxford Handbook of Comparative Politics* (Oxford University Press, 2009) 727.

[3] See, for example, Irwin P. Stotzky (ed.), *Transition to Democracy in Latin America: The Role of the Judiciary* (Baltimore, MD: Johns Hopkins University Press, 1993); Wojciech Sadurski, *Rights Before Courts: A Study of Constitutional Courts in Postcommunist States of Central and Eastern Europe* (Dordrecht: Springer, 2005); Ginsburg, *Judicial Review in New Democracies*.

establishment of the rule of law.[4] Historically, very little work has been done on courts in Africa,[5] although courts in South Africa, both before and after the end of apartheid, have been the subject of some studies.[6]

In the United States, the field has developed in three stages that have produced three main approaches, all of which are still in use today. Starting in 1948, with the publication of Herman Pritchett's study of the Roosevelt Court,[7] political scientists took up the legal realist challenge of proving, by means of empirically testable hypotheses, that judges decide cases according to their 'sincere policy preferences'.[8] The standard method used was to classify the judges of a particular court as being

[4] See J. Mark Ramseyer, 'The Puzzling (In)dependence of Courts: A Comparative Approach (1994) 23 *Journal of Legal Studies* 721; Barry Weingast, 'The Political Foundations of Democracy and the Rule of Law' (1997) 91 *American Political Science Review* 245; Matthew C. Stephenson, '"When the Devil Turns": The Political Foundations of Independent Judicial Review' (2003) 32 *Journal of Legal Studies* 59; Stephen Holmes, 'Lineages of the Rule of Law' in José María Maravall and Adam Przeworski (eds.), *Democracy and the Rule of Law* (Cambridge University Press, 2003) 19; Stephen Holmes, 'Judicial Independence as Ambiguous Reality and Insidious Illusion' in Ronald Dworkin (ed.), *From Liberal Values to Democratic Transition: Essays in Honor of János Kis* (Budapest: Central European University Press, 2004) 3; Georg Vanberg, 'Establishing and Maintaining Judicial Independence' in Keith E. Whittington, R. Daniel Kelemen and Gregory A. Caldeira (eds.), *The Oxford Handbook of Law and Politics* (Oxford University Press, 2008) 99; Rebecca Bill Chavez, 'The Rule of Law and Courts in Democratizing Regimes' in Keith E. Whittington, R. Daniel Kelemen and Gregory A. Caldeira (eds.), *The Oxford Handbook of Law and Politics* 63.

[5] One exception to this general rule is Jennifer Widner, *Building the Rule of Law: Francis Nyalali and the Road to Judicial Independence in Africa* (New York, NY: W. W. Norton, 2001). See also Jennifer Widner, 'Courts and Democracy in Postconflict Transitions: A Social Scientist's Perspective on the African Case' (2001) 95 *American Journal of International Law* 64; Tamir Moustafa, 'Law Versus the State: The Judicialization of Politics in Egypt' (2003) 28 *Law & Social Inquiry* 883.

[6] See, for example, Stacia L. Haynie, *Judging in Black and White: Decision Making in the South African Appellate Division, 1950–1990* (New York, NY: Peter Lang, 2003).

[7] C. Herman Pritchett, *The Roosevelt Court: A Study in Judicial Politics and Values, 1937–1947* (New York. NY: Macmillan, 1948). See also the work done by Martin Shapiro under the rubric of 'political jurisprudence': Martin Shapiro, *Law and Politics in the Supreme Court: New Approaches to Political Jurisprudence* (New York. NY: Free Press, 1964); Martin Shapiro, 'Political Jurisprudence' (1964) 52 *Kentucky Law Review* 294; Martin Shapiro, 'Whither Political Jurisprudence: A Symposium' (1984) 36 *Western Political Quarterly* 533; Martin Shapiro, 'Morality and the Politics of Judging' (1989) 63 *Tulane Law Review* 1555.

[8] The term 'sincere' here simply means 'personal' rather than 'genuinely felt'. It is used to describe the policy preferences that judges who are unconstrained by law or other institutions are able to assert. See Jeffrey A. Segal and Harold J. Spaeth, *The Supreme Court and the Attitudinal Model Revisited* (New York, NY: Cambridge University Press, 2002) 92–3.

either liberal or conservative and then to correlate judicial votes cast in non-unanimous decisions against the ideologically coded outcome of each case.[9] Proceeding in this way, proponents of this method claimed to be able to 'predict' the outcome of US Supreme Court cases.[10] In one well-known study, for example, it was claimed that the method accurately explained 76 per cent of the votes cast in US Supreme Court search and seizure cases from 1962 to 1998.[11] The main explanation offered for these results was that the justices of the US Supreme Court, having been appointed for life with final decision-making power over the content of their docket and the policy outcome of cases, were unconstrained political actors, capable of deciding cases in line with their private political views.[12] 'Simply put,' the two leading proponents of this approach claimed, 'Rehnquist votes the way he does because he is extremely conservative; Marshall voted the way he did because he is extremely liberal.'[13]

The attitudinal model of judicial decision-making, as this approach came to be known, has certain obvious limitations.[14] For the moment, however, it is important to note what its main features are. As a general type of approach the model is behaviouralist in as much as it uses statistical and other quantitative measures to understand how judges respond to the stimuli of their decision-making environment. The model does not ignore broader social, political and economic processes, but reduces these processes to their influence on judicial ideology. Although the immediate impetus behind the development of the attitudinal model was the challenge posed by legal realism and, in particular, the seeming confirmation of the importance of judicial ideology at the end of the *Lochner* era,[15] the emergence of this model may also be understood as a

---

[9] See, for example, Glendon Schubert, *The Judicial Mind: The Attitudes and Ideologies of Supreme Court Justices, 1946–1963* (Evanston, IL: Northwestern University Press, 1965) and Glendon Schubert, *Judicial Policy Making: The Political Role of the Courts* (Glenview, IL: Scott, Foresman, 1974).

[10] The scare quotes are intended to indicate that the predictions were in fact tested against *ex post facto* assessments of decided cases.

[11] Segal and Spaeth, *The Supreme Court and the Attitudinal Model Revisited* 316–20.

[12] Ibid. 92–3.   [13] Ibid. 86.

[14] See Barry Friedman, 'Taking Law Seriously' (2006) 4 *Perspectives on Politics* 261; Frank B. Cross, 'Political Science and the New Legal Realism: A Case of Unfortunate Interdisciplinary Ignorance' (1997) 92 *Northwestern University Law Review* 251, 285–309.

[15] See Barry Friedman, 'The History of the Countermajoritarian Difficulty, Part Four: Law's Politics' (2000) 148 *University of Pennsylvania Law Review* 971, 974.

logical extension to the study of judicial decision-making of broader developments in the social sciences.[16]

The second important feature of the attitudinal model is that it has proved most powerful when applied to explain voting behaviour on the U.S. Supreme Court. Studies of circuit and trial court voting behaviour tend to indicate that legal norms, in the form of precedent and respect for the plain meaning of statutes, are an important determinant of decision-making.[17] In this respect, the attitudinal model conforms to what is known in analytic legal philosophy as 'the selection effect', i.e. the tendency of appellate courts to deal with a higher proportion of hard cases.[18] In addition, although it has been applied in other countries,[19] the attitudinal model is most easily applied in a legal system like the American, where federal judges are appointed by one of two main political parties, and where it is accordingly possible to use the party of the appointing President as a proxy for judicial ideology.[20] The applicability of the model in circumstances where this is not the case, or where judges' tenure and remuneration is not secure, has not been established. By the same token, however, the attitudinal model, by making the independence of judges from external political control a precondition for its application, draws attention to the need to analyse the political context for judicial review when studying courts in other countries.

---

[16] Keith E. Whittington, 'Once More unto the Breach: PostBehavioralist Approaches to Judicial Politics' (2000) 25 *Law & Social Inquiry* 601, 601.

[17] See Lawrence Baum, *The Puzzle of Judicial Behavior* (Ann Arbor, MI: University of Michigan Press, 1997) 23–56 (suggesting a 'pyramid metaphor' to describe the way judges' goals in the United States are more varied the lower down the court hierarchy one goes); Frank B. Cross, *Decision Making in the U.S. Courts of Appeals* (Stanford University Press, 2007) (showing only slight ideological influence on circuit court voting behaviour).

[18] For the relevant citations see Frederick Schauer, *Thinking Like a Lawyer* (Cambridge, MA: Harvard University Press, 2009) 31, n17.

[19] See, for example, Glendon A. Schubert, 'The Dimensions of Decisional Response: Opinion and Voting Behavior of the Australian High Court' in Joel Grossmann and Joseph Tanenhaus (eds.), *The Frontiers of Judicial Research* (New York, NY: Wiley, 1968) and Glendon A. Schubert, 'Two Causal Models of Decision-Making by the High Court of Australia' in Glendon Schubert and David J. Danelski (eds.), *Comparative Judicial Behavior: Cross-Cultural Studies of Political Decision-Making in the East and West* (New York, NY: Oxford University Press, 1969) 335.

[20] There are obviously certain problems with using the party of the appointing President as a proxy for ideology, but these problems may be mitigated to a certain extent by resort to judicial biography.

The main point of contention between the attitudinal model and the so-called 'strategic model' that came to challenge it in the 1990s[21] is precisely this issue, i.e. the extent to which the justices of the US Supreme Court are correctly conceived as politically unconstrained actors. Like the attitudinal model, the origins of the strategic model can be traced to broader developments in the social sciences – in this case, to the rise of rational choice theory.[22] Although the attitudinal model may also be understood as a particular application of this theory,[23] the central difference between the two models is that the strategic model contends that judicial decision-making is politically constrained in various ways, and that judges, as rational actors, must therefore sometimes forgo their sincere policy preferences in order to achieve an outcome as close as possible to their preferred policy.

The first and most important source of constraint on judicial decision-making is the need to secure majority support for an opinion.[24] When faced with a choice between asserting a sincere policy preference in a dissenting opinion and joining a majority opinion that secures an outcome as close as possible to their preferred policy, rational judges are likely to choose the latter option. Extrapolating from this paradigm case, proponents of the strategic model point to other aspects of the institutional and political context that might constrain judicial behaviour, including internal court rules (such as the rule that the vote of four justices is required for a grant of certiorari by the US Supreme Court),[25] 'intrabranch'[26] factors (relationships with judges higher up or lower down the judicial hierarchy), 'interbranch' factors

---

[21] The strategic approach originates in Walter Murphy, *Elements of Judicial Strategy* (Chicago, IL: University of Chicago Press, 1964), but Murphy's work was initially not very influential because it used qualitative rather than quantitative methods. See Lee Epstein and Jack Knight, *The Choices Justices Make* (Washington, DC: Congressional Quarterly, 1998) xi–xii.

[22] See Lee Epstein and Jack Knight, 'Toward a Strategic Revolution in Judicial Politics: A Look Back, a Look Ahead' (2000) 53 *Political Research Quarterly* 625.

[23] See Cross, 'Political Science and the New Legal Realism' 265 (arguing that the attitudinal model may be understood as an application of rational choice theory to the situation where the agent's calculations about how best to maximise his or her self-interest happen to be unconstrained by other agents' like calculations).

[24] See Murphy, *Elements of Judicial Strategy* 37–90; Epstein and Knight, *The Choices Justices Make* 65–79.

[25] See H. W. Perry, Jr, *Deciding to Decide: Agenda Setting in the United States Supreme Court* (Cambridge, MA: Harvard University Press, 1991).

[26] This term and the categorisation of types of constraint are drawn from Friedman, 'The Politics of Judicial Review' 280 ff.

(the capacity of the legislature or the executive either to frustrate the particular decision or to take steps aimed at punishing the assertion of sincere policy preferences) and, finally, external political factors, such as public opinion. In relation to all of these aspects, proponents of the model argue, the same pattern of strategic voting is likely to occur, and may in fact be detected.

Importantly, most proponents of the strategic model do not regard law as a significant constraint on judicial behaviour.[27] Thus, when proponents of the model argue that judges are institutionally constrained actors, what they mean is that judges must take account of the policy preferences of other political actors, and adjust their decisions, as a matter of policy, to ensure that the final outcome of the case is closest to their preferred position. In some versions of the model, to be sure, law is said to exert a moderate constraining influence in as much as a decision that went beyond the realms of legal plausibility would be open to censure, either by a judge higher up the judicial hierarchy or in the form of critical academic commentary.[28] This possibility is not much explored in the literature, however, and tends to be excluded by the strategic model's focus on the output of a judicial decision (the result in policy terms) at the expense of the reasons for the decision (which is where this kind of influence might be detected).

In its application to interbranch conflict, the behaviour that the strategic model tries to capture is described as a 'separation-of-powers game' in which judges formulate legal rules (seen as policy prescriptions) in such a way as to minimise the possibility that the rule will be overturned by legislation.[29] The relative explanatory power of the attitudinal and strategic models is at its most contested in this respect, with proponents of the first model arguing that, at least in relation to *constitutional* interpretation, the capacity of the political branches to frustrate judicial

---

[27] See Friedman, 'The Politics of Judicial Review' 263: 'Most institutionalists believe the restraint on judges comes not so much from law itself as from the other institutions of government with which constitutional judges necessarily interact.'

[28] Baum, *The Puzzle of Judicial Behavior* 115–19.

[29] See Friedman, 'The Politics of Judicial Review' 308–20; William N. Eskridge, 'Reneging on History? Playing the Court/Congress/President Civil Rights Game' (1991) 79 *California Law Review* 613; William N. Eskridge, 'Overriding Supreme Court Statutory Interpretation Decisions' (1991) 101 *Yale Law Journal* 331; John Ferejohn and Barry Weingast, 'A Positive Theory of Statutory Interpretation' (1992) 12 *International Review of Law & Economics* 263; William N. Eskridge and Philip P. Frickey, 'Law as Equilibrium' (1994) 108 *Harvard Law Review* 26; Jeffrey A. Segal, 'Separation-of-Powers Games in the Positive Theory of Congress and Courts' (1997) 91 *American Political Science Review* 28.

rule-making is minimal.[30] In response, proponents of the strategic model have argued that, even though US Supreme Court decisions are very rarely overturned by constitutional amendment,[31] 'the political branches retain a broad arsenal of weapons to use against a troublesome judiciary'.[32] Such weapons include not only the extreme measures of court-packing and impeachment, but also more moderate measures, such as amendment of the Court's jurisdiction, control of the Court's budget, and delays in implementing the Court's decisions.[33] Whether the political branches actually resort to such measures is in turn said to depend on a range of factors, and ultimately on an assessment of the long-term costs and benefits of undermining the Court's independence in this way.[34]

The fact that the strategic model does not depend on the existence of a particular institutional and political context for judicial review, but instead takes this issue into account as a possible determinant of judicial decision-making, makes this model more easily transferable to other institutional and political contexts, including the situation of constitutional courts in new or fragile democracies. The best-known application of the strategic model in this context is that undertaken by Lee Epstein, Jack Knight and Olga Shevtsova on the circumstances leading up to the temporary suspension of the Russian Constitutional Court by President Boris Yeltsin in 1993.[35] Focusing on the separation-of-powers component of the model, the study argues that the Court's suspension may be attributed to a persistent failure on the part of the Court to respect the 'tolerance interval' for the cases analysed.[36] By this term is meant the restricted range of decisions (construed as positions in 'policy space'[37]) open to a constitutional court, taking into account various factors, including the political branches' policy preferences, the importance of the case to the court, the court's capacity to produce a convincing legal

---

[30] See Friedman, 'The Politics of Judicial Review' 313–16; Epstein and Knight, *The Choices Justices Make* 141; Eskridge and Frickey, 'Law as Equilibrium' 42; Keith E. Whittington, 'Legislative Sanctions and the Strategic Environment of Judicial Review' (2003) 1 *International Journal of Constitutional Law* 446, 449.

[31] The Twenty-Sixth Amendment to the US Constitution, which reduced the voting age to eighteen, effectively overturned the decision in *Oregon* v. *Mitchell* 400 U.S. 112 (1970).

[32] Friedman, 'The Politics of Judicial Review' 313.

[33] Ibid. 324, citing Epstein and Knight, *The Choices Justices Make* 142–3.

[34] Vanberg, 'Establishing and Maintaining Judicial Independence' 99.

[35] Lee Epstein, Jack Knight and Olga Shevtsova, 'The Role of Constitutional Courts in the Establishment and Maintenance of Democratic Systems of Government' (2001) 35 *Law & Society Review* 117.

[36] Ibid. 128.   [37] Ibid.

rationalisation of its decision, public opinion, and the extent of the court's institutional legitimacy.[38] In respect of every case, the study argues, a constitutional court will have a choice between various policy positions, some of which will fall within the tolerance interval and others not. Where a court decides a case outside the tolerance interval, the decision triggers a political 'attack'[39] on the court, which weakens its institutional legitimacy and narrows the tolerance interval in future cases.[40] Conversely, deciding cases within the range ensures that the court's decision will be respected, which in turn enhances its institutional legitimacy.[41] Because institutional legitimacy is both a function of a court's respect for the tolerance interval *and* an aspect of its calculation, strategic decision-making of this kind has the potential to set in motion a virtuous circle in terms of which the tolerance interval becomes progressively wider as the court's institutional legitimacy grows.[42]

All the strengths and weaknesses of the strategic approach are apparent in this study. On the one hand, there is the sheer cleverness of the model, and its capacity to produce not only a convincing explanation of why President Yeltsin suspended the Russian Constitutional Court, but also a general account of how constitutional courts might be able to build and maintain their institutional legitimacy.[43] On the other hand, as with all such models, there is the quasi-scientific elaboration of the explanatory variables beyond a point that could be said to be objectively determinable. To give just one example: not all legal decisions by a constitutional court may be reduced to points along a two-dimensional policy space, and even if they could, the precise positioning of a particular decision is an interpretive question that opens the model up to subjective considerations. Likewise, the political branches' preferred policy positions may themselves be a complex function of internal party politics.[44] Underlying all of this, in turn, may be a changing set of social, political and economic circumstances that are impossible to capture within the variables analysed.

The third approach currently being pursued in judicial politics, the historical-institutionalist approach, may be understood both as a reaction to the scientism of the other two approaches and as a return to the earlier qualitative methods these approaches pushed

---

[38] Ibid. 129–30.   [39] Ibid. 128.   [40] Ibid. 130.   [41] Ibid. 130.   [42] Ibid. 130.
[43] Ibid. 131–2.
[44] Epstein, Knight and Shevtsova acknowledge this difficulty (ibid. 140) and claim to have found various 'objective' measures to support their qualitative analysis in this respect.

aside.[45] Although the historical-institutionalist approach shares the strategic model's concern for the broader institutional and political context in which the practice of judicial review is embedded, institutions are conceived in a very different way.[46] Rather than being seen as the source of constraints on judicial behaviour, historical institutionalists regard institutions, including courts, as historically determined sites of purposive activity.[47] On this approach, institutions do not so much constrain what political actors do as constitute the normative environment in which political actors operate. This change in emphasis is significant since it allows much greater scope for consideration of the way legal norms influence judges. Whereas both the attitudinal and the strategic models tend to reduce law to the policy outcome of a case, historical institutionalists are interested in the way legal norms shape judicial behaviour and determine, if not case outcomes, then at least the distinctive role of courts in national political systems.

In its application to courts, the historical-institutionalist approach is generally regarded as having been launched by the publication in 1999 of two volumes of essays edited by Cornell Clayton and Howard Gillman.[48] These two anthologies contain an eclectic mix of chapters, including some that apply rational choice theory.[49] The common thread linking

---

[45] This account draws on Whittington, 'Once More unto the Breach'; Maveety, 'The Study of Judicial Behavior'; Howard Gillman and Cornell W. Clayton, 'Beyond Judicial Attitudes: Institutional Approaches to Supreme Court Decision-Making' in Cornell W. Clayton and Howard Gillman (eds.), *Supreme Court Decision-Making: New Institutionalist Approaches* (University of Chicago Press, 1999) 1.

[46] The strategic and historical-institutionalist approaches thus both owe their origin to the 'new institutionalism' launched by the publication of J. G. March and J. P. Olsen, 'The New Institutionalism: Organisational Factors in Political Life' (1984) 78 *American Political Science Review* 734. The strategic model, however, is much closer to the attitudinal model in the way it conceives of the primary motivation for judicial behaviour as being judicial ideology. See Rogers M. Smith, 'Historical Institutionalism and the Study of Law' in Whittington et al. (eds.), *The Oxford Handbook of Law and Politics* 46, 47.

[47] Whittington, 'Once More unto the Breach' 628; Maveety, 'The Study of Judicial Behavior' 285.

[48] Clayton and Gillman (eds.), *Supreme Court Decision-Making: New Institutionalist Approaches*; Howard Gillman and Cornell W. Clayton (eds.), *The Supreme Court in American Politics: New Institutionalist Interpretations* (University Press of Kansas, 1999). For a penetrating analysis of the way these books distinguished the historical institutionalist approach from the two behaviouralist approaches, see Whittington, 'Once More unto the Breach'.

[49] See, for example, Jeffrey A. Segal, 'Supreme Court Deference to Congress: An Examination of the Marksist Model' in Cornell W. Clayton and Howard Gillman (eds.), *Supreme*

the chapters is nevertheless a rejection of elaborate model-building and quasi-scientific empiricism in favour of more qualitative approaches. For all the authors in these two volumes, judicial behaviour cannot be understood independently of the longer-term, social and cultural factors that condition judges' perceptions of their institutional role and also other political actors' attitudes to law and courts. In many ways, this makes the sort of research collected in these two volumes hard to distinguish from the socio-legal research that has long been conducted under the auspices of the Law & Society Association.[50] If there is a difference, it lies in the fact that the historical-institutionalist approach tends to focus on courts rather than other forms of social control through law, and, within this, on the role of courts in national political systems.

The historical-institutionalist approach should also not be understood as rejecting the attitudinal and strategic models in their entirety. Proponents of this approach do not, for example, deny that judges, in certain institutional and political settings, may decide cases according to their sincere policy preferences, or that judges may take into account the likely political repercussions of their decisions. They merely argue that a proper understanding of these issues depends on more detailed consideration of judges' interpretive practices.[51] The political role of courts as institutions, in other words, is not seen as the 'aggregate consequences of individual [judicial] behaviour',[52] but as a contextually dependent, and historically determined, phenomenon.[53] As Nancy Maveety puts it, the historical-institutionalist approach takes into account the way 'past actions and institutions constitute the powers and preferences of agents in contemporary politics' and 'seeks to discern patterns of historical evolution and political development that demonstrate that conscious, jurisprudential decisions of judicial actors matter'.[54] It is not surprising, therefore, that the rise of the historical-institutionalist approach has prompted a

---

Court Decision-Making: New Institutionalist Approaches (University of Chicago Press, 1999) 237.

[50] For a useful introduction, see Lynn Mather, 'Law and Society' in Whittington et al. (eds.), *Oxford Handbook of Law and Politics* 681. See also Brian Z. Tamanaha, *Law as a Means to an End: Threat to the Rule of Law* (Cambridge University Press, 2006) 123–6.

[51] See Howard Gillman, 'The Court as an Idea, Not a Building (or a Game): Interpretive Institutionalism and the Analysis of Supreme Court Decision-making' in Clayton and Gillman, *Supreme Court Decision-Making* 65.

[52] Smith, 'Historical Institutionalism and the Study of Law' 47 (quoting March and Olsen, 'The New Institutionalism' 734).

[53] See Whittington, 'Once More unto the Breach' 603.

[54] Maveety, 'The Study of Judicial Behavior' 285.

renewed interest in the possibilities of interdisciplinary research on law and politics and, in particular, in the possibilities of combining legal-doctrinal research with more qualitative analyses of the role of constitutional courts in national political systems.[55]

1.2   Criteria of success in political terms

Notwithstanding renewed interest in the role of legal norms as influences on judicial behaviour, judicial politics is still largely descriptive in character: scholars working in this field are concerned to explain why judges behave the way they do and what the role of constitutional courts in national politics systems is. How judges and constitutional courts ought to behave is generally something that judicial politics scholars leave to other fields. Nevertheless, by scratching under the surface a little, it is possible to identify certain criteria by which judicial politics scholars assess the performance of constitutional courts. These criteria are not strictly speaking normative since they are not related to an ideal conception of the purpose and function of constitutional courts. They are, however, evaluative in as much as they derive from a certain conception of what constitutional courts are *designed* to do and what they accordingly need to do if they are to live up to their designers' expectations.

For most judicial politics scholars, constitutional courts are designed to function as an independent check on the abuse of political power. In exercising this function, they are necessarily drawn into politics in as much as their decisions (whatever motivates them) affect political outcomes. This presents constitutional courts with a particular kind of difficulty: in order to be effective, they must make a real difference to political outcomes, but at the same time they must be seen to be above politics, to derive their authority to veto certain types of political outcome from a source other than their own political preferences. The mark of a successful constitutional court on this view is its ability successfully to resolve this conundrum – to continue playing its veto role in national politics without being so drawn into politics that its independence (and therefore its capacity to continue playing this role) is compromised.

From this point, judicial politics scholars tend to diverge into two camps that are related in complex ways to the three methodological approaches discussed in the previous section. For the first camp, a

---

[55] See Whittington, 'Once More unto the Breach'.

constitutional court's capacity to play its appointed veto role in national politics is crucially dependent on its capacity to build widespread public support for its role, to the point where building such support is the mark of its success. For the second camp, the capacity to assert its veto role is the essential factor, whether or not this stems from widespread public support or from other aspects of the political and institutional context for judicial review.

The judicial politics scholar who has done most to promote the first view is James Gibson. In a series of articles and book chapters, Gibson and several others have developed an account of constitutional-court efficacy that goes under the rubric of 'legitimacy theory'.[56] According to this approach, 'to serve effectively as veto players in a democracy, courts must have some degree of legitimacy'.[57] Whatever else a constitutional court might want to achieve, the theory runs, its capacity to play its appointed veto role in national politics depends on widespread public support – support that goes beyond mere agreement with the policy output of a particular decision and extends to generalised public acceptance of the court's moral authority to act as an independent check on the abuse of political power.[58]

The appeal of this theorisation, particularly for those interested in comparative research, is that public support is something that can be measured empirically, through opinion surveys. Thus Gibson and others have extended their initial work on the US Supreme Court[59] to measuring public support for constitutional courts in other countries,[60] including South Africa.[61] By tying the success of constitutional courts to public support in this way, legitimacy theory provides a handy comparative measure for the performance of constitutional courts in political terms. Not just that, but legitimacy theory may also be combined with the strategic model to produce a particular understanding of what

---

[56] See Gibson and Caldeira, 'Defenders of Democracy?' 1, 2.
[57] Ibid. 4.   [58] Ibid. 2.
[59] See Gregory A. Caldeira and James L. Gibson, 'The Etiology of Public Support for the Supreme Court' (1992) 36 *American Journal of Political Science* 635; James L. Gibson, Gregory A. Caldeira and Lester Kenyatta Spence, 'Measuring Attitudes toward the United States Supreme Court' (2003) 47 *American Journal of Political Science* 354.
[60] James L. Gibson, Gregory A. Caldeira and Vanessa Baird, 'On the Legitimacy of National High Courts' (1998) 92 *American Political Science Review* 340.
[61] Gibson and Caldeira, 'Defenders of Democracy?'; Gibson, 'The Evolving Legitimacy of the South African Constitutional Court' in Du Bois and Du Bois-Pedain (eds.), *Justice and Reconciliation in Post-Apartheid South Africa* 229.

constitutional courts need to do in order to play their appointed veto role in national politics. On this theorisation, as we saw in the previous section,[62] what such courts need to do is to respect the 'tolerance interval' for every case they decide. By so doing they ensure that all their decisions are enforced, which in turn builds their institutional legitimacy and eventually allows them to become powerful actors in national politics.[63]

Not all judicial politics scholars condition the success of constitutional courts on the achievement of a certain degree of institutional legitimacy, however. For these scholars, the mark of a successful court is simply whether it is able to decide politically salient cases and have these decisions enforced. Here, for example, is Martin Shapiro, the founder of 'political jurisprudence',[64] and now considered a 'pioneer' of the 'new institutionalist' approach,[65] writing about the lessons that the American experience has to teach those interested in other countries:

> At a minimum successful judicial review would require that constitutional judgments are routinely, if not always, obeyed by both governmental and private actors, and that relatively significant acts of government are judicially invalidated on constitutional grounds, at least occasionally.[66]

Similarly, Tom Ginsburg, writing about the Korean Constitutional Court, refers to a wide range of criteria when evaluating its performance. Included in his list are the Court's ability to 'become a major institution in Korean governance', its ability to function as 'a forum for groups seeking to advance social change as well as for individual disputes', the frequency with which it handed down judgments overturning legislative

---

[62] See Section 1.1.

[63] The same theorisation has thus been used to explain the emergence of judicial review, in the United States. See Jack Knight and Lee Epstein, 'On the Struggle for Judicial Supremacy' (1996) 30 *Law & Society Review* 87.

[64] See Martin Shapiro, *Law and Politics in the Supreme Court: New Approaches to Political Jurisprudence* (New York, NY: Free Press, 1964) and Shapiro, 'Morality and the Politics of Judging'.

[65] See Herbert M. Kritzer, 'Martin Shapiro: Anticipating the New Institutionalism' in Nancy Maveety (ed.), *The Pioneers of Judicial Behavior* (Ann Arbor, MI: University of Michigan Press, 2003) 387.

[66] Martin Shapiro, 'Some Conditions for the Success of Constitutional Courts: Lessons from the U.S. Experience' in Wojciech Sadurski (ed.), *Constitutional Justice, East and West: Democratic Legitimacy and Constitutional Courts in Post-Communist Europe in a Comparative Perspective* (The Hague: Kluwer Law International, 2002) 37. See also Martin Shapiro, 'Judicial Review in Developed Democracies' in Siri Gloppen, Roberto Gargarella and Elin Skaar (eds.), *Democratization and the Judiciary: The Accountability Function of Courts in New Democracies* (London: Frank Cass, 2004) 7.

and executive action, its capacity to hand down such decisions even in politically controversial cases, and its contribution to the consolidation of constitutional democracy.[67] Although the Korean Constitutional Court did at the same time build extensive public support for its role,[68] its success is not attributed to this factor alone, but rather to certain structural features of Korean politics, notably the extent of political fragmentation,[69] and also to the judges' 'decision-making prudence'.[70]

As can be seen from this example, the second way of evaluating the success of constitutional courts in political terms is also capable of comparative application. Although it lacks the seeming power of Gibson's approach, it has the advantage of being able to take account of greater variation in the political conditions for constitutional court efficacy. As we will see in the next section, this is of particular significance to South Africa, where legitimacy theory fails to explain the Chaskalson Court's effectiveness as a veto player in national politics.

The two alternative conceptions of the success of constitutional courts in political terms are related in complex ways to the three methodological approaches currently dominating judicial politics. The attitudinal model, as we have seen, explains judicial behaviour as a function of judicial ideology, and in this sense tries to explode the myth of judicial neutrality that is said to be integral to a constitutional court's success in political terms. If one were to take this model at face value, therefore, the US Supreme Court should not be as successful as it is: there would seem to be no reason why so much power and authority should be accorded to a group of people who decide cases according to their private political ideologies. And yet the US Supreme Court is enormously successful, even when the veil of judicial ideology is spectacularly lifted, as it was at the end of the *Lochner* era and more recently in its decision in *Bush* v. *Gore*.[71]

Proponents of the attitudinal model tend not to be terribly interested in this apparent contradiction. Their primary concern is to find rigorous empirical evidence of the influence of judicial ideology on decision-making, leaving the Supreme Court's capacity to shrug off decisions like

---

[67] Tom Ginsburg, 'The Constitutional Court and the judicialization of Korean Politics' in Andrew Harding and Penelope Nicholson (eds.), *New Courts in Asia* (London: Routledge, 2009) 113, 123. See also Tom Ginsburg, 'The Global Spread of Constitutional Review' in Whittington et al. (eds.), *The Oxford Handbook of Law and Politics*, 81, 93 (examining the criteria for assessing why 'some constitutional courts fail and others succeed').

[68] Ginsburg, 'The Constitutional Court and the Judicialization of Korean Politics' 113, 116.

[69] Ibid. 123.   [70] Ibid. 113.   [71] 531 U.S. 98 (2000).

Bush v. *Gore* to others to explain. To the extent that they do seek to explain the freedom Supreme Court justices have to decide cases according to their own political ideologies, proponents of the attitudinal model tend to make fairly cursory references to the political and institutional context for judicial review in the United States.[72] As noted in the previous section, all of this means that the attitudinal model is not terribly well suited to comparative research. At least, the applicability of this model outside the United States depends on an assessment of the political and institutional context for judicial review in the country concerned. In the abstract, all that the attitudinal model can tell us about the criteria for assessing the performance of constitutional courts is that, in certain political and institutional settings, judges may be able to assert their sincere policy preferences.

The strategic model, on the other hand, can be applied comparatively. It also links directly to one of the two main conceptions of constitutional-court success in political terms. On this approach, as we have seen, a constitutional court is successful to the extent that it is able strategically to assert itself as a major player in national politics. It does this by carefully calibrating its decisions to the politics of each case it decides, ensuring that every time it hands down a decision it is likely to be enforced. The basic standard of success, on this approach, is a constitutional court's capacity to act as a veto player in national politics. The way a court achieves this kind of success, however, is to build its institutional legitimacy, which is seen as a precondition for the court's capacity to assert its veto role. In this way, the building of a certain level of institutional legitimacy becomes a proxy for constitutional-court success, with all the comparative implications set out above.

In its application to the Russian Constitutional Court, this theorisation appears to be quite powerful, providing a convincing explanation for that Court's suspension by President Yeltsin. And yet the theorisation suffers from one fundamental drawback, associated with its sceptical account of the influence on judicial decision-making of legal norms. As we saw in the previous section, Knight, Epstein and Shevtsova do not exclude legal norms entirely from the determination of the tolerance interval,[73] but

---

[72] See, for example, Segal and Spaeth, *The Supreme Court and the Attitudinal Model Revisited* 12–27.

[73] Knight, Epstein and Shevtsova, 'The Role of Constitutional Courts in the Establishment and Maintenance of Democratic Systems of Government' (discussed in Section 1.1).

they do tend, like other proponents of the strategic model, to play down the influence of legal norms as a constraint on judicial behaviour. At least, legal norms are conceived as factors to be taken into account in the court's political strategising rather than independent determinants of judicial behaviour. The problem with this view is that a constitutional court's capacity to rise above politics and found its moral authority on some or other claim to political neutrality ultimately depends on law's capacity to constrain judicial decision-making, or at least on the judges' capacity to convince most of the public most of the time that this is what is happening. It is hard to see how a theorisation that depends on such a sceptical view of law can explain constitutional courts' capacity to acquire this kind of moral authority. While the model may be quite effective in explaining why some constitutional courts fail, therefore, it seems less suited to explaining why other constitutional courts succeed.[74]

For this reason, some combination of the historical-institutionalist approach and the conception of constitutional-court success proposed by Martin Shapiro and Tom Ginsburg would appear to provide the best basis for developing a comparative understanding of the factors that condition the success of constitutional courts in political terms.[75] The historical-institutionalist approach, as we have seen, is better equipped to take account of legal norms as determinants of judicial behaviour, and thus does not suffer from the conceptual problems confronting the strategic model. By combining this approach with a definition of constitutional court success that is not pre-committed to the need for constitutional courts to build their institutional legitimacy, it is possible to take account of the manifold variations in political and institutional context that condition the success of constitutional courts outside the United States. At the same time, this way of proceeding is both more amenable to the sort of interdisciplinary study proposed here and also capable of capturing, as the next section indicates, the particular nature of the Chaskalson Court's success in political terms.

---

[74] But cf. Knight and Epstein, 'On the Struggle for Judicial Supremacy' (using the strategic model to explain the emergence of successful judicial review in the United States).

[75] Ginsburg himself is on record as saying that 'the strategic model has been most successful in explaining the success of courts abroad' (Ginsburg, 'The Global Spread of Constitutional Review' 94). Ginsburg's study of the Korean Constitutional Court, however, is closer to the historical-institutionalist approach in form.

1.3   The Court's success in political terms

An initial impression of the Chaskalson Court's success in political terms may be gleaned by considering two of its early cases. *S v. Makwanyane*,[76] the first case heard by the Court, concerned a challenge to a provision in the apartheid-era Criminal Procedure Act[77] that permitted the imposition of the death penalty in certain circumstances. The case, as Chapter 6 explains in more detail, was not as politically controversial as first appears: the national Government did not support the provision, and the case only came to be litigated as extensively as it was because the invalidation of the death penalty was opposed by the provincial Attorney General, an independent official not connected to the national Government. Nevertheless, the Court's unanimous decision to strike down the death penalty provided an early indication of its institutional self-confidence. Here was a Court, everyone agreed, that was certain enough about its mandate to settle a controversial policy question that the constitutional negotiators had been unable to settle and which South Africans as a whole seemed to want to settle in a different way.

The death penalty case was followed a few months later by a more routine, but in many ways more demanding, case involving a challenge to a presidential proclamation amending an Act of Parliament.[78] The central issue in the case was whether Parliament could delegate to the executive the power to amend a statute in this way. On this occasion, there was no question that the Government opposed the order requested, and therefore that the Court's decision, were it to go against the Government, would be the first real test of the African National Congress's commitment to constitutional democracy. In the event, the Court proceeded to overturn the presidential proclamation as well as the legislative provision on which it was based. In an act that has since become part of South African constitutional folklore, the then President, Nelson Mandela, immediately announced his acceptance of the decision, saying that it was 'not the first nor will it be the last, in which the Constitutional Court assists both the Government and society to ensure

---

[76] 1995 (3) SA 391 (CC), 1995 (6) BCLR 665 (CC).
[77] Section 277(1)(*a*) of Act 51 of 1977.
[78] *Executive Council of the Western Cape Legislature* v. *President of the Republic of South Africa* 1995 (4) SA 877 (CC), 1995 (10) BCLR 1289 (CC) ('local government transition case').

constitutionality and effective governance'.[79] If the death penalty case showed that the Chaskalson Court had the institutional self-confidence to settle a controversial policy question, the local government transition case showed that the ANC might be prepared to allow the Court to perform this role.

The attitudinal model, as we have seen, takes no immediate position on decisions like these. If, after analysis of the political context for judicial review in South Africa, it were concluded that the Chaskalson Court was politically unconstrained, an attempt might be made to test whether the model could be used to predict the outcome of such cases. But it would all depend on the initial analysis of the political context.

The strategic model, on the other hand, could immediately be deployed to analyse the politics of these two cases, and to come to a view on whether the Court had respected the 'tolerance interval' for each case. The Court's decision in S v. Makwanyane – a seemingly bold judgment given the level of public support for the death penalty – might in this way be explained as a case in which major political actors, including the ANC governing elite, were not in fact opposed to the Court's decision. Likewise, it is possible to understand the local government transition case, as Heinz Klug has done, as a Marbury v. Madison-like giving with one hand and taking away with the other.[80] The historical-institutionalist approach could be deployed to the same effect, with perhaps greater attention to the way the judges' legal-professional socialisation pulled them towards a certain conception of the Court's institutional role. Such an analysis would also need to be preceded by more extensive treatment of the institutional history of judicial decision-making and respect for judicial independence in South Africa.

The sticking point for the strategic model, however, comes from certain brute facts about the Chaskalson Court's institutional legitimacy. According to two surveys conducted by Gibson and others in 1996 and 1997, and then again in 2004, the Chaskalson Court never built much public support. In the first survey, conducted shortly after the death penalty decision, it was found that only 27.9 per cent of South Africans supported the Court in the strong sense indicative of institutional legitimacy.[81] This result compares poorly with constitutional courts in other

---

[79] See Klug, *Constituting Democracy: Law, Globalism and South Africa's Political Reconstruction* (Cambridge University Press, 2000) 150.

[80] Ibid. (referring to *Marbury* v. *Madison* 5 US (1 Cranch) 137 (1803)).

[81] Gibson and Caldeira, 'Defenders of Democracy?'.

countries.[82] The second survey, conducted after the Court had been operating for approximately nine years, produced only marginally different results.[83] These figures suggest that, however it came about that the Chaskalson Court was able to assert its veto role in South African politics, it was not because the Court first built its institutional legitimacy in the manner posited by the strategic model. Not only did the Court assert its veto role early on its institutional life, before it could possibly have built the requisite level of public support, it continued to assert that role, even though its institutional legitimacy remained consistently low.

It could be argued, of course, that these figures provide indirect support for the strategic model. The Chaskalson Court's consistently low institutional legitimacy rating might thus be attributed to the fact that it ignored the political constraints impacting on it in its early cases, particularly in the form of public opinion, and that it paid the predicted price for this in institutional terms. Certainly, the death penalty case seems to fit this picture, and perhaps the Court's decisions on same-sex relationships as well.[84] But this still leaves the Court's remarkable effectiveness as a veto player in South African politics unexplained, as well as the fact that the Court was rarely attacked. Indeed, on all the measures mentioned by Ginsburg in his assessment of the Korean Constitutional Court, the Chaskalson Court performed remarkably well. As we have seen, in the local government transition case, the decision went directly against the Government, and yet President Mandela accepted it. This was just the first of numerous adverse decisions, many of them involving politically controversial issues, which were unquestioningly obeyed.[85] On

---

[82] See Gibson, Caldeira and Baird, 'On the Legitimacy of National High Courts'.

[83] Gibson, 'The Evolving Legitimacy of the South African Constitutional Court' 244 (finding 34 per cent public support for the Court).

[84] See National Coalition for Gay and Lesbian Equality v. Minister of Justice and Others 1999 (1) SA 6 (CC), 1998 (12) BCLR 1517 (CC); National Coalition for Gay and Lesbian Equality v. Minister of Home Affairs 2000 (2) SA 1 (CC), 2000 (1) BCLR 39 (CC).

[85] Most dramatic of all, perhaps, was the Court's decision on the compatibility of the draft 'final' Constitution with a schedule of constitutional principles that had been agreed as part of the transition to majority rule (Ex parte Chairperson of the Constitutional Assembly: In re Certification of the Constitution of the Republic of South Africa, 1996 1996 (4) SA 744 (CC), 1996 (10) BCLR 1253 (CC)). The case required the Court to second-guess the outcome of two years of protracted negotiations between the main political parties. Many expected it simply to rubber-stamp what was after all a democratically agreed document. Instead, the Court entertained and accepted several arguments from minority political parties and other interest groups that parts of the text fell short of the far from determinate standards implied by the principles. The text was duly redrafted and re-submitted to the Court, which eventually approved it.

the one occasion that a member of the executive threatened not to implement one of the Court's judgments – Health Minister Manto Tshabalala-Msimang's notorious public statement to this effect before the decision in the *Treatment Action Campaign* case – the executive was quickly forced to back down, and nothing came of the threat.[86]

The Court's ability to function as a forum for public impact litigation was equally impressive. In its early years, gay and lesbian groups were particularly adept at using the Court to translate some of the gains made during the constitutional drafting process into concrete legal reforms. Later on, the Treatment Action Campaign emerged as a major social movement whose strategy to change the Government's approach to the HIV/AIDS pandemic depended crucially on the Court. Other social groups, notably the rural poor, found it harder to use the Court in this way. But overall, the Court's performance according to this measure was undeniably strong.

The Chaskalson Court's contribution to the consolidation of democracy is harder to ascertain. On a minimalist view of democracy, the fact that the Court functioned as a forum in which the rules of the electoral game could be contested would suffice.[87] On a more maximalist view, the Court's consistent support for a range of constitutional rights, not just those pertaining to elections, all contributed to the quality of South African democracy.[88] There were two cases, however, where the Court

---

[86] *Minister of Health and Others* v. *Treatment Action Campaign and Others (No 2)* (2002) (5) SA 721 (CC), 2002 (10) BCLR 1075 (CC). There was some subsequent foot-dragging in the implementation of the Court's order, and in one province the responsible member of the executive had to be sued before compliance was ensured, but the Court's order was never openly defied. See Mark Heywood, 'Preventing Mother-to-Child HIV Transmission in South Africa: Background, Strategies and Outcomes of the Treatment Action Campaign Case against the Minister of Health (2004) 19 *South African Journal on Human Rights* 278, 314–15; Mark Heywood, 'Contempt or Compliance? The TAC Case after the Constitutional Court Judgment' (2003) 4(1) *ESR Review* 7.

[87] See, for example, *United Democratic Movement* v. *President of the Republic of South Africa and Others (African Christian Democratic Party and Others Intervening; Institute for Democracy and Another as* Amici Curiae) *(No 1)* 2003 (1) SA 488 (CC), 2002 (11) BCLR 1179 (CC); *August and Another* v. *Electoral Commission and Others* 1999 (3) SA 1 (CC), 1999 (4) BCLR 363; *New National Party of South Africa* v. *Government of the Republic of South Africa and Others* 1999 (3) SA 191 (CC), 1999 (5) BCLR 489 (CC); *Minister of Home Affairs* v. *National Institute for Crime Prevention and the Re-integration of Offenders (NICRO) and Others* 2005 (3) SA 280 (CC), 2004 (5) BCLR (CC).

[88] It could be argued, for example, that the Court's socio-economic rights jurisprudence promoted democratic participation by requiring that the state direct a reasonable proportion of resources towards meeting the needs of vulnerable and excluded groups, who would otherwise not have been able to participate in the political system.

fared less well. In the so-called 'floor-crossing case', the Court declined to invalidate an amendment to the 1996 Constitution that allowed the ANC to increase its stranglehold on electoral politics.[89] The Court's decision in the *New National Party* case,[90] which conditioned the right to vote on citizens' taking reasonable efforts to comply with voting registration requirements, has also been strongly criticised.[91] But these two cases, though possibly wrongly decided,[92] hardly provide evidence of the Court's failure to contribute to the consolidation of democracy. In the end, the significant thing is that a number of political rights cases were litigated in the Court, and that the Court was a central player in democratic politics to this extent.

The real conundrum presented by the South African case, therefore, is not that the Chaskalson Court failed to build its institutional legitimacy, but that it was able to play such an effective role in South African politics without doing so. As we have seen, legitimacy theory contends that a certain level of public support is a precondition for whatever else a constitutional court may hope to achieve. The South African case appears to defy this rule.

What legitimacy theory misses, it is suggested, is the fact that, in a dominant-party democracy like South Africa, a constitutional court may be insulated from political attack by the governing political party. As explained in Chapter 4 of this study, the single most important feature of South African politics during the Chaskalson Court's term was the ANC's overwhelming dominance of electoral politics. This meant that the Chaskalson Court's lack of public support was not initially troubling to the ANC, even after highly unpopular decisions like that in the death penalty case. Instead, the ANC's propensity to attack the Court depended on other factors, such as the strength and durability of its internal

---

[89] *United Democratic Movement v. President of the Republic of South Africa and Others (African Christian Democratic Party and Others Intervening; Institute for Democracy and Another as* Amici Curiae*) (No 1)* 2003 (1) SA 488 (CC), 2002 (11) BCLR 1179 (CC).

[90] *New National Party of South Africa v. Government of the Republic of South Africa and Others* 1999 (3) SA 191 (CC), 1999 (5) BCLR 489 (CC).

[91] See, for example, R. W. Johnson, *South Africa's Brave New World: The Beloved Country Since the End of Apartheid* (London: Allen Lane, 2009) 159–60 (describing the Court's decision in this case as 'a hotchpotch of circumlocution, factual omission, misstatement and sheer evasion' and criticising the Court's 'failure to stand up to the ANC government' in this and other cases).

[92] See Sujit Choudhry, '"He Had a Mandate": The South African Constitutional Court and the African National Congress in a Dominant Party Democracy' (2009) 2 *Constitutional Court Review* 1, 35–45.

tradition of respect for judicial independence, the interests that an independent Constitutional Court served for the ANC, and the Chaskalson
Court's capacity to decide cases in ways that were respectful of the
democratic legitimacy and moral urgency of the ANC's overarching
policy objectives.

To understand how these factors conditioned the Chaskalson Court's
success in political terms, we will need to examine the political context
for judicial review during Chaskalson's term as Chief Justice and the way
the Court operated within it. This is the task of later chapters.[93] The
point for purposes of this chapter has been to capture the phenomenon
to be explained. What the argument in this section has established is that
the Chaskalson Court's success in political terms was not that it progressively built its institutional legitimacy to the point where it was able to
play a meaningful role in South African politics, but that it was able to
assert its constitutionally assigned role immediately and effectively, without triggering any significant political attack. What the Chaskalson Court
enjoyed, in other words, was not institutional *legitimacy*, but a certain
measure of institutional *efficacy*, i.e. the capacity to assert its constitutionally assigned veto role in national politics without compromising its
institutional independence.

With this understanding of the Chaskalson Court's success in political
terms in place, the second half of this chapter explores its success in legal
terms. The question driving this part of the analysis, it will be recalled, is
whether there is anything in the Court's success in this respect that, when
set alongside its success in political terms, makes its overall achievement
intriguing and difficult to explain except by means of an interdisciplinary
study of the kind here proposed.

1.4   The Court's success in legal terms: four illustrative responses

It may be thought that the place to go looking for an account of the
Chaskalson Court's success in legal terms would be normative constitutional theory. In fact, however, this body of work is not immediately
relevant to this study. While theorisations of the conditions under which
judicial review is morally justified obviously do generate criteria
according to which the performance of constitutional courts may be
assessed, the Chaskalson Court's success in legal terms is a broad

---

[93] See Chapter 4 and Part III.

sociological phenomenon that cannot be captured by any one normative theory of judicial review. As indicated in the Introduction, the Court's reputation in the comparative constitutional law community depends on widespread approval of the way it responded to its mandate under the post-apartheid Constitutions. The members of this community hold divergent, and often quite idiosyncratic, views about the moral justification for judicial review. If we are to capture and accurately represent the Chaskalson Court's success in legal terms, therefore, we need to develop an account of that phenomenon that transcends these differences. What we are looking for is not a particular theory of judicial review, but rather the shared criteria that may be said to have informed the comparative constitutional law community's overwhelmingly favourable assessment of the Chaskalson Court's record.

As a starting point, it will be helpful to analyse some of the comments made by members of this community in more detail. If we can discern in these comments a common appreciation for the way the Court responded to its mandate, we will have the kernel of an idea that can be developed into a fuller account of the Court's success in legal terms.

Writing about the Court's decision on the right to housing in the *Grootboom* case,[94] Cass Sunstein said:

> In the *Grootboom* decision, the Court set out a novel and promising approach to judicial protection of socio-economic rights. This approach requires close attention to the human interests at stake, and sensible priority-setting, but without mandating protection for each person whose socio-economic needs are at risk. The distinctive virtue of the Court's approach is that it is respectful of democratic prerogatives and of the limited nature of public resources, while also requiring special deliberative attention to those whose minimal needs are not being met. The approach of the Constitutional Court stands as a powerful rejoinder to those who have contended that socio-economic rights do not belong in a constitution. It suggests that such rights can serve, not to preempt democratic deliberation, but to ensure democratic attention to important interests that might otherwise be neglected in ordinary debate.[95]

It is clear from this passage that what impressed Sunstein about the Court's decision in *Grootboom* is that it challenged settled views,

---

[94] *Government of the Republic of South Africa and Others* v. *Grootboom and Others* 2001 (1) SA 46 (CC), 2000 (11) BCLR 1169 (CC).

[95] Cass R. Sunstein, 'Social and Economic Rights? Lessons from South Africa' (2000/2011) 11 *Constitutional Forum* 123, 123 (reprinted in Sunstein, *Designing Democracy*) 221).

including his own,[96] about the possible role of constitutional courts in enforcing socio-economic rights. Through its decision, the Court showed that these rights could be meaningfully enforced without encroaching into the political branches' sphere of operation. 'I had my doubts,' Sunstein in effect says, 'but the *Grootboom* decision dispelled them.'

What Sunstein particularly seems to admire is the way the Court's decision not only respected democracy, but actually improved prospects for democratic deliberation about the fulfilment of socio-economic rights. In this way, the decision appeared to solve the great conundrum presented by such rights: their seeming incompatibility with a commitment to majoritarian democracy. The real genius of the Court's decision for Sunstein is that it transformed what seemed like an awkward mandate into a workable review standard. In so doing, the Court extended the comparative constitutional law community's understanding of the possible role of constitutional courts in liberal-democratic systems of government.

Responding to a paper written by Arthur Chaskalson in the *International Journal of Constitutional Law*,[97] Ronald Dworkin had the following to say about the Chief Justice's role in the transition to democracy in South Africa and the contribution made by his Court:

> Since apartheid's end, Chaskalson has rendered what is probably an even more important service to his country [than he did as a lawyer in the struggle against apartheid]. Under his intellectual and administrative leadership, the Constitutional Court has already become one of the most influential such courts in the world. The quality of its craftsmanship and the disciplined imagination with which it has interpreted South Africa's admirable Constitution have helped to ensure a remarkably smooth transition from oppression to a democratic rule of both law and principle, and its opinions are studied with care by lawyers over the world.[98]

Referring to its socio-economic rights jurisprudence, Dworkin went on to argue that, of the two possible 'strategies' for the enforcement of such rights – a 'substantive' strategy that would see the court second-guessing the actual amount of resources devoted to various social programmes, and an 'egalitarian' strategy in terms of which the court reviews whether

---

[96] Cass R. Sunstein, 'Against Positive Rights' in András Sajó (ed.), *Western Rights? Post-Communist Application* (The Hague: Kluwer Law International, 1996) 225.

[97] Arthur Chaskalson, 'From Wickedness to Equality: The Moral Transformation of South African Law' (2003) 1 *International Journal of Constitutional Law* 651.

[98] Dworkin, 'Response to Overseas Commentators' 651, 651–2.

the Government has shown 'equal concern for all in the allocations it does make' – the Chaskalson Court 'properly' chose the second strategy, even though both strategies were 'plausible' as a 'literal reading of the South African Constitution'.[99]

Although similar to Sunstein's remarks in some ways, Dworkin's comments go further in arguing that the Chaskalson Court's approach to socio-economic rights was not only instructive, but also correct in some sense. What he admires is not just that the Court was able to reconcile its duty to enforce socio-economic rights with respect for democracy, but that the Court's interpretation of the Constitution was the best available one, considering the text and the moral principles at stake.

Dworkin's summary of Chaskalson's leadership contribution to the work of the Court makes several other points. First, it identifies the Court as an 'influential' Court, in the sense that 'its opinions are studied with care by lawyers over the world'. This comment must be understood as an attempt to link the work of the Court to the comparative focus of the *Journal*, which was then in the first year of its publication. But it also has independent value as a statement about the Court's reputation in the comparative constitutional law community. We are involved in a 'global conversation'[100] about the role justiciable human rights play in the ongoing project of human emancipation, Dworkin argues, and the Chaskalson Court is a leading participant in that process.

Dworkin then makes a somewhat elliptical comment: 'The quality of [the Court's] craftsmanship and the disciplined imagination with which it has interpreted South Africa's admirable Constitution', he says, 'have helped to ensure a remarkably smooth transition from oppression to a democratic rule of both law and principle.'[101] If we leave aside the slight tautology in this remark,[102] what Dworkin seems to be saying is that there is a causal link between the way the Court responded to its mandate and South Africa's relatively peaceful transition to democracy. Just what this link is, however, is somewhat unclear. Read alongside his comments about the Court's choice of strategy in relation to socio-economic rights, and knowing what we do about Dworkin's theory of adjudication,[103] we

---

[99] Ibid. 652–3.   [100] Ibid. 651.   [101] Ibid. 651–2.

[102] On Dworkin's own approach, a 'democratic rule of ... law' is the same thing as a 'democratic rule of ... principle'. See, for example, Ronald Dworkin, *A Matter of Principle* (Oxford: Clarendon Press, 1986).

[103] See the discussion in Section 1.5.

must understand him to be saying that what he admires about the Chaskalson Court is the way the judges were able to work out a morally convincing understanding of their institutional function in the post-apartheid political system. A court that is able to do this, Dworkin implies, contributes to the consolidation of democracy by subjecting majority rule to the moral restraints that make democracy worth having.

There are clearly some similarities between the things Dworkin and Sunstein admire about the Chaskalson Court and the criteria of success applied by judicial politics scholars. Thus Dworkin's remark that the Court has assisted in South Africa's 'smooth transition from oppression to a democratic rule of both law and principle' is not unlike Tom Ginsburg's emphasis on the Korean Constitutional Court's role in the consolidation of democracy. Sunstein, too, touches on this criterion when talking about the *Grootboom* decision's contribution to democratic deliberation in South Africa. What Dworkin and Sunstein really seem to admire about the Chaskalson Court, however, is not its effectiveness as a political institution, but its ability to solve the riddle of its institutional function. There is a craft being practised here, as Dworkin puts it, one that all constitutional court judges must learn and to which their decisions contribute. That craft is partly technical, but also partly moral. In its technical aspect it consists of skills such as the ability to interpret a text in a way that is faithful to its meaning. In its moral aspect it consists of the ability to justify the exercise by the court of its powers.

In Dworkin and Sunstein's account, in other words, the Chaskalson Court is not being praised for its political acumen – for its ability rationally to calculate how it might best assert its institutional role in the South African political system – but for the *quality of the reasons* it gave in support of its institutional role. In the first instance, those reasons are found to be persuasive as a matter of legal technique – as professionally competent rationalisations of the way the language of the constitutional text ought to be interpreted. In the second instance, those reasons are found to be persuasive in transnational terms, according to the standards applied by the comparative constitutional law community. Indeed, on this level, the Court's reasons are found to be, not merely persuasive, but also *compelling* in some sense – inventive, morally right, and instructive for courts in other countries.

Dworkin and Sunstein, of course, are both liberal legalists – theorists, that is, who are committed to the rule-of-law ideal and who contend that law is in principle capable of constraining the exercise of judicial discretion to a significant degree, significant enough at least to justify the power that judges wield in liberal-democratic systems of government.[104] A major part of what they admire about the Court's decision in *Grootboom* is that it appeared to vindicate this view, and moreover in relation to one of the most institutionally awkward aspects of the Court's mandate. If the Court was able to work out a technically competent and morally persuasive understanding of its mandate in *this* area, Dworkin and Sunstein implicitly argue, we can be that much more confident about its capacity to do so in other areas.

Given their commitment to a liberal-legalist view of law, it is possible that Dworkin and Sunstein are both seeing in the Chaskalson Court's socio-economic rights jurisprudence something that is not really there. To correct for this, it will be helpful to compare their comments to two other assessments of the Court's record by scholars working in the critical legal tradition. If we can discern a common basis for approving the Court's record in their comments, we will be well on our way to understanding the shared criteria informing the Court's reputation. Equally, to the extent that there are any differences, either in the normative standard applied or in the conclusions reached, we will be in a position to give a more focused account of those criteria and the basis for the Court's reputation.

Though less effusive in his praise than Dworkin and Sunstein, one of the doyens of Critical Legal Studies, Mark Tushnet, has also written approvingly of the Chaskalson Court's socio-economic rights jurisprudence. For Tushnet, the significance of *Grootboom* decision is that it showed how the deployment of weaker judicial remedies may allow constitutional courts to play a meaningful rights-enforcing role in areas previously thought, for democratic reasons, to be off-limits to the judiciary.[105] His analysis of *Grootboom* squares with Sunstein's to that extent. But Tushnet was writing after Sunstein, and thus his analysis also needed to take account of the Court's later decision in *Treatment Action Campaign*.[106] In that case, as we shall see,[107] the Court enforced constitutional healthcare rights to drive a significant change to the South

---

[104] Not all liberal legalists, of course, think that the constraining capacity of law is sufficient to justify the institution of *supreme-law* judicial review. See, for example, Jeremy Waldron, 'The Core of the Case against Judicial Review' (2006) 115 *Yale Law Journal* 1346.

[105] Mark Tushnet, *Weak Courts, Strong Rights: Judicial Review and Social Welfare Rights in Comparative Constitutional Law* (Princeton: Princeton University Press, 2008) 242–4.

[106] *Minister of Health* v. *Treatment Action Campaign (No 2)* 2002 (5) SA 721 (CC).

[107] Chapter 7.

African Government's HIV/AIDS treatment policy. Confronted with the Court's more intrusive role in this case, Tushnet reconciled the two decisions by articulating a broad principle of comparative constitutional law supporting stronger judicial intervention in social welfare policies where such policies are inconsistent with any 'reasonable' interpretation of the constitution.[108] For Tushnet, then, the Chaskalson Court's success in enforcing socio-economic rights is associated with its capacity, not so much to work out a single, fit-for-all-occasions review standard, but to work with the legal materials to adjust the level of review to the requirements of democracy. In *Grootboom*, this meant weakly enforcing a right that had been extensively elaborated in government policy, whereas in *Treatment Action Campaign*, the Court was justified in more forcefully correcting the democratic branches' failure to offer a plausible interpretation of the Constitution.

Interestingly, South African legal scholars, as we shall see in Chapter 7, have been far more critical of the Court's socio-economic rights jurisprudence than the three American commentators whose views have just been canvassed. Given the different normative premises from which Dworkin, Sunstein and Tushnet depart, this is in itself intriguing and will need to be explained. For the moment, however, we may conclude the discussion by looking at the views of a fourth American commentator, also working within the critical legal tradition, Karl Klare. Of the four, Klare has been the most influential in the local South African debate, and, with Frank Michelman, is someone who straddles the divide between the South African constitutional law community and the broader comparative constitutional law community.

While pausing to record how 'deeply he and his 'U.S. co-workers ... respect ... the achievements of the Chaskalson Court,[109] Klare is quite critical of the Court's early record and particularly of the style of argument deployed in the three decisions he discusses.[110] As we shall see in Chapter 5, the basis for Klare's criticisms is his reading of the 1996 South African Constitution as inviting a particular interpretive method, one which requires the judges of the Constitutional Court to be honest about the relative indeterminacy of the constitutional text, and to seek public support for the Court's role in the candour with which they go about

---

[108] Tushnet, *Weak Courts, Strong Rights* 245–7, 264.
[109] Karl E. Klare, 'Legal Culture and Transformative Constitutionalism' (1998) 12 *South African Journal on Human Rights* 146, 172 n 56.
[110] Ibid. 172–87.

convincing South Africans of the moral preferability of their decisions. According to this standard, Klare argues, the Court's early record may be criticised for resorting to formalistic arguments, and for its propensity to disguise open, value-laden choices as legally preordained. Rather than taking up the Constitution's invitation to unmask the politics of adjudication, the Court too often resorted to rhetorical strategies aimed at producing an artificial sense of law's constraint.[111]

Klare's assessment of the Court's early record, which was conducted before its decision in *Grootboom*,[112] provides a useful contrast to the other three views. On the one hand, it suggests that the Court's achievement in relation to socio-economic rights may not have been matched in other areas of law. On the other, it highlights both what is common to, and what is different about, the normative standard that liberal legalists and critical legal theorists apply when assessing the performance of constitutional courts. All four theorists thus admire the technical competence with which the Court extrapolated the Constitution's linguistic meaning and its ability to justify the performance of its institutional role in a morally convincing way. The difference between the two sets of theorists mainly concerns the *rhetorical form* in which the Court's decisions were couched, with Klare disappointed by the Court's lack of candour about the openness of the doctrinal choices involved, and Dworkin and Sunstein more inclined to take the Court at its word – to accept that its doctrinal choices were indeed significantly constrained by some combination of the Constitution's language and the force of the moral arguments themselves.

This is not an insignificant difference, to be sure. The impact of the rhetorical form of the Court's decisions on its capacity to mediate the competing demands of law and politics is one of the main themes pursued in this study. But it is worth noting at this early stage the surprising level of agreement between the four theorists over the underlying criteria: technical competence and moral persuasiveness. If the views just canvassed are representative of the spread of views in the comparative constitutional law community, the Chaskalson Court's reputation must have had something to do with its capacity to satisfy these criteria.

---

[111] Ibid.

[112] Klare has updated his assessment in a more recent essay. See Dennis M. Davis and Karl Klare, 'Transformative Constitutionalism and the Common and Customary Law' (2010) 26 *South African Journal on Human Rights* 403.

This does not mean, of course, that the Court's success in legal terms can be determined independently of the assessor's own value-laden assumptions about the purposes and benefits of judicial review. The moral persuasiveness of the Court's decision-making record, for example, probably had a lot to do with the ideological progressivism of the Court's decisions on such issues as the death penalty and gay and lesbian equality, which both liberal legalists and critical theorists found congenial. This fact, in turn, may be ascribed to the non-accidental convergence of the political morality informing the post-apartheid Constitutions and the political views circulating in the comparative constitutional law community.[113] Add to this the tremendous groundswell of international support and goodwill that accompanied South Africa's transition to democracy, and the fact that the Court's decisions were written in English,[114] and the situational contingency, for want of a better term, of the Court's international legal reputation is apparent. This need not concern us, however. The argument of this chapter does not depend on any claim that the Court's success in legal terms is objectively verifiable in any sense, but simply on the claim that the Court was successful according to criteria shared by a broad cross-section of the comparative constitutional law community. The (perhaps surprising) correspondence between Sunstein, Dworkin, Tushnet and Klare's views has done enough to establish that proposition at least.

At the same time, however, the discussion has revealed that the Court's reputation was higher among liberal legalists than it was among critical legal theorists, and that this had something to do with the rhetorical form of its decisions – with the way the Court presented these technically competent and morally persuasive arguments that everyone found so congenial. For CLS scholars like Tushnet and Klare, judges' duty to give technically competent and morally persuasive arguments constrains the

---

[113] As Heinz Klug has shown, the South African constitution-making process was influenced by the models of governance available in 'international political culture'. See Klug, *Constituting Democracy*. The substantive and procedural values informing these models are likely the same as those informing the comparative constitutional law community's assessment of the Court's record. If constitutional language has the capacity to act as a conveyor belt for the transmission of values, and if the Chaskalson Court was technically competent in extrapolating the post-apartheid Constitutions' linguistic meaning, it is not surprising that the comparative constitutional law community should have found the Court's record morally persuasive.

[114] This point was put to me by Wojciech Sadurski during a seminar presentation of this chapter.

exercise of their decision-making discretion only to a limited degree. In hard cases, which includes the vast majority of cases decided at the appellate level under a rights-based constitution, this means that judges have a legally underdetermined choice among competing outcomes. It follows from this that judges have an ethical duty to be candid about the influence of their private political views on their decision-making practices. If the outcome in hard constitutional cases is not in fact determined by law, presenting the outcome as though it *were* is a manifest deception that can only hinder the development of a political culture of respect for judicial independence.[115] For liberal legalists, on the other hand, this sort of candour is not required since their view is that the reasoning methods required to give technically competent and morally persuasive decisions *do* significantly constrain judicial decision-making, and therefore that the duty of judicial candour in fact pulls in the opposite direction, towards the presentation by judges of their decisions as legally required. Indeed, for liberal legalists, it is not just judges' duty of candour that requires them to present their decisions in this way, but also their duty, for rule-of-law reasons, to sustain the legal profession's and the broader political community's faith in the constraining capacity of law, or what we might call *the ideal of adjudication according to law.*

As noted earlier, the difference between critical legal theorists and liberal legalists in this respect has important consequences for how we conceptualise a constitutional court's capacity to mediate the competing demands of law and politics. We must therefore take account of it when articulating the normative criteria informing the Chaskalson Court's reputation and also in the claim we make about the breadth and depth of that reputation. The broadest but shallowest shared normative basis for the Court's reputation was its capacity to hand down technically competent and morally persuasive decisions. The narrower but deeper basis is that it presented its decisions in a way that satisfied liberal legalists' expectations about how it ought to have responded to its mandate.

There are three ways of proceeding from this point. First, we could draw out whatever is common to the liberal-legalist and CLS view of law and articulate a very broad set of normative criteria for the success of

---

[115] For Klare, as we have seen, the added reason in the South African case to eschew this kind of reasoning was that the 1996 Constitution, on his reading, clearly called for a more transparent approach to its mandate. See Klare, 'Legal Culture and Transformative Constitutionalism'.

constitutional courts based on these common features. Alternatively, we might seek to establish, through a social survey of some kind,[116] where the preponderance of views in the comparative constitutional law community lies, and work up our shared normative criteria from there. If such a survey revealed, for example, that the liberal-legalist view of law predominates in this community, we could be fairly confident that the Court could not have built the reputation it did without satisfying the shared normative criteria associated with that view. Finally, we could simply rely on the claim that, whatever the actual spread of views, it is clear that prominent liberal legalists like Sunstein and Dworkin found much in the Court's decision-making record to admire and that their views are likely to be representative of a broad cross-section of the comparative constitutional law community, broad enough at least to account for its reputation.

The first approach has the advantage of breadth but not of depth: it would almost certainly account for the majority of views in the comparative constitutional law community, but it would be unlikely to generate a set of criteria that is sufficiently precise for our purposes. The attitudinal and strategic models in judicial politics, as we have seen,[117] developed out of legal realism, which also in part informs the CLS approach.[118] If the Chaskalson Court's success is defined in terms of the lowest common-denominator criteria shared by CLS and liberal legalism, therefore, the contrast with the judicial politics criteria is likely to disappear: our view of law will collapse into the view of law underpinning the attitudinal and strategic models, making an interdisciplinary approach redundant, or rather reducing the interdisciplinarity of this study to the interdisciplinarity that is already present in the attitudinal and strategic models' adoption of a legal-realist-cum-CLS view of law. That would be one way, of course, of resolving the apparent contradiction between the Court's success in legal and political terms, but it would be a way that proceeded by definitional fiat rather than explanation. If the Chaskalson Court's success in legal terms in fact goes beyond satisfaction of whatever criteria may be common to the CLS and liberal-legalist view of law, to

---

[116] See, for example, Tamanaha, *Law as a Means to an End* 232 (reporting on a survey of judicial attitudes in four state Supreme Courts in the United States in the 1960s in which judges were classified into three categories according to 'their perception of their judicial role' as 'strict law appliers', 'law-makers' or 'pragmatists').

[117] See Section 1.1.

[118] In both cases, the legal realists' insights were developed in a more radically rule-sceptical direction than they themselves would have been comfortable with.

satisfaction of the normative criteria associated with liberal legalism's particular view of law's constraint, we must keep that possibility open.

The second alternative, of conducting a social survey (perhaps backed up by qualitative interviews) to determine in as rigorous a way as possible the actual basis for the Court's reputation, would have been a plausible way of proceeding but sets a higher standard than is necessary for this study. Whether numerically dominant or not, it is reasonable to assume that liberal legalists like Dworkin and Sunstein account for a significant proportion of the membership of the comparative constitutional law community. If the criteria informing their approval of the Court's decision-making record can be shown to be in tension with the judicial politics criteria, that would be an intriguing enough result to warrant further investigation. How did it occur, our question would then become, that the Court was able to satisfy these criteria and the qualitatively different judicial politics criteria at the same time?

This study proceeds on this basis – the third alternative sketched earlier. In particular, the four-part claim on which this study relies is that: (1) liberal legalists conceive of law as capable of constraining the exercise of judicial discretion to a significant degree, sufficient at least to justify the role that judges perform in liberal-democratic systems of government; (2) according to this view of law, judges' legal-professional duty includes a duty, for rule-of-law reasons, to present their decisions as legally constrained and in this way to sustain the legal profession's and the broader political community's faith in the ideal of adjudication according to law; (3) liberal legalists, while not necessarily predominant in the comparative constitutional law community, likely account for a broad cross-section of the membership of that community; (4) the Chaskalson Court's reputation in the comparative constitutional law community, while attributable to a range of factors, including the convergence between the left-progressive values generally espoused by members of that community and the political morality informing the post-apartheid Constitutions, would not have been as high as it was had it not also been able to satisfy the shared normative criteria informing the liberal-legalist ideal of adjudication according to law.

1.5   The ideal of adjudication according to law

To suggest that the Chaskalson Court's reputation in the comparative constitutional law community would not have been as high as it was had it not satisfied the shared criteria informing the liberal-legalist ideal of adjudication according to law is to broach a very large and complex topic.

What keeps this topic within manageable bounds is the fact that we have a fairly limited purpose: our goal, it will be recalled, is to develop an account of the Court's success in legal terms and then to determine whether there is something distinctive enough about this account to make the Court's simultaneous success in legal and political terms intriguing and difficult to explain except by means of a particular kind of interdisciplinary study: one that synthesises the conceptual frameworks and methods of judicial politics and liberal legal theory. It is not being suggested that there is a uniform conception of the ideal of adjudication according to law or even that this is an ideal that all legal theorists espouse. All that is being suggested is that the Court's ability to satisfy the expectations associated with this ideal captures what is common to Dworkin and Sunstein's appreciation of the Court's record, and that their views in this respect are likely to be representative of a broad cross-section of the comparative constitutional law community – broad enough at least to account for the Court's reputation. If that is accepted, the key to understanding the Court's success in legal terms will be to understand what is at stake when liberal legal theorists argue about the ideal of adjudication to law. If we can discern certain commonalities in the way different theorists working in this tradition conceive of this ideal, we should be able to develop an account of the shared criteria informing the Court's reputation.

To this end, consider the latest round in the ongoing debate between Dworkin and the tradition of legal positivism. As is well known, that debate began over forty years ago when Dworkin first started critiquing 'the model of rules' in H. L. A. Hart's *The Concept of Law*.[119] There are several ways of understanding this critique, but for present purposes it may be thought of as a complaint about the paucity of the definition of law in Hart's theory, and therefore about the paucity of Hart's conception of the ideal of adjudication according to law. In particular, Dworkin attacked Hart's notion that, when faced with a hard case, for which there is no plainly applicable legal rule, judges go outside the law, to moral and political considerations, to fashion a new rule to settle the case.[120] This view, Dworkin argued, was both descriptively inaccurate in so far as it purported to explain what lawyers do – and what they think of themselves as doing – when arguing about hard cases, and also normatively

[119] Oxford: Clarendon Press, 1961 (the references to this work are to the first edition unless otherwise specified).
[120] Dworkin, *Taking Rights Seriously* 14–45.

unsatisfying in that it failed to provide an adequate justification for the power judges wield in liberal-democratic systems of government.

In a 2004 essay on Hart's postscript to *The Concept of Law*, Dworkin renewed this attack, this time by constructing an imaginary case.[121] The case involves a woman who takes a generic drug to relieve the symptoms of rheumatoid arthritis. The drug causes permanent damage to her heart and so she sues the various manufacturers of the drug in tort – without, however, being able to prove which of them manufactured the pills she took. The answer to this case, Dworkin says, turns on which of two rival principles should be applied: the principle that no one should be held liable for harm that they cannot be shown to have caused, and the principle that 'those who have profited from some enterprise must bear the costs of that enterprise'.[122] Hart's theory, Dworkin contends, even when understood as a form of inclusive legal positivism,[123] cannot explain how judges decide this kind of case *according to law*. On the positivist approach, for this case to have a *legal* answer, the judge would need to be able to identify, by reference to social sources alone, the relevant moral principle. Since there is no such social source, 'Mrs. Sorenson cannot claim that law is on her side'[124] and thus, '[s]o far as the law is concerned ... she must lose.'[125]

Dworkin's use of this example has been criticised by Brian Leiter as misstating Hart's theory and the legal positivist sources thesis.[126] Hart's theory, Leiter argues, does not entail that a judge would necessarily decide this case against Mrs Sorenson. All that is entailed by his theory is that:

> to the extent that a judge has a duty to decide according to law, then the judge must apply the source-based norms, but it is not part of the sources thesis, or Hart's view, to deny that in some cases, the duty to apply legally valid norms is, and ought to be, overridden by other equitable and moral considerations.[127]

This rebuke is probably deserved. Dworkin does indeed try to make too much of this example and in so doing leaves himself open to the charge

---

[121] See Ronald Dworkin, *Justice in Robes* (Cambridge, MA: Harvard University Press, 2006) 140–86 (first published as Ronald Dworkin, 'Hart's Postscript and the Character of Political Philosophy' (2004) 24 *Oxford Journal of Legal Studies* 1).

[122] Dworkin, *Justice in Robes* 144.   [123] See, for example, Coleman, *The Practice of Principle*.

[124] Dworkin, *Justice in Robes* 164.   [125] Ibid. 144.

[126] The 'sources thesis' is the view that all law is 'source-based' in the sense that 'its existence and content can be identified by reference to social facts alone' (Joseph Raz, *Ethics in the Public Domain: Essays in the Morality of Law and Politics* (Oxford: Clarendon Press, 1994) 194–5).

[127] Brian Leiter, 'The End of Empire: Dworkin and Jurisprudence in the 21st Century' (2004) 36 *Rutgers Law Journal* 165, 176.

that he thinks that Hart's theory entails a particular outcome in cases like this. The central thrust of Dworkin's argument, however, is not that the application of Hart's theory necessarily means that Mrs Sorenson would lose the case. Rather, his point is that she is disadvantaged by the fact that she cannot claim that she has a pre-existing legal right to win. Even if she did go on to win the case, therefore, she would not win because the *law* was on her side, but because the extra-legal considerations, which Hart's theory says the judge would be forced to apply, happened to point in her favour. This seems to run counter, Dworkin contends, to litigants' and legal-professionals' expectations about how this kind of case should be resolved. By failing to satisfy these expectations, Hart's theory fails to satisfy the ideal of adjudication according to law.

Whether Dworkin's own theory of adjudication satisfies this ideal, of course, is itself a controversial question. Even if one accepts his contention that it is possible for judges to fashion moral principles that 'fit' all or most past decisions in particular areas of law,[128] his further contention that conflicts between such principles must be resolved by choosing the principle that best justifies past decisions[129] appears to make the determinacy of law depend on the possibility of objectively correct moral arguments. That part of his theory has been attacked from a number of different angles. Hart himself anticipated the general line of criticism when arguing that, if there is no practical way of showing which of two competing principles is objectively correct, then it is unhelpful to suggest that the exercise of judicial discretion is constrained in this way.[130] Others have disputed the underlying philosophical soundness of Dworkin's theory, arguing that, 'if there are no objectively right answers to moral questions, there can be no objectively right answers to legal questions'.[131]

---

[128] See Ronald Dworkin, *Law's Empire* (Cambridge, MA: Harvard University Press, 1986), 227–8, 245–58. For an early critique of Dworkin's conception of legal principles, see Joseph Raz, 'Legal Principles and the Limits of Law' (1972) 81 *Yale Law Journal* 823. For a useful summary of the CLS critique of this aspect of Dworkin's argument, see Andrew Altman, 'Legal Realism, Critical Legal Studies, and Dworkin' (1986) 15 *Philosophy & Public Affairs* 205.

[129] See, for example, Dworkin, *Law's Empire* 231.

[130] H. L. A. Hart, 'American Jurisprudence through English Eyes: The Nightmare and the Noble Dream' (1977) 11 *Georgia Law Review* 969, 984–5 (citing Kent Greenawalt, 'Discretion and Judicial Decision: The Elusive Quest for the Fetters that Bind Judges' (1975) 75 *Columbia Law Review* 359).

[131] Leiter, 'The End of Empire' 175 (citing John Mackie, 'The Third Theory of Law' in Marshall Cohen (ed.), *Ronald Dworkin and Contemporary Jurisprudence* (Totowa, NJ: Rowman & Allanheld, 1983) 161.

Dworkin has defended himself against these criticisms.[132] The force of his critique of Hart's view of law is in any case not dependent on the persuasiveness of his own theory. There *is* evidently a problem with a purportedly liberal view of law that denies the constraining role of law in hard cases. While it is possible to argue that hard cases constitute only a small fraction of the overall number of cases litigated, let alone the overall number of conceivable 'legal events',[133] this sub-set of cases may include a high proportion of cases where law, on the liberal view, really should make a difference.[134] In constitutional adjudication, especially, this sub-set may include cases involving controversial moral issues and question-able assertions of political power. If law cannot deliver on its promise to constrain judicial decision-making in such cases, judicial review's claim to legitimacy as an apolitical check on the abuse of political power is in jeopardy.

Within the tradition of legal positivism, the most sustained attempt to think through this deficiency in Hart's view of law can be found in the work of Joseph Raz. Raz's approach to the question is complex and it will not be possible to do justice to it here. We can, however, gain an impression of his views by briefly considering his account of legal reasoning and then relating this account to his conception of the rule of law. Through this exercise, in turn, we should be able to discern whatever common elements there might be in the competing Dworkin-ian and legal positivist conceptions of the ideal of adjudication according to law, which we would then be able to use as a basis for understanding the shared criteria informing the Chaskalson Court's reputation.

The main statement of Raz's views on legal reasoning is contained in Chapter 13 of his book, *Ethics in the Public Domain*.[135] In this chapter, Raz distinguishes two forms of legal reasoning: reasoning 'about what the

---

[132] See Ronald Dworkin, 'Objectivity and Truth: You'd Better Believe It' (1996) 26 *Philosophy & Public Affairs* 87, 136–8.

[133] See Frederick Schauer, 'Easy Cases' (1985) 58 *Southern California Law Review* 399, 413.

[134] See Brian Leiter 'Legal Indeterminacy' (1995) 1 *Legal Theory* 481 (responding inter alia to Lawrence B. Solum, 'On the Indeterminacy Crisis: Critiquing Critical Dogma' (1987) 54 *University of Chicago Law Review* 462, 471–2; Ken Kress, 'Legal Indeterminacy' (1989) 77 *California Law Review* 283, 296–7 and Schauer, 'Easy Cases'). Note that Leiter himself thinks that liberal political theory may have an adequate response to the more moderate version of the indeterminacy thesis. See Jules L. Coleman and Brian Leiter, 'Determinacy, Objectivity and Authority' (1993) 142 *University of Pennsylvania Law Review* 549, 579–94.

[135] Raz, *Ethics in the Public Domain* 310–24.

law is' and reasoning 'about how legal disputes should be settled according to law'.[136] Consistently with his exclusivist take on legal positivism,[137] Raz argues that the first type of reasoning occurs independently of moral considerations, whereas the second is 'straightforward moral reasoning'.[138] In this way Raz seeks to preserve legal positivism's 'separability thesis',[139] while at the same time denying that legal reasoning is autonomous from moral reasoning when it comes to the application of a legal rule to decide a case.

The interesting thing about this classification for our purposes is that Raz uses the term 'reasoning according to law' to cover all instances of legal-rule application, including instances where, on the legal positivist view, the law runs out. He does not explain this choice other than to point out that the law 'quite commonly directs the courts to apply extralegal considerations'. As an example of this, he cites instances where the courts are directed to apply the law of a foreign country.[140] But this example hardly accounts for the use of the term 'reasoning according to law' in the situation of 'open texture' identified by Hart.[141] In this kind of situation, as Hart recognised, it is not necessarily the law (in the sense of a valid legal rule) that directs the judge to apply extra-legal considerations, but legal-professional conventions about what judges may do to resolve the case.[142]

In a subsequent essay, Raz offers much the same classification, arguing that legal reasoning is non-evaluative and autonomous in so far as it is used to establish 'the content of the law', but evaluative and non-autonomous in so far as it is used to reason from a premise that the law 'has a certain content' to a particular legal conclusion.[143] On this occasion, however, he does elaborate a little on his choice of terminology.

---

[136] Ibid. 311.

[137] On the distinction between 'inclusive' and 'exclusive' legal positivism, see W.J. Waluchow, *Inclusive Legal Positivism* (Oxford: Clarendon Press, 1994) ch 4.

[138] Raz, *Ethics in the Public Domain* 316–17.

[139] The view, that is, that the identification of a valid legal rule occurs independently of moral considerations.

[140] Raz, *Ethics in the Public Domain* 317.   [141] Hart, *The Concept of Law*.

[142] Ibid. 124 (arguing that the 'criteria of relevance and closeness of resemblance' that judges use when deciding whether or not to apply a legal rule 'depend on many complex factors running through the legal system and on the aims and purposes which may be attributed to the rule. To characterize these would be to characterize whatever is specific or peculiar in legal reasoning.').

[143] Joseph Raz, 'Postema on Law's Autonomy and Public Practical Reasons: A Critical Comment' (1998) 4 *Legal Theory* 1, 5–6.

The second type of type of reasoning, Raz says, 'is (in shape and form) ordinary evaluative reasoning, which is undertaken according to law, *for the law requires courts to reach decisions through such reasoning*'.[144] He then defines reasoning according to law as 'reasoning that imports moral and other premises *in accordance with the role they have by law, or at any rate consistently with the law*'.[145]

As Andrew Halpin has pointed out, Raz's claim that the second type of legal reasoning is reasoning 'according to law' is founded on two separate ideas.[146] The first is that, even where there is no uncontroversially identifiable legal rule that plainly settles the case, the law (in the form of some or other jurisdictional rule) may nevertheless authorise the judge to give an answer. In giving an answer, the judge will reason 'according to law' in the sense that he or she will be acting under a general legal authorisation to resolve the case. The second idea is that, in certain situations, the law might direct judges to resolve a case by recourse to 'moral and other premises' and in so doing specify, or at least delimit, the 'role' that evaluative reasoning is to play.

The first idea, Halpin contends, relies on a 'transferred epithet'.[147] Assuming Raz is correct that reasoning from a premise that the content of the law is such and such to a particular legal conclusion requires no more than ordinary evaluative reasoning, the fact that a judge is authorised by law to settle the case does not justify calling the reasoning in which he or she engages 'legal'. The epithet 'legal' here relates to the source of the judge's authority, rather than to the nature of the reasoning.[148] For the same reason, calling this sort of reasoning 'reasoning according to law' is a little misleading. The law might well authorise the judge to settle the case, but the ideal of adjudication according to law requires more than this. It requires the law to constrain the way the judge decides the case, so that the parties feel that their case was settled according to pre-existing principles and rules rather than the judge's all-things-considered view about who should win.

Raz's second idea seems to accept this point in so far as he acknowledges that the law may circumscribe the role 'moral and other premises' play in legal reasoning. But Raz does not define what he means by 'the law' here. One possibility is that he is referring back to his argument in Chapter 13 of *Ethics in the Public Domain* that judges reason according

---

[144] Ibid. 5 (emphasis added).   [145] Ibid. 6 (emphasis added).
[146] Andrew Halpin, *Reasoning with Law* (Oxford: Hart Publishing, 2001) 39.
[147] Ibid. 38.   [148] Ibid.

to law whenever a valid legal rule directs them to apply extra-legal considerations. As we have seen, however, this argument is not wholly satisfactory, because it ignores instances where the law runs out. In such instances, there may be no 'law' (in the legal positivist sense) that delimits the 'role' that 'moral and other premises' are to play, or that can act as a measure against which evaluative reasoning may be said to proceed 'consistently with the law'.

Left like that, therefore, Raz's account of legal reasoning appears vulnerable to the charge that it lacks a viable conception of the ideal of adjudication according to law. By insisting that there is nothing distinctively legal about the way judges apply valid legal rules to resolve cases, his account seems to deprive law of any independent constraining force. This is not the end of the matter, however. It is clear from other essays that Raz accepts the basic liberal premise that judicial decision-making does need to be constrained if judges are to act as a legitimate check on the abuse of political power. It is just that he does not think that these constraints can be said to emanate from law, at least not law in the sense of an autonomous system of reasoning.

In his essay on the politics of the rule of law in Chapter 16 of *Ethics in the Public Domain*, Raz thus acknowledges that the rule of law 'requires principled, as well as faithful adjudication'.[149] What he means by this, however, is something qualitatively different from Dworkin's conception of these terms. For Raz, '[p]rincipled decisions are reasoned and public. As such they become known, feed expectations, and breed a common understanding of the legal culture of the country, to which in turn they are responsive and responsible'.[150] What constrains the exercise of judicial discretion, on this view, is not the judicial duty to put the law in its 'best' light,[151] but judges' duty publicly to justify their decisions. Legal systems that insist on this duty promote the rule of law in two ways. On the one hand, they subject majoritarian decision-making to judicial control, which is a necessary condition for morally justified democratic government.[152] On the other, they constrain the exercise of judicial discretion by exposing judges' decisions to the possibility of 'public criticism'.[153]

This understanding of the rule of law does not require that every case be settled by recourse to a valid legal rule or a legally immanent principle. Rather, the exercise of judicial discretion is constrained by expectations

---

[149] Raz, *Ethics in the Public Domain* 358.   [150] Ibid.
[151] Dworkin, *Law's Empire* 52–3, 231.   [152] Ibid.   [153] Ibid.

about the sorts of reasons that judges may legitimately give in support of their decisions. These constraints flow naturally from the requirement of 'public, principled justification':[154] since judicial decision-making will always be undertaken within a particular institutional setting, it is inevitable that over time 'common values and shared practices' will develop about how judges may permissibly justify their decisions.[155] These 'common values and shared practices' are transmitted through the relevant legal culture and are susceptible to democratic influence through legislation. Judges need to be 'faithful' to the 'purpose' of the statutes they interpret, but at the same time must seek to integrate them in a principled way with 'the underlying doctrines of the legal system'.[156] They are, in this sense, the 'guardians' of their country's legal 'tradition',[157] even as they are constrained by it.[158]

If we put this argument together with Raz's account of legal reasoning, the outline of a viable conception of the ideal of adjudication according to law begins to emerge. On the one hand, as we have seen, Raz insists that law in the form of a body of valid legal rules cannot constrain the exercise of judicial discretion in every case. This is the formalist fallacy exposed by Hart in his work on the 'open texture' of rules.[159] On the other hand, the requirement of 'public, principled justification' means that judges, when exercising discretion in hard cases, must give reasons that are persuasive according to the legal tradition in which they are operating. It is this duty publicly to justify their decisions, rather than valid legal rules, which both constrains the exercise of their discretion and legitimates the role judges play in liberal-democratic systems of government.

This conception of the ideal of adjudication according to law is not unique to Raz. Most obviously, it resembles Karl Llewellyn's argument about the 'steadying factors' that render appellate-court decision-making

---

[154] Ibid. 358–9.   [155] Ibid. 359,   [156] Ibid.   [157] Ibid.

[158] In another essay ('On the Authority and Interpretation of Constitutions: Some Preliminaries' in Larry Alexander (ed.), *Constitutionalism: Philosophical Foundations* (Cambridge University Press, 1998) 152, 180), Raz argues that there is no such thing as a general theory of constitutional interpretation in the sense of a theory that transcends particular institutional settings. The only 'advice' that can be given to constitutional interpreters, therefore, is that they should 'reason well'. Nevertheless, in particular legal systems at particular times, rules and practices of sound constitutional interpretation will inevitably develop, and these will constrain permissible interpretations to a significant degree.

[159] Hart, *The Concept of Law*, 121–32.

in the United States 'reckonable'.[160] Llewellyn's sceptical account of legal rules, along with American legal realism generally, was of course dismissed by Hart in Chapter VII of *The Concept of Law*.[161] It is now clear from work done by Brian Leiter,[162] however, that the implied theory of law underlying American legal realism was essentially positivist in character, and that Llewellyn differed from Hart mainly in relation to his view of the nature, and therefore the extent, of the indeterminacy of legal rules. Whereas Hart defended law's claim to legitimacy on the grounds that the indeterminacy of legal rules was limited to penumbral cases, and in any case not undesirable,[163] Llewellyn's defence, driven by his more sceptical account of legal rules, depended on showing how judges were constrained by legal-cultural factors such as 'The General Period-Style', 'Known Doctrinal Techniques', and 'Professional Judicial Office'.[164] There is a striking similarity between this argument and Raz's notion of the 'common values and shared practices' underpinning a legal tradition. In both cases, what constrains the exercise of judicial discretion is the fact that judicial decision-making occurs in an institutional setting that is governed by reasonably stable norms and practices. Since these norms and practices may authorise judges to consider moral and policy considerations, there is nothing specifically legal about the reasoning judges use to justify their decisions. The fact that judicial decision-making occurs within this kind of institutional setting, however, means that judges cannot simply give effect to their own policy preferences or to the preferences of third parties. At least, if judges *do* decide cases on that basis, the legal legitimacy of their decisions may be called into question.

When put like that, Raz and Llewellyn's conception of the ideal of adjudication according to law evinces certain similarities to ideas propounded by the American Legal Process School, a group of scholars whose work is typically seen to be quite 'anti-positivist' in

---

[160] Karl Llewellyn, *The Common Law Tradition: Deciding Appeals* (Boston, MA: Little Brown, 1960).

[161] H. L. A. Hart, *The Concept of Law* (Oxford: Clarendon Press, 1961) 132–7. But see Hart, 'American Jurisprudence through English Eyes' 969, where Llewellyn is associated with Dworkin as someone who thought the law always controls. Hart is here evidently responding to Llewellyn's treatment of legal-cultural factors as 'the law'.

[162] See Brian Leiter, 'Positivism, Formalism, Realism' (1999) 99 *Columbia Law Review* 1138, 1153–5.

[163] Hart, *The Concept of Law* 125.

[164] Llewellyn, *The Common Law Tradition* 21–3, 35–45.

character,[165] and as having laid the foundation for Dworkin's theory of adjudication.[166] Far from providing cause for concern, this resemblance suggests that there may be some common ground between the legal positivist conception of the ideal of adjudication according to law and versions of that ideal propounded by legal theorists working in what may loosely be described as the natural law tradition.[167]

The Legal Process School's distinctive contribution to Anglo-American legal theory was to focus on the institutional function of judicial dispute-resolution in the governmental system as a whole.[168] Within that system, members of the school argued, judges had a special role to play: that of settling disputes by way of 'reasoned elaboration'.[169] As Lon Fuller put it,[170] adjudication was a form of social ordering, 'the distinguishing characteristic' of which lay in the fact that it gave litigants the opportunity to present 'proofs and reasoned arguments for a decision in [their] favor'.[171] The role of courts in the governmental system was thus 'to be a voice of reason, charged with the creative function of discerning afresh and of articulating and developing impersonal and

---

[165] See Richard H. Fallon, Jr, 'Reflections on the Hart and Wechsler Paradigm' (1994) 47 *Vanderbilt Law Review* 953, 965 (referring to the Legal Process School's 'anti-positivist principle'). See also Leiter, 'Positivism, Formalism, Realism' 1155 (criticising Anthony Sebok's contrary argument in *Legal Positivism in American Jurisprudence* (New York, NY: Cambridge University Press, 1998) 113).

[166] See Vincent A. Wellman, 'Dworkin and the Legal Process Tradition: The Legacy of Hart & Sacks' (1987) 29 *Arizona Law Review* 413.

[167] Dworkin's status within the natural law tradition is, of course, contested (see, for example, Mackie, 'The Third Theory of Law'), but for present purposes that label will suffice to encompass the broad range of ideas spanning the Legal Process School, Fuller and Dworkin.

[168] See Henry M. Hart, Jr. and Albert M. Sacks, *The Legal Process: Basic Problems in the Making and Application of Law*, ed. William N. Eskridge, Jr. and Philip P. Frickey (New York, NY: Foundation Press, 1994) (first published as a set of mimeographed lecture notes by Harvard Law School in 1958).

[169] See the extract from the 1958 version of Lon Fuller's paper on the 'Forms and Limits of Adjudication' in Hart and Sacks, *The Legal Process* 401 (arguing that the public's faith in the 'essential rationality' of adjudication depends on confining 'the uses adjudication . . . as closely as possible to those where that faith is justified – where, in other words, the process of adjudication is in fact a rational one'). In the published version of this article, Fuller wrote: 'By and large it seems clear that the fairness and effectiveness of adjudication are promoted by reasoned opinions' (Lon Fuller, 'Forms and Limits of Adjudication' (1978) 92 *Harvard Law Review* 353, 388).

[170] Fuller, though not himself a member of the school, is generally understood to have been quite influential on it. See Neil Duxbury, *Patterns of American Jurisprudence* (Oxford: Clarendon Press, 1995) 232.

[171] Fuller 'Forms and Limits of Adjudication' 364.

durable principles'.[172] The legitimacy of the judicial function, on this view, stems not from the determinacy of formally valid legal rules, but from the fact that people living under a liberal-democratic system of government may in theory challenge and subject to rational scrutiny the fairness and appropriateness of the application of general norms to them.[173]

These ideas were famously applied to the role of judges in constitutional adjudication by Herbert Wechsler.[174] Writing in the aftermath of the US Supreme Court's decision in *Brown* v. *Board of Education*,[175] Wechsler argued that principled decision-making consists in the justification of decisions by recourse to reasons that 'transcend the immediate result that is achieved'.[176] Judges' legal-professional duty on this account is to promote the rational coherence of the legal system as a whole rather than a particular political theory. However morally praiseworthy the outcome of the decision in *Brown*, therefore, the decision fell to be criticised on the ground that the reasoning followed was not premised on a principle that could be easily generalised to other cases.[177]

Dworkin, of course, though influenced by these ideas, took them in a different direction. While accepting the need for judges to found their decisions on general principles, he argued that the nature of judicial decision-making was inescapably moral in character.[178] Judges could not avoid choosing between competing political theories in decisions like *Brown*, but rather had to choose the theory that put their country's legal tradition in its 'best' light.[179] With hindsight, it is possible to see how Dworkin was pushed in this direction by the sustained CLS critique of Wechsler's neutral principles idea, as exemplified by Duncan Kennedy's description of American federal-court practice as a function of two rival ideological projects.[180] Faced with this particular line of argument and

---

[172] Henry Hart, 'The Supreme Court, 1958 Term – Forward: The Time Chart of the Justices (1959) 73 *Harvard Law Review* 84, 99 (quoted in Tamanaha, *Law as a Means to an End* 106).

[173] See further Kress, 'Legal Indeterminacy' 327; Gary Peller '"Neutral Principles" in the 1950s' (1988) 21 *University of Michigan Journal of Law Reform* 561.

[174] Herbert Wechsler, 'Toward Neutral Principles of Constitutional Law' (1959) 73 *Harvard Law Review* 1.

[175] 347 US 483 (1954).   [176] Ibid. 15.   [177] Ibid. 31–5.

[178] This theme permeates all of Dworkin's work, but see particularly Ronald Dworkin, *Freedom's Law: The Moral Reading of the American Constitution* (Cambridge, MA: Harvard University Press, 1996).

[179] Dworkin, *Law's Empire* 52–3, 231.

[180] Duncan Kennedy, *A Critique of Adjudication (Fin de Siècle)* (Cambridge, MA: Harvard University Press, 1998).

the peculiarities of the American system of judicial review, Dworkin sought to ground law's claim to legitimacy in a more robust conception of the ideal of adjudication according to law than the one provided by Wechsler. It is not enough, according to Dworkin, that judges play the role of *politically impartial* guardians of their country's legal tradition. They also need to play the role of *moral* guardians. This is true whether or not a particular country's constitution expressly gives them this role (say, by making the validity of legislation subject to compatibility with the moral values underlying a bill of rights). Either way, the ideal of adjudication according to law requires judges to make moral choices between the principles informing a particular legal tradition. Principled adjudication, on this view, is about more than the creation of a rationally coherent body of law that *reflects* the institutionalised norms and practices of a particular legal tradition. It is about the creation of a rationally coherent body of law that *reconstructs* those norms and practices in a morally attractive way.

Dworkin's sustained pursuit of these ideas has had a profound impact on legal academics, constitutional judges and human rights practitioners all over the world.[181] In understanding the Chaskalson Court's reputation in the comparative constitutional law community, therefore, his conception of the ideal of adjudication according to law must be taken into account. While no actually existing constitutional court could be expected to fulfil all the criteria he posits, it is unlikely that the Court's reputation would have been as high as it was had it not managed to satisfy at least those criteria that are compatible with the legal positivist conception.

Despite some important differences, the discussion has revealed that there is indeed a significant amount of overlap between the Dworkinian and legal positivist conceptions of the ideal. Both conceptions thus reject the simple view that the legitimacy of the judicial function in liberal-democratic systems of government stems from the capacity of formal legal rules to eliminate the need for judicial choice. Instead, what legitimates the role judges play in such systems is the fact that judges work within a reasonably stable legal tradition. Such traditions are repositories

---

[181] See, for example, Javier Couso, 'The Transformation of Constitutional Discourse and the Judicialization of Politics in Latin America' in Javier A. Couso, Alexandra Huneeus and Rachel Sieder (eds.), *Cultures of Legality: Judicialization and Political Activism in Latin America* (Cambridge University Press, 2010) 141, 152–3 (testifying to Dworkin's influence on constitutionalist discourse in Latin America).

of the norms and practices governing principled decision-making in the country concerned. Although these norms and practices are subject to creative adaptation by judges (which is a healthy and necessary element in any legal system), they do at the same time impose significant constraints on judicial decision-making, both because judges' legal-professional socialisation makes them want to conform to them, and because they provide a publicly available standard according to which the legitimacy of judicial decisions may be assessed. Any indication that a decision has been influenced by partisan political considerations, for example, is enough to render that decision illegitimate in legal traditions aspiring to this ideal. Shared legal-professional understandings of applicable norms and practices are also often determinate enough to rank one decision as more persuasive than another (a dissenting judgment, say, that eventually wins acceptance). In particularly difficult cases, of course, there is likely to be disagreement about which of two contending decisions is correct. Indeed, that is precisely what renders such cases difficult. But this does not mean that judges are free in such cases to engage in ideological or result-oriented decision-making. At least, if they were to do this, they would tarnish their reputation for principled decision-making and at the same time undermine their community's faith in the ideal of adjudication according to law.

1.6 Translating the common elements of the ideal into shared criteria

Translating these common elements into the shared criteria informing the Chaskalson Court's reputation in the comparative law community is no simple matter. We may begin, however, by revisiting Raz's argument, which was mainly directed at the British situation, and then extrapolate it to the situation in which we are interested: that of a newly established constitutional court interpreting a rights-based constitution.

For Raz, as we have seen, judges are 'guardians' of their country's legal 'tradition',[182] by which he means that they must continually strive to integrate legislation into the underlying doctrines of the legal system. A successful court, on this view, is one that is able to reconcile its duty to be 'faithful' to the purposes of legislation with its duty to safeguard the rational coherence of the law.[183] The former duty stems from the basic

---

[182] Raz, *Ethics in the Public Domain* 359.   [183] Ibid.

commitment to democratic government, whereas the latter is linked to the court's authoritative role in (1) ironing out inconsistencies between the purposes of legislation and other purposes already embedded in the law, and (2) mitigating the potentially distorting effects of legislation on 'long-established traditions'.[184]

If we extrapolate this argument to the situation in which we are interested, the first point to note is that a newly established constitutional court's duty to remain faithful to the purposes of legislation will be complicated by its mandate to strike down legislation that it finds to be inconsistent with the constitution. Not just that, but one of the express (or at any rate, necessarily implied) purposes of the constitution might be to transform the existing legal culture of the country – the very 'common values and shared practices' that Raz says provide the standard against which the legitimacy of judicial decisions is to be measured. In so far as 'the common legal culture ... is shaped by legislation as much as by judicial practices',[185] this means that the court may find itself in the awkward position of having, on the one hand, to be faithful to the purposes of the new constitution, including its transformatory purposes, and, on the other, to justify its decisions according to the very legal-professional norms and practices it is mandated to transform.

The relationship between the constitution, ordinary legislation and legal culture is thus more dynamic and fluid in the situation in which we are interested than it is in the context that Raz was addressing. The new constitution could not simply be treated as an ordinary piece of legislation that needed to be 'tame[d]' to bring it into line with 'existing legal doctrine'.[186] Rather, it would have to be understood as an extraordinary, long-term intervention in the country's legal tradition. As such, every legal rule and principle, and every purpose thought to be embedded in the law, would potentially be up for grabs. The challenge faced by a constitutional court in this situation would be faithfully to implement the constitution's moral vision, while yet justifying its decisions in terms acceptable to the legal-professional community. Meeting this challenge would require the court somehow to take the legal-professional community with it, to transform the 'common values and shared practices' of the existing legal culture even as the justificatory force of its decisions depended on their conformance to these norms.

---

[184] Ibid. 360.   [185] Ibid. 359.   [186] Ibid.

Three criteria in particular would seem to condition the success of a constitutional court in such a situation. First, the court would need to adapt its 'style' of adjudication, in Llewellyn's sense, to the new style required by the constitution. While a constitution cannot dictate the method of its interpretation, the adoption of a constitution that mandated a court to review the conformance of all law to the standards prescribed by a bill of rights would necessarily require the court to adapt its decision-making methods to suit this new institutional function. In particular, where the existing legal culture was predominantly 'formal' in character,[187] the court, especially a newly established constitutional court, would need to give greater interpretive weight to the substantive moral and political considerations informing legal rules. Instead of treating legal rules as conclusive reasons for the resolution of disputes falling within their sphere of application,[188] legal rules would need to be interpreted purposively, as context-sensitive expressions of the moral and political considerations that went into their construction. This change in adjudicative style would be required not just to give content to constitutional rights, but also to understand the operation and effect of existing legal rules, including common-law legal rules, in certain cases.[189]

Secondly, the court would be required to develop a rationally coherent account of the constitutional value system. Whereas the first criterion is essentially a stylistic criterion, relating to the court's ability to transform legal-professional expectations about permissible forms of judicial reasoning, this criterion concerns the substantive content of the 'shared values' that underpin a particular legal-professional culture. Depending on the precise formulation of the constitutional text, it would almost certainly be required that the court should prefer the new constitutional value system to existing legal-cultural values where the two were

---

[187] See P. S. Atiyah and R. S. Summers, *Form and Substance in Anglo-American Law: A Comparative Study of Legal Reasoning, Legal Theory, and Legal Institutions* (Oxford: Clarendon Press, 1987) 5–11 (distinguishing between 'formal' and 'substantive' legal cultures and associated modes of legal reasoning according to the degree to which decisions in the legal system concerned tend to be based on the existence of an authoritative legal rule as opposed to a countervailing 'moral, economic, political, or other social consideration').

[188] See Frederick Schauer, *Playing by the Rules: A Philosophical Examination of Rule-Based Decision-Making in Law and Life* (Oxford: Clarendon Press, 1991).

[189] This would be the case where constitutional rights had so-called horizontal effect, as in South Africa and Germany.

inconsistent. To do this, the court would need to give some type of moral content to constitutional rights.

On the legal positivist conception of the ideal, the court would not need to be 'philosophically ambitious' in this regard.[190] The requirement is not that the court should read into the constitution an elaborate political theory. Rather, the second criterion would require the court to articulate the moral message of the constitution on a case-by-case basis.[191] Thus, for example, a pre-constitutional commitment to the absolute inviolability of property rights might need to be transformed to accommodate the new constitution's concern for the survival needs of the propertyless. In this way, the court would be required to play an active role in bringing legal-cultural values into line with the new constitutional value system.

On the Dworkinian conception, such an incremental, case-by-case approach would not be enough. As we saw when considering Sunstein and Dworkin's comments on the Chaskalson Court's socio-economic rights jurisprudence, the legal positivist and Dworkinian conceptions of the ideal diverge at this point. Whereas Sunstein was content to approve of the Court's approach as providing *a* morally defensible understanding of its institutional function, Dworkin was concerned to argue that it was based on the best available understanding of its institutional function, considering the constitutional text and the moral principles at stake. As Dworkin has argued elsewhere in relation to Sunstein's work, there is no such thing as a 'mid-level principle'.[192] If the justification of the court's institutional function in relation to the enforcement of socio-economic rights requires a full-blown political theory of the relationship between majoritarian democracy and individual rights, then that is what the court must supply, restrained only by the limits of time and imagination.

For both conceptions of the ideal, the success of a newly established constitutional court would also be conditioned by a third and final criterion: the need to develop an account, alternatively (on the Dworkinian conception) a full-blown political theory of its institutional role in the political system – an understanding of the range and limit of its powers that it applied

---

[190] Raz, *Ethics in the Public Domain* 359.

[191] See, for example, Cass R. Sunstein, *Legal Reasoning and Political Conflict* (Cambridge, MA: Harvard University Press, 1995) and W. J. Waluchow, *A Common Law Theory of Judicial Review: The Living Tree* (Cambridge University Press, 2007).

[192] Dworkin, *Justice in Robes* 69 (critiquing this idea as contained in Sunstein, *Legal Reasoning and Political Conflict*).

consistently across all cases. That account would mainly need to be articulated through its separation of powers doctrine. The essential requirement here would be for the court to develop a rationally coherent and morally defensible understanding of how far its constitutionally mandated function of protecting fundamental rights permitted it to intrude into the political branches' sphere of operation. Once again, this criterion would not require the court to develop determinate tests that made its decisions entirely predictable, in the manner of legal formalism. Rather, the ideal of adjudication according to law requires the court to develop standards of review that force it to be clear about the substantive moral and political considerations justifying its decisions. The third criterion would in this sense re-enforce the first. The difference between the two, however, would be the need in relation to the third to develop an account of the nature and importance of particular constitutional rights, and the circumstances in which the court's views of how they should be fulfilled could be substituted for the political branches' views on the same issue.

This list is not meant to be exhaustive, but rather illustrative of the kinds of criteria that the ideal of adjudication according to law generates when extrapolated to the type of situation in which we are interested. Enough, at least, has been said to show that the criteria are meaningful and capable of conditioning the success of constitutional courts in this situation. It should also by now be apparent how these criteria relate to Dworkin and Sunstein's comments on the Chaskalson Court's record and how, by elaborating on the common theme running through these comments, the criteria may be said to inform the Chaskalson Court's reputation in the comparative constitutional law community. The final section concludes the argument by drawing out the difference between these criteria and the criteria applied by judicial politics scholars.

1.7   The distinctiveness of the criteria and the justification for this study

As we saw in the first section, judicial politics scholars work with two main standards of success when assessing the performance of constitutional courts: an *institutional legitimacy* standard, in terms of which a constitutional court is successful to the extent that it builds public support for its veto role in national politics, and an *institutional efficacy* standard, which simply requires the court to be able to assert (and get away with asserting) that role. Studies conducted by Gibson and others show that the Chaskalson Court was not successful according to the first standard.[193] The second standard, however, captures much of what is remarkable about the political dimension of the Court's achievement. For whatever reason, the Court was able to decide a number of politically controversial cases, secure compliance with its decisions, and in this way act as an effective veto player in South African politics. Most remarkable of all, it did all of this without triggering any significant political backlash.

We are now in a position to set this aspect of the Court's achievement alongside its success in legal terms, to see whether there is anything puzzling about the co-existence of these two phenomena and, if so, whether an interdisciplinary approach might be best suited to resolving that puzzle. On the one hand, we have the Court's efficacy as an institution – its capacity to do what it was designed to do without endangering its institutional independence. On the other, we have its reputation in the comparative constitutional law community – a reputation that this chapter has argued would not have been as high as it was had the Court's decision-making record not satisfied certain criteria associated with the ideal of adjudication according to law.

Stated in this abstract form, the two aspects of the Court's achievement appear fairly ordinary. Sustained institutional efficacy and a reputation for principled decision-making are after all phenomena that are commonly encountered side by side in mature constitutional democracies. Indeed, the very notion of a mature constitutional democracy is that of a polity in which the courts have built the capacity to decide politically controversial cases in a legally principled way without sacrificing their institutional independence.

But the Chaskalson Court was not operating in a mature constitutional democracy. On the contrary, the Court began its work in very uncertain political circumstances, after a dramatic transition from authoritarian rule to democracy. Moreover, that transition took the form, not of a revolutionary transfer of power, but of a negotiated political compromise, in which the outgoing white minority Government was able to influence the content of the new constitution in a way that would not have been possible had it been forced to rely on its share of the popular vote.[194] Even after the first democratic elections in 1994, when the ANC was elected with close to two-thirds of the votes cast, the white minority still continued to exercise a disproportionate influence over the final constitution-making process.[195] In effect, this situation required the

---

[193] See the discussion in Section 1.3.   [194] See Chapters 4 and 6.   [195] See Chapter 4.

Chaskalson Court to enforce the terms of a less than fully democratic constitution against the wishes of a democratically elected government, and moreover one that was overwhelmingly popular and without a realistic competitor.

In circumstances like these, comparative experience suggests, the Chaskalson Court should not have been able to assert its institutional role as quickly and as forcefully as it did, at least not without triggering an attack on its independence. The Court's closest post-1989 analogue, the Hungarian Constitutional Court, was reined in after the original justices had served their first term of office, with none of them re-appointed to serve a second term.[196] Like the Chaskalson Court, the first Hungarian Constitutional Court had built a reputation for bold, principled decision-making; only in the Hungarian case, the Court paid the predicted price for its uncompromising approach to its mandate. Why did the same not happen to the Chaskalson Court? Why was it allowed to continue thwarting the implementation of the ANC's policies with only the occasional, and in the end quickly abandoned, threat to its independence?

Neither the attitudinal nor the strategic model in judicial politics is capable of explaining this achievement. Even if it could be shown that the institutional and political preconditions for the first model's application in South Africa were satisfied, we would be left with the Court's reputation in the comparative constitutional law community to explain, one that went far beyond the assertion by the judges of their sincere policy preferences. The strategic model, too, would be hard pressed to explain the Court's success in legal terms. Although it might be able to show, as we saw in relation to the death penalty decision, that the Court was not as politically constrained as might first appear, the strategic model's underlying conception of law precludes it from being interested in, let alone explaining, how it was that the Court built a reputation for principled decision-making. The historical-institutionalist approach would fare better than the other two approaches on this score, but it would be parasitic on the liberal-legalist conception of law to explain the legal dimension of the Court's achievement, and thus any explanation it offered would collapse into the approach suggested here.

---

[196] See Kim Lane Scheppele, 'Guardians of the Constitution: Constitutional Court Presidents and the Struggle for the Rule of Law in Post-Soviet Europe' (2006) 154 *University of Pennsylvania Law Review* 1757.

As to liberal legal theory itself, the difficulty lies in the general aversion of theorists working in this tradition to factoring in the real-world political constraints on constitutional adjudication. This does not mean that liberal legalists deny the existence of these constraints. Dworkin, for example, in what is almost a throwaway line in *Law's Empire*, remarks that:

> [a]n actual justice must sometimes adjust what he believes to be right as a matter of principle, and therefore as a matter of law, in order to gain the votes of other justices and to make their joint decision sufficiently acceptable to the community so that it can continue to act in the spirit of a community of principle at the constitutional level.[197]

This passage seems positively to invite consideration of the circumstances in which judges committed to principled decision-making may legitimately make some concession to the constraints of the political environment in which they are working. Dworkin does not go on to consider these circumstances, however, contenting himself with the statement that the importance of his approach lies in allowing us to see 'the compromises actual justices think necessary as compromises with the law'.[198] The unfortunate (because false) impression created is that of someone who is happy to leave the messy business of real-world constitutional adjudication to others.

Perhaps there is something in Richard Posner's notion of pragmatic adjudication that may be of assistance. Consider, for example, his controversial views on the US Supreme Court's decision in *Bush v. Gore*.[199] On Posner's reading, that decision, despite its seeming disregard for principle, was justified on the grounds that it averted a constitutional crisis.[200] Does this approach not provide a framework for explaining how constitutional courts in new or fragile democracies might go about reconciling their commitment to principle with the real-world political constraints under which they operate?[201] Not really. According to Posner, satisfying legal-professional expectations about how a case ought to be decided is simply one pragmatic consideration among many – something that judges must do in the interests of legal certainty, but a

---

[197] Dworkin, *Law's Empire* 380–81.   [198] Ibid. 381.   [199] 531 U.S. 98 (2000).

[200] Richard A. Posner, *Law, Pragmatism, and Democracy* (Cambridge, MA: Harvard University Press, 2003) ch 9.

[201] See my earlier attempt to explain the Chaskalson Court's record in these terms: Theunis Roux, 'Principle and Pragmatism on the Constitutional Court of South Africa' (2009) 7 *International Journal of Constitutional Law* 106.

consideration that may be outweighed by other factors.[202] This is hardly
an approach to judging, as Dworkin's powerful critique of Posner's work
demonstrates,[203] that satisfies any defensible conception of the ideal of
adjudication according to law. Once again, therefore, the Chaskalson
Court's reputation in the comparative constitutional law community
would be hard to explain. At the same time, if all it ever did was make
pragmatic compromises on principle, it would hardly have been the
efficacious institution it was.

So we must try to explain the Chaskalson Court's achievement in some
other way. Perhaps the explanation lies instead in the fact that the criteria
generated by the ideal of adjudication according to law are fairly easy to
satisfy? According to these criteria, after all, a constitutional court is not
required to give an objectively correct answer to the cases it decides, but
merely an answer that is principled and persuasive according to the
norms and practices of the legal tradition in which it is working. It
follows that constitutional courts are not absolutely constrained by law
in any practical sense. In any particular case, there may be several ways of
satisfying the criteria set out in Section 1.6. Does it not then also follow
that the criteria conditioning a court's ability to assert its institutional
role, though different from the criteria in Section 1.6, are not really in
tension with them? If constitutional courts are not absolutely constrained
by law, surely it is an easy enough matter for judges to defer to the wishes
of powerful political actors whenever necessary, and to camouflage their
decisions under a mass of legalist rhetoric, as both the strategic model
and critical legal theorists contend? If so, is the Chaskalson Court's
achievement really that remarkable?

Seductive as this argument is, it does not do justice to the criteria in
Section 1.6 or to the nature of the Chaskalson Court's reputation in the
comparative constitutional law community. The Court's reputation is not
that it cleverly manipulated the law in politically controversial cases so as
to avoid political attack, but that it frequently took courageous stands on
principle. In so doing, the Court did more than simply rationalise its
decisions in legally plausible ways. If Sunstein and Dworkin's comments
are anything to go by, it often gave quite compelling answers to the
questions that were put to it – answers that were not just competent in
some legal-technical sense but also morally appealing and instructive
about the role that constitutional courts may play in liberal-democratic

---

[202] Posner, *Law, Pragmatism, and Democracy* ch 9.
[203] See, for example, Dworkin, *Justice in Robes* 60–65, 75–104.

systems of government. Most importantly, the Court's reputation (even among critical legal theorists) is that of one committed to the ideal of adjudication according to law. If the criteria in Section 1.6 are indicative of the things a constitutional court needs to do in order to build such a reputation, then the simple 'law is politics' explanation for the Chaskalson Court's achievement rings hollow. There must be a richer explanation, one that has to do with the political context in which the Court found itself, the legal tradition in which it was working, the challenge to this tradition posed by the Court's duty to give effect to the post-apartheid Constitutions, the comparative constitutional law community's role in providing the resources needed to respond to this challenge, and ultimately the Court's doctrinal choices in the cases that came before it. The next chapter develops a conceptual framework for an interdisciplinary explanation of this kind.

2

A conceptual framework for assessing the performance of constitutional courts

As Chapter 1 has endeavoured to show, the criteria that judicial politics scholars and liberal legal theorists use to evaluate the performance of constitutional courts are different and not obviously related. In large part, this has to do with the factors these two fields have traditionally been prepared to countenance as actual or permissible influences on constitutional adjudication. While judicial politics scholars have tended to emphasise, mainly as a descriptive matter, a wide range of contextual factors, liberal legal theorists have primarily been interested in the nature and permissible scope of judicial reasoning. The separation between the two fields is not absolute, however, and the last fifteen years have seen a number of calls for interdisciplinary research in this area.[1] The challenge laid down in such calls, to liberal legal theorists in particular, has been to ground normative theorisations of judicial review in realistic accounts of the political contexts in which constitutional courts operate.[2]

This chapter must be understood against this background. For reasons given in the previous chapter, however, the aim is not so much to provide a contextually grounded theory of judicial review as to develop an interdisciplinary conceptual framework for assessing the performance of constitutional courts. In order to do this, the chapter argues, what we need is a mediating concept – some way of conceiving of the factors that judicial politics scholars and liberal legal theorists respectively emphasise that brings them into relation with each other, allowing their mutual interaction to be

---

[1] See, for example, Cross, 'Political Science and the New Legal Realism' 252; Whittington, 'Once More unto the Breach' 601.

[2] See Barry Friedman, 'The Politics of Judicial Review' (2005) 84 *Texas Law Review* 257, 259 (arguing that 'much, if not most, normative constitutional theory … still fails to come to grips with the lessons of positive scholarship'); Keith E. Whittington, 'Constitutionalism' in Whittington et al. (eds.), *The Oxford Handbook of Law and Politics* 281, 294–5 ('normative constitutional theorists who drive a great deal of explicit interest in constitutional institutions often rest their arguments on assumptions about constitutions that require greater conceptual and empirical work to adequately unpack and examine').

explored. The most appropriate candidate for such a concept is the notion of 'constraint', which is defined here as a particular type of influence on judicial behaviour disregard for which entails a loss in legal or political terms. Following the argument in Chapter 1, the legal constraints under which constitutional courts operate are conceived as emanating from judges' legal-professional duty to give principled reasons for their decisions in accordance with the norms and practices of the legal tradition in which they are working. The political constraints, in turn, are seen to derive from the capacity of political actors to attack the court in ways that undermine its independence.

When the influences on constitutional adjudication are conceived as interacting forms of constraint in this way, the Chaskalson Court's achievement may be understood as consisting in its capacity to respond to each form of constraint without compromising its ability to respond to the other. This would have been possible, of course, only if the relationship between the two forms of constraint had been one of tension rather than necessary contradiction. To keep open this possibility, the chapter introduces a two-dimensional matrix depicting the relative strength of the constraints under which constitutional courts operate. The chapter then sets out the indicators of constraint along each axis of the matrix according to which a court's relative position may be mapped. This way of proceeding makes it possible to see that the nature of the law/politics tension impacting on a constitutional court is contingent on its proximity to one of four ideal types, corresponding to the four sectors of the matrix. It also makes it possible to see how a constitutional court may be able to negotiate the legal and political constraints impacting on it, either so as to maintain its position within a particular sector, or so as to manoeuvre itself across the matrix.

2.1   Two forms of constraint

For all their differences, most scholars working in judicial politics and liberal legal theory would likely agree that both legal and political factors *potentially* exert an influence on constitutional adjudication. At the extreme end of these fields, to be sure, the influence of one or the other of these two types of factor is denied.[3] In between these extremes,

---

[3] Thus, the attitudinal model denies, as an empirical matter, the influence of legal factors on US Supreme Court adjudication, and restricts the influence of political factors to the formation of judicial ideology. Likewise, critical legal theorists deny, as an interpretive matter, the

however, there is a sizeable middle ground in which different theories about the respective influence of legal and political factors are propounded – either as a descriptive matter in relation to a particular court, or as a normative matter in relation to some or other ideal conception of the role of constitutional courts in liberal-democratic systems of government.

For those tilling this middle ground, the key interdisciplinary question is how to conceive of the influence of legal and political factors in a way that makes sense to both fields while allowing for the possibility of some interaction between them. In relation to the second part of this question, the further issue is whether the two sets of factors pull in opposite directions, in the sense that the influence exerted by legal factors always (as a descriptive matter) and necessarily (as a conceptual matter) contradicts the influence exerted by political factors, or whether it is possible to conceive of the influence exerted by legal and political factors in a more nuanced way – as sometimes contradictory, at other times mutually re-enforcing, and at yet other times neutral in relation to each other.

The approach adopted here is to conceive of the legal and political factors impacting on constitutional adjudication as two distinct but inter-related forms of constraint, and then to address the question of the interaction between these two sets of factors as being about the court's capacity to respond to each form of constraint without compromising its ability to respond to the other. This approach will not satisfy everyone. Brian Tamanaha, for example, in his assessment of 'the slant in the "judicial politics" field',[4] has argued that conceiving of legal factors as constraints concedes too much to the political science view of judges as policy-preference maximisers. Rather than viewing law as a form of constraint, Tamanaha argues, law should be seen as a set of 'guideposts [judges] are actively searching for and following to reach their destination'.[5] The idea of law as a constraint on adjudication is also the idea, as we have seen,[6] against which the historical-institutionalist school in judicial politics has reacted,[7] in a move many think has improved prospects for productive interdisciplinary exchange.[8]

---

constraining influence of legal doctrine on appellate-court adjudication in the United States – at least in the strong, legitimacy-conferring sense maintained by liberal legalists.

[4] Brian Z. Tamanaha, *Beyond the Formalist-Realist Divide: The Role of Politics in Judging* (Princeton University Press, 2010) 111–31.

[5] Ibid. 118–19.   [6] Chapter 1.

[7] See, for example, Whittington, 'Once More unto the Breach' 615.

[8] See the references in notes 1 and 2.

Thinking about law in this way is nevertheless common practice in liberal legal theory. As we saw in Chapter 1, the debate between Dworkin and the legal positivist tradition over the ideal of adjudication according to law assumes the need for judicial decision-making to be constrained – if not by formal legal rules and principles, then at least by the institutionalised norms and practices of the legal tradition in which the judge is operating. When put in this way, the idea of law as a constraint on adjudication is not antithetical to the idea of adjudication as an institutionally embedded social practice. Even if judges view law as a set of 'guideposts' they are 'actively searching for', institutionalised norms and practices still function as constraints in so far as they inform the standards of principled decision-making in the legal tradition concerned. The required correction to the political science conception of judging, in other words, is to conceive of legal constraints, not as constraints on the maximisation of judges' *policy preferences*, but as constraints on the *character and quality of the reasons* judges may offer in support of a decision without damaging their reputation for principled decision-making.

Conceiving of political factors as constraints on adjudication likewise has a long history in judicial politics. The strategic model, as we have seen, is premised on a view of judges as politically constrained actors who must sometimes forgo their sincere policy preferences in order to achieve an outcome closest to their preferred policy.[9] Historical institutionalists, while stressing that judges respond to legal-professional norms, also take account of the wider political context in which judges operate – a context they conceive as constraining a court's capacity to assert its constitutionally assigned role.[10] Finally, proponents of the attitudinal model, in denying the influence of external political factors on the US Supreme Court, premise their argument on a particular understanding of the political context for judicial review in the United States, rather than a blanket denial of the relevance of external political factors in all contexts.[11]

Even if it does not capture every kind of influence on constitutional adjudication, the idea of legal and political factors as constraints captures

---

[9] See, in general, Epstein and Knight, *The Choices Justices Make*. For an application of this idea outside the United States, see Gretchen Helmke, *Courts under Constraints: Judges, Generals, and Presidents in Argentina* (Cambridge University Press, 2005).

[10] See Gillman and Clayton (eds.), *The Supreme Court in American Politics*.

[11] See, for example, Segal and Spaeth, *The Supreme Court and the Attitudinal Model Revisited*.

a very important kind of influence, viz., those influences that, if disregarded, entail a loss of some kind – in the case of legal constraints, a loss in legal terms, and in the case of political constraints, a loss in political terms. That at least is the conceptualisation offered here. The power of this conceptualisation is that it allows us to define the law/politics tension in terms of a court's capacity to respond to the sometimes contradictory legal and political constraints impacting on it, and to see how, in situations where the two sets of constraints indeed pull in different directions, a court's enforced prioritisation of one or the other set of constraints entails a loss in legal or political terms. Not just that, but each type of loss may also be seen to entail certain consequences for a court's long-term capacity to negotiate the law/politics tension.

The nature of the loss associated with each form of constraint and the interaction between the two sets of constraints will be explained below.[12] For the moment, the general point may be illustrated by means of an example. Suppose a court were asked to decide a constitutional challenge to an abortion law, and that the court's powers included not just the power to grant or deny the claim, but also to fashion an order that effectively rewrote the law in accordance with the court's view (voting by majority) of the constitution. Suppose further that the judges each held strong, but differing views on the morality of the measures proposed, and that there were also the usual array of political actors in the country (a president, the governing party, an opposition party in theory capable of winning power at the next election, lobby groups and so on) with a range of equally strongly held views. The judges' discretion would be legally constrained to the extent that legal-professional norms and practices curtailed the otherwise potentially infinite set of justificatory arguments that each of the judges, and the court acting collectively by majority vote, could deploy in support of a particular outcome without incurring a loss in legal terms.[13] Likewise, the judges' discretion would be politically constrained to the extent that its failure to abide by the views of powerful political actors on the various policy measures proposed entailed some or other loss in political terms.

---

[12] See Section 2.2.

[13] Note that in this instance it is the range of *justificatory arguments* not *policy outcomes* that must be restricted.

When the legal and political factors impacting on constitutional adjudication are conceived as constraints in this way, all constitutional courts enforcing a supreme-law constitution on the liberal-democratic model may be thought of as occupying a position on the following matrix:

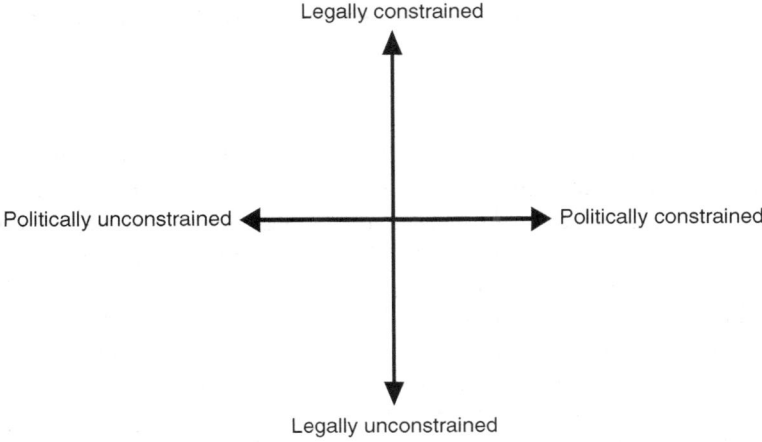

Figure 2.1

The two axes of the matrix represent the hypothetical range of all possible constitutional courts according to the relative strength of the legal and political constraints impacting on them, with each court's position in a particular sector determined by the coordinates of its position along the vertical and horizontal axes. A court in the bottom left-hand sector is thus a court whose decision-making discretion is both legally and politically unconstrained relative to other courts, whereas a court in the top right-hand sector is one whose discretion is both legally and politically constrained, and so on. More will be said below about the indicators of constraint used to position a court along each axis and therefore in a particular sector of the matrix. For the moment, the point to be grasped is that each axis represents the hypothetical range of constitutional courts in respect of the type of constraint concerned, and that a court's position along each axis is a relative position, i.e. it is not determined by any kind of absolute measure, but rather by considering the circumstances of the court in relation to the circumstances of other courts.

The significance of representing the hypothetical range of all possible constitutional courts in this way may be seen by contrasting Figure 2.1 to an alternative depiction based on the idea that the constraints exerted by legal and political factors pull in diametrically opposed directions. If that were the case, then all possible constitutional courts would occupy a point somewhere along the following continuum:

Legally constrained ◄————————————————► Politically constrained

Figure 2.2

According to this depiction, the legal and political constraints under which constitutional courts operate are locked in a zero-sum game such that a politically constrained court is to that extent legally unconstrained and vice versa. But the legal and political constraints under which constitutional courts operate are not necessarily correlated in this way. It is thus possible to conceive of a court that is both politically and legally unconstrained. (This is the way, for example, that the attitudinal model asks us to conceive of the US Supreme Court.) Conversely, a new constitutional court in a country with a well-developed legal tradition but no previous history of rights-based judicial review may be both politically and legally constrained. Even where a court is legally constrained and politically unconstrained, or politically constrained and legally unconstrained, the degree of its legal constraint may have nothing to do with the degree of its political constraint. At least, it cannot be assumed that the relationship between these two forms of constraint is of the zero-sum type depicted in Figure 2.2 without begging the question as to the nature of the interaction between them.

Accepting, then, that the hypothetical range of all possible constitutional courts is best expressed in the form of Figure 2.1, how should we conceive of the two sets of constraints, and with what degree of confidence might we be able to map a particular court on the matrix? The first question relates to the indicators of constraint along the two axes, the second to our ability meaningfully to apply them.

Recall that the point of developing this conceptual framework is to explain the Chaskalson Court's achievement, and that this achievement was said to consist in its simultaneous success in legal and political terms. The forms of constraint represented by each axis must therefore be conceived in a way that reflects the criteria for success identified in Chapter 1. At the same time, the conceptual framework must allow us to explore the relationship between these two forms of constraint and how it might be possible for a court to achieve success in legal and political terms at the same time. In the case of the vertical (legal constraints) axis, this means that the constraints in which we are interested, and which provide the basis for determining a court's relative position along this axis, are the constraints impacting on the court's capacity to build a reputation for principled decision-making. In the case of the horizontal (political constraints) axis, this means that the relevant constraints are those impacting on a court's capacity to play an effective veto role in national politics. The types of loss associated with each set of constraints may in turn be conceptualised, in the case of the legal constraints axis, as a loss in legal legitimacy, and, in the case of the political constraints axis, as a loss in institutional independence. The rest of this section fleshes out these somewhat crudely asserted ideas a little more.

Starting with the vertical axis: what are the indicators of constraint along this axis and how might we use them to determine a court's relative position? The basic conceptual distinction here is between courts above the midpoint, where the legal-professional culture maintains a relatively strong attachment to the ideal of adjudication according to law, and where law is thus seen to be separate from politics in the sense explained in Chapter 1,[14] and courts situated below the midpoint, where the legal profession's attachment to the ideal of adjudication according to law is relatively weak, and where the dividing line between law and politics is thus more blurred. As discussed below,[15] the position of a particular court just above or just below the midpoint of the vertical axis may be debatable and beyond the capacity of any defensible methodology to determine. The bright-line distinction marked by the midpoint is nevertheless that between courts in countries where both ideological and partisan political decision-making are strongly censured, and courts in countries where this proposition does not hold, either because legal institutions in the country concerned have not yet developed to the point where law is seen to be autonomous from politics,[16] or because the legal-professional culture, though well-developed, has undergone some sort of transformation that weakened its earlier attachment to the ideal of adjudication according to law.[17]

---

[14] See Sections 1.5, 1.6 and 1.7 in particular.

[15] See text accompanying note 25.

[16] A system of 'repressive law' in other words, as imagined in Philippe Nonet and Philip Selznick, *Toward Responsive Law: Law and Society in Transition* (New Brunswick, NJ: Transaction Publishers, 2001) (first published in 1978).

[17] As, for example, is generally thought to have occurred in the Unites States in the 1920s and 1930s under the influence of the legal realist movement. See the discussion in Section 2.3.

On the CLS view, of course, the fact that a particular legal-professional culture maintains a relatively strong attachment to the ideal of adjudication according to law does not mean that constitutional judges are *actually* significantly constrained by law, or that ideological or partisan political considerations do not *in fact* play a role in constitutional decision-making. Whatever the strength of a particular legal-professional culture's attachment to this ideal, critical legal theorists contend, judges will always be able to rationalise their decision in a way that satisfies applicable legal-professional norms and practices, at least in the sort of case that typically comes before a constitutional court. On the liberal-legalist view, however, the posited connection between the strength of the attachment to the ideal and the strength of the actual constraints exerted by law *does* follow, both because judges' legal-professional socialisation conditions them to search out the most legally satisfying answer to the case, and also because legal-professional norms and practices constitute an externally verifiable standard for assessing the quality of the reasons judges offer in support of their decisions. By correlating the strength of the constraints along the vertical axis to the strength of the relevant legal-professional culture's attachment to the ideal of adjudication according to law, the conceptual framework presented here assumes the correctness of the liberal-legalist view. Since the framework aims to capture the liberal-legalist criteria for the success of constitutional courts, this is as it should be.

What about some of the other categorisations of legal-professional culture in the literature and the norms of judicial reasoning with which they are associated? Do any of these other categorisations overlap with the categorisation offered here and, if so, might we be able to use them to locate a court on the vertical axis?

One of the best-known existing categorisations is that proposed by Patrick Atiyah and Robert Summers. In English legal-professional culture, they famously argued, norms of judicial reasoning tend towards the 'formal' in the sense that judges mostly are expected to rely on the authority of a settled rule to resolve a case, even where it is clear that there are strong 'moral, economic, political, institutional, or other social considerations' pointing to a different outcome.[18] In American legal-professional culture, by contrast, norms of judicial reasoning tend towards the 'substantive' in the sense that these considerations have greater weight, and may negate the application of a settled rule.

---

[18] Atiyah and Summers, *Form and Substance in Anglo-American Law* 1.

When considering the position of a court along the vertical axis, it might be tempting to think that formal legal-professional cultures by definition maintain a stronger attachment to the ideal of adjudication according to law than substantive legal-professional cultures, and therefore that a court in a formal legal-professional culture should automatically be placed above the midpoint of the axis and a court in a substantive legal-professional culture automatically below. This does not necessarily follow, however. A substantive legal-professional culture may be associated with just as strong an attachment to the ideal of adjudication according to law as a formal legal-professional culture. The dominant mode of legal reasoning in Germany, for example, underwent a transformation from formal to substantive after 1948, but German legal-professional culture did not abandon its historically strong attachment to the ideal of adjudication according to law.[19] The same is arguably true of Canada after 1982. On the other hand, the high formalism of Australian legal culture *is* associated with a strong attachment to the ideal of adjudication according to law, while the United States remains the paradigmatic case of a substantive legal-professional culture in which a high degree of ideological (but not result-oriented) decision-making is tolerated, at least on the Supreme Court.[20] All that can be said in the abstract, therefore, is that formal legal-professional cultures tend to be associated with a relatively strong attachment to the ideal, but that substantive legal-professional cultures may or may not be, depending on other factors.[21]

Another well-known categorisation is that offered by Phillipe Nonet and Philip Selznick between 'repressive', 'autonomous' and 'responsive' law.[22] According to this categorisation, political systems may be

---

[19] See Donald P. Kommers, *The Constitutional Jurisprudence of the Federal Republic of Germany* (Durham, NC: Duke University Press, 1989); Sweet, *Governing with Judges* 78 (referring to 'the deeply embedded legalism that is said to infect German political culture').

[20] The American example suggests that there may be a difference between the strength of a particular legal-professional culture's attachment to ideal of adjudication according to law in non-constitutional cases and in constitutional ones, in which case it would make sense to use the narrower constitutional culture in these instances.

[21] One of the preconditions for the co-existence of a substantive legal-professional culture with a strong attachment to the ideal of adjudication according to law, for example, might be broad societal consensus over the meaning and content of constitutional values, sufficient at least to determine the outcome of constitutional disputes in a high proportion of cases.

[22] Nonet and Selznick, *Toward Responsive Law.*

conceptualised as developing from an early stage of state-building in which law is used essentially as an extension of political power, through an intermediate phase in which law's autonomy from politics is increasingly tolerated for purposes of legitimation, and finally (and not at all necessarily) to a stage in which law and politics are once again connected, only in this case by a more sophisticated acceptance of the need for judges and administrative decision-makers openly to give effect to the political purposes embedded in legal rules and the substantive values running through the legal system.

The bipartite classification used here is obviously too crude to capture these three types of politico-legal order. But there is also a normative difference between the two conceptualisations that explains this fact. On the liberal-legalist view, 'responsive law', unless it can be stabilised by a high degree of consensus over the substantive values running through the legal system, inevitably leads to a greater degree of toleration for ideological decision-making than is compatible with the ideal of adjudication according to law, and thus courts operating in such politico-legal orders are correctly categorised as falling below the midpoint. By the same token, where a politico-legal order *is* premised on a high degree of consensus over the substantive values running through the legal system, it will be possible for judges to take account of these values in a way that satisfies the liberal-legalist understanding of the separability of law and politics. Courts operating in such politico-legal orders will therefore be categorised as falling above the midpoint. On the liberal-legalist approach, in another words, Nonet and Selznick's notion of responsive law either collapses back into the second type of legal-professional culture falling below the midpoint (i.e. that of a well-developed legal-professional culture in which a previously strong attachment to the ideal of adjudication according to law has for some historical reason weakened) or is coterminous with the sort of legal-professional culture, like that in Germany, where a substantive mode of legal reasoning is associated with a strong attachment to the ideal.

A third existing categorisation that it is worth briefly mentioning is Brian Tamanaha's distinction between 'instrumental' and 'non-instrumental' views of law and their associated legal-professional cultures.[23] According to this categorisation, a politico-legal order departs from the rule-of-law ideal to the extent that it condones the use of law as

---

[23] Tamanaha, *Law as a Means to an End.*

a value-neutral instrument for the achievement of political ends. This is chiefly because law in such politico-legal orders loses its capacity to discipline the abuse of political power – to impose limits on what can be done through and in the name of law. Instead, law is seen as a means to whatever end political parties, interest groups, legislatures, administrators, legal professionals and ultimately also judges seek to put it. Where this view of law predominates, Tamanaha argues, the rule-of-law ideal is seriously threatened and may even be said to have been compromised.

To a certain extent, Tamanaha's argument may be read as a liberal-legalist critique of Nonet and Selznick's overoptimistic reading of various trends in American judicial, legal-professional and administrative practice, about whose existence they are nevertheless all in agreement.[24] Tamanaha's conception of the law/politics distinction, however, is stricter than the one proposed in Chapter 1. Properly understood, the ideal of adjudication according to law does not condemn all instrumental uses of law. Indeed, it is central to this ideal that law be an effective tool for the implementation of legitimately determined political ends. This is one of the main reasons, after all, why liberal legalists are interested in law's capacity to constrain judicial decision-making. At the same time, liberal legalists think that law has a morally defensible role to play in determining both the procedural preconditions for the legitimate determination of political ends and also the substantive standards of political morality that otherwise legitimately determined political ends must meet.

As these three examples show,[25] other categorisations of types of legal-professional culture do not necessarily map onto the categorisation offered here and cannot therefore be used to locate a court's position on the vertical axis. This is not the same, however, as concluding that the only viable distinction is that between constitutional courts above and below the midpoint. It may be possible to make finer distinctions, at least between courts in legal-professional cultures where the attachment to the ideal of adjudication according to law is very strong and courts where the

---

[24] Ibid. 124–5, 233.

[25] The other obvious example is Max Weber's argument that European civil law systems evince greater 'formal rationality' than the English common-law system. See Max Weber, *Economy and Society: An Outline of Interpretive Sociology*, ed. Guenther Roth and Claus Wittich (Berkeley: University of California Press, [1921] 1978) 656–7, 890. This argument, if it was ever persuasive, holds little water today, and certainly cannot be used as a basis for a general rule that civil law systems are more strongly attached to the ideal of adjudication according to law than common-law systems.

ideal is less strictly maintained. The same may be true of courts below the midpoint. The only real doubt concerns whether it is possible to distinguish a court operating in a legal-professional culture where the attachment to the ideal is moderately strong (just above the midpoint) from one where the attachment to the ideal is moderately weak (just below the midpoint). In practice, these conceptual possibilities may amount to the same thing, meaning that a court's position along the vertical axis becomes indeterminate as it approaches the midpoint.

As indicated earlier, the loss a court incurs when it disregards the constraints imposed by the norms and practices of the legal tradition in which it is operating is a loss in legal legitimacy. For the court to incur such a loss, its decision – as a matter of justificatory adequacy rather than policy outcome – must fail to satisfy the standards of principled legal argument in the legal tradition concerned. This means, at the very least, that the court's decision should be *plausible* according to applicable norms and practices, i.e. it should not stray beyond the outer limits of permissible judicial reasoning by, for example, appealing to religious forms of authority in a legal tradition in which such appeals were not countenanced, or by deploying plainly irrational or self-contradictory arguments.[26] It also means more than this, however. Since law on the liberal-legalist view is capable of conditioning the relative persuasiveness of a decision, a court will also incur a loss in legal legitimacy whenever it justifies its decision in a way that is less than fully persuasive according to applicable legal-professional norms and practices.

While there would be many cases in which it would not be possible to say that the court's decision was illegitimate in this sense, there would be others in which the court's failure to provide a fully persuasive answer would *not* be subject to serious legal-professional disagreement. This would be the case, for example, where a dissenting judgment was generally agreed to have been more persuasive than the majority judgment, or where the overwhelming weight of legal academic opinion revealed that another, more persuasive way of justifying the majority judgment was available. Equally, there would be other cases in which a court was able to exceed legal-professional expectations about how its decision ought to have been justified – by writing a particularly persuasive judgment, say, which produced a strong rhetorical effect of legal necessity in a case in which the contending arguments were thought to be evenly matched.

---

[26] This is the definition of legal legitimacy used in Richard H. Fallon, Jr, 'Legitimacy and the Constitution' (2005) 118 *Harvard Law Review* 1787, 1817–18.

Legal legitimacy thus understood is a form of social capital: it is lost when the court fails to provide a fully persuasive decision, but it may be regained when the court hands down a particularly persuasive decision, one that revitalises the legal profession's faith in the ideal of adjudication according to law. Indeed, on this conceptualisation, as more fully elaborated below,[27] a constitutional court may be able to build up something like a store of legal legitimacy that allows it to weather the political storms of particularly controversial cases.

Following the procedure adopted in relation to the vertical axis, the next step is to translate the criteria for success in political terms discussed in Chapter 1 into indicators of constraint along the horizontal axis. Given the focus of the relevant judicial politics standard on a constitutional court's ability effectively to assert its veto role in national politics, the factors in which we are interested are factors relating to the external political environment for judicial review. We may, in other words, immediately exclude internal political factors – such as the influence of judicial ideology – from the indicators of constraint along this axis. Although the attitudinal model, as we have seen, is preoccupied with establishing the influence of such factors on the US Supreme Court, this model takes no particular position on the factors conditioning the success of constitutional courts in other countries. Rather, it is concerned with explaining judicial behaviour in the United States by reference to a particular conception of the political context for judicial review in that country. As we saw in Chapter 1, proponents of the strategic model challenge the accuracy of this conception. It is not necessary to take one or the other side in this dispute, however, to see that the cardinal issue when assessing the political constraints impacting on constitutional courts from a *comparative* perspective is variation in the external political environment for judicial review.

How should the political context for judicial review be conceived so as to capture the criteria for success in political terms developed in Chapter 1? The conceptualisation offered here is that the strength of the constraints exerted by the external political environment may be reduced to the court's relative degree of insulation from political attack *when asserting its constitutionally assigned veto role*. A court is thus strongly constrained in political terms where it is not so insulated (i.e. where its capacity to assert its veto role in politically controversial cases is

---

[27] See the discussion in Section 2.2.

minimal), and weakly constrained where it is so insulated (where it enjoys a relatively high degree of actual independence from political control, even in politically controversial cases). The corresponding loss in political terms that results from a court's disregarding these constraints is a loss in actual independence from political control, which may also (but need not necessarily) be reflected in changes to the formal institutional arrangements guaranteeing its independence.

The central notion in this conceptualisation is the notion of 'political attack' and thus it is this notion that must be explained first. As used here, the term refers to action taken by a political actor, as a response to, or in anticipation of, a particular court decision or a series of decisions, which has the effect of undermining the court's actual independence from political control.[28] The phrase 'has the effect of undermining' is used deliberately. It means that, in order to qualify as a political attack, the action must actually reduce the court's independence from political control. Action that does not have this result amounts to an attempted or threatened political attack, and will be referred to in these terms.

Political attacks may be of varying levels of severity. Examples of severe political attacks include changes to the judicial appointments process that make it more likely that judges appointed to the court will be less independent of the executive; changes to the rules relating to judges' security of tenure or remuneration, or to the court's budgetary independence; changes to the court's jurisdiction and powers that undermine its capacity to function as an independent check on the abuse of political power (e.g. the removal of the court's jurisdiction in respect of certain matters, or the removal of its power to make certain types of order); and the appointment of politically compliant judges (including by way of court-packing), or the non-reappointment of judges with a reputation for independence from the executive. Other forms of political attack include public statements intended to cow the court into submission, but only where these statements actually have the effect of undermining the court's independence, i.e. where they influence the court to decide the case (if the attack occurs before the decision) or future cases (if the attack occurs after the decision) in line with the policy preferences of the political actor making the attack.

---

[28] See Epstein, Knight and Shevtsova, 'The Role of Constitutional Courts in the Establishment and Maintenance of Democratic Systems of Government' 128; Whittington, 'Legislative Sanctions and the Strategic Environment of Judicial Review'.

Given this definition, a court's relative degree of insulation from political attack consists, not in its capacity to prevent all attempted attacks, but in its capacity to withstand them. Thus, the fact that a court is subject to repeated attempted political attacks does not mean that it is not insulated if none of these attacks actually reduces its independence from political control. In fact, quite the reverse is true: a pattern of repeated attempted (but failed) attacks would be indicative of a fairly high degree of insulation. Other indicators of insulation from political attack include: the level of respect for judicial independence in the political culture concerned (as assessed by qualitative analysis of that culture and the extent of compliance with court decisions), the institutional arrangements for judicial review, including judges' security of tenure and remuneration and the process of judicial appointment, but only to the extent that these arrangements actually raise the costs to political actors of attacking the court; the interests of major political actors, and whether these interests incline them to support the court's independence or not; and diffuse public support for the court as measured in social surveys (i.e. its institutional legitimacy).

The loss in political terms that a court incurs when it fails to abide by the constraints of the political context in which it is working amounts to a loss in institutional independence. This point follows conceptually from the above discussion: a failure to abide by these constraints necessarily triggers a political attack, which by definition results in a reduction in the court's actual independence from political control. The assumption, in other words, is that every time a court takes a decision that disregards the political constraints impacting on it, it will be successfully attacked. Whether or not a particular decision is constrained in political terms therefore depends on whether or not other political actors actually have the capacity and the inclination to attack the court in consequence of the decision.

The extent of a court's actual independence from political control is affected by, but not equivalent, to its institutional legitimacy. Institutional legitimacy may thus contribute to the court's capacity to withstand attempted political attacks,[29] but a court's capacity to withstand such attacks is also a function of the other factors listed above. It is therefore

---

[29] As is the case, for example, in India, where the Supreme Court enjoys a high degree of public support. See Pratap Bhanu Mehta, 'India's Unlikely Democracy: The Rise of Judicial Sovereignty' (2007) 18 *Journal of Democracy* 70.

possible for a court to enjoy a significant degree of independence from political control without building its institutional legitimacy.

Assessing a court's relative position on the horizontal axis requires qualitative analysis of all these factors. So, for example, a court whose judges were appointed for life and which operated in a political culture in which there was general respect for judicial independence would be a court that was relatively insulated from political attack. Conversely, a court whose judges were vulnerable to dismissal in consequence of their decisions, and which operated in an environment where powerful political actors had no interest in supporting its independence, would be a court that was relatively exposed to political attack.

2.2   Four central cases

A detailed methodology for mapping a court's position on the matrix is provided in Chapter 3. Depending on the depth of the analysis, it may be possible to make fairly fine-grained distinctions, and to identify a particular court as being, say, highly exposed to political attack, or only moderately so exposed. For present purposes, however, it is enough to say that the above discussion generates four central cases, as depicted by the following figure:

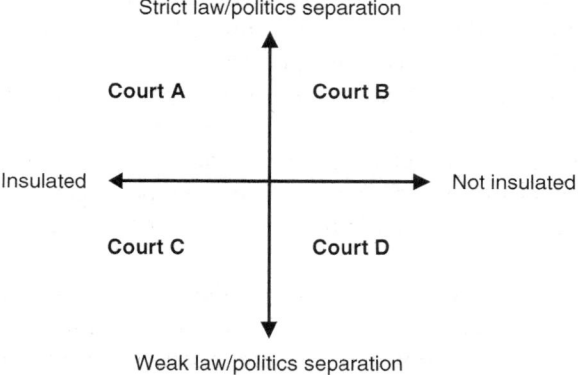

Figure 2.3

Figure 2.3 helps us to see that the precise interaction between the two forms of constraint will depend on a court's position on the matrix and the degree to which it approaches one of the four central cases. Where the court is weakly constrained in one or both senses, the likelihood that the two forms of constraint will contradict each other is reduced. This occurs either where the legal-professional culture maintains a fairly weak attachment to the ideal of adjudication according to law (Courts C and D), or where the court is relatively well insulated from political attack (Courts A and C).

The central cases represented by Courts A and D correspond to two immediately recognisable ideal types: the well-functioning constitutional court in a mature constitutional democracy (Court A), and the court in a new or fragile constitutional democracy with weakly developed legal institutions and no political tradition of respect for judicial independence (Court D). In most mature constitutional democracies,[30] where the legal-professional culture is premised on a relatively strong attachment to the ideal of adjudication according to law, and where all major political actors support the need for judicial independence, the tension between law and politics recedes to the background, arising only in isolated cases when a particularly controversial case brings it to the surface.[31] In situations like this, it will usually be possible for the court to negotiate its way through the period of heightened tension by justifying its decision in a way that the legal profession, and by extension, the broader political community, finds acceptable. It is only in rare cases, where the court fails to justify its decision in this way, that it will suffer a loss in legal legitimacy. Even in this exceptional kind of case, however, a loss in legal legitimacy rarely translates into a loss in institutional independence because the extent of support for judicial independence in the political culture is typically strong enough to enable the court to withstand any attempted political attack.

In the typical new or fragile constitutional democracy, there is also no real tension between law and politics, although in this instance this is for exactly the opposite reason, i.e. because the legal tradition has not yet developed to the point where judges are significantly constrained by law. In this situation, the legal profession and the broader political community *expect* the court to decide politically controversial cases in line with the wishes of the dominant political grouping (whether that grouping is currently in power or about to assume power[32]). While politically

---

[30] The major exception is the United States. See the discussion below.

[31] See, for example, Waluchow, *A Common Law Theory of Judicial Review* 5 (listing 'controversial' Canadian cases that have caused 'initial misgivings' about the Canadian Charter of Rights and Freedoms to 'flare up from time to time in public discourse').

[32] See Helmke, *Courts under Constraints*.

controversial cases may therefore give rise to even greater cynicism in the legal profession and the broader political community about the independence of the judiciary and the rule of law, they do not pose insurmountable problems for courts in the position of Court D. Such courts, as Epstein, Knight and Shevtsova argue,[33] must simply render decisions that conform to the policy preferences of powerful political actors. In this way they can ensure that their decisions are enforced and their institutional legitimacy progressively enhanced.

The law/politics tension also does not present significant problems for courts in the position of Court C. Here, the ideal of adjudication according to law is relatively weak but the court is at the same time relatively secure, either because fortuitous political conditions, such as a situation of political fragmentation, happen to insulate the court from political attack or because the political culture has adjusted to the partial collapse or blurring of the law/politics distinction. In both these cases, judges are relatively unconstrained by both law and politics, and consequently have greater freedom to decide cases in line with their own policy preferences. Courts conforming to the first variant of this ideal type, however, are by definition vulnerable to a sudden change in the political conditions that conduce towards their insulation from political attack. Courts in such a situation may therefore seek to consolidate their position by developing a style of legal reasoning that both constrains their discretion and at the same time contributes towards building a political culture of respect for judicial independence.[34]

The really interesting case is Court B, because it is in this sector of the matrix that the two forms of constraint operate at their strongest, and where law and politics may therefore appear to be in a permanent state of contradiction (in the manner depicted by Figure 2.2). If this is indeed the case, then, depending on the form of constraint the court disregards, it may either suffer repeated losses in legal legitimacy or be subject to repeated political attacks. If this is not the case, however – if the relationship between the legal and political constraints impacting on a constitutional court, even in this sector of the matrix, is better described as one of tension rather than permanent contradiction – then it might be possible for the court to negotiate that tension and eventually manoeuvre itself into the safer confines of the top left-hand sector.

---

[33] Epstein, Knight and Shevtsova, 'The Role of Constitutional Courts in the Establishment and Maintenance of Democratic Systems of Government'.
[34] See further Section 2.3.

The first reason why we might suppose that courts in the position of Court B might not be caught in a permanent state of contradiction is that the interaction between the legal and political constraints impacting on constitutional courts is case-specific. In any particular case, therefore, the constraints imposed by judges' legal-professional duty to give principled answers and the constraints emanating from the court's exposure to political attack may coincide. This would be the case, for example, where the outcome preferred by political actors with the inclination and capacity to attack the court could be justified by principled arguments. This would also be the case where the decision was not particularly controversial, and where the court was accordingly free to justify either outcome without triggering a political attack. In certain legal systems, it might also be possible for the court to avoid politically controversial cases altogether, either by declining to decide the case or by delaying the onset of the case until the controversy had been settled through the political process.[35] If these docket-management decisions were not subject to legal constraints, the court could do these things without any loss in legal legitimacy.

Only in some cases, therefore, would there be a stark contradiction between law and politics – between compliance with the justificatory standard set by the legal tradition in which the court was working and the policy outcome required by powerful political actors with the capacity and inclination to attack the court. Where a constitutional court in the position of Court B is presented with such a situation, the conceptual-isation offered here dictates that the court will suffer the loss associated with whichever form of constraint it disregards. Not just that, but a loss of either type would have certain predictable consequences for the court along the other dimension. Thus, a decision that complied with the political constraints impacting on the court at the expense of the legal constraints impacting on it would entail a loss in legal legitimacy, with possible knock-on effects for the court's institutional independence. Conversely, a decision that complied with the legal constraints impacting on the court at the expense of the political constraints would entail a loss in institutional independence, with possible knock-on effects for the strength of the legal profession's commitment to the ideal of adjudication according to law.

Where a court in the position of Court B disregards the legal con-straints impacting on it, the crucial question is how frequently this occurs

---

[35] The classic American case study is Perry, Jr., *Deciding to Decide*.

and how serious a loss in legal legitimacy it is able to sustain. On the one hand, the stronger the attachment to the ideal of adjudication according to law in the legal-professional-culture, the more damaging to the court's reputation for principled decision-making any capitulation to the political constraints impacting on it would be. On the other, the more entrenched the court's reputation for principled decision-making, the greater the court's capacity might be to survive the damaging reputational effects of politically driven decision-making, especially if such instances were restricted to a small number of cases. Just as the strategic model posits a court's capacity to build a store of institutional legitimacy, so, too, there might be something like a store of legal legitimacy on which a court in the position of Court B could draw to survive losses in politically controversial cases. If so, it might be possible for the court to compromise on principle in a few particularly awkward cases, without endangering its overall reputation for principled decision-making. Much would depend on how frequently such cases occurred and on the extent to which the court was able to exploit opportunities, either before or after these cases were presented, to build its overall reputation.

Where a court prioritises the legal constraints impacting on it, the conceptualisation offered here dictates that the court will be attacked and that it will consequently suffer a loss in institutional independence. In this instance, too, the crucial question is how severe each particular loss in institutional independence is and how frequently the court suffers this kind of loss. While a court might be able to sustain some degree of loss to its institutional independence (for example, greater politicisation of the judicial appointments process), repeated, severe political attacks would reduce its institutional independence to the point where it was unable to perform its constitutionally assigned veto role. Where this happened, the court's capacity to sustain the legal-professional culture's commitment to the ideal of adjudication according to law might also decline. This would be the case, for example, where the loss in institutional independence took the form of the appointment of politically compliant judges who were by definition less committed to the maintenance of that ideal. Repeated political attacks might also have a chilling effect on judges previously committed to principled decision-making. In both cases, the ironic result of the court's prioritisation of the legal constraints impacting on it would be a weakening of the legal-professional culture's commitment to the ideal of adjudication according to law, pushing the court down to the bottom right-hand sector of the matrix.

The interaction between the legal and political constraints impacting on a court is thus both context- and case-specific. 'Context-specific', because the political context for judicial review and the nature of the prevailing legal-professional culture will determine the sector of the matrix the court finds itself in and the general nature of the law/politics tension impacting on it. 'Case-specific', because the micro-politics of each case, and the applicable legal-professional norms and practices, will determine the precise nature of the law/politics tension in any particular case. Since the political context for judicial review is subject to change, both in response to the court's decisions and independently of them, we must also allow for the possibility of a change in the court's position over time. Indeed, the simultaneous success of a constitutional court in legal and political terms will in the end depend on its conformance to some or other normatively preferred view of its movement across the matrix from time T_1 (the commencement of the analysis, with the appointment of a new Chief Justice, say) to time T_2 (the Chief Justice's retirement). While the court's position on the matrix at T_1 and other factors beyond its control will obviously condition its success, we might be particularly interested in a court's capacity to negotiate the law/politics tension impacting on it and in this way alter its position on the matrix. It is to this question that the discussion now turns.

2.3   Judge-driven changes to a court's position on the matrix

Although changes to the law/politics tension over time are conditioned by a number of factors,[36] including factors beyond the court's control, most scholars agree that constitutional judges have a not insignificant role to play in this process. Epstein, Knight and Shevtsova, as we have seen, conceive of constitutional judges as masters of their own destiny with the capacity, through politically strategic decision-making, progressively to build their court's institutional legitimacy.[37] Liberal legal theorists tend not to address this issue specifically, but would presumably argue that judges, by consistently and from the very outset resisting the siren call of politics, may progressively mark out their

---

[36] See the discussion in Sections 3.1.2 and 3.2.
[37] Epstein, Knight and Shevtsova, 'The Role of Law in the Establishment of Democratic Systems of Government'.

court as a 'forum of principle'[38] and in this way contribute to its insulation from political attack. For critical legal scholars, for whom ideological decision-making is an ineradicable side-effect of adjudication under a rights-based constitution, the role of judges is not so much to manage the law/politics tension as to be open and honest about the political nature of their function.[39] To the extent that they fail to do this, CLS scholars tend to argue, judges are engaged in a permanent game of deception, in which they use various technical legal devices to mask the influence of political factors on their decisions.[40]

That courts can alter their position on the matrix, however, is beyond dispute. The Australian High Court, for example, having achieved a position comfortably in the top left-hand sector of the matrix over the course of the last century,[41] broke with settled interpretive methods in the 1980s and 1990s in an apparent attempt to transform the Australian Constitution into a more robust instrument for the protection of human rights. In place of the 'strict and complete legalism'[42] that had characterised the influential Dixon Court's jurisprudence, the High Court under Sir Anthony Mason embraced a more substantive method of constitutional interpretation in drawing out the Constitution's implications for such matters as the freedom of political communication and indigenous land rights.[43] The change in method precipitated a long period of

---

[38] See Dworkin, *A Matter of Principle*, 33–71. Dworkin, of course, does not deny that Supreme Court decision-making is political in the sense that the Court often settles controversial issues of political morality. Rather, by means of his distinction between 'principle' and 'policy', he tries to separate a class of legitimate political decision-making (decisions about what rights people have) from illegitimate political decision-making (utilitarian reasoning about the general welfare) (ibid. 69). On the Razian approach, the strict Dworkinian distinction between policy and principle is dropped (see Raz, 'Legal Principles and the Limits of Law'), but a weaker notion of 'public principled' reasoning is nevertheless maintained. See the discussion in Section 1.5.

[39] See Klare, 'Legal Culture and Transformative Constitutionalism'.

[40] This feature of research in the tradition of critical legal theory is sufficiently well known as not to require a detailed list of examples. For a representative sample, see David Kairys (ed.), *The Politics of Law: A Progressive Critique* 3rd edn (New York, NY: Basic Books, 1997).

[41] See Brian Galligan, *The Politics of the High Court* (Brisbane: University of Queensland Press, 1987).

[42] See address by Sir Owen Dixon on his appointment as Chief Justice, reprinted in Tony Blackshield and George Williams, *Australian Constitutional Law & Theory: Commentary and Materials* 5th edn (Sydney: Federation Press, 2010).

[43] Haig Patapan, *Judging Democracy: The New Politics of the High Court of Australia* (Cambridge University Press, 2000); Jason L. Pierce, *Inside the Mason Court Revolution: The High Court of Australia Transformed* (Durham, NC: Carolina Academic Press, 2006).

political turbulence for the Court, including threats by the executive, which were eventually carried out, to appoint judges of a more conservative political disposition.[44] This phase in the High Court's institutional life may thus be thought of as a rightwards drift across the matrix as the Court became relatively less insulated from political attack. Over the last fifteen years, judges more sensitive to Australian legal-professional culture's traditional distaste for substantive reasoning have returned the High Court to its former place squarely in the top left-hand sector.[45]

This example not only illustrates that judges are capable of changing the position of their court on the matrix, but also that action undertaken by a court in relation to one set of constraints may affect its position along the other axis. The impact of such action will not necessarily be adverse, in the sense of increasing the court's exposure to political attack or weakening the legal profession's commitment to the ideal of adjudication according to law. This is because, as seen in Section 2.2, the same action may be required by both sets of constraints.

Although judges may be conscious of the impact of their response to one set of constraints on their court's position along the other axis, this need not be the case. A group of judges who were collectively committed to the ideal of adjudication according to law might thus disregard the political constraints impacting on their decisions without any conscious appreciation of the impact of their decisions on their court's capacity to withstand political attack. Where their decisions happened to coincide with outcomes that were politically required, this would have no adverse impact on their court's position along the horizontal axis, and could, indeed, have a beneficial impact. Where, however, this type of commitment resulted in the court's flouting the political constraints impacting on it, the court would move rightwards along the horizontal axis, until such time as repeated political attacks resulted in changes that conclusively undermined its institutional independence. This, for example, is what happened to the Hungarian Constitutional Court, whose uncompromising (and some would say, institutionally short-sighted) pursuit of legal principle under Chief Justice Sólyom eventually resulted in the appointment of judges who were more susceptible to political control.[46]

---

[44] Haig Patapan, 'High Court Review 2001: Politics, Legalism and the Gleeson Court' (2002) 37 *Australian Journal of Political Science* 241; Haig Patapan, 'High Court Review 2002: The Least Dangerous Branch' (2003) 38 *Australian Journal of Political Science* 299.
[45] Ibid.   [46] See Scheppele, 'Guardians of the Constitution'.

Where judges *are* conscious of the impact of their decisions on the court's position along the two axes, it is not unreasonable to suppose that they might seek to use this knowledge to negotiate the law/politics tension in a particular case and to influence their court's position on the matrix over time. Whether unconscious or deliberate, the capacity of a court to alter its position on the matrix is determined by the nature of the sector in which it finds itself, how close to the central case for that sector it is, and its actions in response to the particular legal and political constraints impacting on it.

The top left-hand sector (Court A), apart from being the sector preferred by liberal legalists, is also a relatively desirable place for a court to be. For courts in this sector, as seen in Section 2.2, the tension between law and politics is latent rather than real. Provided they respect the legal constraints under which they are operating, there is every possibility that they will be able to remain in this sector indefinitely. Success for this type of court consists in staying where it is. By the same token, however, courts that find themselves at T_1 in this position have little to gain and everything to lose. Since their position at T_1 is attributable to factors for which they cannot take any credit (actions of predecessor judges combined with pre-existing features of the political context), the scale of achievement open to them is lower.

But there *is* room for movement, and thus reason to attribute some degree of success to a court if it manages to stay in this sector of the matrix. The duty to give principled decisions is not one that is easy to discharge and requires judges with the necessary technical skill and the requisite commitment to the ideal of adjudication according to law. Where the court disregards applicable legal-professional norms and practices, or creatively tries to reconceive them without taking the legal profession along with it, things can start to go wrong, as the Australian example shows. It is not impossible that the court might begin to slide both downwards and across the matrix, in a mutually reinforcing process that pushes the court towards the bottom right-hand sector. Avoiding this fate is a not inconsiderable achievement for courts in this sector.

There is also the possibility of the converse trajectory as the court adheres to prevailing legal-professional expectations about how it ought to fulfil its mandate, strengthens its reputation for principled decision-making, and becomes ever more institutionally secure. In this case, a virtuous circle may apply: the more the court satisfies the standards of principled decision-making, the more its decisions are seen to be 'legal' and not 'political', the more politically insulated the court becomes. This process may be visualised as a movement towards the top left-hand corner of the matrix – the ideal point in liberal legal theory, subject only to whatever reservations liberal legalists might have about the desirability of a constitutional court's being absolutely immune to political control (i.e. the requisite degree of democratic accountability).

As discussed in Section 2.2, a court that is solidly within the top left-hand sector of the matrix is not one that only receives politically uncontroversial cases. The left-hand sector of the matrix does not presuppose the absence of politics – just the fact that the court is insulated from whatever political repercussions its decisions might trigger. In comparative judicial politics terms, the court is one that has built the capacity to deal with politically controversial cases without risking its institutional independence. Indeed, the virtuous circle trajectory assumes that the more the court is seen publicly to decide politically controversial cases according to law, the greater its insulation from political attack will be.

In contrast to the top left-hand sector, the top right-hand sector of the matrix (Court B) is not a particularly desirable place for a court to be. In this sector, courts are relatively strongly constrained in both legal and political terms. As discussed, this does not mean that every case will present an irreconcilable choice between law and politics. A court's position on the horizontal axis is a measure of its overall exposure to political attack rather than a depiction of its exposure in every case. There might thus be many routine cases where the political stakes were not high. Even in politically controversial cases, it might be possible for the court to respect the legal constraints impacting on it without triggering a political attack. Given the relatively strong attachment to the ideal of adjudication according to law posited for a court above the midpoint, however, it is inevitable that, at some point, a case would be presented to the court where the politically required outcome, while plausibly justifiable according to applicable legal-professional norms and practices, could not be justified without some loss to the Court's reputation for principled decision-making. In this situation, the court would be forced to prioritise one set of constraints over the other: to trade off its commitment to principled decision-making against its need to protect itself from political attack.

This feature means that the top right-hand sector of the matrix is a fairly unstable place for a court to be. Indeed, the only reason why a court would find itself there in the first place would be a circumstantial change that thrust it into this sector (the adoption of a new constitution, say, or the ousting of a long-dominant political party). Finding itself there, one of two things could be expected to happen: the court might, by dint of its decision-making practices or a fortuitous change to the political context, move to the top left-hand sector of the matrix; or, before this happened, the court might be confronted by a politically controversial case, or series of politically controversial cases, the (combined) effect of which was to force it down the matrix into the bottom right-hand sector.

Where the judges on the court had some understanding of their court's situation, their capacity and inclination to manoeuvre their court into the top left-hand sector would depend on a number of factors: the timing of the cases that came to the court and its ability to manage its docket; the micro-politics of particular cases and the interaction between these micro-politics and the legal constraints impacting on the court; the judges' backgrounds, training and legal-professional socialisation; their preparedness to take account of the long-term institutional consequences of their decisions; and the judges' legal-technical skills in deciding cases in ways that minimised losses in legal or political terms. Although some of these factors would be beyond the judges' capacity to control, many would not be. Indeed, one might think of the judges as possessing various navigational tools that allowed them, if not immediately to move their court to calmer waters, at least to avoid some of the political storms that came their court's way.

This conceptualisation of what the judges of a court in the position of Court B need to do resembles the strategic model in certain respects. Both conceptualisations thus require judges to negotiate the legal and political constraints impacting on them to maximise their court's chances of reaching a preferred institutional position. There are two key differences, however. First, on the conceptualisation offered here, the position to which the judges would need to manoeuvre their court is not equivalent to some or other minimum degree of institutional legitimacy necessary for their effective functioning, but rather to the particular combination of insulation from political attack and attachment to the ideal of adjudication according to law characteristic of courts in the top left-hand sector. Secondly, the motivating force behind any such deliberate effort on the judges' part to manoeuvre their court to this position is not a desire progressively to expand their capacity to decide cases in line with their own policy preferences. Rather, judges engaging in this type of behaviour are conceived as being motivated by a commitment to the ideal of adjudication according to law and an appreciation that a political culture in which judges are allowed to pursue this ideal has to be carefully nurtured. On this conceptualisation, judges' legal-professional socialisation may actually predispose them to *want* to be constrained by law, and thus to pursue a strategy of putting their court in a position where (a) these constraints are real and meaningful; and (b) they are able to respond to them without fear of political attack.

Despite its association with rational choice theory, the term 'strategy' is still the best term to describe this type of behaviour, provided that what we understand by the term in this context is a deliberate process, within and through the constraints imposed by law, of improving prospects for principled decision-making over time. If the rational choice sense of the term is adapted in this way it is both compatible with, and complementary to, a commitment to the ideal of adjudication according to law. 'Compatible with' because the goal of improving prospects for legally principled decision-making over time is the concrete instantiation of this ideal, and 'complementary to' because the use of this term adds to the liberal-legalist conception the idea that judges may be able to shape the law in ways that enhance their court's capacity to assert its institutional role over the long run. To signal the difference between the two senses of the term, we might call a strategy of the second type an 'adjudicative strategy' and a strategy of the first type 'a purely political strategy'.

The list of such adjudicative strategies is open-ended, depending as it does on the political context in which the court finds itself and the nature of the legal-professional culture in which it is operating. As an example of what is meant by this term, however, consider the way in which a new constitutional court in the position of Court B might go about establishing a review standard in respect of a particular right. One approach might be to develop a full-blown political theory of the content and importance of the right in the very first case litigated under the right, and then to proceed to fit all subsequent decisions into this theorisation. Such an approach, however, would not be particularly strategic in the sense just defined – at least, the strategy associated with such an approach would be the all-or-nothing strategy of immediately and boldly asserting the court's institutional role as a 'forum of principle'[47] in the hope that this would insulate it from political attack. This kind of strategy might possibly work in certain circumstances, but it would be more likely to backfire given that, for courts of this type, the political community would by definition not yet be ready to accept such a role for the court. An alternative approach might thus be to develop a more

---

[47] See Dworkin, *A Matter of Principle*, 33–71.

context-sensitive review standard, one that depended less on providing a full-blown political theory and more on a case-by-case drawing out of the implications of the right. The court could then give further content to the right over time, concretising the review standard as it did so. While not fully principled in the Dworkinian sense, such an adjudicative strategy would satisfy the Razian requirement of 'public, principled justification'[48] and might also put the court in a better position to play a meaningful checking role over the long run.

In addition to developing context-sensitive review standards of this kind, another adjudicative strategy that a court in the position of Court B might conceivably use would be to develop a flexible separation of powers doctrine that allowed it to defer to the political branches in controversial cases, at least until such time as it had manoeuvred itself into the top left-hand sector of the matrix. Too flexible a doctrine, of course, would lead to allegations that the court had abdicated its responsibility to protect constitutional rights. But if the doctrine could be developed in such a way that it allowed the court to respond to the politics of particular cases, the court could enforce rights in a large enough number of cases to ensure that this did not occur, whilst at the same time avoiding political attack. Such a strategy would again compromise on principle in the Dworkinian sense since there would necessarily be instances where the court would fail to enforce a particular right that ought to have been enforced according to the best interpretation of the Constitution. Provided such instances were kept to a minimum, however, the court's overall reputation for principled decision-making might not be damaged, particularly if these deferential decisions were interspersed with bolder assertions of judicial power.[49]

If the supposition that a constitutional court would find itself in the position of Court B only after some extraordinary change to the political context is correct, the very fluidity of this situation might also work to the court's advantage. Certainly, where the court found itself in this position in consequence of a constitutional change from parliamentary sovereignty to rights-based judicial review, it would have significant scope to

---

[48] Raz, *Ethics in the Public Domain* 358–9 (discussed in Chapter 1).

[49] A court in the position of Court B would thus need to do more than cultivate the 'passive virtues' made famous in Alexander M. Bickel, *The Least Dangerous Branch: The Supreme Court at the Bar of Politics* 2nd edn (New Haven, CT: Yale University Press, 1986). It would also need to exploit the opportunities provided by the micro-politics of particular cases to build its reputation for principled decision-making.

shape the law. As we have seen,[50] the shift from a formal to a substantive legal-professional culture would give it numerous opportunities to engage in the types of adjudicative strategy just described.

The situation of courts in the bottom left-hand sector of the matrix (Court C) is quite different. In this sector, courts are relatively unconstrained by both law and politics, leaving the judges notionally free to decide cases in line with their policy preferences.[51] At first blush, this suggests that this might be quite a stable sector of the matrix. The judges themselves, lacking as they would any socialised attachment to the ideal of adjudication according to law,[52] might feel no particular compulsion to move. But there are reasons to doubt that this situation could last for very long, at least where the court conformed to the first variant of this ideal type: the court in a new or fragile constitutional democracy that was insulated from political attack by fortuitous political circumstances, such as a situation of political fragmentation. By definition, such circumstances would not include a well-developed political culture of respect for judicial independence, and thus the court would not enjoy the more durable shield that such a culture provides. One possible scenario, therefore, is that the judges, even in the absence of a strong legal-professional commitment to the ideal of adjudication according to law, would begin – for self-interested reasons – to develop norms of judicial reasoning that progressively reduced their ability to decide cases in line with their sincere policy preferences. In this way, both a stronger attachment to the ideal and a stronger political culture of respect for judicial independence might develop, lifting the court into the top left-hand sector.[53] If the court failed to do this, any change to the circumstances conducing towards its insulation from political attack could be expected to have a fairly immediate and dramatic effect, pushing it rightwards to the position of Court D.

---

[50] See Chapter 1.

[51] Both the attitudinal model and critical legal theory place the US Supreme Court in this sector of the matrix.

[52] The assumption, in other words, is that below-the-midpoint legal-professional cultures would not produce judges committed to the ideal of adjudication according to law, and that the building of a legal-professional culture in which this ideal mattered would thus require some independent change to the political context for judicial review.

[53] The process envisaged here is akin to the movement from 'repressive' to 'autonomous' law described by Nonet and Selznick, *Toward Responsive Law* 29–52 (focusing on the reasons why a repressive regime might tolerate such a shift).

This conceptual logic does not apply, however, to the alternative variant of this ideal type: the court in a mature constitutional democracy in which the legal-professional culture at some point in its history has undergone a transformation from a relatively strong to a relatively weak attachment to the ideal of adjudication according to law. The paradigm case here, as noted earlier, is the US Supreme Court, which, at least since the influence of the legal realist movement and the end of the *Lochner* era,[54] has operated in a legal-professional culture relatively tolerant of consequentialist, policy-based reasoning. In such a situation, decision-making according to the authority of settled rules is de-emphasised in favour of judges' legal-professional duty to give effect to the substantive moral and political commitments running through the legal system.[55] While it is possible still to maintain an attachment to the ideal of adjudication according to law in such a situation, as the German example shows, what is different about the American situation is a deep division in the political culture, and consequently also in the substantive moral and political commitments running through the legal system, between competing liberal and conservative conceptions of the good. In such a situation, substantive moral and political commitments (or higher-order principles) are less able to constrain constitutional adjudication, and US Supreme Court decision-making and to a lesser extent federal-court-of-appeals adjudication as well are open to greater influence by judicial ideology (though not by result-oriented decision-making).[56]

[54] Tamanaha, *Law as a Means to an End* 82–3 (identifying the Court's reversal of its opposition to the New Deal in response to President Roosevelt's court-packing plan as the defining moment when American legal-professional culture abandoned its faith in the constraining capacity of law). Tamanaha (*Beyond the Formalist-Realist Divide*) has recently cast doubt on the conventional version of this 'story', according to which American legal-professional culture was dominated by legal formalism from the 1870s to the 1920s and then underwent a dramatic transformation towards a radically rule-sceptical version of legal realism. The true situation, Tamanaha argues, is rather one of a more continuous commitment to 'balanced legal realism' over the last 150 years.

[55] Atiyah and Summers, *Form and Substance in Anglo-American Law* (on the characteristic mode of legal reasoning in the United States), Schauer, *Playing by the Rules* (on the implications of a commitment to rule-based decision-making).

[56] The strongest version of this thesis is presented in the attitudinal model literature discussed in Chapter 1 and in the CLS literature by Kennedy, *A Critique of Adjudication* (arguing that judges' personal commitment to either a liberal or conservative political ideology informs the 'ideological projects' they pursue in gap-filling, ambiguity-resolving judicial law-making). In recent years, a number of empirical studies have cast doubt on the strong version of this thesis, particularly at the federal court of appeals level, suggesting instead that judicial decision-making, while open to influence by judicial

The peculiar American combination of a weak attachment to the ideal of adjudication according to law and a relatively strong commitment to the independence of the judiciary is nevertheless highly stable, based as it is, not on a fortuitous and consequently fragile situation of political fragmentation, but on a long process of legal and political development in which the two-party political system has driven a mutually reinforcing acceptance by the legal profession and the political culture of a higher degree of ideologically driven decision-making than has been accepted in other countries.

The bottom right-hand sector (Court D), as we have seen, is quite a typical place for a constitutional court in a new or fragile democracy with an underdeveloped or politically compromised legal-professional tradition. Because the norm against result-oriented, partisan-political decision-making in this sector is by definition weak, there will be no discernible law/politics tension. By the same token, however, a court in this sector might find it very difficult to build a political culture of respect for judicial independence. Certainly, a purely political strategy of the kind posited by the strategic model would be unlikely to build such a culture. On the contrary, decision-making of this kind might simply entrench the court's reputation as a naked political actor. The best that a court engaging in this type of strategy could hope for, therefore, would be to move to the bottom left-hand sector of the matrix by building its institutional legitimacy in the manner prescribed by the strategic model, and from there to try to develop self-limiting norms as discussed in relation to Court C. The worst-case scenario is that a court in the position of Court D might get itself into a downward spiral – the mirror image of Court A's virtuous circle – as its exposure to political attack forced it into ever more desperate political strategising, further damaging its reputation for principled decision-making.

These various possibilities for judge-driven movement across the matrix may be expressed in the form of the following figure:

ideology, is also constrained by external political factors and by legal doctrine. See, for example, Cass R. Sunstein, David Schkade, Lisa M. Ellman and Andres Sawicki, *Are Judges Political? An Empirical Analysis of the Federal Judiciary* (Washington, DC: Brookings Institution Press, 2006); Cross, *Decision Making in the U.S. Courts of Appeals*; and Michael A. Bailey and Forrest Maltzman, *The Constrained Court: Law, Politics, and the Decisions Justices Make* (Princeton University Press, 2011).

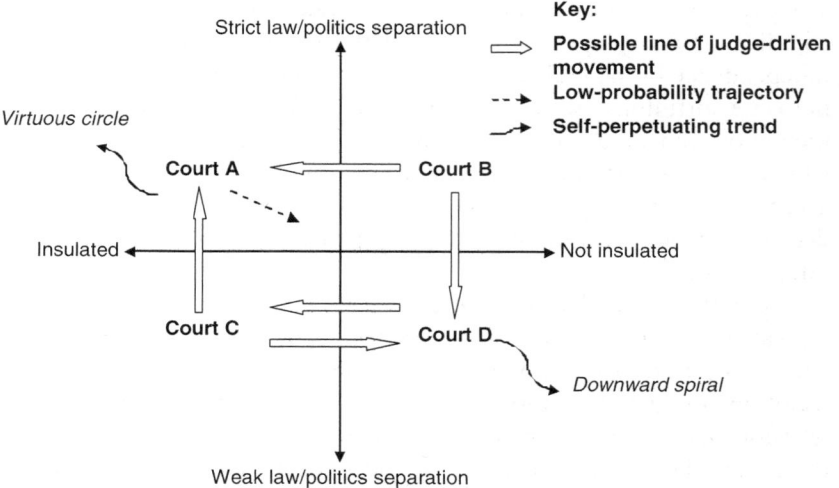

Figure 2.4

2.4   Constitutional courts in new and old democracies

Although this framework of analysis could be applied to evaluate the performance of constitutional courts in both new and old democracies, there would be some differences in emphasis. In mature constitutional democracies, as we have seen, the law/politics tension at T_1 would be a latent tension – the product of a reasonably stable political context for judicial review based on a well-developed political culture of respect for judicial independence. Under these conditions, the court's position on the left-hand side of the matrix would be in no doubt and the focus of the analysis would fall on the more subtle changes in adjudicative style associated with a new chief justice. One might think here, say, of the Burger Court's more moderate than expected retrenchment of the Warren Court's liberal activism,[57] or the High Court of Australia's still developing interpretation, under Chief Justice Robert French, of the separation of judicial power in Chapter III of that country's Constitution.[58]

---

[57] See, for example, Richard Hodder-Williams, 'Is There a Burger Court?' (1979) 9 *British Journal of Political Science* 173.

[58] See, for example, *South Australia* v. *Totani* (2010) 242 CLR 1.

Where, on the other hand, a court in an established democracy was given new powers of judicial review that drew it into politics in ways that required adjustment to the prevailing political culture, the court's position at T_1 would be less certain. Here, the political drivers behind the change to the court's powers might be important to establish. Were they, as was the case in the United Kingdom in 1998, the product of a single-party legislative rather than cross-party constitutional change? If so, to what extent did the country's membership of a supranational political organisation make up for this fact? If, instead, the change to the court's powers was effected through constitutional amendment, as was the case in Canada in 1982, how durable was the political coalition responsible for this change, and to what extent was the court able to exploit any accompanying public support for its institutional role to manage the required adjustment to the prevailing political culture?

In all such cases, the precise nature of the change to the court's powers would be important to establish. A change from a system of parliamentary sovereignty to one of weak-form judicial review could thus be expected to present fewer challenges than a change to a system of strong-form judicial review.[59] A change from a system of court-monitored federalism to rights-based judicial review would present different challenges again. Common to all these examples, however, would be the fact that, in a mature democracy, the court could draw on a well-established political culture of respect for judicial independence to see it through the initial period of turbulence. Even though the court would be required to take the lead in transforming this culture in line with its new institutional role, the existence of such a culture would be more of a help than a hindrance. As Martin Shapiro has long argued, it is easier for a court to engage in rights-based judicial review where a political culture of respect for judicial independence has already been established than it is for a court to engage in this form of review from scratch.[60]

In the case of a new constitutional court, established at T_1 after a transition from authoritarian rule, the legal and political constraints impacting on the court would initially be in a tremendous state of flux,

---

[59] These changes may nevertheless still be quite considerable. See Murray Hunt, 'The Human Rights Act and Legal Culture: The Judiciary and the Legal Profession' (1999) 26 *Journal of Law and Society* 86 (describing the changes required in the United Kingdom if the legal-professional culture envisaged by the Human Rights Act is to be instantiated in practice).

[60] Shapiro, *Courts: A Comparative and Political Analysis*; Martin Shapiro, 'Judicial Review in Developed Democracies' (2003) 10 *Democratization* 7, 8–12.

and thus harder to describe with precision. Many issues would be open for analysis. The support of newly powerful political actors for judicial independence, for example, might be unclear, and certainly untested. Where law had come to be associated in the public mind as a tool of oppression rather than a guarantor of human freedom, notions of judicial independence might be treated with cynical disdain, and the court expected to play a quiescent role in the implementation of the new political power-holders' democratic mandate. At the same time, the capacity of the existing legal-professional culture to adjust to the new constitutional order would be unknown and slow to reveal itself.[61] Any political tradition of judicial independence that had been able to establish itself under, or survive, the period of authoritarian rule, would be weak and contested at best, with every instance of heroic judicial resistance to the dictates of the previous regime likely matched by ten other examples of abject capitulation.

Still, even a court that began functioning at T_1 after a transition from authoritarian rule would inherit something – a distinct legal-professional culture and an accompanying political culture that would exert a structuring influence on the environment in which it began its work.[62] Depending on the nature of the transition, the existing legal-professional culture might be more impervious to change than the political culture. Where the transition to democracy was marked by the inclusion of previously excluded groups, for example, the legal profession could be expected to be dominated by members of the previous elite, with perhaps little inclination to change settled ways of thinking about the law. The same might be true of lower ranks of the judiciary, especially where a newly created constitutional court was staffed by judges who were seen as political appointees rather than legal-professional experts. The political culture, on the other hand, might be subject to more rapid and radical change, with the new incumbents keen to stamp their authority on politics and drive a more populist agenda. If governmental institutions were at the same time headed by new appointees, settled relationships between the three branches of government might be disrupted. Depending on the extent of transformation of the civil service, this sort of disruption might occur lower down the ranks of the bureaucracy as well.

---

[61] This is the sort of question investigated in Ruti Teitel, 'Transitional Jurisprudence: The Role of Law in Political Transformation' (1997) 106 *Yale Law Journal* 2009.

[62] This is the question of path-dependency explored in relation to South Africa in Meierhenrich, *The Legacies of Law*. Meierhenrich's argument is discussed at greater length in Chapter 5.

All of this might make it quite hard to locate a newly established constitutional court on the matrix. Along the vertical axis, the difficulty would be to know how the legal-professional culture would cope with a radical challenge to entrenched legal-professional views on the purposes and possibilities of law. So, for example, where that culture had come to associate the ideal of adjudication according to law with a fairly deferential role for judges, it might take that culture some time to adjust to what it saw as their new 'activist' function. The court would be most vulnerable at this stage of its life, as its early decisions – however appropriate to the new constitutional arrangements – might be seen as inappropriately political in the eyes of the legal profession.

A constitutional court that found itself in this situation could be expected to do several things to protect itself. It might, for example, rely quite heavily on the citation of foreign judicial decisions, both as a legitimating device and as a means to reach out to other legal-professional cultures. A court that inherited a fairly formalist legal-professional culture could also be expected to try to convert the open-ended moral inquiries invited by the new constitution into more familiar rule-based tests. Indeed, the inertial force of the existing legal-professional culture might be strong enough to contradict a clear constitutional injunction to change settled ways of thinking about the law, meaning that the full possibilities of the legal-cultural transformation envisaged by the constitution would not be realised. A new constitutional court might even aid and abet this process, or at least not actively oppose it, as a way of preventing legal legitimacy losses. If that happened, a place in the top left-hand sector of the matrix might be won at the expense of giving full effect to the transformatory promise of the new constitution.

Along the horizontal axis, the main question would be whether the driving force behind the transition to constitutional democracy was the need for 'political insurance'[63] or whether the constitutional negotiators' choice of this form of constitution stemmed from a more deep-seated commitment to the value of liberal constitutionalism. If the former, the court's insulation from political attack might be greatly influenced by the result of the first democratic election, and what that revealed about prospects for ongoing multi-party political competition. If the latter, the court might be able to rely on a certain degree of respect for its institutional role even in the absence of a credible electoral alternative.

[63] Tom Ginsburg, *Judicial Review in New Democracies: Constitutional Courts in Asian Cases* (Cambridge University Press, 2003).

The extent to which the new political power-holders' policy objectives were tied to the reintegration of the country's economy into the global economy might also have a role to play here, with the threat of international market censure substituting for the absence of genuine political competition. The possibility that the turn to liberal constitutionalism might have been driven by 'hegemonic' political, economic and judicial elites could also not be excluded, in which case the court's insulation from political attack would depend on the durability of the relevant elite political pact and its capacity to withstand populist pressures from below.[64]

Despite these differences in emphasis, the conceptual framework for the evaluation of a constitutional court's performance in new and old democracies would be the same. In each case, evaluating that performance would depend on an initial assessment of the court's position on the matrix at T_1 and an investigation of the strategies the court deployed, against the backdrop of a dynamically evolving political context, to change or maintain its position on the matrix. By focusing on the possibilities of judge-driven movement in this way, the framework presented in this chapter provides a way of isolating the court's contribution to its success from the political and institutional factors conditioning its position on the matrix. But in which direction should the court ideally move? It is to this question that the final section turns.

2.5   The success of constitutional courts in interdisciplinary law/politics terms

The success of constitutional courts in interdisciplinary law/politics terms, we have been assuming, is bound up with their capacity to negotiate the law/politics tension – a task that is more easily performed in certain sectors of the matrix than in others. Indeed, it is only really in the top right-hand sector that courts experience this tension to the full extent. Since this sector is inherently unstable, a court that was able to maintain a commitment to principled decision-making from within that sector, and at the same time safeguard what institutional independence it did enjoy, would likely to be met with critical acclaim. If, in addition, such a court were able to assert its institutional role through the sorts of adjudicative strategies described in Section 2.3, this would be an

---

[64] See Hirschl, *Towards Juristocracy.*

impressive achievement. Ideally, of course, such a court should try to manoeuvre itself to the top left-hand sector. The circumstances favouring such a movement, however, might not be within its power to control. Where this was generally understood, a court of this type might be regarded as successful – indeed, as particularly successful – even if it remained where it was. Its achievement would then consist in its capacity to play its constitutionally mandated role without compromising its institutional independence.

What about the other three sectors, each of which is characterised by a certain degree of equilibrium? Should we count as successful a court that managed to negotiate the law/politics tension from within any one of these three sectors? Why, for example, should we not count as successful a court that remained within, or manoeuvred itself towards, the position of Court D? After all, a court in this situation might be able, by means of a purely political strategy, to avoid institution-threatening conflict for a considerable time. Would such an achievement not constitute success of a kind?

The answer to this question, it should by now be clear, is that a court that remained within, or manoeuvred itself towards, the bottom right-hand sector would be capable of achieving very little in legal or political terms. Its capacity to avoid attack would depend on its preparedness to capitulate, in every case that truly mattered, to the demands of politics. Institutional survival would in this way be purchased at the cost of institutional irrelevance. The constitution, in turn, would be a constitution in name only – its elaborate system of checks and balances, its independent state institutions, its democratic procedures, and its aspirational rights and freedoms nothing but abstractions, with little bearing on actual politics.

The same could be said of courts corresponding to the first variant of the Court C ideal type (the bottom left-hand sector). Such courts would enjoy a relatively high degree of insulation from political attack, but their position in this sector would depend either on a fortuitous set of circumstances (a particular alignment of political power, say) or on their having pursued, from the position of Court D, a purely political strategy of calibrating their decisions to the policy preferences of major political actors. Such a strategy, as noted earlier,[65] could not conceivably contribute to building a strong legal-professional attachment to the ideal of

---

[65] See Section 2.3.

adjudication according to law. Success in legal terms would accordingly remain elusive, its achievement dependent on whether the judges on the court were prepared to adjust their strategy to give greater weight to legal norms, and in this way build their court's reputation as a legally constrained actor.

The second variant of the Court C ideal type, we have said, represents the court in a mature constitutional democracy in which the ideal of adjudication according to law has for some historical reason weakened. The paradigmatic example of such a court is the US Supreme Court after the influence of the legal realist movement. While this type of court, as the US experience indicates, represents a highly stable model, it is not, on the liberal-legalist view, a desirable end state for constitutional courts in new or fragile democracies to try to reach. This conclusion, of course, depends on the attractiveness of liberal legal theory's particular understanding of the required separation of law and politics. According to the alternative ideal of 'responsive law' proposed by Nonet and Selznick, the bottom left-hand sector is normatively preferable to the top left-hand sector in several respects, including an improved capacity on the part of judges and administrative decision-makers to do substantive justice in the individual case. Nonet and Selznick acknowledge, however, that any movement towards responsive law is a high-risk undertaking that carries with it the threat that the politico-legal order will default back to the cruder kind of instrumentalism characteristic of repressive law (Court D).[66] This threat is all the more real in countries where law's autonomy from politics has not been solidified, i.e. in countries that have never known the liberal rule of law, or where the liberal rule of law has only been partially realised, or realised on behalf of a privileged section of the population only. For this reason, Nonet and Selznick would likely counsel against constitutional judges in such countries trying to drive a movement to the bottom left-hand sector from either the bottom right-hand sector (Court D) or the top right-hand sector (Court B). On the contrary, their advice would likely be that judges in such countries ought to try first to stabilise the politico-legal order around a commitment to law's autonomy from politics (Court A).

It is only in the top left-hand sector, then, that a constitutional court would be able, not only to negotiate the law/politics tension, but also to do so in a way that satisfied both the ideal of adjudication according to

---

[66] Nonet and Selznick, *Toward Responsive Law* 26.

law and the institutional efficacy standard favoured by judicial politics scholars. By building or maintaining a legal-professional culture in which law exerted significant constraints on judicial decision-making, a court could both reduce the risk of political attack and maintain the degree of independence from political control required to allow it to play its constitutionally assigned veto role.

It follows that assessing a particular constitutional court's performance according to the conceptual framework presented in this chapter requires us to do four things: (a) analyse the factors relevant to mapping the court's starting position on the matrix; (b) analyse the changing political context for judicial review and the changing strength of the legal profession's attachment to the ideal of adjudication according to law over the time period of the assessment; (c) to the extent possible, isolate the contribution made by the court to these changes; and (d) identify and describe the strategies deployed, or the other actions taken, by the judges to negotiate the law/politics tension and, if this is indeed what is seen to happen, manoeuvre their court into the top left-hand sector. The next chapter discusses some of the methodological issues attendant on undertaking an assessment of this kind.

3

Operationalising the conceptual framework to explain the Court's achievement

The conceptual framework developed in Chapter 2 invites assessment of the Chaskalson Court's achievement in terms of its capacity to negotiate the legal and political constraints impacting on it. This assessment, it was suggested, is tantamount to tracking the Court's movement across a two-dimensional matrix reflecting the relative strength of these constraints.

The usefulness of conceiving of the Court's achievement in these terms is that it provides us with a shorthand way of expressing what it is that we need to explain, viz. that the Court found itself at the end of Chaskalson's term as Chief Justice in the top half of the quadrant – working in a legal-professional culture strongly attached to the ideal of adjudication according to law and at the same time effectively able to assert its veto role. What we do not as yet know is whether the Court's capacity to assert its role in this way was a consequence of its fortuitous location in the top left-hand sector or of the strategies it deployed to negotiate the law/politics tension from within the top right-hand sector. We also do not know where the Court started on the matrix and what actions it took, if any, to change or maintain its position. The extent of the judges' contribution to their Court's achievement is further unclear. Were the judges the agent of the Court's success or merely the fortunate benefi-ciaries of improved circumstances?

The first of these questions requires analysis of the legal and political constraints impacting on the Court in 1995. Whatever weight we end up giving to long-run institutional and cultural factors, we need to assess the Court's situation as it stood when it began its work. In relation to the Court's position on the vertical axis, this means that we must take a view on the nature of South African legal-professional culture at this time, including the impact on that culture of the instrumental use of law under apartheid, the role played by law in the transition to democracy, and the legal-cultural changes triggered by the adoption of the 1993 Constitution. The Court's starting position on the horizontal axis will likewise depend on our assessment of a number of long-run institutional factors – such as the strength of South Africa's political tradition of respect for judicial independence – and a range of other factors, such as the ANC's sense of whether its interests were best served by support for the Court's independence, the personal commitment to judicial independence of a charismatic leader like Nelson Mandela, and the extent of political fragmentation in South Africa at the time the Court began its work.

Having fixed the Court's starting position on the matrix, the second question requires analysis of the way the Court responded to the legal and political constraints impacting on it and how these responses in turn affected the Court's position on the matrix. Was the Court somehow able to reduce the political constraints impacting on it by establishing a reputation for principled decision-making? If so, how did it avoid political attack in the first part of its institutional life, before that reputation had been established? Conversely, if the Court pursued a purely political strategy of the kind posited by the strategic model, how do we explain its legal-professional reputation?

In conducting this assessment, we will need to take account of the fact that the political context for judicial review might have been changing independently of the Court's actions. Perhaps the explanation for its achievement lies not so much in what the Court did but in fortuitous changes to the external political environment – changes that enhanced its institutional independence and allowed it to play a progressively more influential role in the post-apartheid political system. This would be the case, for example, if South African politics became more fragmented over the time period covered in the investigation, giving all major political parties an incentive to respect the Court's independence.

To the extent that conscious strategising on the part of the judges forms part of the explanation, we will also need to find some evidence that the judges were aware of the changing political context for judicial review and of the impact of their actions on the Court's institutional independence. Is there any indication that the judges adjusted their account of the post-apartheid Constitutions according to their perception of how their decisions might be received? If so, is it possible to think of the Court as a composite political actor in this respect, or should the Court's actions be seen simply as the sum total of the actions of the individual judges?

The purpose of this chapter is to set out the methods used in this study to answer these questions. The first two sections track the sequence suggested by the conceptual framework in Chapter 2. Section 3.1 thus addresses itself to the analysis of the Court's starting position on the matrix, while Section 3.2 details the methods used in the analysis of the Court's movement across the matrix, from the commencement of the Court's work in 1995 to Justice Chaskalson's retirement in 2005. Given the focus of the dynamic analysis on the Court's written opinions, the final section discusses the criteria used for choosing the cases for detailed discussion in Part III.

3.1   The Court's starting position on the matrix

3.1.1   The vertical axis: South African legal-professional culture

The term 'legal culture' was defined in Chapter 2 as the set of institution-alised, legal-professional norms and practices regulating permissible forms of judicial reasoning in a particular legal system. Whatever the formal legal rules and principles which have been adopted or are other-wise identifiable in a legal system, this definition assumes, their con-straining effect depends on the existence of a reasonably well-established tradition of reasoning about the law that both delimits the outer bound-aries of permissible justificatory argument, provides an idiom and accepted form of argumentation, and determines the relative persuasive-ness of a judicial decision.

On the spectrum of definitions of legal culture from wide to narrow, this definition falls towards the latter end. Lawrence Friedman, for example, has defined the term in a much broader way as referring to 'ideas, values, expectations and attitudes towards law and legal institutions, which some public or some part of the public holds'.[1] On this approach, institutional-ised legal-professional norms and practices are just one, albeit important, aspect of a particular society's legal culture, constituting what Friedman elsewhere refers to as its 'internal' dimension.[2] As Friedman himself has

---

[1]   Lawrence M. Friedman, 'The Concept of a Legal Culture: A Reply' in in David Nelken (ed.), *Comparing Legal Cultures* (Aldershot: Dartmouth, 1997) 33.

[2]   Lawrence M. Friedman, *The Legal System: A Social Science Perspective* (New York, NY: Russell Sage Foundation, 1975) 223. There are many other definitions of legal culture, most of them distinguishing between a broad and narrow use of the term. See, for example, Austin Sarat, 'Studying American Legal Culture: An Assessment of Survey Evidence' (1977) 11 *Law & Society Review* 427, 427 (defining legal culture as 'public attitudes toward law and the legal system'); Susan S. Silbey, 'Legal Culture and Legal Consciousness' in Neil J. Smelser and Paul B. Baltes (eds.), *International Encyclopaedia of the Social & Behavioural Sciences* (Amsterdam: Elsevier, 2001) 8623, 8623 ('[l]egal *culture* refers to an aggregate level (macro or group) phenomenon; legal *consciousness* usually refers to micro level social action, specifically the ways in which individuals interpret and

argued,[3] however, what matters is not what definition is best in the abstract, but whether the chosen definition is coherent and suited to the purposes of the study in which it is used.

The virtue of the narrow definition offered here is that it bolsters the conceptual distinction in Chapter 2 between the legal and political constraints under which constitutional courts operate. By restricting legal culture to institutionalised legal-professional norms and practices, attitudes to law on the part of other political actors may be excluded from the assessment of a court's position on the vertical axis. Those factors, on the approach taken here, are relevant to the assessment of the court's position on the horizontal axis. To keep the distinction between the two sets of factors clear, the first set of factors will be referred to as aspects of 'legal-professional culture' and the second as part of South Africa's 'political culture of respect for judicial independence', or just 'political culture' for short.

The relative strength of a legal-professional culture thus defined must be distinguished from the actual constraints exerted by legal-professional norms and practices in any particular case. The claim here is not that legal-professional cultures generate a consistent level of constraint according to the strength of their attachment to the ideal of adjudication according to law. Rather, as argued in Chapter 2, the force of the constraints exerted by legal-professional norms and practices in any particular case is a function of the nature of that case, the norms and practices implicated by it, and the extent of reasonable legal-professional disagreement about the correct answer. The determinacy of law, in other words, is one thing, the relative strength of a legal-professional culture's attachment to the ideal of adjudication according to law another. Taking account of this distinction, this study first assesses the relative strength of South African legal-professional culture (Chapter 4) and then considers the constraints exerted by legal-professional norms and practices in the cases decided by the Chaskalson Court (Part III).

Even with all these qualifications, it might be contended that legal culture is just too vague and unmeasurable a concept to be deployed in the way envisaged in this study. Roger Cotterrell, for example, has

---

mobilize legal meanings and signs'); David Nelken, 'Using the Concept of Legal Culture' (2004) 29 *Australian Journal of Legal Philosophy* 1, 1 ('[l]egal culture, in its most general sense, is one way of describing relatively stable patterns of legally oriented social behaviour and attitudes').

[3] Friedman, 'The Concept of a Legal Culture: A Reply' 38.

criticised Friedman's use of the concept along these lines.[4] For Cotterrell, the difficulty with Friedman's use of legal culture is not just that his particular usage is inconsistent, but that there are certain 'general problems in using "culture" as an explanatory concept in theoretical analysis of law'. As Cotterrell has argued:

> It may, indeed, be impossible to develop a concept of legal culture with sufficient analytical precision to give it substantial utility as a component in legal theory and, especially, to allow it to indicate a significant explanatory variable in empirical research in sociology of law.[5]

Given these problems, a potentially more helpful concept might be the concept of 'legal ideology', which Cotterrell defines as the 'value elements and cognitive ideas presupposed in, expressed through and shaped by the practices of developing, interpreting and applying legal doctrine within a legal system'.[6] To the extent that legal culture might still be a useful concept in certain contexts, its use should be restricted to the development of ideal types, which could then be used to develop 'methods of measuring, observing or experiencing specific social, including legal, phenomena.'[7]

Cotterrell's reservations about the use of legal culture as an analytic concept in legal theory and comparative sociology of law are important, but can be overcome. First, the notion of legal-professional culture as used in this study is restricted to institutionalised legal-professional norms and practices of judicial reasoning. This understanding is not so different from Cotterrell's idea of 'legal ideology' or, indeed, from Friedman's notion of 'internal legal culture'.[8] At any rate, the term legal-professional culture will be consistently used in this sense, and thus the problem of variations in meaning does not arise. Secondly, legal-professional culture is deployed here for the most part as an element in an ideal type, in just the way Cotterrell endorses. The only part of the argument that treats legal-professional culture as a measurable phenomenon is that part that contends that it is possible to distinguish between

---

[4] Roger Cotterrell, 'The Concept of Legal Culture' in Nelken (ed.), *Comparing Legal Cultures* 13. For a more recent consideration of this issue, see Alexandra Huneeus, Javier Couso and Rachel Sieder, 'Cultures of Legality: Judicialization and Political Activism in Latin America' in Couso et al. (eds.), *Cultures of Legality* 3, 7 (accepting that the concept of legal culture is 'amorphous' but nevertheless deploying it as an explanatory factor in a 'social-constructivist' account of the judicialisation of politics in Latin America).
[5] Cotterrell, 'The Concept of Legal Culture' 14.
[6] Ibid. 21–2.   [7] Ibid. 25.   [8] Friedman, *The Legal System* 223.

legal-professional cultures that are strongly attached to the ideal of adjudication according to law and those that are not. But here, too, we will be able to address Cotterrell's concerns if we can develop indicators of the relative strength of a legal-professional culture in this sense, and analyse those indicators rather than the legal-professional culture directly.

On the definition used here, the indicators of the strength of a particular legal-professional culture's attachment to the ideal of adjudication according to law include such variables as the length of time judicial decision-making has been institutionalised in the country concerned; the degree of independence of the legal profession from governmental control; attitudes to law on the part of the legal profession, and particularly any indication that law is regarded as a technical discipline that is properly immune to ideological or partisan-political influence; the criteria for judicial appointment, including the extent to which a reputation for impartiality and legal-professional competence is valued over allegiance to the political party making the appointment; and the nature of law teaching and legal-academic writing in the society concerned, with the emphasis again falling on attitudes to law as a technical discipline.

Given these indicators, the questions we will need to ask in order to locate the Chaskalson Court's starting point on the vertical axis are: How long had judicial decision-making been institutionalised in South Africa by the time the Court began its work? What was the nature of the organised legal profession at this time? How closely regulated was that profession? Did advancement within the legal profession depend on connections to the governing regime or on the person's standing within the legal profession? What were the criteria for appointment to judicial office? Were technical skills stressed more than political allegiance? What was the nature of law teaching? How was the law presented in classes and academic textbooks? How, in short, were legal professionals socialised?

The secondary literature on these questions is fortunately quite rich,[9] and thus there will be no need to start from scratch. The main difficulty is rather the question of the impact of apartheid on South African legal-professional culture. Although that culture had already have been influenced by 300-odd years of colonial rule, it was under apartheid that racial segregation was legally formalised and driven as a deliberate policy of

---

[9] See, for example, Martin Chanock, *The Making of South African Legal Culture 1902–1936: Fear, Favour and Prejudice* (Cambridge University Press, 2001).

government. The instrumental use of law in this way is likely to have had a profound effect on legal professionals' faith in the capacity of law to constrain judicial decision-making.[10] On the conceptualisation offered here, legal-professional cultures shift from strong to weak at the point at which that faith becomes discernibly weaker relative to other legal-professional cultures. The indicators of the impact of apartheid on the strength of South African legal-professional culture are thus such issues as: observable changes in the style and quality of judicial reasoning that reflect a decline in the legal profession's faith in the capacity of law to constrain judicial decision-making; contemporaneous legal-academic accounts confirming this impression; and judicial statements, either in the text of judgments themselves or extra-curially, to the same effect.

Once again, there is a great deal of literature on all of these questions already,[11] and thus it will not be necessary to investigate them afresh. Rather, the focus of the inquiry must fall on whether the ideal of adjudication according to law was thought to have been compromised and, if so, to what extent. In particular, was the ideal completely undermined by apartheid, in the sense that the instrumental use of law associated with that system was thought to have infected all aspects of South African legal-professional culture and all areas of law? Or did the ideal survive in attenuated form? If the latter, how plausible is it to think that the ideal might have been revitalised by the transition to democracy?

The last of these questions flows naturally into the next part of the assessment: the question of how South African legal-professional culture would have been affected by the process of negotiating and adopting the post-apartheid Constitutions. There are two distinct issues here. The first relates to the impact on South African legal-professional culture of the confidence placed in law by those involved in the negotiations process, and the second to the impact of the adoption of the post-apartheid

---

[10] For a related argument in the American context, see Tamanaha, *Law as a Means to an End*.

[11] See, for example, Hugh Corder, *Judges at Work: The Role and Attitudes of the South African Appellate Judiciary, 1910–50* (Cape Town: Juta, 1984); C. F. Forsyth, *In Danger for their Talents: A Study of the Appellate Division of the Supreme Court of South Africa 1950–80* (Cape Town, Juta, 1985); Stephen Ellmann, *In a Time of Trouble: Law and Liberty in South Africa's State of Emergency* (Oxford: Clarendon Press, 1992); David Dyzenhaus, *Hard Cases in Wicked Legal Systems: South African Law in the Perspective of Legal Philosophy* (Oxford: Clarendon Press, 1991); Richard L. Abel, *Politics by Other Means: Law in the Struggle Against Apartheid 1980–1994* (New York, NY: Routledge, 1995); Meierhenrich, *The Legacies of Law*.

Constitutions on the existing style of judicial reasoning. In respect of the first issue, the two main arguments already in play are: (1) that the ideal of adjudication according to law had been thoroughly undermined by apartheid, but that the transition to democracy provided an opportunity for political actors to draw on the more positive image of law in 'international political culture' and in this way to restore confidence in the ideal;[12] (2) that the ideal of adjudication according to law had survived the impact of apartheid in attenuated form, and that 'the memory of formally rational law . . . created the conditions for the emergence of trust between democracy-demanding and democracy-resisting elites'.[13] On both these views, the transition to democracy would have had a positive impact on South African legal-professional culture's attachment to the ideal of adjudication according to law. It may not be necessary, therefore, to decide between them, but simply to assess what their respective implications are for the assessment of the Chaskalson Court's starting position on the vertical axis.

The second issue relates to the potentially destabilising effect of the move to rights-based constitutionalism on South African legal-professional culture. The particular question here is whether the associated shift from formal to substantive legal reasoning created something like a legal-cultural lag-effect. Did the fact that the fairly formalist style of reasoning that had dominated South African legal-professional culture under apartheid was clearly incompatible with the style of reasoning required to give effect to the post-apartheid Constitutions prevent the Chaskalson Court from embracing the transformative possibilities of the new constitutional order? Or is it better to think of the Court as in effect free to devise new forms of reasoning?

These questions will be difficult to answer in the abstract and may thus have to be deferred to the case discussion in Part III. A close reading of the Chaskalson Court's decision-making record may reveal the dominant style of reasoning it adopted, and this in turn may give us an indication of the extent to which its discretion was constrained by the old and the new styles. Indeed, it may even be possible to observe the process of legal-cultural transformation in the text of the Court's judgments, as the judges progressively shifted their style of reasoning from one form to the other.

Our assessment of the impact on South African legal-professional culture of the shift to rights-based constitutionalism will also depend

---

[12] Klug, *Constituting Democracy*.   [13] Meierhenrich, *The Legacies of Law* 4.

on the role we ascribe to foreign legal actors. If the adoption of the 1993 interim Constitution signalled the re-entrance of South Africa into the international community, it is not implausible to suppose that South African legal-professional culture underwent some sort of international-isation process as well, to the point where it is no longer really sensible to speak of a distinct South African legal-professional culture.[14] If we can find some evidence of this – for example, in the existence of ties between the judges and their colleagues in other jurisdictions – then the legal-cultural lag-effect argument might lose some of its force. Any evidence that the members of the Chaskalson Court were responsive to debates within the comparative constitutional law community would tend to suggest that the judges would have been constrained by their desire to satisfy this community's expectations about the reasoning methods required to give effect to their mandate.

3.1.2   The horizontal axis: the Court's relative insulation from political attack

The Chaskalson Court's starting position on the horizontal access, Chapter 2 argued, is a function of its exposure to political attack or, put positively, its actual independence from political control. Since the Court's position is determined relative to the position of other courts, the focus of the assessment must fall on the external political environment for judicial review. In particular, the factors relevant to the assessment are: the political culture of respect for judicial independence; the formal institutional safeguards of judicial independence (to the extent that such safeguards actually insulated the Court from political attack); the interests of major political actors in respecting the Court's independence; and the extent of public support for the Court.

There are two main approaches to the assessment of these factors in the literature: a fairly well-defined rational choice approach that seeks to calculate their aggregate effect on the propensity of major political actors to attack the court; and a more eclectic, culturalist approach, which emphasises the broader social and economic processes impacting on the establishment of a political culture of respect for judicial

---

[14] For scepticism about the coherence of the concept of a national legal culture, see Roger Cotterrell, 'Law and Culture – Inside and Beyond the Nation State' (2008) 31 *Retfaerd: Nordisk Juridisk Tidsskrift* 23.

independence. These two approaches are not necessarily incompatible, as others have argued.[15]

On the rational choice approach, the governing assumption is that a court's actual independence from political control depends on the capacity and inclination of major political actors to attack it.[16] Assessing a court's exposure to political attack thus involves, first, identification of the major political actors capable of attacking the court and, secondly, a cost-benefit analysis of these actors' interests in doing so. Such an assessment may be carried out individually, in relation to a particular policy issue, or globally, in relation to all politically salient cases.[17] Both types of assessment are potentially relevant to this study: the second to the assessment of the Chaskalson's Court's starting position on the horizontal axis, and the first to the assessment of the politics of particular cases.

In the case of the global assessment, the analysis typically proceeds by considering each factor in turn to see whether it tends to raise the costs to major political actors of attacking the court.[18] For example, where the institutional arrangements for safeguarding judicial independence include measures that require cross-party support for appointments to the court, the costs of appointing a politically compliant judge may be assumed to increase in proportion to the political capital spent in overcoming any resistance to the appointment. Similarly, where public support for the court is high, the costs of attacking the court may be assumed to increase in proportion to the relevance of this issue to electoral outcomes.[19]

The primary interest most political actors have in respecting judicial independence is the court's role in the maintenance of a competitive electoral system.[20] By guaranteeing the conditions for free and fair

---

[15] On the potential for these two approaches to complement each other, see Robert H. Bates, Rui J. P. de Figueiredo, Jr and Barry Weingast, 'The Politics of Interpretation: Rationality, Culture and Transition' (1998) 26 *Politics & Society* 603.

[16] See, for example, Whittington, 'Legislative Sanctions and the Strategic Environment of Judicial Review'; Holmes, 'Lineages of the Rule of Law'; Holmes, 'Judicial Independence as Ambiguous Reality and Insidious Illusion' et al.; Vanberg, 'Establishing and Maintaining Judicial Independence' 103–13.

[17] See Whittington, 'Legislative Sanctions' 448.

[18] See Vanberg, 'Establishing and Maintaining Judicial Independence' 106; Ginsburg, 'The Global Spread of Constitutional Review' 94.

[19] See Weingast, 'The Political Foundations of Democracy and the Rule of Law' 254 (referring to President Franklin D. Roosevelt's failed court-packing plan).

[20] Stephenson, '"When the Devil Turns"'.

elections, constitutional courts serve the long-term interests of political parties whose strategies for maintaining or winning back political power are focused on the ballot box.[21] In situations where a single political party is assured of long-term electoral dominance, this consideration obviously carries less weight.[22] Even a dominant political party, however, may have an interest in respecting the independence of a constitutional court if the court is seen to perform some function useful to it. This would be the case, for example, where the dominant party's legislative programme was controversial and likely to be resisted by economically powerful groups, or where the approval of external actors, such as foreign investors, was required for the success of the programme.[23] In this type of situation, a dominant political party would have an interest in an independent court's capacity to legitimate its legislative programme by occasionally vetoing some aspects of it.[24]

Political actors' interests in attacking a constitutional court are similarly bound up with the court's capacity to frustrate the achievement of their policy goals. Given the potential long-term benefits of respecting the court's independence, the benefits of attacking the court in anticipation of, or in response to, a particular decision need to be weighed against both the immediate costs of launching the attack and the long-term costs of undermining the court's independence. Only if the combined short- and long-term costs of attacking the court are less than the net benefits of respecting its independence will a political actor's interests be served by attacking the court.[25] Alternatively, the political actor may seek to limit its attack to undermining the implementation of the court's decision.[26] The advantage of this option is that the political actor may be able to

---

[21] See Vanberg, 'Establishing and Maintaining Judicial Independence' 109; Ginsburg, 'The Global Spread of Constitutional Review' 90.

[22] See J. Mark Ramseyer, 'The Puzzling (In)dependence of Courts' and Pilar Domingo, 'Judicial Independence: The Politics of the Supreme Court in Mexico' (2000) 32 *Journal of Latin American Studies* 704.

[23] On the role of foreign investors in securing judicial independence in new democracies, see Moustafa, 'Law versus the State'.

[24] On the role of the US Supreme Court in legitimating the New Deal in this way, see Charles L. Black, Jr, *The People and the Court: Judicial Review in a Democracy* (New York, NY: Macmillan, 1960).

[25] Vanberg, 'Establishing and Maintaining Judicial Independence' 109; Ginsburg, 'The Global Spread of Constitutional Review' 104.

[26] See Georg Vanberg, *The Politics of Constitutional Review in Germany* (Cambridge University Press, 2005).

achieve its policy goals without incurring the costs of a full-scale assault on judicial independence.

In contrast to the rational choice approach, the culturalist approach emphasises the broader social and economic processes impacting on the establishment of a political culture of respect for judicial independence.[27] On this approach, political actors' propensity to attack the court is not purely a matter of strategic calculation but also a function of their commitment to the value of judicial independence. At the very least, such commitments may shape preferences and consequently affect the outcome of any strategic calculation.

Since a political culture of respect for judicial independence is something that requires many years to build, it may be thought that the culturalist approach would invariably record a low institutional independence rating for newly established constitutional courts. Value-laden commitments to judicial independence may, however, develop in pre-democratic or sub-national settings, even in the absence of a generalised political culture to this effect. A particular political party, for example, might have its own internal tradition of respect for judicial independence. This internal tradition, in turn, might be strong or weak, or associated with a particular leader or faction within the party. In such cases, the impact of this internal tradition on the court's institutional independence could be assessed by analysing the importance of the political actor to the court's institutional independence, the strength of its internal tradition of respect for judicial independence, and the balance of political power between different factions within the party.[28]

In other instances, there might simply be ideological ties between members of the court and influential players within one of the major political parties. Indeed, such a situation is almost guaranteed where political parties play a significant role in the judicial appointments process. For the most part, ideological ties like this could be expected to narrow the policy gap between the court and these

---

[27] See, for example, Martin Krygier, 'Institutional Optimism, Cultural Pessimism and the Rule of Law' in Martin Krygier and Adam Czarnota (eds.), *The Rule of Law after Communism* (Aldershot: Ashgate/Dartmouth, 1999) 77; Marina Kurkchiyan, 'Russian Legal Culture: An Analysis of Adaptive Response to an Institutional Transplant' (2009) 34 *Law & Social Inquiry* 337.

[28] If it could in addition be shown that the judges were aware of the party's internal tradition, and of the impact of their decisions on the balance of power within the party, this factor would also be relevant to the dynamic analysis of the court's movement across the matrix.

parties.[29] In situations of one-party dominance, however, it is not inconceivable that judges who are known to members of the governing political elite may actually find it easier to assert their court's independence. This possibility would be heightened where the dominant political party was the prime mover in a transition to democracy and where the judges had had some role within the party, either as office bearers or as lawyers representing party members.

It is possible, of course, to collapse some of these broader considerations into the rational choice framework by exploring their impact on political actors' interests in attacking the court. So, for example, a well-developed political culture of respect for judicial independence could be said to raise the costs to political actors of attacking the court. Likewise, where there existed a strong internal tradition of respect for judicial independence in a particular political party, the cost to a member of that party of attacking the court would include the potential loss of influence within the party. Not every consideration is susceptible to assimilation in this way, however. Ideological ties between members of the judiciary and the political elite, for example, are not easily translated into the language of cost-benefit analysis. Even if they could be, the complex calculations required to take account of such factors might undermine the utility of the model, giving it a spurious sense of accuracy when in fact the application of the model would depend on a number of controversial assumptions. This study will accordingly maintain a two-pronged approach, or what may be understood as a modified rational choice approach. Where it makes sense to think about a particular factor impacting on the Chaskalson Court's independence in rational choice terms, the factor will be analysed in that way. But the analysis will also attempt to capture the ideas, personalities, traditions and broader social processes that could be said to have influenced the Court's relative exposure to political attack.

Recall that our aim in the first instance is to assess the Chaskalson Court's starting position on the horizontal axis. This means that our methodology must enable us to place the Court on either the left- or the right-hand side of the matrix with some confidence. The most straightforward way of conducting this assessment is to treat the institutional independence enjoyed by a typical constitutional court in a mature democracy as the baseline for the left-hand side of the matrix, and then

---

[29] The classic study is Robert A. Dahl, 'Policy-making in a Democracy: The Supreme Court as a National Policy-maker' (1957) 6 *Journal of Public Law* 279.

to assess how closely the external political environment in which the Chaskalson Court began its work approached this situation. Following the discussion in Chapter 2, this means that the baseline for the left-hand side of the matrix is not a situation of absolute independence, but one in which the court would on occasion have needed to weather the storm of a controversial case by relying on broad-based support for its institutional role.

As a newly established constitutional court, the Chaskalson Court would obviously not have been in this exact situation. Whatever the political culture of respect for judicial independence under apartheid, the transition to democracy and the adoption of a rights-based constitution would have disrupted it. But perhaps there were other aspects of the political context for judicial review that might have made up for this fact, meaning that the Court's situation was functionally equivalent to that of a typical constitutional court in a mature democracy.

Even at this early stage of the analysis, we know enough about the situation in which the Chaskalson Court found itself to surmise that the two most important issues affecting its relative exposure to political attack are likely to have been the ANC's domination of South African politics and the Court's lack of public support. As the dominant political force in South Africa after the 1994 elections, the ANC was the political actor with both the greatest capacity to attack the Court and also the most effective means of protecting it. In the absence of meaningful political opposition, the ANC's interest in respecting the Court's independence would not have been the Court's potential role in assisting it to regain power in the event that it was voted out of office. Nevertheless, the ANC might have had other reasons to desist from attacking the Court. Most obviously, the ANC's primary interest in the Court's independence would have been its potential role in legitimating the ANC's social transformation project. That project, touching as it did on vested interests (including property rights), was inherently controversial. At the same time, the ANC's macro-economic strategy depended on attracting foreign investment. Both of these factors might have counteracted the independence-reducing effects of the ANC's political dominance.

As we have seen,[30] studies by Gibson and others show that public support for the Court was low in comparative terms shortly after it began its work, lower at least than the level that is ordinarily thought to provide

---

[30] Section 1.3.

a buffer against political attack. But perhaps this factor, too, should not automatically be read to mean that the Court was politically vulnerable. The hypothesis about the impact of public support on a court's independence depends on an underlying assumption about the functioning of multiparty politics. Political costs in attacking a court are incurred where the court is popular and where the electoral system is capable of registering public disapproval of an attack.[31] Neither of these conditions obtained in South Africa. Indeed, in the absence of a credible opposition party, the ANC might actually have been able to protect the Court against the effects of its low public support, particularly if the Court served some useful purpose for the ANC, as suggested in the preceding paragraph.

Still, the fact that the situation in which the Court found itself in 1995 could not be described as one of political fragmentation in the ordinary sense, together with the Court's low public support, are weighty considerations. Without further investigation, neither looks promising for the Court's institutional independence. Going into the assessment, therefore, it is probably fair to say that the burden of persuasion is on the side wanting to show that the Court's starting position was equivalent to that of a typical constitutional court in a mature democracy. What were some of the features of the South African political context that might convince us that this burden could be discharged?

Four main arguments suggest themselves: (1) that the political environment in which the Court began its work was marked, if not by political fragmentation, then at least by a fair measure of political uncertainty; (2) that the strength of the ANC's internal tradition of respect for judicial independence, and especially President Mandela's charismatic leadership on this issue, would have made up for any deficiencies in the broader political culture, especially given the ANC's dominance of South African politics; (3) that the close personal and ideological ties between the judges and members of the ANC political elite would have restrained the ANC from attacking the Court; and (4) that the strength and diversity of South African civil society, and especially the tradition of cause lawyering that had developed under apartheid, would have made up for the centralisation of political power in the hands of the ANC.

As to the first issue, it will be necessary to investigate just how uncertain the ANC's hold on political power was after the first

---

[31] Vanberg, *The Politics of Constitutional Review in Germany* 21.

democratic elections in 1994. It had won a resounding victory, but was it really assured of its future political dominance? In the transitional moment that still characterised South Africa at that time, would the ANC not have required the co-operation of other political parties, especially given the procedures in the interim Constitution for adoption of the final Constitution? And what about the fact that the interim Constitution gave the Chaskalson Court a central role in the certification of the final Constitution? How would that have played into its exposure to political attack? On the one hand, the ANC might have been predisposed to control the Court to ensure that the procedural and substantive safeguards for the protection of minority rights in the final Constitution did not pose an obstacle to the achievement of its policy goals. On the other, the Court's legitimating stamp of approval was surely necessary to cement the transition to democracy.

The second issue relates to the strength of the ANC's internal tradition of respect for judicial independence and the extent to which this might have made up for the absence of a broader political culture to this effect. As is well known, the ANC had a long history as a liberation movement in which the use of the courts to advance its goals was contested but never wholly abandoned.[32] It is quite possible that the ANC's post-1994 leadership was influenced by this history, and that key players within the organisation might have had a profound commitment to the value of judicial independence. The figure of Nelson Mandela, an attorney and someone who had personal experience of the capacity of law to place limits on political power, looms particularly large here. He, more than any other ANC leader, might have had the ability to restrain the organisation from undermining the Court's independence.

Thirdly, the fact that the members of the Chaskalson Court had close personal and ideological ties to the ANC political elite must surely have made a difference to the ANC's inclination to attack it. It is one thing to be told to amend a policy by a known ideological opponent, another to be told the same thing by a person who has lost a limb in the course of a shared liberation struggle.[33]

Finally, the potentially insulating effect of South Africa's diverse and robust civil society will need to be examined. Although public support for the Chaskalson Court was low, the struggle against apartheid had produced a wide variety of civil society organisations. Some of these

---

[32] Abel, *Politics by Other Means*; Ellmann, *In a Time of Trouble*.
[33] The reference here, of course, is to Albie Sachs.

organisations, while remaining loyal to the ANC, might have had an interest in using the Court to influence ANC policy in ways that the party's own internal policy-formulation processes did not allow. This would have been particularly true of organisations whose vision for South Africa's future was closely aligned to the post-apartheid Constitutions' vision of a non-racial, democratic society. The ANC political elite, in turn, might have had a corresponding interest in allowing these organisations to contest policy in this way – either because their own ideological views were aligned with these outcomes, or simply because the Court could be used for the resolution of issues that would have been politically costly to resolve through the ANC's internal policy-formulation processes.[34] Whatever the reason, these organisations' use of the Court to promote their agendas would have given the Court the opportunity to show its support for the ANC's broader social transformation project, and in this way enhance its institutional independence.

3.2   Tracking the Court's movement across the matrix

The dynamic analysis of the Court's movement across the matrix, we have said, involves an examination of the Court's responses to the changing legal and political constraints impacting on it. But what do we mean by 'responses' here? Only the Court's official actions, in the form of its written opinions, or also any other actions it might have taken to manage the law/politics tension? And should we think about the Court's actions as the actions of a goal-directed political actor, or simply as the sum total of the individual actions of the judges, all of them guided by their own judicial lights?

The legalist approach, of course, concentrates on a court's written opinions. In particular, the analysis falls on the court's progressive elaboration of legal doctrine, as though the court's decision-making record were a slowly unfolding narrative or, in another suggested metaphor, a musical performance in several acts.[35] Judicial politics scholars, for their part, have tended to focus on the policy *output* of decisions, dismissing formal written opinions, in crude legal realist fashion, as mere ex post facto rationalisations of decisions reached on other grounds. Ever

---

[34] See Holmes, 'Lineages of the Rule of Law' 25–8 (on the considerations that might prompt 'politicians to cede some of their power to judges').

[35] See David M. Beatty, *Talking Heads and the Supremes: The Canadian Production of Constitutional Law* (Toronto: Carswell, 1990).

since Walter Murphy's seminal study of the US Supreme Court,[36] however, there have been some judicial politics scholars who have been prepared to range more widely. In this tradition, any action through which a group of judges' may conceivably control their decision-making environment is worthy of scholarly attention. Thus, actions such as a court's docket management decisions,[37] the allocation of majority opinion writing responsibility,[38] bargaining between judges during the opinion writing process,[39] and even the judges' public speaking engagements[40] have all been thought to be significant in various ways.

While acknowledging the value of this broader approach, this study concentrates for the most part on the Chaskalson Court's written opinions. There are two main reasons for this. First, by maintaining a narrower focus, this study hopes to counteract some of the residual bias in the judicial politics literature against considering the internal constraints exerted by law.[41] If this set of constraints is an important influence on judicial behaviour, as many judicial politics scholars now concede, the reasoning in written opinions matters – not because written opinions can be taken at face value, but because they reflect (even when the reasoning is supplied ex post facto) the judge's view of the required standard of public justification. Indeed, on the approach taken here, the writing of a judicial opinion is not so much a process of formally recording the reasons thought to be dispositive of a case as it is a legal-cultural act, in which the judge both responds to and on occasion transforms the tradition of reasoning about the law in which he or she is working. Formal written opinions are, in this sense, legal-cultural artefacts, which can be analysed as evidence of the internal constraints exerted by law.[42]

---

[36] Murphy, *Elements of Judicial Strategy*.   [37] See Perry, Jr, *Deciding to Decide*.

[38] Epstein and Knight, *The Choices Justices Make*.

[39] Murphy, *Elements of Judicial Strategy*; Epstein and Knight, *The Choices Justices Make*; James F. Spriggs II, Forrest Maltzman and Paul J. Wahlbeck, 'Bargaining on the U.S. Supreme Court: Justices' Responses to Majority Opinion Drafts' (1999) 61 *Journal of Politics* 485.

[40] See Jeffrey K. Staton, *Judicial Power and Strategic Communication in Mexico* (Cambridge University Press, 2010) 5, 22 (arguing that judges 'construct their power' in part through judicial 'public relations').

[41] See Friedman, 'Taking Law Seriously'.

[42] This view of formal written opinions is logically entailed by the argument in Chapter 1 that the constraints exerted by law are not a function of the determinacy of formal legal rules and principles, but a function of the legal-professional norms and practices that determine how formal legal rules and principles are to be applied.

The second reason for focusing on the Chaskalson Court's written opinions is the intuition that they were of more than usual importance to the way the judges sought to manage their Court's relationship with key political actors. All judges try to write carefully, of course, but there is a sense in which the Chaskalson Court's opinions were intended as diplomatic missives of some sort, alternately praising the political branches for their efforts in realising the post-apartheid Constitutions' vision for South Africa and admonishing them for not trying hard enough. This feature of the Court's record stems in part from its comparatively low caseload and the time the judges consequently had to craft their opinions.[43] But it also appears to reflect, or so this study will argue,[44] a deliberate strategy – as though the judges thought that, whatever the policy implications of a particular decision, they could control its impact by their astute choice of words. At the same time, the judges were careful to keep controversial extra-curial communications to a minimum. Although they certainly did not shy away from public speaking engagements,[45] most of the speeches delivered on these occasions consisted of fairly cautious recitations of the reasons for past decisions, together with very general exhortations about the need to safeguard the constitutional project.[46] If there is a theme running through these speeches, it is the repeated assertion of law's claim to neutrality as an apolitical check on the abuse of political power. In this sense, the judges' speaking engagements *were* part of their overall 'public relations' strategy,[47] but the effort the judges put into this aspect of their work was relatively insignificant when compared to the effort put into their written opinions.

---

[43] The Chaskalson Court decided on average twenty-three cases per year. See Dugard and Roux, 'The Record of the South African Constitutional Court in Providing an Institutional Voice for the Poor: 1995–2004' 108.

[44] See Section 10.3.

[45] In August 1999, the Court was publicly criticised by then Justice Minister, Penuell Maduna, for being inefficient and taking too much paid leave (see 'Maduna Attacks Constitutional Court' (*IOL News*, 30 August 1999) www.iol.co.za/news/south-africa/maduna-attacks-constitutional-court-1.9368). For a summary of the debate about extra-curial speaking engagements in the United States, see Leslie Dubeck, 'Understanding "Judicial Lockjaw": The Debate over Extrajudicial Activity' (2007) 82 *New York University Law Review* 569 (arguing that both proponents and opponents of extrajudicial activity use indeterminate policy arguments and questionable historical support for what is in the end a necessary public function).

[46] See, for example, Arthur Chaskalson, 'Human Dignity as a Foundational Value of Our Constitutional Order' (2000) 16 *South African Journal on Human Rights* 193.

[47] See Staton, *Judicial Power and Strategic Communication in Mexico*.

Accepting, then, that the Chaskalson Court mainly acted through its written opinions, how should we think about the Court: merely as the sum total of its individual judicial parts or as a composite political actor in some sense? Once again, the legalist approach is clear: judges are individual actors, deciding each case according to their good-faith interpretation of the law. The attitudinal and strategic models likewise concentrate on the actions of the individual judge, although here the focus falls on judicial ideology, and the conditions that either allow that ideology to be sincerely acted upon or require the judge to act strategically. Of the three judicial politics approaches, it is the historical-institutionalist approach that is most inclined to see courts as composite political actors – as institutions with their own distinctive political presence in a network of other political actors.[48]

This study is a study of the Chaskalson Court, and thus it is precommitted to thinking about the Court, if not as a composite political actor, then at least as a corporate institution. But does the phrase 'Chaskalson Court' really connote a meaningful unit of analysis, or is it just a convenient label for a group of individuals whose actions were not coordinated in any way?[49] After all, the appointment of a new chief justice may not be accompanied by any other change in the court's personnel.[50] And the question whether a particular chief justice gave a distinct style to a court, or controlled its behaviour in some way, is not one to which a positive answer may simply be assumed. Nevertheless, there are reasons to think that the conventional bracketing off of a period in the life of a court by reference to the name of its chief justice may not be entirely artificial. Chief justices do inevitably exert an influence on their colleagues, even where (and perhaps especially where) that influence is exerted through personal loyalty rather managerial commands.[51] In any case, the designation of a period in the life of a court by reference to the tenure of a

---

[48] See further the discussion in Section 1.1.

[49] On the different ways in which it may be sensible to distinguish a court by reference to the tenure of a particular Chief Justice, see Hodder-Williams, 'Is There a Burger Court?'.

[50] If the Chaskalson Court were defined by the influence exerted by a group of like-minded judges, for example, it might have been more sensible to regard the Chaskalson era as having ended with the resignation of the last remaining members of the original Court (Chief Justice Langa and Justices Mokgoro, Sachs and O'Regan) at the end of 2009.

[51] On the distinction between 'task leaders' and 'social leaders' in this context, see Hodder-Williams, 'Is There a Burger Court?' 186 n 65 (citing David Danelski, 'The Influence of the Chief Justice in the Decisional Process of the Supreme Court' in Walter H. Murphy and C. Herman Pritchett (eds.), Courts, Judges, and Politics 2nd edn (New York, NY: Random House, 1974) 525.

particular chief justice does not imply that it was the chief justice who gave the court its corporate identity. Courts are institutions, after all, and the actions of other political actors are often directed at courts *qua* institutions rather than at the individuals who happen to staff them.

To the extent that the argument of this book depends, not just on bracketing out the Chaskalson Court as the object of study, but on attributing to it coordinated actions in the form of distinct adjudicative strategies, the evidence for this will largely be found in the text of the Court's opinions. In particular, this study will examine the forms of justificatory argument, approaches to the use of authority, legal doctrines, standards of review, and general rhetorical style the members of the Court collectively adopted, over and above their own unique judicial styles.

The interplay between individual judicial styles and a court's overarching adjudicative strategy is typically seen as a question of small-group dynamics.[52] Rather than conducting a statistical or psychological analysis of this issue, this study will attempt to draw a richly detailed picture of the various individual styles on the Chaskalson Court, and then feed these judicial profiles into the analysis of particular decisions. Was a particular judge's reputation for uncompromising adherence to legal principle, for example, partly dependent on the existence of a prudential majority on the Court who could be relied on to manage the law/politics tension in controversial cases? What function did dissents play in the Court's case law?[53] Is it conceivable that, rather than evidencing a lack of coordination, they could have formed part of its overarching strategy? How united, in short, was the Court, despite differences at the level of individual judicial style?

So much, then, for the way this study proposes to approach the general question of how to understand the actions the Chaskalson Court judges took in response to the legal and political constraints impacting on the Court. The next question is how these actions interacted with the changing political context for judicial review. Were the judges' actions influenced by their perceptions of the Court's institutional situation and,

---

[52] Eloise C. Snyder, 'The Supreme Court as a Small Group' (1958) 36 *Social Forces* 232; Epstein and Knight, 'Toward a Strategic Revolution in Judicial Politics: A Look Back, a Look Ahead'.

[53] There is a vast literature on the role of dissents. See, for example, Paul J. Wahlbeck, James F. Spriggs II, Forrest Maltzman, 'The Politics of Dissents and Concurrences on the U.S. Supreme Court' (1999) 27 *American Politics Research* 488.

if so, did they seek to influence it? Even if the judges did not consciously seek to influence the Court's institutional situation, how should we understand the impact of their decisions on the changing political context?

It will be helpful as a starting point to separate out the judges' awareness of the Court's institutional situation into their awareness, first, of the legal constraints impacting on it and, secondly, their awareness of the political constraints impacting on it. For various reasons, the first issue is less problematic than the second. Judges are *expected* to be conscious of the constraints exerted by law and to respond to them accordingly. The only controversial question, as we have seen,[54] is whether the term 'constraint' distorts the analysis by predisposing us to think of judges primarily as political actors, in which case the law, if it is experienced as a constraint at all, would be experienced as a constraint on the achievement of the judges' *political* objectives rather than on their good-faith attempts to give the correct legal answer to a case.

As argued in Chapter 2, this study's use of the term 'constraint' should not be understood in this way. The term was chosen as the best available mediating concept – its particular usefulness being that it allows us to focus, in the case of both legal and political influences on constitutional adjudication, on a particular type of influence, disregard for which entails a loss in legal or political terms. The chapter accepted that the totality of the law's influence on constitutional adjudication could not be reduced to this issue. In particular, judges who are socialised to view law as a technically rigorous, politically neutral method for the resolution of disputes are motivated, not just by a desire to respect the boundaries of permissible forms of legal argument, but also by a desire to give the most persuasive answer possible to the question put to them. This wider view of the 'pull' of the law on the Court is important to the dynamic analysis of the Court's movement across the matrix because it affects our understanding of the compromises the judges were prepared to make when seeking to manage the law/politics tension. If avoiding impermissible reasoning methods had been the only requirement, fewer such compromises would have been necessary than if the judges were socialised to view their duty as being to give the most persuasive answer to every case, whatever the political repercussions.

It follows that it is crucially necessary, when exploring the way the Chaskalson Court sought to manage the law/politics tension, to understand the judges' legal-professional socialisation and their corresponding

---

[54] Section 2.1.

judicial ethic. To what extent did that ethic allow the judges to compromise on principle, both in relation to the immediate political repercussions of a decision and in relation to the impact of a decision on the Court's long-term capacity to manage the law/politics tension?

This study addresses this question in two stages. First, the chapter on South African legal-professional culture (Chapter 5) includes a section on the backgrounds and legal-professional socialisation of the members of the Court. While relevant to the determination of the Court's independence from political control, the primary purpose of this section is to build personal profiles of the members of the Court in order to get a sense of their judicial ethic. These profiles are then fed into the discussion of the Chaskalson Court's decision-making record in Part III. Here, the method is necessarily a legal-interpretive one. In respect of each case discussed, this study adopts an internal perspective on the requirements of principled legal reasoning in each case, and offers its own interpretation of the constraints exerted by applicable legal-professional norms and practices. This interpretation is then used to critique the reasons offered for the decision by the Court and to identify respects in which those reasons may be said to have compromised on principle. As with all legal-interpretive analysis, the persuasiveness of the critique in each case will depend on the persuasiveness of the rival interpretation offered.[55] The only advantage this study has is that which comes from being able to offer an interpretation unaffected by any external political constraints that might have influenced the Court. The aim, in other words, is to offer a 'pure' legal analysis, which can be used as an interpretive standard against which to analyse the Court's reasoning.

Any compromises on principle thus identified would not necessarily have been politically motivated, of course. Even on a Dworkinian approach, judges sometimes make mistakes. Likewise, on the legal positivist approach, deviation from applicable legal-professional norms and practices need not be indicative of political decision-making in the strong sense. Any inference about the *cause* of such compromises, therefore, would need to be independently substantiated. Here, the evidence will necessarily be circumstantial. Short of interviewing the judges and getting them to acknowledge the impact of institutional-independence concerns on their judgments, we are unlikely to find any direct evidence that their decisions were influenced by this kind of consideration. We will therefore need to do the best we can by painting a detailed picture of the

[55] See Cross, *Decision Making in the U.S. Courts of Appeals* (dismissing legal-interpretive analyses of the correctness of decisions as lacking in objectivity and therefore unreliable).

micro-politics of each case, from which a reasonably reliable inference about the extent to which the decision was influenced by institutional-independence concerns may be drawn. While some of these case discussions might be unpersuasive, either as a matter of legal interpretation or as an assessment of the political constraints impacting on the Court, the cumulative effect of the argument might be quite convincing.

To a certain extent, the application of the conceptual framework in Chapter 2 does not depend on conclusive evidence that the judges were consciously motivated by institutional-independence concerns. All that we have posited is the existence of two sets of constraints, with a particular kind of loss associated with each. If the Court was indeed alive to cases where the two sets of constraints contradicted each other, then it would be appropriate to understand its decision in these cases as a conscious choice to respond to one set of constraints rather than the other. But the conceptual framework would work just as well on a descriptive level if the Court were not assumed to be alive to the political constraints impacting on it and where the cause of its decision was instead ascribed to legal factors or judicial ideology. If the conceptual framework is solid, the posited loss in political terms would still follow.

But we are trying to do more than describe. We are also trying to explain, and to this extent the plausibility of identifying the judges' conscious awareness of the political constraints impacting on their court as a causal factor in their decision-making processes does matter. There can be no such thing, after all, as an unconscious strategy. If the Chaskalson Court's achievement is attributable, in whole or in part, to the Court's actions rather than coincidental changes to the political context in which it was working, and if one of the possibilities we are exploring is that the Court sought to manage the impact of its decisions on its institutional independence, we will need to find some way of establishing this.

Given that we will be reliant on circumstantial evidence, it may be necessary to soften the claim somewhat. There is a difference, we might say, between attributing to a group of judges a general awareness of the political context in which they are operating and explaining a particular decision as a function of the court's institutional-independence concerns *in that case*. Any compromise on principle in an effort to avoid the political repercussions of a *particular* decision is anathema to the ideal of adjudication according to law.[56] If the judicial biography section of

---

[56] See the discussion in Section 1.7.

this study finds that the members of the Chaskalson Court were committed to this ideal, therefore, purely political strategising of this sort is likely to have been the exception rather than the norm. In any case, as we have said, it is hard to reconcile the pursuit of such a strategy with the Court's reputation in the comparative constitutional law community.

But the objection would be less strong if the conscious awareness we attributed to the judges was a conscious awareness of the Court's overall vulnerability to political attack. This sort of political wisdom, after all, is something that we may reasonably expect any competent group of judges to have, let alone a group of judges with the sort of legal-professional experience that the members of the Chaskalson Court had. This being so, the attribution to the judges of a conscious awareness of the Court's situation would hardly be contentious. Nor would it be contentious to suggest that this conscious awareness influenced, not the outcome of particular decisions, but the general way in which the judges sought to reconcile their commitment to the ideal of adjudication according to law with their understandable (and quite legitimate) concern for the Court's institutional independence.

It is one thing, however, to attribute to the judges a conscious awareness of their Court's institutional situation, another to show that they were able to act on this awareness to influence the external political environment for judicial review. The final part of the dynamic analysis of the Court's movement across the matrix is devoted to this issue, i.e. to investigating the way in which the Court's actions, whatever motivated them, interacted with the changing political context for judicial review. As we have said, the goal here is to separate out the judges' contribution to their Court's achievement from fortuitous changes to the political context – not because this is what academic lawyers with a blinkered commitment to the legalist model like to do, but because understanding what the Chaskalson Court did to improve its situation may generate important lessons for constitutional courts in other countries.

We need to distinguish between two levels of the changing political context here: a broader level, reflecting major changes to the external political environment for judicial review associated with, say, a change in government or a change in the leadership of a dominant political party, and what has been referred to as the micro-politics of particular cases. The changing political context, in other words, may be broken up into more gradual shifts away from the situation that obtained when the Court began its work in 1995, and more volatile, case-specific shifts, not necessarily reflective of these broader changes. In both instances, our concern is to find a way of exploring whether the Court was able to manage these changes in any way.

In this study, the broader level will be accommodated in the general discussion of the political context for judicial review during the Chaskalson Court era. After analysing the political context in which the Court began its work, Chapter 5 goes on to develop an argument about how that context changed over the years, particularly as the Mandela-led racial reconciliation era gave way to the period of technocratic centralism under President Thabo Mbeki. The discussion includes an analysis of the way the Court positioned itself, and of the broader institutional-independence concerns the Court may be understood to have had. For example, during Mandela's presidency, the dominant concern was that the Court not be type-cast, on the one hand, as an institution for the maintenance of minority-group privilege, and on the other, as an ANC-court, especially given the close personal and ideological ties between members of the Court and the ANC political leadership. This analysis inevitably anticipates some of the case discussion in Part III, but only to the extent required to show how the judges sought to position the Court in relation to broader changes in the political context.

The question of the Court's ability to manage the micro-politics of particular cases is addressed in Part III. Each case discussion is organised around a composite assessment of the determinacy of the legal-professional norms impacting on the Court and the case-specific political constraints under which it operated. The focus of the analysis falls on how the Court managed the legal and political constraints impacting on it in each case. As indicated in Chapter 2, the analysis sometimes reveals that there was in fact no contradiction between the two sets of constraints, even in cases that were thought at the time to have been controversial. Either the legal constraints impacting on the Court's decision were sufficiently indeterminate so as to pose no conflict with the political constraints under which the Court operated, or the Court was able to manage the micro-politics of the case so as to reduce the political constraints impacting on it (for example, by delaying its judgment until the issue had been settled at a political level). In other instances, the analysis reveals that the Court was indeed caught between contradictory legal and political constraints. In these instances, the discussion tries to show which set of constraints the Court prioritised, and what the impact of its decision was on its institutional situation. In the final type of situation, the discussion reveals that the case itself was not controversial, but that it fell into an area of law that was likely to be productive of controversial cases down the line. Here, the discussion focuses on the Court's development of legal doctrine, trying to show how the Court's doctrinal choices might have been influenced by institutional-independence concerns in the manner discussed earlier.

3.3   Choosing the cases

The Chaskalson Court handed down its first judgment on 5 April 1995.[57] Between this point and Justice Chaskalson's retirement on 31 May 2005, the Court delivered a further 240 written judgments.[58] In addition, after his retirement, the Chief Justice was party to three judgments in two cases in which he had sat before 31 May 2005.[59] As we have said, the text of the written opinions making up these judgments constitutes the primary object of study. Clearly, however, it will not be possible to discuss all of these judgments. A trade-off will have to be made between the breadth of this study's coverage and the depth of its analysis of particular cases. What criteria should we use for this purpose?

In the judicial politics literature, this issue manifests itself in the debate over how to identify 'politically salient' cases. That category of cases is thought to be important because judicial behaviour may be influenced by the degree of political controversy surrounding a case. Thus a chief justice's decision to assign the majority opinion to a particular judge or the tendency of the court to write unanimously have both been found to be affected by this variable.[60] In order to standardise the identification of

---

[57]   *S v. Zuma and Others* 1995 (2) SA 642 (CC), 1995 (4) BCLR 401 (CC).

[58]   This number is based on the official list of judgments available on the Court's website: www.constitutionalcourt.org.za/site/judgments/judgments.htm. The term 'judgment' in this context refers to all of the written opinions collectively produced by the Court in settlement of a particular legal issue or series of legal issues put to it. Depending on the nature of the matter, there might have been several judgments in one case. Although identified by the same case number, each of these judgments would generally have been delivered on a different day. They are also distinguishable by discrete citations in the law reports.

[59]   *S v. Basson* 2007 (3) SA 582 (CC), 2005 (12) BCLR 1192 (CC) and *Minister of Health and Another NO v. New Clicks South Africa (Pty) Ltd and Others (Treatment Action Campaign and Another as Amici Curiae)* 2006 (2) SA 311 (CC), 2006 (1) BCLR 1 (CC) and *Minister of Health and Another v. New Clicks South Africa (Pty) Ltd and Others: In re: Application for Declaratory Relief* 2006 (8) BCLR 872 (CC).

[60]   See, for example, Elliot E. Slotnick, 'The Chief Justices and Self-assignment of Majority Opinions: A Research Note' (1978) 31 *The Western Political Quarterly* 219; Saul Brenner and Harold J. Spaeth, 'Issue Specialization in Majority Opinion Assignment on the Burger Court' (1986) 39 *The Western Political Quarterly* 520; Laura Krugman Ray, 'The Road to *Bush* v. *Gore*: The History of the Supreme Court's Use of the Per Curiam Opinion' (2000) 79 *Nebraska Law Review* 517.

such cases, judicial politics scholars have developed various proxy measures for political salience, most notably, in the case of the US Supreme Court, whether the judgment was reported the next day on the front page of the *New York Times*.[61]

In the legal-academic literature, by contrast, the importance of a case depends on whether the case produces new judge-made law or changes existing understandings of legal doctrine. There is no necessary correlation between the importance of a case assessed in this way and its political salience as assessed by judicial politics scholars. A judgment in a politically controversial case may thus tell us a great deal about the court as a political actor but very little about the way a particular section of the constitution ought to be interpreted, and vice versa.

This study combines aspects of both approaches. Without proposing a single proxy measure for political salience, the discussion in Part III provides qualitative reasons for treating certain cases as more politically salient than others. This is a natural side effect of the focus on the micropolitics of cases. At the same time, Part III does not attempt to provide a comprehensive treatment of every doctrinal issue in the nature of a constitutional law textbook. Rather, the discussion focuses on the legal-interpretive issues mentioned in Section 3.2. The idea, in other words, is to identify cases in which the outcome mattered from the point of view of the Court's institutional independence, and to examine closely how the Court managed the law/politics tension in those cases, if indeed it had to.

As a recent study of the influence of public opinion on the US Supreme Court has shown, however, the politics of judicial behaviour is not confined to politically salient cases.[62] Some cases that may be regarded as routine may thus have a bearing on the court's behaviour in politically salient cases. Indeed, the court's actions in these cases may form a crucial part of its overall strategy, especially if that strategy is conceived as being an adjudicative strategy of the kind discussed in Chapter 2. This study accordingly supplements its discussion of politically salient cases with an examination of cases in which the area of law may be said to have had a bearing on the court's capacity to manage the law/politics tension in future cases. This is the third set of cases mentioned at the end of the preceding section. The study also includes a chapter on 'cross-cutting

---

[61] See Lee Epstein and Jeffrey A. Segal, 'Measuring Issue Salience' (2000) 44 *American Journal of Political Science* 66.

[62] Christopher J. Casillas, Peter K. Enns and Patrick C. Wohlfarth, 'How Public Opinion Constrains the U.S. Supreme Court' (2010) 54 *American Journal of Political Science* 1.

strategies, such as the Court's separation of powers doctrine, which were relevant to a large proportion of the cases it decided. In this way, the case discussion does turn out to be fairly comprehensive, although not as comprehensive perhaps as some would have liked.

The other foundational choice that needs to be made is whether to discuss the cases chronologically or thematically. The legalist approach, as we have seen, is to discuss the cases more or less in chronological order and in this way to tell the story of the court's progressive elaboration of legal doctrine, whether in a particular area of law or across the board. This rationale does not apply here, but there may be other reasons for following a chronological approach. In particular, the advantage of a chronological approach is that it would allow us to correlate the case discussion with the discussion of the changing political context for judicial review in Chapter 4. This approach, however, also has a downside, viz. that any insights into the Court's overarching response to its mandate, whether conceived as a distinct adjudicative style, political strategy or something else, must inevitably await the end of the discussion. From this perspective, a thematic approach would be better, although here the danger is exactly the opposite, i.e. that the choice of themes might pre-empt or distort the explanation offered for the Court's achievement.

On balance, the thematic approach seems like the better option, particularly since the aim of this study is not to provide a comprehensive account of the Chaskalson Court's doctrinal output but to explore the way the Court dealt with the three types of case discussed at the end of the preceding section. Although this means that the chapter division in Part III reflects prior analytic conclusions about the major themes in the Court's jurisprudence, the reasons for these conclusions are made clear in the relevant chapters.[63] In the end, the relevant question is not how comprehensive this study's coverage of the Chaskalson Court's case law is but whether the cases that *are* discussed provide adequate support for the explanation offered and, conversely, whether any cases that are not discussed may be said to cast doubt on that explanation.

---

[63] Part III thus starts with a chapter on cases in which social morality came into conflict with the moral values expressly promoted by the post-apartheid Constitutions. This theme conveniently allows us to start with the first case heard by the Court (*S v. Makwanyane and Another* 1995 (3) SA 391 (CC), 1995 (6) BCLR 665 (CC)) while also permitting discussion of the Court's apparently strategic disavowal of the influence of public opinion on its judgments.

PART II

Context

4

The political context for judicial review, 1995–2005

It has become customary in a particular strand of the post-apartheid politics literature to classify South Africa in the first ten years of democracy as a dominant-party democracy.[1] Whether or not this classification is technically correct,[2] the ANC was unquestionably the most important political party in South Africa during this time. Indeed, more than a political party, the ANC was a national liberation movement whose popular appeal transcended any particular policy or political creed. Although its constituency was largely restricted to black South Africans,[3] the ANC drew votes from the urban working class as well as the rural poor, from democratic socialists as well as free-marketeers, from liberal progressives as well as religious conservatives and African traditionalists. The ANC, in short, was a party whose electoral support was unaffected by the cyclical shifts in sentiment that account for the regular rotation of political power in a conventional multi-party democracy.

---

[1] See Hermann Giliomee and Charles Simkins (eds.), *The Awkward Embrace: One-Party Domination and Democracy* (Cape Town: Tafelberg, 1999); Hermann Giliomee, 'South Africa's Emergent Dominant-Party Regime' (1998) 9:4 *Journal of Democracy* 128; Roger Southall, 'The Centralization and Fragmentation of South Africa's Dominant Party System' (1998) 97 *African Affairs* 443; Roger Southall, 'Opposition in South Africa: Issues and Problems' (2001) 8 *Democratization* 1; Hermann Giliomee, James Myburgh and Lawrence Schlemmer, 'Dominant Party Rule, Opposition Parties and Minorities in South Africa' (2001) 8 *Democratization* 161.

[2] See Raymond Suttner, 'Party Dominance "Theory": Of What Value?' 2006 (33) *Politikon* 277 (associating the theory of party dominance with conservative, anti-democratic bias on the part of its proponents). Perhaps in sympathy with Suttner's critique, Heinz Klug prefers the term 'unipolar' democracy. See Klug, *The Constitution of South Africa: A Contextual Analysis* (Oxford: Hart, 2010) 219. It is not entirely clear, however, how Klug's analysis of the underlying issues differs from that of Giliomee and Southall. For a recent deployment of the idea of South Africa as a dominant-party democracy in a progressive liberalist critique of the Constitutional Court's jurisprudence, see Choudhry, '"He Had a Mandate"'.

[3] See Giliomee, Myburgh and Schlemmer, 'Dominant Party Rule, Opposition Parties and Minorities in South Africa'.

Given this salient feature of South African politics, this chapter argues, the main determinant of the Chaskalson Court's insulation from political attack must have been the ANC's interest in its independence. From 1995 to 1996, that interest was bound up with the Court's role in stabilising the transition, and particularly its role in certifying the 1996 Constitution. For the transfer of political power to South Africa's black majority to be properly consolidated, and for the certification process to be seen to be legitimate, the ANC needed an independent constitutional court. After the adoption of the 1996 Constitution, however, this rationale fell away, and the ANC's interest in the Court's independence shifted to its role in overseeing the party's social and economic transformation programme. Since the legitimacy of that programme was in any case supported by the ANC's overwhelming democratic mandate, the Court's instrumental value to the ANC declined from this point. At the same time, the ANC's respect for the Court's independence became less certain, contingent as it was on changes to the presidency, factional shifts within the party, and the perceived political advantages to be had from association with the negotiated settlement.

As this overview of the argument indicates, the political context for judicial review during Chaskalson's term as Chief Justice cannot be understood separately from the institutional and cultural factors that structured the ANC's capacity and inclination to attack the Court. In addition to the two-stage constitution-making process, three issues of this sort are discussed: (1) South Africa's pre-democratic tradition of judicial independence, and the extent to which this tradition may be said to have supported the development of a political culture of respect for judicial independence after 1994; (2) the ANC's character as a political party, and the role of factional politics within the organisation, both in its turn to rights-based constitutionalism and in the ANC's fluctuating support for judicial review; and (3) the procedure for the appointment of Constitutional Court judges in the 1993 and 1996 Constitutions.

For the most part, the chapter argues, these institutional and cultural factors simply reinforced the trajectory set by the two-stage constitution-making process. The procedure for the appointment of Constitutional Court judges under the 1993 Constitution thus enhanced the Court's early insulation from political attack by ensuring that the ANC had control of the judicial appointments process at a time when it was inclined for strategic reasons to respect the Court's independence. The procedure under the 1996 Constitution, on the other hand, by giving the ANC the power to appoint the original judges' successors at a time when its respect for judicial independence was less certain, had exactly the opposite effect. Likewise, the inability of the bureaucracy effectively to implement the Court's decisions, especially those on socio-economic rights, contributed to the general deterioration of the political environment for judicial review after 1996.

The picture was not completely bleak. The practice of public impact litigation that had developed under apartheid continued after the transition and ensured a steady flow of cases to the Court in which it was able to demonstrate its relevance to the new regime. It is also arguable that South Africa's pre-democratic tradition of judicial independence, though weak, was in fact quite well suited to a situation in which a dominant political party sought to use law to implement a major programme of social and economic reform. Still, the overarching trajectory was one of steady decline as Chaskalson's term as Chief Justice progressed. Far from undermining the Court's achievement, the chapter concludes, this finding suggests that the Court's continued capacity to assert its institutional role in South African politics must be attributable to something that the Court itself did.

4.1   South Africa's pre-democratic tradition of judicial independence

At the time of the transition to democracy, South Africa had almost no experience of constitutional judicial review.[4] It did, however, have a distinct tradition of judicial independence – a relatively long history, that is, of political contestation and institutional practice relating to the need for the courts to be independent from partisan political control. The purpose of this section is to assess the nature and strength of this tradition and its likely impact on the political context for judicial review after 1994. When the Court began operating, was its capacity to assert its

---

[4] The 1854 Constitution of the Orange Free State contained a list of individual rights, but these were applied to the judicial review of legislation (unsuccessfully) in only one case. In the South African Republic, Chief Justice J. G. Kotze's attempted assertion of the power of judicial review in *Brown* v. *Leyds NO* (1897) 4 Off Rep 17 famously resulted in his dismissal. See Klug, *Constituting Democracy* 32–4. After the manner and form provisions of the 1910 Union of South Africa Constitution were used to resist the removal of Coloured voters from the Cape voters' role (see below), the 1961 and 1983 South African Constitutions expressly excluded the power of judicial review. Shortly before the transition, bills of rights were adopted in the former Bantustans of the Ciskei and Bophuthatswana. See Klug, *Constituting Democracy* 75.

institutional role enhanced by well-developed politico-cultural norms favouring respect for judicial independence? If not, did the transition to democracy and the turn to liberal constitutionalism make the development of such norms more likely? How relevant to the new constitutional order was the limited (but never abandoned) practice of using the courts to oppose apartheid? And did the turn to liberal constitutionalism necessarily mean that this aspect of the tradition would be strengthened, or did the post-apartheid Constitutions pose fresh challenges to the tradition that human rights lawyers and others committed to the ideal of judicial independence would have to overcome?

Before attempting to answer these questions, a threshold decision must be made about how far back to go. In as much as the starting point for South Africa's tradition of judicial independence consisted of ideas that the white settlers brought with them from Europe, one approach might be to go all the way back to the seventeenth century, to the emergence of the separation of powers doctrine in England,[5] and then to trace the attempt to instantiate this doctrine at the Cape after the second British occupation in 1806 and in Natal and the two Boer Republics after that.[6] With some effort, it might then be possible to follow the tradition as it developed in the first forty years of the Union of South Africa, when it briefly thrived as a side-effect of the contest between Afrikaner nationalists and cultural assimilationists for white minority support.[7] The additional effort put into such an exercise, however, would probably not be rewarded by any significant increase in return. For two reasons, the vital period for purposes of this study is the period of National Party rule from 1948 to 1994.

First, whatever the nature of the earlier part of the tradition, the political context for judicial review from 1995 to 2005 is likely to have been far more powerfully influenced by norms and practices that developed in the latter stages of the tradition's development. It was primarily these norms and practices, after all, that informed the design of the post-apartheid Constitutions and conditioned the way in which the ANC and other political actors sought to relate to the Court.

---

[5] The 1701 Act of Settlement was the first English statute to recognise the principle of security of judicial tenure.

[6] See H. R. Hahlo and Ellison Kahn, *South Africa: The Development of its Laws and Constitution* (London: Stevens & Sons, 1960) 51–127; Albie Sachs, *Justice in South Africa* (Berkeley: University of California Press, 1973) 68–94.

[7] See Corder, *Judges at Work*; Chanock, *The Making of South African Legal Culture 1902–1935*, 517–18.

Secondly, there is an obvious similarity between certain aspects of the National Party's rule under apartheid and the ANC's rule in the first decade of democracy. In both cases, a dominant political party gained effective control of the state and attempted to use law to implement a major programme of social reform. Notwithstanding the important difference that the ANC was voted into office in a series of democratic elections, this similarity suggests that the latter part of the tradition might have been doubly influential: not only was it recent, it was also highly relevant.

Focusing, then, on the period of National Party rule from 1948 to 1994, what was the nature and strength of the tradition during this time? According to the fairly extensive literature on this topic,[8] the story is one of steady decline associated with decreasing fragmentation in white minority politics. Whereas three different political parties had held office in the first forty years of the Union of South Africa,[9] the National Party was able to exploit white South Africans' fear of black domination after 1948 to exclude all other political parties from power for close to fifty years. During this extended period of single-party dominance, the relatively vigorous tradition of judicial independence that had developed before the National Party took office was progressively eroded. At the same time, the political rationale for the tradition underwent a fundamental transformation. In the absence of effective political competition, the National Party's respect for judicial independence came increasingly to depend on the legitimating function served by the courts – on the National Party's strategic need, that is, to be able to claim that its hold on political power, however undemocratic, was at least partially justified by black South Africans' ability to challenge the application of apartheid legislation before an independent and impartial tribunal.

In keeping with this rationale, the National Party's commitment to judicial independence was ambivalent at best. On the one hand, it was clearly prepared to subdue the courts in matters thought to be vital to the implementation of apartheid. The most notorious of these incidents occurred in the 1950s when it packed the Appellate Division to secure

[8] Dugard, *Human Rights and the South African Legal Order*; Forsyth, *In Danger for their Talents*; Ellmann, *In a Time of Trouble*; Chanock, *The Making of South African Legal Culture* 517–19.

[9] The South African Party (from 1910 to 1924), the National Party and Labour Party coalition (from 1924 to 1933) and the United Party, an alliance of the SAP and the NP (from 1933 to 1948). See Corder, *Judges at Work*, xxvii–xxviii.

the removal of Coloureds from the Cape voters' roll.[10] At around the same time, the Appellate Division's assertion of a limited (but still politically awkward) 'separate but equal' doctrine was met by the enactment of the Reservation of Separate Amenities Act, which ousted the courts' jurisdiction from reviewing subordinate legislation on this ground.[11] There were other, more insidious attacks as well. Over the years, the judicial appointments process became increasingly politicised, with several qualified but ideologically unpalatable candidates either not asked to serve on the Bench or not promoted once there.[12] Other candidates, whose loyalty to the regime had been demonstrated at the bar or in the civil service, were promoted faster than they otherwise would have been.[13] Towards the end of the apartheid era, in the turbulent 1980s, clear evidence of the manipulation of the Appellate Division's panel system emerged. This was particularly true of cases heard under the emergency regulations, where a group of five judges under Chief Justice Rabie took effective control.[14] In an unprecedented step, Rabie was asked to serve as Acting Chief Justice for two years after reaching retirement age, with no permanent appointment made.[15]

On the other hand, the National Party never completely turned the courts into an instrument of the executive. Apart from a brief hiatus in the 1950s,[16] liberal judges continued to be appointed and were not dismissed when they handed down inconvenient judgments. Instead, the apartheid Government typically responded to such judgments by

---

[10] For fuller accounts of this episode, see Forsyth, *In Danger for their Talents*, 63–7; Leonard Thompson, *A History of South Africa* rev. ed. (New Haven, CT: Yale University Press, 1995) 190–91; Meierhenrich, *The Legacies of Law* 134–6.

[11] Act 49 of 1953. See Dugard, *Human Rights and the South African Legal Order* 64–5; Meierhenrich, *Legacies of Law* 116; Klug, *Constituting Democracy* 42–3.

[12] Schreiner JA, for example, was not elevated to the chief justiceship of the Appellate Division, on most accounts because of the stand he took in the third Cape franchise case. See Dugard, *Human Rights and the South African Legal Order* 286.

[13] See Edwin Cameron, 'Legal Chauvinism, Executive-Mindedness and Justice: L. C. Steyn's Impact on South African Law' (1982) 99 *South African Law Journal* 38.

[14] Ellmann, *In a Time of Trouble* 57–69, citing Nicholas Haysom and Clive Plasket, 'The War against Law: Judicial Activism and the Appellate Division' (1988) 4 *South African Journal on Human Rights* 303, 310. See also Michael Kidd, 'Internal Security and Specialist Judges: A Study of the Composition of the Appellate Division in Internal Security Cases from 1986 to the Present' (1990) 6 *South African Journal on Human Rights* 417.

[15] Ellmann, *In a Time of Trouble* 60–61, citing Edwin Cameron, 'Nude Monarchy: The Case of South Africa's Judges' (1987) 3 *South African Journal on Human Rights* 338, 344–6.

[16] Dugard, *Human Rights and the South African Legal Order* 285.

amending the statute concerned. This practice drew liberal judges into a morally testing game in which they tried to secure some sort of justice for those targeted by apartheid legislation without triggering even more draconian measures.[17] If a statutory loophole was too obviously exploited, or the more egalitarian values of the common law too strongly asserted, the legislative screw would invariably be tightened. At no point, however, did the National Party abandon its commitment to legality, even when, as in the case of the Group Areas Act, liberal judges succeeded in making the system unworkable.[18]

In tolerating a measure of judicial independence in this way, the National Party behaved in a manner similar to other authoritarian regimes that have sought to dress up oppressive measures in legal garb. What marks the South African case out as exceptional is the sheer scale and ambition of the apartheid legal order. The National Party was also in the somewhat unusual position (for a non-European authoritarian regime) of claiming to represent the interests of a civilised European people. When combined with South Africa's dependence on foreign trade, this yearning to be accepted by the West made the apartheid Government relatively more susceptible to international criticism.

It was precisely this susceptibility, of course, that liberal judges exploited when trying to soften the impact of apartheid legislation. The occasional victories they won would not have been possible had the National Party not had self-interested reasons for self-restraint. Even this limited degree of toleration, however, crucially depended on the fact of parliamentary sovereignty. As we have seen, on the one occasion when the Appellate Division exercised something like an American-style power of judicial review – the Cape franchise case – the National Party immediately attacked it, with little regard for the consequences of its actions on South Africa's international standing. That there were not more such occasions had less to do with the fact that the National Party eventually

---

[17] On the debate over whether liberal judges under apartheid should have resigned rather than participate in this game, see Raymond Wacks, 'Judges and Injustice' (1984) 101 *South African Law Journal* 266; John Dugard, 'Should Judges Resign? A Reply to Professor Wacks' (1984) 101 *South African Law Journal* 286. For an in-depth treatment of the moral choices facing liberal judges in apartheid South Africa, see David Dyzenhaus, *Hard Cases in Wicked Legal Systems*.

[18] By requiring magistrates to inquire into the availability of alternative accommodation before making an order for eviction, Goldstone J's decision in *S v. Govender* 1986 (3) SA 969 (T) effectively put a halt to the implementation of this Act.

learned to be more restrained than with the fact that the Westminster system largely obviated the need to attack the courts directly.

Such, then, was the state of South Africa's tradition of judicial independence when the constitutional negotiators met to discuss the mechanics of the transition. Given the fragility of the tradition, just why the negotiators placed so much trust in law – to the point of giving judges the power of judicial review – is an intriguing question.[19] Of primary interest here, however, is the narrower issue of the impact that the turn to rights-based constitutionalism had on the tradition, and what this would have meant for the Chaskalson Court's capacity to withstand political attack. On the one hand, there is reason to think that the adoption of a higher-law constitution would have strengthened that part of the tradition that had seen the courts used as a check on the abuse of political power. On the other, the turn to rights-based constitutionalism – by giving judges the power to review democratic decisions – posed challenges to the tradition of a kind that had not been encountered before.

As to the first point, the use of the courts in the struggle against apartheid must be understood as having been driven partly by human rights lawyers committed to a liberal vision of law as separate from politics and partly by political activists for whom recourse to the courts was mainly a matter of strategy.[20] The enduring contribution of this work to South Africa's tradition of judicial independence therefore depended on the continuities human rights lawyers were able to draw between the apartheid and post-apartheid eras. For Chaskalson himself, the record of human rights lawyering under apartheid, and the partial receptivity of the South African judiciary to such cases, was an important legacy that could be used as the foundation stone on which to build a more robust

---

[19] While one of the main drivers of the turn to liberal constitutionalism was the National Party's desire for 'insurance' (see Ginsburg, *Judicial Review in New Democracies* 55–7), the outgoing apartheid government's confidence that the ANC would abide by the terms of the constitutional compact must still be explained. For contending views on this question, see Klug, *Constituting Democracy* (attributing South Africa's turn to liberal constitutionalism to the ascendancy of rights-based constitutionalism in 'international political culture') and Meierhenrich, *The Legacies of Law* (attributing the negotiators' ability to place their trust in law to the 'memory' of 'formally rational law' as applied in the apartheid 'dual state').

[20] See the contrasting views taken on this issue in Stephen Ellmann, *In a Time of Trouble* and Richard L. Abel, *Politics by Other Means: Law in the Struggle against Apartheid, 1980–1994* (New York, NY: Routledge, 1995). For an interesting recent return to this debate, See Stephen Ellmann, 'Learning from "The Making of South African Legal Culture"' (2012) 28 *Law in Context* (forthcoming).

tradition.[21] For others, the development of such a tradition depended on the frankness with which South Africans, and legal professionals in particular, were prepared to confront the failings of the apartheid era and the general capitulation of legal elites to the imperatives of white minority rule. On this view, the mere fact that South Africa had adopted a higher-law constitution was no guarantee that it would develop a political culture capable of supporting it.[22] Indeed, there was a real danger of complacency, of a tendency to think that such a culture would develop by itself when in fact it would have to be fought for.

This concern was all the more pressing given the extraordinary powers conferred on the courts by the post-apartheid Constitutions. Even the weak tradition of judicial independence that had developed before 1995 was, as we have seen, contingent on the limited role given to the courts under the Westminster system. The post-apartheid Constitutions, by contrast, thrust the courts into the centre of politics, and in so doing required them to develop a more nuanced understanding of the judicial function, both as a matter of legal reasoning and as a contribution to the broader political culture. Just how the courts would respond to this challenge was far from certain.[23]

Against this, however, must be weighed the fact that the transition to democracy was associated with the political ascendancy of a party that for the first time in South Africa's history had a defensible moral claim to govern on behalf of all its people. If the 'right degree of independence'[24] is contingent on the democratic legitimacy of the ruling regime, this change arguably reduced the need for the courts to be entirely free from political influence. Whereas the role of the courts under apartheid, in other words, should ideally have been to resist the National Party's unjust and authoritarian rule – and jealously guard their independence – the post-apartheid courts needed to seek out a less confrontational relationship with the political branches, one that acknowledged the democratic legitimacy of the ANC's mandate and the corresponding need for the

---

[21] Arthur Chaskalson, 'The Past Ten Years: A Balance Sheet and Some Indicators for the Future' (1989) 5 *South African Journal on Human Rights* 293.

[22] See David Dyzenhaus, *Judging the Judges, Judging Ourselves: Truth, Reconciliation and the Apartheid Legal Order* (Oxford: Hart Publishing, 1998) 174 (quoting from Edwin Cameron's submission to the TRC's Legal Hearing).

[23] See further Section 5.2.

[24] Owen Fiss, 'The Right Degree of Independence' in Irwin P. Stotzky, *Transition to Democracy in Latin America: The Role of the Judiciary* (Boulder, CO: Westview Press, 1993) 55.

courts to be at least somewhat accountable to the people. When this consideration is taken into account, there may after all have been sufficient resources in the tradition to support the development of the required political culture. At least, the destabilising effect of the increase in the courts' powers associated with the turn to liberal constitutionalism may have been off-set by the simultaneous transition to democracy.

Even so, the required political culture still needed to be nurtured, and thus the conclusion must be that South Africa's pre-democratic tradition of judicial independence did not significantly enhance the Chaskalson Court's capacity to withstand political attack. While human rights lawyers and liberal judges had done enough to keep the ideal of judicial independence alive, the tradition's main politico-cultural legacy was the lesson the National Party had taught about the advantages to a dominant political party of tolerating a measure of judicial independence. Given the similarity alluded to earlier between the National Party and the ANC's use of law, it was this aspect of the tradition that was always likely to prove most influential.

4.2   The character of the ANC and its commitment to liberal constitutionalism

South Africa's first democratic elections in 1994 brought to power a political party with a fundamentally different character to that of the National Party. Founded in 1912, the ANC's identity had been forged by eighty years of extra-parliamentary struggle, first as a relatively conservative lobby group representing the interests of the emerging African middle class, and then, from 1949,[25] as an increasingly militant, mass-based political organisation demanding the full inclusion of the African majority in a non-racial, unitary state.[26] As an extra-parliamentary movement, the ANC had experienced none of the burdens of governing and all of the considerable moral appeal of an organisation dedicated to

---

[25] 1949 was the year in which the ANC adopted the more radical programme of the ANC Youth League, founded in 1944 by Anton Lembede, Oliver Tambo, Walter Sisulu and Nelson Mandela.

[26] For a succinct history of the ANC, see Saul Dubow, *The African National Congress* (Stroud: Sutton Publishing, 2000). See also Tom Lodge, *Black Politics in South Africa Since 1945* (London: Longman, 1983); Dale T. McKinley, *The ANC and the Liberation Struggle: Critical Political Biography* (London: Pluto Press, 1997); and William Mervin Gumede, *Thabo Mbeki and the Battle for the Soul of the ANC* rev. ed. (Cape Town: Zebra Press, 2007) 1–32.

the overthrow of an unjust regime. It was also much more ideologically diverse than its long-term political rival, including within its ranks the full spectrum of South African political opinion, from communists on the left to religious conservatives and African traditionalists on the right.

Throughout the course of its long extra-parliamentary history, the ANC's vision for a future South Africa was kept deliberately vague in order to accommodate the diverse views within its ranks. The ANC's central demand for the inclusion of the African majority in a non-racial, unitary state was thus compatible with a liberal vision of South Africa as a Westminster-style parliamentary democracy, but it was also not incompatible with an understanding of the ANC's core political programme as amounting to the creation of a one-party socialist state. The 1955 Freedom Charter lay at the centre of this carefully managed ambiguity. Drafted by a Marxist, and containing such proposals as a call for the nationalisation of South Africa's 'mineral wealth beneath the soil, the banks and monopoly industry', the Freedom Charter was nevertheless also amenable to a more capital-friendly reading. In a 1956 article, Nelson Mandela famously glossed the Charter's references to the need to break up South Africa's mining and other monopolies as a necessary step to 'open up fresh fields for the development of a prosperous non-European bourgeois class'.[27] As a political manifesto, it was clear, the Charter was more important for its commitment to non-racialism than it was for any concrete statement of the ANC's political and economic philosophy.

The ANC's relationship with the South African Liberal Party reflected this ambivalent attitude, although the Liberal Party, it must be said, gave the ANC little reason to forge an alliance with it. Stung by its refusal to call for universal adult suffrage, Mandela dismissed the Liberal Party in a 1953 essay as inflexibly committed to the maintenance of white privilege.[28] The Party's decision not to participate in the drafting of the Freedom Charter tended to confirm the correctness of this view,[29] and from this point on white influence on the ANC was mainly exerted by members of the banned South African Communist Party, which the

---

[27] Nelson Mandela, 'Freedom in Our Lifetime' *Liberation*, June 1956, 4–8 (cited in Anthony Sampson, *Mandela: The Authorised Biography* (London: Harper Collins, 1999) 95.

[28] Sampson, *Mandela* 90.

[29] Ibid. 91 (citing Randolph Vigne, *Liberals against Apartheid: A History of the Liberal Party of South Africa, 1953–68* (Basingstoke: Macmillan, 1997) 24).

ANC rightly saw as less ambiguously committed to black majority rule.[30]

Notwithstanding this somewhat fractious relationship with the liberal tradition in white politics, the ANC had for much of its history been led by political moderates, who had managed to unify the party around the shared goal of defeating white minority rule while successfully avoiding categorisation as either left or right. The ANC's early demand for African representation in the Union Parliament was thus premised on the progressive extension of rights of political participation to all.[31] After a radical take-over of the presidency in 1927, an alliance of conservatives and chiefs quickly regained control of the organisation.[32] It was not until the ANC Youth League succeeded in convincing the organisation to adopt its more militant Programme of Action in 1949 that the ANC finally shook off its image as a party of polite protest. Even then, however, pragmatic centrists continued to hold the balance of power in the organisation, mediating between the ANC's left faction, which was aligned with the Communist Party, and its right faction, which was African nationalist in orientation and inclined to think of the Communist Party as the source of undue white influence. At two points in the organisation's history, a perceived leftwards shift in the ANC's political centre of gravity triggered African nationalist-inspired breakaways, the first in 1959, when the Pan Africanist Congress was formed, and the second in 1973, when the so-called 'gang of eight' briefly set up a rival version of the party, claiming allegiance to the imprisoned Mandela.[33] On both occasions, however, centrists were able to re-assert control of the organisation, and the members of the breakaway factions either disappeared into the political wilderness or rejoined the ANC suitably chastened.

If there was a single defining feature of the ANC's political character before 1994, then, it was its capacity to dominate the centre ground of South African politics by co-opting or seeking out alliances with parties of the left and right, and by adapting its policies to counter any perceived threat from factions intent on better expressing popular African sentiment. The ANC's post-1955 commitment to non-racialism was a core part of this strategy, allowing it as it did to utilise the talents of white and Indian communists while sacrificing the support of only the most radical

---

[30] The Communist Party had accepted African members from the 1920s (Gumede, *Thabo Mbeki and the Battle for the Soul of the ANC* 10).
[31] Ibid. 5.   [32] Ibid. 11.   [33] Sampson, *Mandela* 266.

of the African nationalists, whose exclusivist views were in any case awkwardly reminiscent of the National Party's doomed ideology.[34]

In keeping with this centrist tradition, the ANC developed a commitment to human rights that straddled the left and right wings of the party. Neither wholly liberal in its emphasis on socio-economic rights, nor wholly socialist in its call for the extension of civil and political rights, the ANC's human rights tradition was rather a complex amalgam of the two dominant international human rights traditions.[35] Starting with the 1943 African Claims document, which applied the principles of the Atlantic Charter to the call for political equality in South Africa, and reaching full expression in the Freedom Charter, the ANC repeatedly committed itself to a rights-based conception of democracy in which all South Africans would be able to participate to the full extent of their capabilities. Recognising the link between the fulfilment of socio-economic rights and meaningful political participation, the tradition stressed that the attainment of political freedom in South Africa would need to be matched by economic emancipation. For communists, the stressing of this link was code for a planned two-stage revolution, in which the ANC as a national liberation movement would first throw off the yoke of imperialism before leading South Africans into a one-party people's democracy. For African nationalists, on the other hand, the link between the two sets of rights was more akin to the one that the National Party was beginning to demonstrate in its capacity to use its political dominance to uplift the newly urbanised Afrikaner community.

Either way, the ANC's human rights tradition was not initially committed to the idea of judicial rights protection under a supreme-law constitution. In the case of the socialist element in the tradition, this was because of the long-standing belief on the part of the left that

---

[34] The ANC's commitment to non-racialism was not purely strategic, of course. A succession of leaders, including Albert Luthuli in the crucial period from 1952 to 1967, were committed South Africans, whose nationalism was neither ethnic nor racial. (See Scott Couper, *Albert Luthuli: Bound by Faith* (Scottsville: University of KwaZulu-Natal Press, 2010).) Mandela's own political evolution from radical African nationalism to the ideals of the Freedom Charter occurred on the back of the genuine friendships he formed with Indian, Coloured and white South Africans in the cultural melting pot of mid-century Johannesburg. (See Tom Lodge, *Mandela: A Critical Life* (Oxford University Press, 2006) 48.) Along with the other founding members of the Youth League, Mandela's capacity to reach out to, and genuinely empathise with, members of all race groups was an important component of the ANC's centrist tradition.

[35] See Kader Asmal with David Chidester and Cassius Lubisi (eds.), *Legacy of Freedom: The ANC's Human Rights Tradition* (Johannesburg: Jonathan Ball, 2005).

socio-economic rights were best realised through forms of participatory
democracy in which the judiciary had no meaningful role to play. In the
case of the liberal element, this was because the American model of
judicial review had yet to capture the world's imagination, with the
dominant understanding of the role of courts in enforcing individual
rights still being that of the British Westminster tradition.

The ANC's shift towards accepting the need for judicial review under a
supreme-law constitution was a progressive development that occurred,
as Heinz Klug has argued, through the gradual interweaving of its
struggle against apartheid with the evolving models of governance in
'international political culture'.[36] As the American model of judicial
review gradually gained the ascendancy, and as the apartheid Government began to reach out to the ANC in the 1980s, the ANC came under
increasing pressure to articulate its vision for a future South Africa in
concrete institutional form. The proposed role of the judiciary became
crucial in this respect, since it was here that the tension between the
socialist and liberal elements in the ANC's human rights tradition was
hardest to resolve.

The start of the ANC's attempt to deal with this challenge can be
traced to the party's June 1985 Kabwe conference.[37] Occurring in the
midst of widespread unrest in South Africa, at a time when it was clear,
not only that the apartheid state was beginning to unravel, but that the
ANC would need to take decisive steps to control the process of its
unravelling, the Kabwe conference saw the launching of two alternative
and ultimately competing strategies for the expedition of the transition to
democracy: a military strategy, in terms of which the ANC would infil-
trate and direct the popular uprising so as to effect the violent overthrow
of the apartheid regime, and a negotiations strategy, in terms of which
the ANC would reach out to moderate Afrikaners and South African
businessman in an attempt to convince the regime to hand over power
peacefully. The idea of combining military and non-military strategies in
this way was not new.[38] What was different was the sense that, on this
occasion, one strategy would ultimately play a more important role in the

---

[36] Klug, *Constituting Democracy*.

[37] See Mark Gevisser, *The Dream Deferred: Thabo Mbeki* (Johannesburg: Jonathan Ball,
2007) 527–35; Klug, *Constituting Democracy* 77.

[38] See Padraig O'Malley, *Shades of Difference: Mac Maharaj and the Struggle for South
Africa* (London: Penguin, 2007).

transition than the other, thus enhancing the position of those leaders who were seen to have supported it.

The then President of the ANC, Oliver Tambo (a pragmatist who is credited with having kept the divergent elements of the ANC in exile together[39]), played a key role in each strategy. On the one hand, he was party to, and fully backed, the Kabwe conference's decision to intensify the armed struggle.[40] On the other, he managed to secure a mandate to set up a commission to explore possible constitutional options for a future South Africa as a basis for negotiations with the National Party. In its first report to the ANC in December 1985, the commission recommended the establishment of a standing Constitutional Committee. This proposal was duly accepted, and the Committee began work under the auspices of the ANC's department of legal and constitutional affairs, which had itself been established just six months earlier.[41]

The two most prominent members of the Committee, Albie Sachs and Kader Asmal, were both legal academics who had spent considerable time living abroad, in Sachs's case in the United States, and in Asmal's case in the Republic of Ireland.[42] Neither could be described as a mainstream liberal,[43] but both had had extensive experience of the workings of a modern constitutional democracy, and were thus in a position to adapt the ANC's human rights tradition to the requirements of the post-Cold War era.[44] Starting in January 1986, the Committee set about translating the aspirational ideals of the Freedom Charter into concrete constitutional proposals.[45] The Committee made rapid progress, producing a

---

[39] See Lulu Callinicos, *Oliver Tambo: Beyond the Engeli Mountains* (Claremont: David Philip, 2004); Gumede, *The Battle for the Soul of the ANC* 36.

[40] Gevisser, *The Dream Deferred* 527–35.   [41] Ibid. 535.

[42] On the influence of Sachs's American experience, see R. W. Johnson and David Welsh (eds.), *Ironic Victory: Liberalism in Post-Liberation South Africa* (Cape Town: Oxford University Press, 1998) 24.

[43] In his later role as judge of the Constitutional Court, Sachs's sympathy for the identity-politics strand of liberalism was plain to see, with Sachs often handing down the most progressive of the Court's judgments on gender and sexual equality. Asmal, by contrast, is on record as saying that '[l]iberalism ... has become South Africa's last credible instrument of privilege' (Kader Asmal and Ronald Suresh Roberts, 'Liberalism's Hollow Core' *Sunday Times* (1 October 1995) quoted in Patrick Laurence, 'Liberalism and Politics' in Johnson and Welsh (eds.), *Ironic Victory* 45, 50). Towards the end of his life, however, as a vocal critic of the ANC's descent into factionalism, Asmal revealed himself to be, if not a liberal, then at least an advocate of political moderation and tolerance of opposing views. See Kader Asmal and Adrian Hadland, with Moira Levy, *Politics in My Blood: A Memoir* (Johannesburg: Jacana, 2011).

[44] Gevisser, *The Dream Deferred* 535.   [45] Asmal, *Politics in My Blood* 105.

comprehensive set of Constitutional Guidelines in September 1986. Even so, the internal process within the ANC of accepting the need for limited government under a supreme-law constitution took a further five years. The Guidelines themselves, which were publicly released in 1987, committed the organisation to the adoption of a Bill of Rights, but made no mention of an independent judiciary.[46] It was only in the Constitutional Committee's 1991 draft Bill of Rights that the subjection of 'the State and organs of government at all levels' to the authority of a judicially enforced constitution was finally proposed.[47]

In his magisterial biography of Thabo Mbeki, Mark Gevisser argues that the Constitutional Committee was 'the dynamo for the revision of the ANC's clunky statism'.[48] His own account, however, suggests that the real drivers of the process were Tambo and Mbeki. It was Tambo, as we have seen, who first floated the idea of converting the Freedom Charter into a more concrete statement of the ANC's preferred constitutional model, and Mbeki who began talking to the National Party's emissaries at a time when a more hardline faction, led by Chris Hani and Joe Slovo, was still plotting the violent overthrow of the apartheid regime.[49] In parallel with these developments, Nelson Mandela, in a series of talks with the National Party during the last five years of his imprisonment, also showed himself to be a pragmatist who was prepared to countenance the idea of constitutional guarantees for minority rights.[50] After his release in February 1990 and the return of the exiled leadership in June of that year, Mandela sided with the Tambo/Mbeki faction, enhancing its control of the organisation and ensuring the ultimate success of the negotiations strategy.

---

[46] Instead, the Guidelines stated vaguely that the Bill of Rights 'shall guarantee the fundamental human rights of all citizens . . . and shall provide appropriate mechanisms for their enforcement' (African National Congress, 'Constitutional Guidelines for a Democratic South Africa, 1988' reprinted in (1989) 21 *Columbia Human Rights Law Review* 235, clause (h)).

[47] African National Congress, 'Draft Bill of Rights', published in (1991) 7 *South African Journal on Human Rights* 110.

[48] Gevisser, *The Dream Deferred* 536.

[49] Ibid. 535. In the dying days of apartheid, Slovo was the prime mover behind Operation Vula, an underground operation aimed at creating the conditions for a people's revolution. The operation was sanctioned by the ANC's National Executive Committee, and Mbeki knew of it. This was later to cause much resentment in the organisation, especially on the part of those, like Mac Maharaj, who had been arrested. See Gevisser, *The Dream Deferred* 528.

[50] See Hermann Giliomee, *The Afrikaners: Biography of a People* (Cape Town: Tafelberg, 2003) 627–8.

A similar process played itself out on the side of the National Party, whose turn to negotiations was likewise driven by pragmatists keen to broker a constitutional settlement at a time of relative strength.[51] From the National Party's perspective, an independent judiciary enforcing the widest possible range of civil and political, but especially also cultural rights, was the next best option to its preferred constitutional model of heightened federalism and group rights. Spurred on by the ANC's need to re-assure the National Party's constituency of its concern for their interests, the negotiations process led inexorably to the adoption of the American model of judicial review. The adoption of the American Constitution's *substantive* vision of rights was not similarly inevitable, however, and here the ANC was able to use its popular support, particularly after the first democratic elections, to ensure that its unique blend of liberal and socialist rights was reflected.

The combination of the American model of judicial review with an expanded list of justiciable rights was something of a mixed blessing. On the one hand, the fact that the ANC had been drawn into concretising its human rights tradition in the course of negotiations with the National Party helped it to sidestep what would otherwise have been an intractable conflict between its left and rights factions. Presented as a necessary political compromise, the centrist faction was able to overcome both the institutional objections of the left wing of the party to the idea of judicial rights enforcement and the culturalist objections of the right wing to Western notions of gender equality. Indeed, viewed in its most positive light, the centrist faction successfully used the constitutional negotiations process as a crucible within which to melt down and combine the competing elements of the ANC's human rights tradition.

On the other hand, the fact that the ANC had been forced to accept a system of rights-based judicial review as part of a political compromise entailed certain awkward consequences, both for the centrist faction and for the future stability of the new constitutional order. By nailing its political colours to this particular mast, the centrist faction assumed responsibility for the delivery of the ANC's long-awaited social transformation project, and moreover through means which were always going to be constrained by the terms of the negotiated settlement and the international political order that lay behind it. It was one thing for pragmatic centrists to have held the broad church of the ANC together

---

[51] Ibid. 585–634.

during its time in exile, quite another for them to maintain the unity of the organisation when the mantle of government was thrust upon it. Governing entails choices, and with those choices come assessments, in the centrist faction's case, not just of the wisdom of the policies it would be pursuing but also of the wisdom of the negotiated settlement that undergirded and constrained those policies.

Despite the ultimate success of the centrist faction's negotiations strategy, therefore, the ANC's commitment to liberal constitutionalism was fragile. In particular, the strength of that commitment depended on the centrist faction's continued control of the party, which in turn depended on public perceptions about the long-term benefits of the negotiated settlement.[52] To the extent that the new constitutional order came to be perceived as hindering the ANC's ability to deliver on its promise of a 'better life for all',[53] the centrist faction's hold on the party was vulnerable to challenge, and with it the ANC's commitment to a constitutional system that for the left and right factions seemed alien to its long-established traditions and political objectives.

Given the ANC's domination of South Africa politics after 1994, this internal political dynamic was the single-most important determinant of the Chaskalson Court's institutional independence. For as long as the centrist faction retained control of the party, the Court's independence was at least partly secured by this faction's strategic interest in the success of the negotiated settlement.[54] On the other hand, any perceived hindrance posed by the negotiated settlement to the achievement of the ANC's social transformation project threatened to generate political attacks on the Court, either from the centrist faction itself (in an attempt to dissociate itself from the consequences of the political compromise it had brokered) or from the left or African nationalist factions in the ANC (seeking to take advantage of the centrist faction's vulnerability in this respect).

This aspect of the political context, the next section argues, was reinforced by certain structural features of the post-apartheid

---

[52] For a recent consideration of this issue, see Dikgang Moseneke, 'Striking a Balance Between the Will of the People and the Supremacy of the Constitution' Claude Leon Public Lecture, University of Cape Town (29 September 2011) 2.

[53] This was the slogan adopted in the ANC's 1994 election campaign.

[54] Cf. Barry Friedman, *The Will of the People: How Public Opinion Has Influenced the Supreme Court and Shaped the Meaning of the Constitution* (New York, NY: Farrar, Straus and Giroux, 2009) 137–66 (on the early US Supreme Court's need for a 'constituency' – in the South African case, this need was met by the ANC's centrist faction).

Constitutions. In particular, the provision in the 1993 Constitution for a two-stage constitution-making process, in which the Constitutional Court was to play a central role, gave the centrist faction an immediate interest in its independence. This feature was in turn supported by the judicial appointments process, which allowed the ANC to choose the first judges of the Court at a time when its support for judicial independence was relatively strong. After the adoption of the 1996 Constitution, however, the ANC's support for judicial review declined in line with the perceived advantages to be had from association with the negotiated settlement.

4.3   Constitutional provisions affecting the Court's independence from political control

A constitutional court's insulation from political attack, Chapter 2 argued, is equivalent to its *actual* rather than *formal* independence from political control. Whether a constitutional provision aimed at protecting the independence of the judiciary indeed has this effect is contingent on its capacity to raise the costs to political actors of attacking the court. By the same token, a provision need not have been intended to serve a protective purpose for it to contribute to the court's independence from political control in fact.

The post-apartheid Constitutions contained several provisions of both these sorts, including provisions setting out the procedure for the appointment of Constitutional Court judges,[55] guarantees of security of tenure and remuneration,[56] a series of provisions setting out the Court's jurisdiction and powers,[57] and an express prohibition on interference with the independence of the courts.[58] Of all these various provisions, the most important from the point of view of the Court's insulation from political attack were the provisions in the 1993 Constitution relating to the adoption of the final Constitution and the procedure laid down in the 1993 and 1996 Constitutions for the appointment of Constitutional Court judges. In combination, these two sets of provisions exerted a profound influence on the political context for judicial review,

---

[55] These are discussed in detail below.
[56] Sections 104(2) and (4) of the 1993 Constitution and ss 176 and 177 of the 1996 Constitution.
[57] Section 98 of the 1993 Constitution and ss 167 and 172 of the 1996 Constitution.
[58] Section 165(3) of the 1996 Constitution.

structuring the ANC's interest in the Court's independence and ensuring that the Court, at least in the first two years of its existence, was relatively secure from political attack.

4.3.1   The two-stage constitution-making process

South Africa's constitutional transition from apartheid to democracy famously took place in two stages. First, the 1993 Constitution was enacted into law by the old-order Parliament after 'sufficient consensus' had been reached by the political parties involved in the Multi-Party Negotiating Process ('MPNP').[59] The 1996 Constitution was then deliberated upon and adopted by the first democratic Parliament, sitting as a Constitutional Assembly. The crucial link between these two stages was provided by the specification in the 1993 Constitution that the 1996 Constitution should conform to a list of agreed principles and that the newly created Constitutional Court should have the power to certify whether this condition had been met.[60]

At first blush, the Court's role in certifying the 1996 Constitution might appear to have thrust it into the centre of politics too early, before it had had an opportunity to establish itself. In fact, the impact on the Court's insulation from political attack of its role in the certification of the 1996 Constitution was just the reverse. By giving the ANC an early interest in the Court's independence, the two-stage constitution-making process negated any potential threat from the most powerful political actor in post-apartheid politics and bought the Court precious time in which to prove its usefulness to the new regime.

The ANC's interest in the legitimacy of the two-stage constitution-making process rested on two main grounds. First, and most obviously, the legitimacy of the ANC's democratic mandate after 1996 depended on the legitimacy of the underlying constitutional order. Secondly, to the extent that the 1996 Constitution imposed significant limits on the ANC's political power, the legitimacy of the process through which these limits were imposed needed to be established. For black South Africans, in particular, the fact that the Constitutional Assembly's power to draft the 1996 Constitution had been fettered by the political deal struck during the MPNP represented an ongoing compromise with the

---

[59] For a comprehensive history of the MPNP, see Spitz with Chaskalson, *The Politics of Transition*.
[60] Section 71(2) read with Schedule 4 to the 1993 Constitution.

principle of majority rule. For that compromise to endure, and for the centrist faction in the ANC that had supported it to maintain its hold on the party, the two-stage constitution-making process needed to be seen to be legitimate.

This primary interest in the legitimacy of the two-stage constitution-making process drove the ANC's secondary interest in the independence of the Court. Before the certification of the 1996 Constitution, it was important for the ANC, not just to respect the Court's independence, but actively to promote the idea that the Court was a politically neutral body whose decisions were guided solely by legal considerations. President Mandela's decision to appoint a number of non-ANC-aligned judges to the Court,[61] while indicative of his general emphasis on the need for national reconciliation, is thus more persuasively explained as a function of the ANC's interest in the establishment of a Court whose members would be seen to be impartial and independent. Likewise, Mandela's famously accommodating response to the Court's 1995 decision on local government,[62] while attributable to his personal commitment to the ideal of judicial independence, is also explicable as a consequence of the ANC's strategic need at the time to send a strong signal of support for the Court.

After the adoption of the 1996 Constitution, this rationale for the ANC's support for the Court's independence fell away. There were several reasons, however, why an independent constitutional court remained strategically important to the ANC. First, the centrist faction that had supported the political compromise struck during the MPNP had an ongoing interest in the Court's capacity to demonstrate the wisdom and practical benefits of that compromise. One might mention here the Court's contribution to such issues as national reconciliation and nation-building, state formation, economic growth, and the enhancement of South Africa's standing in the international and regional African community.[63] All of these functions were useful to the centrist faction. They could also only be performed by a Court that was genuinely independent of political control.

---

[61] See Chapter 5.

[62] *Executive Council of the Western Cape Legislature* v. *President of the Republic of South Africa* 1995 (4) SA 877 (CC) ('local government transition case') (discussed in Chapter 1).

[63] See Wilson, *The Politics of Truth and Reconciliation in South Africa*: (describing the role of human rights and constitutionalism in nation-building and state formation in post-apartheid South Africa).

Secondly, notwithstanding the overwhelming electoral support that the ANC had received in the 1994 elections, much of the ANC's legislative reform programme was inherently controversial. Reform of the education sector, for example, inevitably touched on vested interests in the distribution of state resources to particular population groups. Through its power to review the procedural and substantive fairness of policy decisions in this area, the Court performed a vital legitimating function and helped to secure minority cooperation in the implementation of the measures concerned.[64]

Finally, there were several moral and social issues, apart from the already-settled death penalty question, that the ANC found it politically convenient for the Court to decide. The conformance of African customary law to Western liberal standards of gender equality, for example, was an issue that had the potential to cause division in the party and one that was therefore better left for resolution by the Court. The same might be said of the recognition of gay and lesbian rights, which the 1996 Constitution mandated but whose detailed working out the ANC was content to leave to public impact litigation.

Given these additional considerations, it would be wrong to suggest that the ANC's support for the Court's independence simply collapsed after the adoption of the 1996 Constitution. Nevertheless, the political rationale for that support did fundamentally shift once the Court had performed its certification function. Whereas the period before the adoption of the 1996 Constitution had been marked by political uncertainty and the ANC's need to secure the cooperation of smaller parties, the period after 1996 saw the ANC take increasing control of the levers of state power and extend its influence into the furthest reaches of the economy. In these circumstances, as further discussed in Section 4.4, the ANC's interest in the Court's independence became less certain, varying as it did with the particular policy goals being pursued and changes to the party leadership. It therefore makes sense, when analysing the political context for judicial review, to divide the eleven-year period of Chaskalson's chief justiceship into these two sub-periods. Such a division is also supported by the structuring influence exerted by the

---

[64] On the legitimating function of judicial review in the United States after the New Deal, see Black, Jr, *The People and the Court* 52; Keith E. Whittington, *Political Foundations of Judicial Supremacy: The Presidency, the Supreme Court, and Constitutional Leadership in U.S. History* (Princeton University Press, 2007) 152–7.

procedure for the appointment of Constitutional Court judges, to which the discussion now turns.

4.3.2   The judicial appointments process

In liberal constitutional theory, there is no particular requirement that the procedure for the appointment of constitutional court judges should be entirely free from political influence. Indeed, it may be vital to the capacity of a constitutional court to withstand political attack that the governing party be involved in the appointment of its members. Rather, the ideal is that the appointments process should be designed in such a way as to ensure that judges, while inevitably sharing the broad ideo-logical outlook of the appointing party, are possessed of the necessary qualities of impartiality and independence.[65]

The choice of procedure to achieve this goal depends on whether the constitution is drafted in the expectation that it will operate in a well-functioning multi-party democracy. In countries where this *is* the governing expectation, the majority party's inclination to appoint parti-san judges may reasonably be assumed to be counteracted by the fear of 'revenge' appointments. In such countries, therefore, a process in which the majority party has the overriding say in the appointment of judges may be both a rational and workable constitutional-design choice.[66] The situation is different in countries where there is no effective political opposition. In such situations, an executive or parliamentary appoint-ments process allows the majority party to capture the judiciary and turn it into its quiescent agent, restrained only by whatever legitimating function the courts are expected to perform. Where such dominance is anticipated at the constitutional-design stage, therefore, rational negoti-ating parties may try to limit the role of the majority party in the appointments process by requiring some degree of co-operation from

---

[65] See Howard Gillman, *The Votes that Counted: How the Court Decided the 2000 Presiden-tial Election* (University of Chicago Press, 2001) 174–5.

[66] This is well illustrated by the American example. In the United States, the process for appointing Supreme Court justices is open to majority-party capture in as much as candidates are nominated by the President and ratified by the Senate, both of which institutions may from time to time be in the hands of the same party. As the Court became more interventionist during the 1960s, there was a move to appoint justices whose allegiance to the appointing party's political values was thought to be absolutely guaranteed. Ever since the Bork nomination debacle, however, there has been cross-party support for the nomination of political moderates.

smaller parties, to the point of giving them an effective veto power over the appointment of partisan judges.

Against this background, the South African case provides an interesting illustration of the impact on constitutional design of shifting assumptions about the post-transitional balance of power. According to a leading commentary,[67] the National Party's chief negotiator on legal issues at the MPNP, Justice Minister Kobie Coetsee, was initially convinced that the outgoing apartheid Government would have a significant role in the first democratic Cabinet. Operating on this assumption, Coetsee suggested to his ANC counterpart, Dullah Omar, that the executive should have the exclusive power to appoint judges to the Constitutional Court. After some initial disbelief that the National Party was ceding control of this important institution so easily, the ANC entered into a bilateral agreement with the National Party to this effect. When the agreement was made public, however, the Democratic Party, the only truly liberal party involved in the MPNP, strenuously objected to it. Knowing that it had little chance of representation in the new Government, and correctly anticipating that the first democratic Cabinet would be controlled by the ANC, the Democratic Party insisted that the Judicial Service Commission ('JSC') be given a role in the appointment of Constitutional Court judges. The National Party, realising its mistake, switched sides, and a new agreement was eventually brokered.[68]

As encapsulated in ss 97(2)(a) and 99 of the 1993 Constitution, the agreement provided for the judges to be appointed in three tranches. First, the President of the Constitutional Court (as the head of the Court was then known) was to be appointed by the national President 'in consultation with the Cabinet and after consultation with the Chief Justice' (i.e. the head of the judiciary, who was then not the head of the Constitutional Court). Next, four judges were to be appointed from among the sitting judiciary by the national President 'in consultation with the Cabinet and with the Chief Justice'. Finally, the remaining six judges were to be appointed by the national President 'in consultation with the Cabinet and after consultation with the President of the Constitutional Court'. In this case, however, the 1993 Constitution stipulated that the national President's choice should be made from a list of

---

[67] Spitz with Chaskalson, *The Politics of Transition* 204–5.

[68] See further Tony Leon, 'Etienne Mureinik's Role in Securing and Constitutionalising the Independence of the Universities and Judicial Selection' (1998) 14 *South African Journal on Human Rights* 190, 194–6; Ginsburg, *Judicial Review in New Democracies* 56–7.

ten names submitted by the JSC, subject to the proviso that the national President had the power to refuse to appoint one or more of the people on the list, in which case the JSC would be under a duty to supplement it.[69]

In theory, this system provided for a measure of minority-party influence on the judicial appointments process. The vast majority of the sitting judges at the time the Constitutional Court was established had been appointed before the transition to democracy. It was thus likely that the second tranche of four appointments would include at least some judges who had been elevated to the Bench by the National Party.[70] The fact that these four appointments had to be made 'in consultation with' the head of the judiciary was also significant. In effect it meant that this tranche of appointments could not be made without the sitting Chief Justice's concurrence.[71] The third tranche, too, was open to minority-party influence in as much as the 1993 Constitution stipulated that four of the JSC's seventeen members should be appointed by a two-thirds majority of the Senate, thus requiring minority-party co-operation.[72] Finally, all eleven appointments, to the extent that they required the concurrence of the Cabinet, were subject to minority-party influence through the stipulation that there should be a Government of National Unity, which resulted in the appointment of several non-ANC Cabinet ministers. In practice, however, the ANC controlled seven of the eleven appointments: the President of the Court, through its power to appoint the national President and its control of the Cabinet's decision-making processes,[73] and the six judges appointed

---

[69] Section 99(4) read with s 99(5)(a).

[70] There was a small window period between the coming into effect of the 1993 Constitution and the finalisation of the composition of the Constitutional Court during which the ANC was responsible for the appointment of judges to the Supreme Court, making them eligible for appointment to the Constitutional Court under s 99(3) of the 1993 Constitution. Justice Tholie Madala, who was appointed to the Eastern Cape Provincial Division of the Supreme Court after the transition to democracy, was appointed to the Constitutional Court via this route. The other three judges (Ismail Mahomed, Laurie Ackermann and Richard Goldstone) had all been appointed by the National Party – in Mahomed's case, in 1991, after Nelson Mandela's release from prison.

[71] The terms 'in consultation with' and 'after consultation with' were defined in s 233(3) and (4) of the 1993 Constitution as meaning with the 'concurrence' of and 'after consulting and giving serious consideration to views of' the named functionary.

[72] Section 105(1)(h).

[73] Section 233(3) provides that where a decision is required to be taken 'in consultation with' a body consisting of a group of persons, that body shall express its occurrence through its own decision-making procedures'.

from the JSC's list, through its power to control the majority of appointments to that body, and by reason of the fact that the national President would in any case have the final say in these appointments.

At first blush, then, it would seem that the National Party's blunder at the MPNP, despite the Democratic Party's attempts to save the situation, must have undermined the Chaskalson Court's capacity to resist political attack: by miscalculating the *post-transitional* balance of power, the National Party agreed to an appointments process that was subject to greater ANC control than was necessary given the balance of political power *at the time the 1993 Constitution was negotiated*. This conclusion follows too quickly, however. The problem with an executive-controlled judicial appointments process in a dominant-party democracy is that it facilitates the appointment of partisan judges. Whether the dominant political party in fact makes use of its control of the appointments process in this way, however, is contingent on the party's strategic calculations about the benefits to it of an independent judiciary and the extent of the party leadership's non-instrumental commitment to the ideal of judicial independence.

When these considerations are taken into account, the National Party's blunder is better seen as having been quite propitious. By giving the ANC control of the judicial appointments process at a time when its interest in the Court's independence was at its highest, the 1993 Constitution ensured that the Court was composed of judges who were broadly sympathetic to the ANC's policies but who were not so closely aligned to it as to be tarred with the brush of partisanship.[74] At the same time, the fact that the ANC had had effective control of the judicial appointments process made it difficult for factions within the ANC opposed to liberal constitutionalism to depict the Court as a reactionary institution bent on the preservation of minority-group privilege.[75] Far from undermining the Court's insulation from political attack, therefore, the

---

[74] In *President of the Republic of South Africa* v. *South African Rugby Federation* 1999 (4) SA 147; 1999 (7) BCLR 725, several members of the Court were asked to recuse themselves on the basis of their close relationship with the ANC and President Mandela. The Court was able convincingly to rebut this allegation. The charge of partisanship was subsequently repeated (somewhat scurrilously) in Johnson, *South Africa's Brave New World* 152–60.

[75] To see the force of this point, one need only imagine what the situation would have been had the National Party succeeded in winning a minority party veto over the appointments process. Had that been the case, the Chaskalson Court would almost certainly have been differently composed, with a greater proportion of old-order judges.

procedure for the appointment of the original members of the Court, more by accident than design, enhanced it.

The same cannot be said, however, for the procedure specified in the 1996 Constitution. Although no more obviously subject to ANC control than the original procedure, the 1996 Constitution's procedure was applied in a very different political setting, one in which the ANC's strategic interest in the Court's independence was less certain.[76] On this occasion, therefore, the openness of the procedure to majority-party control did pose a threat to the Court's institutional independence.

As amended in 2001, s 174(3) of the 1996 Constitution provides that both the Chief Justice and the Deputy Chief Justice of the Constitutional Court must be appointed by the national President after consulting with the JSC and the leaders of the parties represented in the National Assembly. The remaining nine judges are appointed by the President after consulting with the Chief Justice and the leaders of the parties represented in the National Assembly. As was the case in the 1993 Constitution, these further appointments must be made from a list of names produced by the JSC, subject to the requirement that the list should contain at least three more names than the number of vacancies.[77] The majority party's capacity to control the appointment of Constitutional Court judges therefore depends on its capacity to control the JSC.

The relevant provision here is s 178, which provides for an expanded, 23-member body, of whom up to seven may be representatives of the majority party in Parliament (three from the lower and four from the upper house) and four direct Presidential appointees.[78] The other member aligned to the majority party is the Cabinet member responsible for the administration of justice.[79] In addition to these members, the section provides that the national President must appoint two members from the attorneys' profession and two from the advocates' profession, as nominated by their respective professional bodies. As Richard Calland has pointed out,[80] at least one of these members, too, is likely to be sympathetic to the majority party, giving it effective control of the JSC.

---

[76] See Section 4.4.2. [77] Section 174(4)(a).
[78] See s 178(1)(h), (i) and (j). [79] Section 178(1)(d).
[80] Richard Calland, *Anatomy of South Africa: Who Holds the Power?* (Cape Town: Zebra Press, 2006) 218.

Together with the President's power to disapprove some or all of the names on the JSC's list, the ANC's control of the JSC gave it the power to control the composition of the Constitutional Court. The ANC was only able to exercise this power once vacancies started to arise, of course. But the possibility that it might seek to attack the Court through the appointment of partisan judges was a constant threat to the Court, from the adoption of the 1996 Constitution until Justice Chaskalson's retirement and beyond.

As had been the case under the 1993 Constitution, this threat was tempered by the ANC's strategic interest in the Court's independence. As we shall see in the next section, however, this variable changed over the course of Justice Chaskalson's term in a way that made it more likely that the ANC would seek to appoint partisan judges. By facilitating this possibility, the 1996 Constitution's procedure for the appointment of Constitutional Court judges fed into the deteriorating political environment for judicial review, and contributed to the overall decline in the Court's insulation from political attack.

4.4   The changing political context for judicial review

The post-apartheid Constitutions, the previous section has argued, structured the ANC's interest in the Court's independence, such that the political context for judicial review during Chaskalson's term as Chief Justice is best divided into two sub-periods: the two years from 1995 to 1996, when the Court's role in certifying the 1996 Constitution guaranteed it a measure of independence, and the period after 1996, when a range of other considerations came into play. This periodisation is further justified, this section will argue, by changes to the presidency and the ANC's policy priorities. Before the adoption of the final Constitution in December 1996, South African politics was marked by President Mandela's emphasis on national reconciliation and the ANC's attempts to establish itself in government. After 1996, the focus shifted to the centralisation of governmental power under Thabo Mbeki, first as Deputy President and then, after 1999, as Mandela's successor. While an independent constitutional court remained strategically important to the ANC during this time, the continued lack of an effective political opposition, Mbeki's strident and constitutionally incompatible views on HIV/AIDS, and the ANC's failure to deliver on its economic growth and job creation promises led to a gradual deterioration in the political environment for judicial review.

4.4.1   Racial reconciliation, 1994–1996

When the ANC entered office in May 1994, it was at once a very old political movement and a very new political party. Indeed, the ANC had had little more than five years to prepare for power, from the late-1980s, when it first became clear that the National Party was serious about ending white minority rule. During this brief period, the ANC's formal policy commitments had undergone a dramatic transformation from the Freedom Charter's vague rhetoric about the nationalisation of the monopoly industries to something more akin to social-democratic market managerialism.[81] Although a tremendous amount of hard thinking had been done, the policy frameworks that the ANC developed from 1989 to 1994 were necessarily constructed with no real understanding of the actual mechanisms of government. In addition, on entering office, the ANC was confronted with a divided civil service: in the former South Africa, largely white and, if not openly hostile to the ANC, then at least decidedly suspicious of its new political master; and, in the former Bantustans, more representative of South Africa's population but badly compromised by the absurdities of administering that artificially maintained system. Transforming the culture of these two components of the civil service would have been a daunting task even for a party with considerable experience of government. For the ANC, it was to absorb much of its initial energy.

Despite its overwhelming election victory, then, the ANC in 1994 was far from being in control of all the levers of state power. Complicating matters further was the fact that the political agreement struck during the MPNP had included a stipulation that the first democratic Government should be a Government of National Unity. In terms of this arrangement, any party that won more than 80 seats in the National Assembly was entitled to appoint a Deputy President,[82] and any party that won more than 20 seats was entitled to appoint as many members of the 27-member Cabinet as were equivalent to its share of the total number of seats.[83] Whether this arrangement really gave the two participating parties, the National Party and the Inkatha Freedom Party ('IFP'), a significant say in policy-making was debatable.[84] From the ANC's

---

[81] Whether this is a correct description of the ANC's post-1989 political programme is disputed. See Raymond Suttner, 'Provocative Introduction to ANC', H-Net Reviews, January, 2003 www.h-net.org/reviews/showrev.php?id=7123.

[82] Section 84(1) of the 1993 Constitution.   [83] Ibid. s 88(2).

[84] In June 1996, the National Party withdrew from the GNU, citing its lack of influence as the main reason.

perspective, however, the presence of opposition-party politicians in the Cabinet likely restrained its capacity for decisive political action.

Some measure of cooperation between the ANC and other political parties was in any case dictated by the ANC's failure to win two thirds of the votes in the 1994 elections.[85] According to the complicated scheme set out in Chapter 5 of the 1993 Constitution,[86] this result meant that the ANC required the support of either the National Party or the IFP to pass the final Constitution, alternatively the support of two or more of the smaller minority parties. After the IFP withdrew from the Constitutional Assembly in 1995, the drafting of the final Constitution took on the character of a negotiated pact between the ANC and the National Party.[87] When considered together with its failure to win control of two provinces, the ANC's inability to dictate the content of the final Constitution meant that South African politics from 1994 to 1996 was characterised by much the same spirit of political compromise that had marked the transition to democracy.

Feeding into this political climate was President Nelson Mandela's particular leadership style. From the outset, Mandela maintained a very small office and left detailed policy issues to his deputy, Thabo Mbeki, to determine.[88] Instead, Mandela focused on promoting national reconciliation, as famously demonstrated by his support for the Springbok rugby team during the 1995 World Cup. Mandela's concern for assuring Coloured, Indian and white South Africans that they still had a place in South Africa was not purely altruistic, of course; such an approach also made sense in the context of the ANC's inability to take immediate control of the civil service and the economy's dependence on minority-group skills. Mandela's obviously sincere commitment to the creation of a unified, non-racial South Africa nevertheless encouraged many to believe that this ideal was indeed achievable – that South Africans could transcend their differences and that a flourishing multi-party democracy would eventually develop.

---

[85] The ANC won 62.65 per cent of the vote, giving it 312 of the 490 seats in the Constitutional Assembly. See Katharine Savage, 'Negotiating South Africa's New Constitution: An Overview of the Key Players and the Negotiation Process', in Penelope Andrews and Stephen Ellmann (eds.), *The Post-Apartheid Constitutions: Perspectives on South Africa's Basic Law* (Johannesburg: Witwatersrand University Press, 2001) 164, 164 n 2.

[86] See s 73, according to which it would have been possible for the final Constitution to have been passed at a national referendum with 60 per cent support.

[87] See Savage, 'Negotiating South Africa's New Constitution' 164.

[88] See Calland, *Anatomy of South Africa* 43; Gevisser, *The Dream Deferred* 659.

At the same time, Mandela had a deep personal attachment to the value of judicial independence. In addition to his work as an attorney, Mandela had been on the receiving end of the apartheid legal system as a criminal accused in both the 1958–1961 Treason Trial and the 1963–1964 Rivonia Trial. Mandela was evidently impressed by the conduct of the judges in the former case, commenting in his autobiography that they were 'exemplars of human decency under adversity'.[89] The Rivonia Trial was more tightly controlled,[90] but it was here that Mandela got to know Chaskalson, one of the advocates for the defence. The mutual respect that developed between the two men was an important element in the mix of factors that conditioned the ANC's early relationship with the Court. For as long as Mandela was President, there was a sense that the sincerity of the judges' commitment to decision-making according to law would be taken on trust.

In its 1994 election manifesto, the Reconstruction and Development Programme ('RDP'), the ANC had committed itself to an ambitious strategy of rights-based development.[91] Among the ANC's major policy goals were the provision of affordable housing 'to even the poorest South Africans',[92] the redistribution of 30 per cent of agricultural land within five years,[93] and the extension of health care services and education to all on an equal basis.[94] The first two and a half years of democracy saw a sustained effort to lay the legislative basis for this programme, with over 200 statutes passed between April 1994 and December 1996.[95] .

The influence of this massive law-making effort on the political context for judicial review needs to be carefully assessed. On the one hand, the ANC's rights-based development programme was closely aligned to the social and economic philosophy underlying the 1993 Constitution. To this extent, the constitutional limits that the ANC had been required to accept during the MPNP looked less like a straightjacket and more like

---

[89] Nelson Mandela, *Long Walk to Freedom: The Autobiography of Nelson Mandela* (London: Abacus, 1995) 309 (as quoted in Meierhenrich, *The Legacies of Law* 137).

[90] See Stephen Clingman, *Bram Fischer: Afrikaner Revolutionary* (Cape Town: David Philip, 1998) 299–322.

[91] See the African National Congress, *The Reconstruction and Development Programme: A Policy Framework* (Johannesburg: Umanyano Publications, 1994).

[92] Ibid. 2.5.5.   [93] Ibid. 2.4.14.   [94] Ibid. 2.12 and 3.3.

[95] Some of the more important statutes included: the Restitution of Land Rights Act 22 of 1994, the Labour Relations Act 66 of 1995, the Development Facilitation Act 67 of 1995, the South African Police Service Act 68 of 1995, and the Promotion of National Unity and Reconciliation Act 34 of 1995.

a blueprint for reform.[96] This in turn meant that the chances of a major political contest developing between the ANC and the Court were much reduced. Given the correspondence between the ANC's early policy commitments and the 1993 Constitution's vision for social and economic transformation, there was every prospect that the Court would be able to position itself as a partner in the ANC's social transformation project.

On the other hand, many of the new statutes threatened vested rights. The converse possibility, that the Court might be drawn into the politically awkward role of protecting minority-group privileges, was therefore very real. In this context, as argued earlier,[97] it was fortunate that the ANC had had effective control of the judicial appointments process. This fact undoubtedly helped the Court to monitor the constitutionality of the ANC's legislative reform programme without itself becoming drawn into the political conflict over the redistribution of resources. In any case, delays in the implementation of the programme meant that relatively few cases challenging the constitutionality of post-apartheid legislation came to the Court from 1995 to 1996.[98] Instead, the Court's docket during the first two years of its life was mostly filled with cases involving old-order criminal procedure legislation.[99] As South Africa's crime wave grew, this aspect of the Court's work became more important. But in the first two years of democracy the focus on criminal procedure cases meant that the Court was able to assert its review power in relation to statutory provisions that the ANC had little interest in defending.

The leading example of such a case, of course, was *S v. Makwanyane*.[100] As more fully explained in Chapter 6, the Court's decision in this case was made considerably easier by the fact that the ANC political leadership was not committed to the maintenance of the death penalty. That South Africans overwhelmingly supported the contrary view had no

---

[96] This was particularly true of the provisions on land restitution, where a detailed framework was spelled out. See ss 121–123 of the 1993 Constitution.

[97] See above.

[98] Apart from the local government transition case, the first challenge to an ANC statute occurred in *Transvaal Agricultural Union* v. *Minister of Land Affairs and Another* 1997 (2) SA 621 (CC), 1996 (12) BCLR 1573 (CC) (decided on 18 November 1996).

[99] Seven of the Court's first 10 cases were of this type, and 15 out of the 32 cases it decided before its *First Certification Judgment* (*Ex parte Chairperson of the Constitutional Assembly: In Re Certification of the Constitution of the Republic of South Africa, 1996* 1996 (4) SA 744 (CC)). A list of the Court's judgments is available at www.constitutionalcourt.org.za/site/judgments/judgments.htm.

[100] 1995 (3) SA 391 (CC) 1995 (6) BCLR 665 (CC).

immediate impact on the Court in a context in which the ANC cushioned it from the effects of adverse public opinion.[101]

Just how long the Court could survive without extensive public support was a different question. On the analysis offered here, the Court's failure to build its institutional legitimacy, as recorded in the two social surveys discussed in Chapter 1,[102] posed no immediate threat to it in a situation where (a) the ANC was politically dominant; and (b) the party was controlled by a centrist faction that saw certain strategic benefits in respecting the Court's independence. By the same token, however, the stability of this arrangement depended on the durability of these two conditions: on the ANC's capacity to continue winning elections and on the capacity of the centrist faction to maintain control of the party.

The possibility that the first condition would cease to hold was extremely remote. After the 1994 elections, it was clear that the ANC would be in power for some time to come and that opposition politics would be dominated by competition for the Coloured, Indian and white vote. Quite apart from the fact that they had little chance of ever winning an election, the main representatives of these groups, the National Party and the Democratic Party, had no interest in exploiting public disaffection with the Court for political gain. Whatever their constituents' views of the legitimacy of the Court's death penalty decision, they were far outweighed by the Court's potential role as a bulwark against the abuse of majoritarian power. The smaller African parties, the IFP and the Pan Africanist Congress, might in theory have been able to get some political mileage out of the Court's lack of public support, but were confronted after 1994 by the ANC's ability to use its position as the incumbent party of government to monopolise the African vote.[103]

The second set of factors conditioning the Court's capacity to survive without extensive public support was less stable. As we have seen, the ANC's commitment to a negotiated settlement was contentious within the organisation. Although the organisation's centrist faction ultimately persuaded it to make the political concessions necessary to expedite the transition, this faction's continued leadership of the ANC was not assured. Rather, its long-term control of the party depended on whether

---

[101] On the more powerful role of public opinion in the United States, see Friedman, *The Will of the People*.

[102] See Gibson and Caldeira, 'Defenders of Democracy?'; Gibson, 'The Evolving Legitimacy of the South African Constitutional Court' 229.

[103] See Thompson, *A History of South Africa* 268.

the constitutional settlement was seen by the ANC's mass support base to have produced the promised 'better life for all'. To the extent that it failed to do that – to the extent that the constitutional settlement was seen instead to have taken the form of an 'elite transition'[104] – the centrist faction was vulnerable to challenge, and with it the constitutional project with which the centrist faction was inevitably associated.

In the first two years of the Court's institutional life, this threat was still on the distant horizon. Buoyed by the appointment of Thabo Mbeki over Cyril Ramaphosa as Mandela's heir apparent,[105] the centrist faction set about reining in the RDP and preparing the way for the more fiscally conservative Growth, Employment and Redistribution strategy ('GEAR'), which replaced the RDP as official ANC policy in June 1996.[106] GEAR's provenance and democratic legitimacy have been much debated.[107] For the moment,[108] it is enough to note that the adoption of this strategy confirmed the centrist faction's almost complete control of the ANC by the end of 1996. Even as the final Constitution, with its impressive list of social rights, was being drafted, the ANC's formal policy commitments were moving decidedly rightwards. In time, the divergence between the final Constitution's commitment to some degree of statism and the neo-liberalism of GEAR was to prove politically awkward for the Court.[109] Under the 1993 Constitution, however, there was no such tension. Instead, as we have seen, the Court was fed a steady diet of mostly criminal procedure cases.[110] Far from threatening the Court's independence, these cases allowed the Court to demonstrate its usefulness to the centrist faction as the prime embodiment of the ANC's commitment to orderly, law-driven social transformation.

In summary, the political environment in South Africa from 1995 to 1996 was relatively favourable to judicial review: the ANC's inexperience

---

[104] See Patrick Bond, *Elite Transition: From Apartheid to Neo-Liberalism in South Africa* (London: Pluto, 2000).

[105] See Gevisser, *The Dream Deferred* 638; Anthony Butler, *Cyril Ramaphosa* (Johannesburg: Jacana, 2007) 314.

[106] GEAR was adopted by Cabinet in May and announced to the media on 14 June 1996.

[107] See, for example, Bond, *Elite Transition*; Alan Hirsch, *Season of Hope: Economic Reform under Mandela and Mbeki* (Scottsville: University of KwaZulu-Natal Press, 2005).

[108] The origins and provenance of GEAR are discussed in more detail in Section 8.1.2.

[109] See the more extended discussion in Section 4.4.2.

[110] See, for example, *S v. Mbatha; S v. Prinsloo* 1996 (2) SA 464 (CC) (challenge to s 40(1) of the Arms and Ammunition Act 75 of 1969); *Brink v. Kitshoff NO* 1996 (4) SA 197 (CC) (challenge to s 44 of the Insurance Act 27 of 1943); *S v. Julies* 1996 (4) SA 313 (CC) (challenge to s 21(1)(*a*)(iii) of the Drugs and Drug Trafficking Act 140 of 1992).

in government and its dependence on the support of minority political parties meant that, despite its overwhelming election victory, the situation in the country was closer to one of political fragmentation than one-party dominance; Mandela's leadership style and his personal commitment to the ideal of judicial independence reinforced this general political climate; and the ascendancy of a centrist, rule-of-law-friendly faction within the ANC helped the Court to position itself as the facilitator of the ANC social transformation project. By the same token, the terms of the Court's continued institutional independence were set. For as long as the centrist faction retained control of the ANC, and for as long as GEAR's promises of economic growth and job creation were believed, the Court could afford to ignore its lack of popular support. Any significant change to these conditions, however, threatened to expose it to political attack. Indeed, to a certain extent, the fates of the centrist faction and the Court were linked, with each dependent on the other's survival.

4.4.2 Technocratic centralism, 1997–2005

After the adoption of the final Constitution in December 1996, Mandela still had a further two and a half years to serve as President.[111] It is generally agreed, however, that Mbeki was the *de facto* head of Government from this time.[112] The long Mbeki presidency therefore dates from January 1997 or, at the latest, from the end of that year, when Mbeki was elected as President of the ANC.[113]

On the surface, the combination of factors that had guaranteed the Court a measure of insulation from political attack in the first two years of its life remained unchanged under Mbeki: the ANC was returned to power with even greater majorities in the 1999 and 2004 elections[114] and, if anything, the ANC's centrist faction appeared to tighten its grip on the party. Underneath the surface, however, the transition from Mandela to Mbeki was associated with three developments that eventually destabilised the political context for judicial review. First, the virtually

---

[111] Mandela's term as President ended in June 1999.

[112] From the outset, Mbeki chaired meetings of Cabinet and built a formidable team of advisers around him. See Gevisser, *The Dream Deferred* 659; Calland, *Anatomy of South Africa* 43.

[113] See Adrian Hadland and Jovial Rantao, *The Life and Times of Thabo Mbeki* (Johannesburg: Zebra Press, 1999).

[114] The ANC's share of the vote in 1999 was 66 per cent, and 70 per cent in 2004.

simultaneous adoption of the fiscally conservative GEAR framework and the 1996 Constitution, with its comprehensive list of social rights, presented the Court with a contradiction between ANC economic policy and constitutional norms that it had not had to face under the 1993 Constitution. Secondly, the ANC's policy of 'cadre deployment', which had started under Mandela but which was much more aggressively pursued under Mbeki, meant that the Court became increasingly isolated as the only real counterweight to the ANC's political hegemony. Finally, a series of what can only be described as moral failures, including the so-called Arms Deal, the ANC's passivity in the face of the human rights abuses occurring in Zimbabwe, and Mbeki's own personal failings in response to the HIV/AIDS crisis, cast serious doubts on the ANC's trustworthiness as a partner in the constitutional project.

The impact of each of these developments is worth examining in its own right. As to the GEAR framework, we have already seen how the centrist faction's cautious, law-driven approach to social transformation in theory favoured the maintenance of the constitutional project. That positive relationship, however, only applied for as long as GEAR in fact delivered on its promises of economic growth and job creation. To the extent that it did not, or was otherwise seen as a hindrance to thorough-going social reform, the identification of the constitutional project with GEAR threatened to take the Constitutional Court down with it.[115]

All of this was doubly awkward for the Court since the 1996 Constitution's conception of law-driven social transformation is in fact quite progressive. Far from mandating the absolute protection of property rights,[116] the 1996 Constitution seeks a nuanced balance between the

---

[115] As just one example of this, the ANC's willing buyer/willing seller approach to land reform was frequently attributed by the left to the restraints imposed on the government by the property clause (s 25 of the 1996 Constitution). This gave rise to persistent calls in the land reform lobby to amend or even abolish the property clause. In fact, as pointed out in Chapter 8, the property clause in the 1996 Constitution does not prevent the expropriation of property for purposes of land reform, or even mandate the payment of market value compensation. Rather, the willing buyer/willing seller approach to land reform was driven by the centrist faction's GEAR-related desire to retain foreign investor confidence.

[116] Cf. Ran Hirschl, *Towards Juristocracy* 89–97, arguing that the transition to democracy in South Africa was driven by political, economic and judicial elites intent on 'preserving' their 'hegemony'. The content of the rights guarantees in the 1996 Constitution simply does not bear this thesis out. The ANC's drift into neo-liberalism occurred independently of the constitution-making process, and was in fact in tension with the economic philosophy underlying the 1996 Constitution.

level of negative protection required for economic growth and the level of positive provision required for meaningful citizenship. By tying the Government to an inflexible policy of fiscal restraint, the GEAR framework arguably conflicted with this constitutional balance. On a purely practical level, too, adherence to GEAR's strictures arguably starved the ANC's RDP-inspired social reform statutes of the funding they required to make a meaningful impact on poverty.

Just why ANC economic policy under Mbeki came to move so dramatically rightwards is a question that lies outside the scope of this study.[117] For our purposes, the significance of the disjuncture between GEAR and the 1996 Constitution is that it placed the Constitutional Court in a difficult situation. On the one hand, its continued insulation from political attack depended on its capacity to manage its relationship with the ANC's centrist faction, which had driven the constitution-making process and supported the Court in the first two years of its life. On the other, the centrist faction's persistent pursuit of policies that made it vulnerable to left-wing critique threatened the constitutional project, and by extension the Court itself. To survive in this awkward environment, the Court needed somehow to enforce the more progressive economic philosophy underlying the 1996 Constitution whilst at the same time maintaining its working relationship with its most important constitutional partner.

Part III of this study contains a detailed analysis of how the Court went about this delicate task. Of relevance here is an understanding of the constraints imposed on the Court by this particular feature of South African politics. To what extent was the Court's institutional fate really in its own hands? Or, putting the same question in its opposite form, to what extent did the Court's future fall to be determined by political factors beyond its control?

Given the preceding analysis, the answer must be that the Court's room for manoeuvre was fairly limited. One option open to it was to attempt to force a change in the Mbeki Government's macro-economic

---

[117] On one view, GEAR was attributable to Mbeki's personal determination to prove that a black-led government could manage the South African economy and to his background as a member of the aspirant black middle class whose economic aspirations had been thwarted by the restrictions imposed on black business by the apartheid state. See Gevisser, *The Dream Deferred*. On another view, the adoption of GEAR was compelled by the parlous state in which the apartheid government, after decades of international isolation and conflict, had left the South African economy, coupled with the realities of economic globalisation after the end of the Cold War. See Hirsch, *A Season of Hope*.

strategy by alerting it to the disjuncture between GEAR and the 1996
Constitution's vision for social and economic transformation. In effect,
this would have required the Court to extend the reach of socio-
economic rights to the macro-economic sphere. As we shall see in
Chapter 7, there were certain doctrinal avenues through which the Court
might have done this, and thus any such intervention could have been
presented, not as a political strategy to rein in the centrist faction's
sidelining of the ANC's left flank, but as a strictly legal interpretation
mandated by the 1996 Constitution. In reality, however, contesting the
ANC's macro-economic framework in this way would have been institutionally risky for the Court; while perhaps advantageous to the Court in
the long run, exercising this option would almost certainly have precipitated a damaging conflict with the centrist faction in the short term.

An alternative option open to the Court was therefore to resist all
invitations to review the constitutionality of GEAR and instead to continue to position itself as the facilitator of the ANC's social transformation project. This option, however, had its own limitations. Quite apart
from the fact that GEAR's fiscal constraints would be left in place, the
achievement of the ANC's social transformation project was constrained
by the inefficiency of the civil service. Indeed, on one view, it was never
really GEAR that restricted the implementation of the original RDP
programmes, but the ANC Government's inability effectively to utilise
even the resources that it did have.[118] If so, there was really very little that
the Court could have done about this. To a certain extent, it was open to
it to attempt, through due process review and the issuing of robust
remedies, to contribute to improving the delivery of social services. The
Court was also in a position to encourage certain types of public impact
litigation to assist it in this respect.[119] But there are limits on the extent to
which even skilled public impact lawyers can litigate a dysfunctional civil
service into efficiency. Even if the Court had been asked to play this role
(for example, by way of structural interdicts), it could hardly have taken
on the burden of managing the entire civil service. In the final analysis,
therefore, the negative impact on the Court's insulation from political
attack of the ANC's rightwards drift under GEAR must be understood to
have been largely outside the Court's power to control.

The second development that destabilised the political environment
for judicial review after 1996 had to do with the ANC's policy of

---

[118] See Section 4.5.   [119] See the discussion of structural interdicts in Chapter 10.

'deployment'.[120] As we have seen, when the ANC took office in 1994 the civil service was deeply divided and in many ways unsuited to its purposes. While Mandela focused on national reconciliation, Mbeki set about turning the civil service into a more reliable vehicle for the ANC's social transformation project.[121] Despite charges of undue centralisation of power, many of the initiatives undertaken during this time were arguably necessitated by the lack of capacity in the President's office.[122] The deployment policy, however, stood apart from these initiatives. In stark contrast to the 'bureaucracy speak' in which the reforms to the presidency were couched,[123] the language of deployment was unapologetically Leninist. As formally adopted by the National Executive Committee of the ANC in December 1997,[124] the policy called for the placement of so-called 'cadres' in key positions in national, provincial and local government. Not just that, but the ANC also sought to bring all public sector bodies, including the supposedly independent Chapter 9 institutions, under its control. In its fully developed form, the policy even saw the ANC exerting its influence over civil society, including the South African National Civic Organisation, the wider NGO sector (through the attempted control of foreign funding) and key private sector companies.[125]

Once again, a full analysis of the origins and political effects of this development lies outside the scope of this study. For our purposes, the key question is the impact that the ANC's cadre deployment policy had on prospects for liberal constitutionalism and independent judicial review. In particular, to what extent were the potentially positive effects of the ANC's support for the Court's independence undermined by its seeming insensitivity to the need to maintain the distinction between party and state?

---

[120] As adopted at the ANC's Mafikeng policy conference in 1997.

[121] In 1997, for example, Mbeki drove the establishment of a Presidential Review Commission to investigate capacity requirements in the presidency. The Commission's report recommended the establishment of a number of different bodies aimed at better coordinating the delivery of the ANC's social reform programmes.

[122] See Calland, *Anatomy of South Africa* 22; Hein Marais, *South Africa Pushed to the Limit: The Political Economy of Change* (Claremont: University of Cape Town Press, 2011) 409.

[123] See Maphai Commission Report, quoted in Calland, *Anatomy of South Africa* 23-6.

[124] See Choudhry, "'He Had a Mandate'" 13-15.

[125] See Brian Pottinger, *The Mbeki Legacy* (Cape Town: Zebra Press, 2008) 37-41; Gumede, *Thabo Mbeki and the Battle for the Soul of the ANC*.

The conventional wisdom in comparative judicial politics has it that the emergence of independent judicial review is dependent on a well-functioning multi-party democracy.[126] As different political parties compete for power, so their interest in the establishment of a politically neutral body tasked with the maintenance of the state system and the conditions for free political competition grows. It is in the enforcement of this distinction between the higher law of the state and the competing goals of political parties that a constitutional court finds both its *raison d'être* and its institutional legitimacy.

The Chaskalson Court, as we have seen, could not rely on the fulfilment of this precondition, but it did enjoy the benefit of what seemed for some time like an adequate substitute: a strong, apparently stable governing party led by a centrist faction favourably disposed towards the institution of judicial review. Indeed, on one view, the Constitutional Court was actually better off under this arrangement. Given the formidable challenges facing the South Africa, a fully competitive multi-party political system might have undermined the policy continuity the country required for meaningful social transformation, which was the precondition for, rather than the end result of, a flourishing liberal democracy.[127]

The potentially positive relationship between the ANC's political dominance and the Court's institutional independence, however, was crucially dependent on the maintenance of the party/state distinction. To the extent that state institutions came instead to be seen as devices through which the ANC could assert its political hegemony, the Court's task became immeasurably more difficult. As one of the last remaining independent state institutions,[128] the Court was required to maintain the conditions for multi-party political competition even as it was denied the protective benefits that such a system is capable of producing.

Adding to the difficulty of the Court's situation was the fact that, as Mbeki's term as President progressed, the ANC's policy of cadre deployment came increasingly to be seen as a device used by the centrist faction

---

[126] Ramseyer, 'The Puzzling (I)ndependence of Courts'; Stephenson 'When the Devil Turns'; Vanberg, 'Establishing and Maintaining Judicial Independence' 99, 109.

[127] See Adam et al., *Comrades in Business* 90; Heribert Adam, 'Corporatism as Minority Veto under ANC Hegemony in South Africa' in Hermann Giliomee and Charles Simkins (eds.), *The Awkward Embrace: One-Party Domination and Democracy* (Cape Town: Tafelberg, 1999) 261, 278; Giliomee, 'South Africa's Emergent Dominant-Party Regime' 131 (raising this possibility, but dismissing it as unlikely).

[128] The other being (arguably) the Reserve Bank.

to maintain its hold on the party. Although this charge was only expressly made after Chaskalson's retirement as Chief Justice,[129] the notion that state institutions were being abused for factional purposes was current from December 1997, when the ANC's National Executive Committee took control of the appointment of provincial premiers.[130] The threat posed by this development, of course, was that popular disaffection with the centrist faction's abuse of state institutions would, in a process analogous to the political dynamic unleashed by GEAR, come to be deflected onto the constitutional project.

The particular way in which the Chaskalson Court sought to deal with this difficulty is discussed in Part III. It is once again useful, however, to frame the analysis by examining the alternatives open to the Court. In essence, the preceding paragraphs have argued, the political environment for judicial review during Mbeki's presidency deteriorated as the state/government distinction blurred and as the centrist faction's hold over the ANC became increasingly tenuous. Clearly, then, the option that had been open to the Court during the early years of Chaskalson's tenure – of cleaving to the centrist faction and allowing it to mediate the Court's relationship with the ANC's mass support base – was no longer available to it. Instead, the Court needed to demonstrate its ongoing relevance to the changing political context by turning itself into a forum in which the ANC's various factions could compete with each other, either over particular policy issues or for control of the organisation. In the absence of genuine multi-party political competition, the Court's continued reputation for impartiality depended on its capacity to distance itself from any particular faction in the ANC, and instead to function as the guardian of the ANC's internal democratic processes. If it succeeded in this endeavour, the Court would stand a chance of fostering the pluralist democracy on which its long-term institutional independence ultimately depended.

As we shall see in Part III, there is some evidence that the Chaskalson Court was able to change tack in the way, with its judgment in *Treatment Action Campaign*[131] providing the leading example of a case in which it functioned as a forum for intra-ANC policy contestation. The switch in the Court's institutional role from that of facilitator of the ANC's social

---

[129] In the period of intense political infighting following Jacob Zuma's sacking as Deputy President in June 2005.

[130] At the party's Mafikeng policy conference.

[131] *Minister of Health* v. *Treatment Action Campaign (No 2)* 2002 (5) SA 721 (CC) (discussed in Chapter 8).

transformation project to guardian of the ANC's internal democratic processes was always going to be difficult, however. For one, the 1996 Constitution was not designed for this purpose. The use of the Court in this way also depended on the amenability of internal ANC policy disputes to resolution through judicial review, as well as the ability of social movements like the TAC to exploit the ANC's factional politics in a way that precluded the need for the Court to take sides. Prospects for countering the ANC's political hegemony through the development of a more robust constitutional conception of democracy were better,[132] but were once again confronted by the 1996 Constitution's underlying assumption about the existence of multi-party competition.[133] As was the case with the ANC's macro-economic strategy, therefore, the conclusion must be that its cadre deployment policy unleashed a political dynamic that was largely beyond the Court's power to control.

The third development impacting on the political context for judicial review after 1996 was the ANC's loss of its moral compass. Three separate issues are worth briefly reflecting on here: the Arms Deal; Mbeki's interference with the ANC's otherwise quite admirable policies on HIV/AIDS; and the ANC's failure to take decisive action in relation to the human rights abuses occurring in Zimbabwe. Of these three, only the second surfaced in the form of a constitutional case during Chaskalson's term as Chief Justice.[134] Nevertheless, all three issues, in their own way, played into the deteriorating political environment.

The impact of the Arms Deal, whose byzantine complexities would take too long to rehearse here,[135] was essentially twofold: first, reaching as far into the interstices of the ANC's leadership structures as it did, the

---

[132] See Theunis Roux, 'Democracy' in Stuart Woolman, Theunis Roux and Michael Bishop (eds.), *Constitutional Law of South Africa* 2nd edn (Cape Town: Juta, 2006) ch 10; Choudhry, "'He Had a Mandate'" 34–80 (proposing a series of constitutional doctrines that might plausibly have been developed by the Court to counteract the effects of the ANC's political dominance).

[133] See Chapter 9.

[134] In *Treatment Action Campaign*. During Chaskalson's term, an unsuccessful challenge to the Arms Deal was launched by activist Terry Crawford-Browne in the Cape High Court. In 2011, an application to the Constitutional Court for an order that the President launch a judicial commission of inquiry into the Arms Deal triggered the establishment of such a commission. The closest the events in Zimbabwe came to being considered in the Court was in *Kaunda v. President of the Republic of South* Africa 2005 (4) SA 235 (CC) (application for order compelling the South African government to intervene on behalf of alleged mercenaries arrested in Zimbabwe en route to Equatorial Guinea).

[135] For a detailed account, see Andrew Feinstein, *After the Party: A Personal and Political Journey inside the ANC* (Johannesburg: Jonathan Ball, 2007); Paul Holden, *The Arms*

Arms Deal set an early and unfortunate precedent for the party's capacity to deal with corruption; secondly, the political fall-out from the Arms Deal inevitably became intertwined with the factional struggles consequent on the adoption of GEAR, making the resolution of those struggles increasingly impossible.

As to the first point, the success of the constitutional project, as we have seen, was crucially dependent on the capacity of the civil service to deliver on the ANC's legislative reform programme. By tainting senior ANC members with the charge of corruption, the Arms Deal undermined the civil service's commitment to impartiality and professionalism. The progressive intertwining of the Arms Deal with the ANC's factional struggles exacerbated this situation by contributing to the general trend in terms of which state institutions became sites of patronage rather than public service. And, of course, in the spectacular dismissal of Jacob Zuma over allegations of corruption related to the Arms Deal,[136] the allegations of abuse of state institutions that had been building through the latter part of Mbeki's presidency reached their crescendo.

The effects of Mbeki's intervention in the ANC's HIV-prevention strategy are discussed in Chapter 7. Here, it is merely worth highlighting the way in which the *Treatment Action Campaign* case presented the Court with a valuable opportunity to demonstrate its usefulness to the ANC's left faction. Before this case, it is fair to say, neither COSATU nor the SACP had really seen the potential role that constitutional litigation could play in the furtherance of their objectives within the tripartite alliance. Although the adoption of the extensive social rights guarantees in the 1996 Constitution had largely been driven by the ANC's left faction,[137] it lacked a tradition, outside the sphere of labour relations, of public impact litigation. It was not until the Treatment Action Campaign actively sought out COSATU's support for its application against the Minister of Health that the labour movement saw how constitutional litigation might be used to promote its interests.[138] As mentioned earlier,

---

Deal in Your Pocket (Johannesburg: Jonathan Ball, 2008); Klug, *The Constitution of South Africa* 178–81.

[136] In June 2005. See Jeremy Gordin, *Zuma: A Biography* (Johannesburg: Jonathan Ball, 2008).

[137] Dixon and Ginsburg, 'The South African Constitutional Court and Socio-Economic Rights as "Insurance Swaps"'.

[138] See Mark Heywood, 'Preventing Mother-to-Child HIV Transmission in South Africa: Background, Strategies and Outcomes of the Treatment Action Campaign Case against the Minister of Health' (2003) 19 *South African Journal on Human Rights* 278.

this was a crucial development for the Court, since it gave it an opportunity to demonstrate its relevance to intra-ANC policy struggles. In this sense, Mbeki's meddling in the ANC's HIV-prevention strategy actually had a fortuitously positive impact on the Court's insulation from political attack. The potential trend started by the *Treatment Action Campaign* case, however, was not sustained, and subsequent events saw a return to the orthodox left-wing critique of the constitutional project as a neo-liberal constraint on genuine social reform.[139]

While not in the nature of things giving rise to constitutional litigation, the significance of Zimbabwe's political and economic meltdown after 2000 is that it exposed the uncertain nature of the ANC's commitment to human rights. By consistently failing to do anything to stop the politically motivated campaign of murder and torture that followed the rejection of President Robert Mugabe's constitutional reform proposals,[140] the ANC gave the lie to the lofty ideals of the Freedom Charter. In matters of foreign policy, it was clear, the ANC was an all-too-ordinary political party, motivated more by strategic interests and past loyalties than any concern for social justice. The exposure of the ANC's less-than-wholehearted embrace of the values underlying the post-apartheid Constitutions in this way added to the sense that, under Mbeki, the ANC was no longer the ideal constitutional partner that it had once been.

If the Mandela presidency had constituted something of a honeymoon period for the Court, then, the long Mbeki presidency presented more complex challenges. The end of South Africa's relatively short-lived, and somewhat artificial, period of racial reconciliation in December 1996 exposed the constitutional settlement, and with it the institution of judicial review, to the possibility of sustained political attack. With the ANC not just politically dominant, but rampant, the ordinary guarantor of respect for judicial independence – the regular transfer of power between competing political parties – was lacking. Although the ANC's centrist faction still sheltered the Court from the ordinary political effects of its failure to build its public support, the centrist faction's continued

---

[139] In June 2008, for example, in the political turmoil over the prosecution of Jacob Zuma on charges of corruption, ANC Secretary-General, Gwede Mantashe, attacked the Court as a 'counter-revolutionary' force in South African politics.

[140] This is well documented in Peter Godwin, *The Fear: The Last Days of Robert Mugabe* (London: Picador, 2010).

capacity to play this role was undermined by its increasingly tenuous position within the ANC.

Despite this deterioration in the political environment, however, very few attacks on the Court were in fact launched, and none that could be described as successful. During the *Treatment Action Campaign* case, as we shall see,[141] the Minister of Health threatened to disobey the Court's order. More ominously, in December 2005, a package of legislation, including a proposed amendment to the 1996 Constitution and a new Superior Courts Bill, was published.[142] If passed, the amendment and bill would have given the executive greater control over the administration of the judicial system, including the Constitutional Court.[143] The legislative package also contained a specific proposal that the Court should be divested of its power to declare legislation unconstitutional before commencement.[144]

Although deeply concerning at the time, the significant point about these attempted attacks is that they were both effectively thwarted. After a public outcry, the Minister of Health's threat to disobey the Court's order in the *Treatment Action Campaign* case was quickly retracted, and Chaskalson himself, in a post-retirement speech given at a meeting of the General Council of the Bar, did much to dissuade the ANC from proceeding with the Constitution Fourteenth Amendment Bill.[145] Notwithstanding the deteriorating political environment, therefore, the formal constitutional provisions protecting the Court from undue political control remained intact.

Of course, the real test of the Constitutional Court's capacity to survive in this environment still lay in the future, in the turbulent two-and-a-half-year period in which Jacob Zuma was first dismissed as Deputy President, then unsuccessfully charged with corruption, and finally elected as ANC President at its Polokwane conference in December 2007.[146] The final chapter of this study reflects on these events, and asks whether the Chaskalson Court's achievement ought to be reassessed in light of the threats now facing the Court. One of the questions that any such assessment must face is the extent to which actions taken after Chief

---

[141] Chapter 8.

[142] Constitution Fourteenth Amendment Bill (GN 2023 in GG 28334 of 14 December 2005).

[143] Ibid, clause 1.   [144] Ibid, clause 7(b).

[145] See Cathi Albertyn, 'Judicial Independence and the Constitution Fourteenth Amendment Bill' (2006) 22 *South African Journal on Human Rights* 126, 126.

[146] For a succinct account of these events, see Gordin, *Zuma.*

Justice Chaskalson's retirement, including the judges' decision to bring allegations of improper interference with the Court's processes against Cape High Court Judge President John Hlophe,[147] have contributed to the Court's current troubles. Against this must be weighed the fact that several of the original members of the Chaskalson Court, including Pius Langa, Albie Sachs, Yvonne Mokgoro and Kate O'Regan, continued to serve until 2009. As much as the long Mbeki presidency must be assessed from 1997, it might be argued, so should the long Chaskalson Court be regarded as having lasted until these other judges' retirement. It would also in any case be artificial to terminate the analysis of the political effects of the Chaskalson Court's record in May 2005. As this chapter has been at pains to emphasise, the impact of judicial decisions on the creation of a political culture of respect for judicial independence may only really be assessed over the *longue durée*.

Nevertheless, there is enough in the fact that the Chaskalson Court was able to survive until May 2005 without triggering a debilitating attack on its independence to suggest that its reputation as one of the most successful of the post-Cold War constitutional courts is not unwarranted. If further support for this assertion is required, then reference might be made to the Constitutional Court's continued capacity after Justice Chaskalson's retirement to resist attempts to amend its jurisdiction,[148] and to the fact that the Zuma-led ANC Government has not as yet conclusively moved to undermine the Court's independence through its control of the judicial appointments process.[149] Given the even more volatile political environment in which the current Court is operating, this fact must at least have something to do with the foundation laid by the Chaskalson Court in the first ten years of democracy.

---

[147] See Theunis Roux, 'The South African Constitutional Court and the Hlophe Controversy' paper presented at the Centre for Comparative Studies 21st Anniversary Celebration, *International and Comparative Perspectives on Constitutional Law*, Melbourne (November 2009).

[148] At the time of writing, the amendments proposed in the original Constitution Fourteenth Amendment Bill had still not been passed.

[149] In September 2011, there was considerable public outcry over the appointment of Mogoeng Mogoeng as South Africa's fourth Chief Justice, following the premature resignation of Sandile Ngcobo in July of that year. Among the charges made at the time were allegations that Mogoeng Mogoeng was a sweet-heart appointment, chosen more for his ideological proximity to Zuma than for his record as a judge. Other Zuma-era appointments, however, including Edwin Cameron, hardly suggest a general trend in this direction.

4.5 Conclusion

The political context for judicial review during Chaskalson's term as Chief Justice, this chapter has argued, was structured by the two-stage constitution-making process. Before the adoption of the 1996 Constitution, the ANC had a strong, strategic interest in the Court's independence. When coupled with the ANC's inexperience in government, its reliance on smaller political parties to adopt the Constitution, and Mandela's personal commitment to the value of judicial independence, the Constitutional Court is best thought of as having been relatively insulated during this period. After the certification of the 1996 Constitution, however, the political environment for judicial review steadily deteriorated. Thabo Mbeki, who took over *de facto* control of the Government from this point, was less personally committed to the value of judicial independence. At the same time, the ANC's political strategy under his presidency, while still dependent on the Court's perceived independence from political control, was aimed at the centralisation of state power in service of its social transformation project. There were important continuities between the ANC's rule in this respect and the National Party's rule under apartheid. On the one hand, this meant that the fragile tradition of judicial independence that had survived under apartheid was in fact quite well suited to the dominant-party democracy that developed under the ANC. On the other, the absence of a credible opposition party continued to prevent a robust political culture of respect for judicial independence from developing.

As the ANC's inability to deliver on its promise of thoroughgoing social and economic transformation became more apparent, the strategic alliance that had developed between the Court and the ANC's centrist faction weakened. Whereas that alliance in the beginning had sheltered the Court from populist attacks on its independence, the Court's association with the failing experiment in law-driven social transformation became more and more of a liability for it. This situation was exacerbated by the ANC's control of the judicial appointments process under the 1996 Constitution. At just the time when the ANC's commitment to judicial independence was declining, the procedure for the appointment of the Chaskalson Court's successors exposed the Court to the possibility of attack.

And yet, when the next tranche of appointments was made, it was clear that the ANC had not attacked the Court through this route. Chaskalson himself also played a pivotal role in forcing the ANC to rethink the draft Constitution Fourteenth Amendment Bill. Although a final assessment of the Court's achievement depends on consideration of later events, including events yet to happen, these incidents suggest that, despite the deteriorating political environment, the Court had managed somehow to prevent its institutional independence from being undermined. This conclusion in turn suggests that the Court's achievement is attributable to some or other capacity on its part to negotiate the law/ politics tension. The next chapter examines the other side of this tension, and in particular the impact of apartheid and the turn to liberal constitutionalism on South African legal-professional culture.

5

Constraints and opportunities: The law/politics distinction in South African legal-professional culture

Throughout the process of colonial state formation and the rise and fall of apartheid, the legal profession in South Africa remained strongly attached to an idea of law as separate from politics. For the most part, this attachment was driven by narrow class and race interests. The dominant legal-professional view of law in South Africa before 1994 was thus a crude form of positivism that originated in the profession's self-serving need to distance itself from the injustices of white minority rule. There was, however, also an oppositional tradition that made a profound contribution to the struggle against apartheid. The adherents of this tradition maintained a sincere and tenacious faith in law as a form of anti-politics – in the capacity of law to act as a bulwark against the abuse of political power.

Many of the members of the Chaskalson Court, in their previous work as practising lawyers and judges, had been leading exponents of this tradition, and all of them embraced its fundamental premises. They would thus have been predisposed to see the transition to liberal constitutionalism both as a conclusive vindication of their view of law and as a mandate to act on it. This predisposition would have been reinforced by the political context in which the Court found itself and also by the institutional form of the post-apartheid Constitutions. Founded as it was on the separation of powers, the Court's role under the post-apartheid Constitutions would have seemed to the judges to require them to sustain the law/politics distinction as a necessary precondition for the Court's independence.

The difficulty confronting the judges in this respect, of course, was that the transition from a system of parliamentary sovereignty to one of rights-based judicial review meant that the legal profession's sense of what counted as a legally legitimate decision was in the process of being remade. Although the precise implications for legal-professional practice of such a transition are disputed, it is clear that so fundamental a change as the one that occurred in South Africa after 1994 must have had at least a momentarily a destabilising impact. Settled institutional practices and forms of legal reasoning would inevitably have been thrown into flux as the legal profession, and with it, the broader legal and political culture, adjusted to the very different institutional function the judiciary was expected to perform.

This situation would have presented the Court with certain challenges. It is not unreasonable to suppose, for example, that the dominant mode of legal reasoning that had prevailed under apartheid would have exerted an inertial force on the legal professional's capacity to adjust to the new forms of reasoning required. The judges themselves, notwithstanding their involvement in the oppositional tradition, would have been susceptible to this tendency. At the same time, however, the transition to a system of rights-based judicial review would have presented the Court with certain opportunities. Precisely because of the destabilising impact of the post-apartheid Constitutions, the transitional moment would have allowed the judges to decide cases in ways that would not have been regarded as legally legitimate in the past, but which were plausibly justified by the Court's role in the new constitutional system.

The discussion that follows elaborates this argument in three sections. The first section begins by rehearsing the story of the development of South African legal-professional culture before 1994 and shows how the two versions of this story – the external version that concentrates on the role of law in the process of state formation, and the internal version that focuses on lawyers' reasoning methods – both have implications for South African legal-professional culture's future trajectory. The next section examines the likely impact of the post-apartheid Constitutions on the crude positivist view of law that developed before 1994 and sets out the opportunities presented to the Court to drive either a wholesale transformation of that view or a more limited set of adjustments in support of its institutional role. The final section sketches an outline of the Chaskalson Court's judicial ethic: the common features of the judges' legal-professional socialisation that would likely have informed the Court's adjudicative practices.

5.1   The received tradition: South African legal-professional culture before 1994

The dominant mode of legal reasoning in South Africa before 1994, most commentators agree, was a crude or 'low' version of positivism, tending towards formalism.[1] The consensus in the literature on this point,

---

[1] See, for example, Dugard, *Human Rights and the South African Legal Order* 374; Dyzen-haus, *Hard Cases in Wicked Legal Systems*; Ellmann, *In a Time of Trouble* 231–2; Chanock,

however, masks certain differences about how best to tell the story of the development of South African legal-professional culture and also about the extent to which the dominant mode was open to contestation and creative manipulation. These differences are significant to the argument of this chapter since they entail divergent assessments of the legal constraints under which the Chaskalson Court operated: how one tells the story of the development of South African legal-professional culture before 1994 clearly has implications for the continuation of that story after the transition, and the view one takes of the contestability and manipulability of the dominant mode of legal reasoning necessarily informs one's assessment of the freedom the Court had to adapt that mode to the demands of the new constitutional order.

The first difference is primarily a matter of disciplinary perspective. As told by social scientists, looking at law mainly from the outside, the story of the development of South African legal-professional culture is a sub-chapter of a more extended story about the role of law in the construction of the colonial and apartheid states. For proponents of this account, legal-professional culture tends to be seen as an epiphenomenon – as the contingent by-product of the social, political and economic processes in which legal professionals were embedded. For legal academics, on the other hand, reflecting on law mainly from the inside, the emphasis falls on the way in which the imperatives of white minority rule affected (and infected) the dominant style of legal reasoning. On this approach, the influence of broader social, political and economic processes is reduced to the impact of racially-based legislation on the egalitarian values of the common law, with particular emphasis falling on the way in which judges, especially liberal judges, struggled to reconcile their personal commitment to individual freedom with their judicial duty to give effect to clearly worded statutes.

In the nature of things, the second way of telling the story provides a more detailed account of the particular styles of legal reasoning that developed under colonialism and apartheid. Whereas the first version is content with a broad-brush depiction of a legal-professional class that was generally unwilling to acknowledge, even less to expose, the moral failings of the legal rules it was asked to apply, the second version shows that the retreat into formalism was not entirely uncontested, and that a

The Making of South African Legal Culture 1902–1936 25; Klare, 'Legal Culture and Transformative Constitutionalism'; Alfred Cockrell, 'Rainbow Jurisprudence' (1995) 11 *South African Journal on Human Rights* 1.

more substantive, human-rights-regarding style of legal reasoning developed in opposition to the dominant mode. By the same token, of course, the second version of the story – by reducing the influence of colonialism and apartheid to the impact of racially-based statutes – has little to say about the way nominally extra-legal factors defined the outer boundaries of permissible legal argument. By bringing these factors into play, the first version arguably has more explanatory power: if its account of the dominant mode of legal reasoning is a little thin, it compensates by telling a richer story about how the development of South African legal-professional culture was shaped by the political and economic context in which lawyers found themselves. In so doing, the first version also makes a methodological point that this study would do well to heed, viz. that even where the focus falls on the relative strength of the law/politics distinction in a particular legal-professional culture, explaining the nature of that distinction, and the role of the courts in maintaining and developing it, requires some attention to be paid to broader social, political and economic processes.

That said, the two versions of the story are not irreconcilable: their differences mostly amount to differences of emphasis rather than substance. In the review of the literature that follows, therefore, an attempt is made to weave the two versions together, using the one to complement the other. The purpose of this exercise, in turn, is to set up the account in the next section of South African legal-professional culture's post-1994 trajectory. The underlying assumption is that, notwithstanding the transition to democracy and the turn to liberal constitutionalism, there were important continuities in both the external and the internal versions of the story, and that a proper appreciation of the legal constraints impacting on the Chaskalson Court depends on an understanding of what went before.

The leading example of the first version of the story is Martin Chanock's magisterial study of the use of law in the construction of the South African state in the early part of the twentieth century.[2] Using a broad definition of legal culture as extending to 'a set of assumptions, a way of doing things, a repertoire of language, of legal forms and institutional practices',[3] Chanock argues that the development of South African legal culture from 1902 to 1936 was mainly driven by the dynamic interaction between the imposed colonial legal system and African customary law.

---

[2] Chanock, *The Making of South African Legal Culture.*   [3] Ibid. 23.

On this view, the origins of white attitudes to law are to be found, not just in the two legal traditions inherited from Europe, but also in white South Africans' self-legitimating need to define the rationality of their system in contradistinction to the primitive other. 'The image of legalism,' Chanock writes, 'its justice, discernment and restraint, is a counterpoint of the opposing image of savagery, impulse and transgression.'[4]

Central to Chanock's argument is the claim that lawyers and judges were fairly marginal players in this process. Rather, it was the bureaucracy and, to a lesser extent, politicians whose discursive practices informed the dominant societal view of law. Given the use of law in the construction of the colonial state, this view was necessarily quite instrumentalist.[5] Law was 'a way of creating powers, of endowing officials with regulated ways of acting, a weapon in the hands of the state rather than a defence against it'.[6] Black South Africans, on the receiving end of the colonial legal system, were inclined to think of law in the same way.[7]

The heightened formalism of South African *legal-professional* culture, Chanock argues, must be understood as a reaction against this broader societal view. In a country where law was so obviously deployed as an instrument of social control and oppression, lawyers' discourse on law played the role – common to most legal-professional cultures, but intensified in the particular circumstances of South Africa – of separating the realm of the legal from the political.[8] Precisely because of law's instrumental deployment in the creation and maintenance of a morally unjust system, legal-professional discourse resisted any sense that the moral worth of a legal rule should inform an understanding of its content. In the case of conservative judges, this attitude was supported by an unquestioning acceptance of the political premises underlying the colonial legal system's differential operation according to race. Even liberal judges, however, tended to avoid direct engagement with the malign purposes of racist legislation, choosing instead to hold the executive to the precise terms of the empowering statute – a tactic of 'obstructive literalism' that Chanock argues liberal South African judges learned from their conservative British counterparts, who had attempted to resist the implementation of early twentieth-century welfare legislation in much the same way.[9]

For Chanock, then, the formalism of South African legal-professional culture was a contingent by-product of the dual role of law as both a limitation on the abuse of state power (in relation to white sub-society)

---

[4] Ibid. 127–8.   [5] Ibid. 23–4.   [6] Ibid. 22.   [7] Ibid. 42.   [8] Ibid. 25.
[9] Ibid. 518.

and an instrument of the exercise of state power (in relation to the indigenous African majority).[10] This idea has subsequently been developed by Jens Meierhenrich in a study of the role of law in the transition to democracy. Drawing on the émigré-German theorist Ernst Fraenkel's account of the Nazi state as a 'dual state',[11] Meierhenrich argues that the pre-democratic South African state was also a classic 'dual state' consisting, on the one hand, of a 'prerogative state', in which law functioned as an instrument of arbitrary power,[12] and, on the other, of a 'normative state', in which law exerted constraints on power.[13] In the particular case of South Africa, 'substantively irrational' law (in the Weberian sense) was used in the prerogative state to exert social control over the black majority, whilst in the normative state 'formally rational law' regulated the commercial and other activities of white South Africans.[14]

The key insight Meierhenrich draws from Fraenkel's theory is the claim that the dual state is 'in permanent tension with itself'[15] in as much as the imperatives driving the prerogative state (social control through law) must sometimes give way to the imperatives driving the normative state (equal treatment under law).[16] In pre-democratic South Africa, this tension meant that black South Africans' attitudes to law were influenced not only by the substantively irrational law that was the main instrument of their oppression, but also by the formally rational law in which they were occasionally allowed to participate.[17] Reinforced by deeply held religious views on both sides of the racial divide,[18] the positive memory of formally rational law played a crucial role in the transition to democracy, functioning as a shared 'mental model' that supplied the 'trust' required to drive the negotiations process forward.[19]

Like Chanock, Meierhenrich does not explore the precise nature of the formal rationality he identifies as being integral to the operation of the normative state. His primary concern is the role of law in the transition, and for this purpose a fairly general typification of South African

---

[10] Ibid. 32, 37.

[11] Ernst Fraenkel, *The Dual State: A Contribution to the Theory of Dictatorship* trans. E. A. Shils (New York, NY: Oxford University Press, 1941).

[12] Meierhenrich, *The Legacies of Law* 63–5.

[13] Ibid. 65–6.   [14] Ibid. 4.   [15] Ibid. 75.

[16] Ibid. 75 (on the 'conflicting imperatives' faced by the dual state in Nazi Germany).

[17] Ibid. 129–74.   [18] Ibid. 239–58.

[19] Ibid. 59, 76, 190, 319. The term 'mental model' derives from Arthur T. Denzau and Douglass C. North, 'Shared Mental Models: Ideologies and Institutions' (1994) 47 *Kyklos* 3.

legal-professional culture as an off-shoot of the English common-law tradition is sufficient.[20] For a more detailed account of the nature of South African legal-professional culture and the forms of legal reasoning associated with it, it is necessary to turn to the debate conducted in the 1970s and 1980s among legal academics about the role of the courts under apartheid, and in particular about such questions as whether the judiciary might have done more to frustrate the implementation of apartheid legislation, and whether judges had a duty to resign. Though in the nature of things mostly conducted from an internal perspective, these debates have bequeathed a rich literature on the different styles of legal reasoning available to judges under apartheid, and in this way have much to say about the state of South African legal-professional culture at the time of transition.

For many years, the standard legal-academic account was John Dugard's narrative about the arrival of positivism in 1806 with the British occupation of the Cape.[21] From this time on, Dugard argued, legal-professional practice was heavily influenced by a Benthamite and Austinian view of law, which eventually replaced the natural-law tradition of Grotius and Voet. The core positivist notions of law as the command of the sovereign and the separation of law and morality became frozen in the conditions of colonial and apartheid South Africa, so that South African legal professionals largely missed out on the Hartian development of positivism in the 1950s and 1960s.[22] As far as most South African judges, attorneys and advocates were concerned, 'statutory interpretation [was] ... a mechanical operation in which value judgments play[ed] no part.'[23] After 1948, Afrikaans-speaking legal academics and judges developed an historical jurisprudence in the form of the purist movement, which was aimed at rooting out English influence on Roman-Dutch private law. But Afrikaner jurists, like L. C. Steyn, accepted the basic tenets of positivism in public law, regarding it in this context as a more favourable legal theory.[24]

Dugard's account came to be challenged in the 1980s, with several scholars arguing that the South African tradition of positivism was not as crude as he had made out.[25] Focusing on the question whether judges

---

[20] Meierhenrich, *The Legacies of Law*.
[21] See John Dugard, 'The Judicial Process, Positivism and Civil Liberty (1971) 88 *South African Law Journal* 181; Dugard, *Human Rights and the South African Legal Order* 393–7.
[22] Dugard, *Human Rights and the South African Legal Order* 395.
[23] Ibid. 374. [24] Ibid. 396.
[25] See Christopher Forsyth and Johann Schiller, 'The Judicial Process, Positivism, and Civil Liberty II' (1981) 98 *South African Law Journal* 218; Wacks, 'Judges and Injustice'; Forsyth, *In Danger for their Talents* 228–30.

had a moral duty to resign, the debate split into two camps: those who, relying on a revamped, Hartian version of positivism, argued that there were enough spaces in South African law, including especially the rules of statutory interpretation, from which to contest and occasionally rein in the repressive effects of apartheid legislation,[26] and those who argued, from a Dworkinian perspective, that the cancer of racism had so infiltrated the legal tradition that there was no option for liberal judges but to resign.[27] Other Dworkinians – in agreement with positivists on the prescription, but differing in the diagnosis – argued that there was still enough in the South African legal tradition to justify a 'best interpretation' of that tradition resistant to repressive legislation.[28]

At the tail end of this debate, in a major study of the performance of the South African Appellate Division under the 1985–1990 state of emergency, Stephen Ellmann argued that there had long been a minority, but nevertheless fairly vigorous, human rights tradition in South African legal-professional practice, and that this tradition had been able to exploit a certain flexibility in the dominant positivist mode of reasoning:

> [W]idespread adherence to positivist argumentation in South African courts has also made a contribution to the rise of more rights-minded decisions. It has done so by providing an agreed-upon framework for argument, within which a considerable range of human rights contentions can be presented as legitimate grounds for decision. And it has been able to offer this opportunity in good part because the central positivist dictate of South African law, the supremacy of Parliament, has proved to be a relatively unconfining doctrinal constraint ... The result is that the South African judiciary does not have to fundamentally restructure its jurisprudence, with all the doctrinal and even moral strain that might entail, in order to render a range of decisions in favour of human rights.[29]

The thrust of Ellmann's point, the rest of his book makes clear, is that, faced with a strategic choice between developing a rival natural-law

---

[26] See John Dugard, 'Should Judges Resign? A Reply to Professor Wacks' (1984) 101 *South African Law Journal* 286, 289–90 (arguing that 'many of the principles of equality and liberty immanent in Roman-Dutch law have been recognized as positive rules of law by our courts') (cited in Ellmann, *In a Time of Trouble* 238).

[27] Wacks, 'Judges and Injustice'.

[28] Etienne Mureinik, 'Dworkin and Apartheid' in Hugh Corder (ed.), *Essays on Law and Social Practice in South Africa* (Cape Town: Juta, 1988) 181; Etienne Mureinik, 'Pursuing Principle: The Appellate Division and Review under the State of Emergency' (1989) 5 *South African Journal on Human Rights* 60; David Dyzenhaus, 'The Disappearance of Law?' (1990) 107 *South African Law Journal* 227.

[29] Ellmann, *In a Time of Trouble* 233.

tradition, in which the rules of positive law would have been subjected to higher-order moral norms, and working within the dominant positivist tradition to exploit the opportunities for human-rights-regarding decisions that it provided, liberal South African judges correctly chose the latter approach. By framing their decisions as decisions based on legally immanent principles rather than extra-legal moral values, liberal judges were able to immunise their decisions from the charge of fundamental illegitimacy – of going beyond 'the normal parameters of South African legal argument'.[30] The further advantage of this approach, Ellmann contended, was that it 'largely avoided [the] danger [illustrated by the example of American anti-slavery jurisprudence] of polarizing potentially sympathetic judges'.[31] Thus, even fairly conservative judges would sometimes make use of the human rights line of argument.[32]

David Dyzenhaus, whose study of the lessons apartheid law had to teach about the rival claims of positivism and natural law was published more or less contemporaneously with Ellmann's work,[33] took a less sanguine view of the contribution made by positivism to the cause of human rights in South Africa. Distinguishing between a 'plain fact' approach, which he defined as a 'doctrine of judicial responsibility' in terms of which ambiguity in legislation ought to be resolved according to facts appearing in the public record,[34] and a 'common law' approach, according to which such ambiguity ought to be resolved on the assumption that Parliament intended to act in conformity with common-law values,[35] Dyzenhaus argued that the second approach, had it been more vigorously pursued, would have been far more protective of human rights. By holding the legislature to the values on which law's claim to legitimacy depends, the common law approach would have kept open a space for human rights lawyering that the plain fact approach mostly closed down. At least, if the apartheid regime had continued to see some strategic benefit in adhering to the rule of law, the common law approach would have supported this tendency by making explicit the legislature's

---

[30] Ibid. 239.

[31] Ibid. 238 (referring at 233–7 to Robert M. Cover, *Justice Accused: Antislavery and the Judicial Process* (New Haven, CT: Yale University Press, 1975).

[32] Ibid. 238–9.

[33] Dyzenhaus, *Hard Cases in Wicked Legal Systems*. See also David Dyzenhaus, 'Law's Potential' (1992) 7 *Canadian Journal of Law & Society* 237.

[34] Dyzenhaus, *Hard Cases in Wicked Legal Systems* 57. See also Dyzenhaus, *Judging the Judges, Judging Ourselves* 77.

[35] Dyzenhaus, *Hard Cases in Wicked Legal Systems* 155–8.

choice between statutory language that abandoned any pretensions towards fairness, and language that allowed liberal judges to read such assumptions in.[36]

In arguing thus, Dyzenhaus was seeking to contribute not only to the South African debate about the appropriate role of the judiciary under apartheid, but also to the wider jurisprudential debate about the respective merits of positivism and natural law in the face of a 'wicked legal system'.[37] For Dyzenhaus, what the South African experience showed was that positivism, lacking as it does a 'political doctrine of judicial responsibility',[38] had no particular counsel to offer judges when confronted with Hartian-style 'gaps' in the law. Liberal judges, to be sure, could exploit such gaps to make liberal law, but had no defence against a repressive legislature determined to undo their efforts. Worse, judges who espoused a positivist view of law unwittingly assisted the apartheid regime by collapsing the requirements of the rule of law into the requirements of legality.[39] By contrast, those judges who saw their role as being to hold government to a substantive, rights-based conception of the rule of law were far more effective, both in exposing apartheid law for what it was and in keeping open a space for human rights lawyering.

When directed at the question of the appropriate strategy to be pursued by liberal judges under apartheid, this argument led naturally into a critique of Ellmann's work.[40] Whereas Ellmann, as we have seen, argued that liberal judges were wise not to abandon the basic framework of positivism, Dyzenhaus thought that this strategy had potentially damaging side-effects. In two important respects, however, Ellmann and Dyzenhaus were in broad agreement: first, that the dominant mode of legal reasoning under apartheid was best described as a crude form of positivism;[41] and, secondly, that judges committed to human rights ought to have adopted, and did in fact adopt, an oppositional mode of legal reasoning. In Ellmann's case, that oppositional mode was typified as a particular doctrinal approach within the boundaries of permissible legal argument set by positivism, whereas in Dyzenhaus's case, the

---

[36] For a succinct expression of this point, see Dyzenhaus, 'Law's Potential' 250.
[37] See H. L. A. Hart, 'Positivism and the Separation of Law and Morals' (1958) 71 *Harvard Law Review* 593; Lon L. Fuller, 'Positivism and Fidelity to Law: A Reply to Professor Hart' (1958) 71 *Harvard Law Review* 630.
[38] Dyzenhaus, *Hard Cases in Wicked Legal Systems* 10.   [39] Ibid. 254.
[40] See Dyzenhaus, 'Law's Potential'.
[41] See Dyzenhaus, *Judging the Judges* 77 (equating the plain fact approach to Robert Cover's idea of a 'retreat to a mechanistic formalism').

oppositional mode took the form of a natural-law style of argument that saw judges holding the apartheid legislature to respect the moral values that alone could render its enactments legitimate, or at least as legitimate as they were ever going to be in a system of white minority rule. Over and above their differences, therefore, what Ellmann and Dyzenhaus's studies share is a sense that liberal judges were in a position to make strategic choices about the sorts of legal argument that would best further the cause of human rights in South Africa.

This notion of the strategies open to liberal judges, the next section argues, is important to an understanding of the Chaskalson Court's capacity to adapt the received mode of legal reasoning to suit its institutional role under the post-apartheid Constitutions. On the one hand, the turn to liberal constitutionalism presented the Court with an opportunity to cast off the crude positivist view of law that had long dominated South African legal-professional culture. On the other, the constraints of the external political environment, and of the Court's need to maintain some version of the law/politics distinction, meant that the Court needed to proceed cautiously. Just as liberal judges under apartheid had had to make strategic choices about how best to keep open the space for human rights lawyering, so too did the Chaskalson Court need to make strategic choices about how best to adapt the received mode to the requirements of the new constitutional order.

5.2 The impact of the post-apartheid Constitutions on South African legal-professional culture

In theory, the changes to a legal-professional culture consequent on the adoption of a new constitution may be conceptualised as falling into two main categories: changes that were necessarily entailed, in the sense that legal-professional practice under the new constitution could not conceivably have continued absent those changes, and changes that were supported, or in some other way triggered, by the adoption of the new constitution, but whose occurrence was contingent on other factors. In practice, the distinction between these two sets of changes may be hard to draw and subject to reasonable disagreement. For one, the characterisation of the constitution itself – its jurisprudential implications and political commitments, including especially its commitments to a particular conception of the role of the judiciary and the legal profession – may be in dispute. Even if agreement could be reached on these matters, the link between the various general theories of law and particular constitutional systems is notoriously contested, with some purportedly general theories dismissed by other theorists as mere rationalisations of a particular country's constitutional practice.[42]

Despite these difficulties, the distinction between a new constitution's necessarily entailed and contingent impacts may be useful as a rough framework for analysis, especially if it is deployed with a limited purpose in mind. From the perspective of this study, the usefulness of the distinction is that it allows us to separate out those adaptations to the dominant mode of legal reasoning that the Chaskalson Court necessarily had to make if it was to develop a legally credible understanding of its institutional role under the post-apartheid Constitutions, and those adaptations that were open to it as a plausible construction of its institutional role, but which were in the end dependent on the Court's strategic choices (if that is indeed what they were) about how best to position itself in the new constitutional order. If that limited purpose is kept in mind, it may be possible to deploy the distinction in a way that helpfully elucidates the opportunities presented to the Court by the constitutional transition.

To this end, this section begins by characterising the post-apartheid Constitutions as liberal-democratic constitutions of a particular type, and then examines whether any changes to the prevailing legal-professional view of law were necessarily entailed by the adoption of the Constitutions thus understood. Concluding that the crude form of positivism that had prevailed during the apartheid era clearly had to be abandoned, the section moves on to consider the two main views of law that might be said to have been at least minimally supported by, or jurisprudentially compatible with, the post-apartheid Constitutions. Each alternative view is then assessed on the basis of its capacity to assist the Court in managing the law/politics tension. Finding neither of the views more obviously better equipped in this respect than the other, and questioning the capacity of the Court in any event to develop a uniform strategy of wholesale legal-cultural transformation, the section ends by considering various other, more limited strategies that might have been available to the judges in defining and defending the Court's institutional role.

---

[42] Legal positivism's dismissal of Ronald Dworkin's theory of law as integrity is the most obvious case in point here. See Brian Leiter, 'The End of Empire: Dworkin and Jurisprudence in the 21st Century' (2004) 36 *Rutgers Law Journal* 165.

5.2.1 The character of the post-apartheid Constitutions

As noted above, the characterisation of the jurisprudential implications and political commitments of a constitution is open to reasonable disagreement. Determining the impact of the post-apartheid Constitutions on South African legal-professional culture nevertheless requires us to give some determinate content to these documents. In attempting this initial task, the discussion that follows tries to strike a balance between the need, on the one hand, to develop an understanding of the post-apartheid Constitutions that is sufficiently detailed to serve as the basis for examining their impact and the need, on the other, to resist imposing too controversial an understanding – one that would be better offered as a contribution to the ongoing debate over the meaning of the Constitutions.

To begin with the least contentious matters: the post-apartheid Constitutions clearly signalled a shift away from a system of parliamentary sovereignty to one of constitutional supremacy, and established a Constitutional Court with the power of judicial review over both intergovernmental and rights issues. The range of rights in the 1993 Constitution was initially intended to be restricted to rights that were necessary to guarantee free and fair political competition in the lead-up to the first democratic elections. The negotiations process over the transitional Constitution took on its own logic, however, and a much wider range of rights was included than initially intended.[43] By the time the 1996 Constitution came to be drafted, the ANC's overwhelming electoral support helped it to ensure that the Bill of Rights reflected its hybrid human rights tradition.[44] Not only civil and political rights, but also a number of socio-economic rights were included.[45] In this way, the 1996 Constitution extended the liberal constitutionalist tradition of rights-based judicial review into unchartered waters. Although the basic institutional form of the Constitution was quite familiar, the scope of the Bill of Rights was wider than in any previous liberal-democratic constitution. The political thrust of the rights was also much more obviously weighted towards a left-wing view of politics. In addition to socio-economic rights, the Bill of Rights in the 1996 Constitution contains the right 'to make decisions concerning reproduction',[46] the right to non-discrimination on

---

[43] See Lourens M. Du Plessis and Hugh Corder, *Understanding South Africa's Transitional Bill of Rights* (Cape Town: Juta, 1994).
[44] See the discussion in Chapter 4.   [45] See Chapter 8.   [46] Section (2)(a).

the grounds of sexual orientation,[47] the right to strike,[48] and the right to a non-harmful environment,[49] few of which had been expressed in any other constitution quite so forcefully.

The 1996 Constitution is also, as Cass Sunstein put it, a 'never again' Constitution.[50] If there is a consistent theme that runs through the Constitution it is a focus on the past as a lesson for the future. In the section on property rights, for example, the Constitution provides that '[a] person or community whose tenure of land is legally insecure as a result of past racially discriminatory laws or practices is entitled, to the extent provided by an Act of Parliament, either to tenure which is legally secure or to comparable redress'.[51] In the next section, on housing rights, the Constitution invokes South Africa's history of forced removals and forbids the eviction of people from their home 'without an order of court made after considering all the relevant circumstances'. Most clearly of all, the equality clause expressly insulates measures aimed at benefiting those disadvantaged by past discrimination from challenges based on the right to equal treatment. In this way, the 1996 Constitution unambiguously commits itself to a substantive rather than formal conception of equality.[52]

Despite references in the 1993 Constitution to the concept of *ubuntu*,[53] the post-apartheid Constitutions do not reflect a particularly African ethos. Indeed, anyone reading them without any knowledge of the country from which they originated might be forgiven for thinking the Constitutions to have been enacted by the Parliament of a modern Western liberal democracy, albeit one where for some reason the constitutional moment had produced a remarkable consensus on the political left. Apart from the preamble, the languages clause,[54] and the short chapter on traditional leadership,[55] the 1996 Constitution bears little trace of a specifically African conception of government. Various provisions lean towards a participatory or dialogical understanding of democracy, but none is phrased in such a way as to invoke the African tradition of participatory democracy and consensual decision-making. Most significantly, the equality clause makes no attempt to reconcile Western

---

[47] Section 9(3).   [48] Section 23(2)*(c)*.   [49] Section 24(a).
[50] Sunstein, *Designing Democracy* 221–37.   [51] Section 25(6).
[52] See Cathi Albertyn and Beth Goldblatt, 'Facing the Challenge of Transformation: Difficulties in the Development of an Indigenous Jurisprudence of Equality' (1998) 14 *South African Journal on Human Rights* 248.
[53] 1993 Constitution, Postamble.   [54] Section 6.   [55] Chapter 12.

notions of gender equality with traditional African notions of the extended family, reciprocal relationships of support, and the system of male primogeniture in the customary law of succession.

Apart from the establishment of a system of rights-based judicial review itself, the most significant provisions in the 1996 Constitution from the point of view of its impact on legal practice are the provision in s 8(2) that 'the Bill of Rights binds a natural or juristic person if, and to the extent that, it is applicable, taking into account the nature of the right and the nature of the duty imposed by any right' and the provision in s 39 (2) that the courts, and other tribunals and forums, 'when developing the common law or customary law, must promote the spirit, purport and objects of the Bill of Rights'. In combination, these provisions clearly signal that the Bill of Rights should be horizontally applicable, and that the reasoning methods necessary to its interpretation should be deployed, not only in facial challenges to legislation, but also in the ordinary process of common-law development.

So much is clear from the text of the post-apartheid Constitutions and the history of their enactment. Beyond this point, however, the characterisation of the two Constitutions becomes more controversial. In an influential article published two years after the 1996 Constitution was enacted, Karl Klare, pointing to the above-mentioned features, sought to describe it as 'postliberal', by which he meant that it was a constitution 'that may plausibly be read not only as open but as committed to a large-scale, egalitarian social transformation'.[56] '[I]n sharp contrast to the classical liberal documents', Klare argued, the 1996 Constitution was '*social, redistributive, caring, positive,* at least partly *horizontal, participatory, multicultural,* and *self-conscious* about its historical setting and transformative role and mission.'[57] Having described the 1996 Constitution's political character in this way, he then went on to argue that it invited a particular interpretive method, one that could only properly be effected through a fundamental transformation of South African legal-professional culture from its dominant formalist mode to something approximating the methods and political commitments of the Critical Legal Studies ('CLS') movement in the United States.[58]

The problem with Klare's argument is not that his depiction of the political ideology informing the Bill of Rights is inaccurate, but that it is not entirely clear whether the term 'postliberal' is larger than the sum of

---

[56] Klare, 'Legal Culture and Transformative Constitutionalism' 151.
[57] Ibid. 153 (footnote omitted).   [58] Ibid. 156–72.

its parts.[59] Klare's label may also be criticised for its implication that the 1996 Constitution went beyond the conceptual limits, not only of classical liberalism, but also of the liberal constitutionalist tradition.[60] That the 1996 Constitution, in its comprehensive list of socio-economic rights and its subjection of private power to the discipline of the Bill of Rights, went further than any previous liberal-democratic constitution is not in dispute. But the 1996 Constitution, in institutional form, clearly falls into the tradition of liberal constitutionalism that began with the adoption of the American Constitution in 1789. At least, it is less controversially understood as a development of that tradition than as a fundamental departure from it.

Most obviously, the 1996 Constitution is premised on the quintessentially liberal doctrines of the separation of powers and judicial independence. Section 165(1) thus provides that '[t]he judicial authority of the Republic is vested in the courts'. Section 165(2) continues by providing that '[t]he courts are independent and subject only to the Constitution and the law, which they must apply impartially and without fear, favour or prejudice'. Section 165(4) enjoins all organs of state 'to assist and protect the courts to ensure the independence, impartiality, dignity, accessibility and effectiveness of the courts'. By playing down these features of the 1996 Constitution in favour of the political ideology informing the Bill of Rights, Klare asks us to accept that the Chaskalson Court was somehow in a position to escape the law/politics tension and win support for its role by openly declaring the political nature of its function.[61] As further explained below,[62] this argument fundamentally misconstrues the nature of the 1996 Constitution and the essentially liberal commitment to the rule of law that underpinned it. However progressive the political ideology informing the Bill of Rights, the Court could not escape the fact that its institutional role, and thereby also its

---

[59] See further Theunis Roux, 'Transformative Constitutionalism and the Best Interpretation of the South African Constitution: Distinction without a Difference?' (2009) 20 *Stellenbosch Law Review* 258.

[60] Klare is careful to say that by 'liberal' he means 'classic liberal', as exemplified by the US Constitution (Klare, 'Legal Culture and Transformative Constitutionalism' 152). The thrust of his argument, however, is that the 1996 Constitution goes beyond the limits of the liberal tradition of constitutionalism by collapsing the law/politics distinction and inviting a conception of the judicial function, and of the Constitutional Court's function in particular, as thoroughly political.

[61] Ibid. 164.   [62] See Section 5.2.3.

institutional independence, was premised on the Court's capacity to sustain the public's faith in the impartiality of its interpretive practices.[63]

5.2.2 The necessarily entailed impact of the post-apartheid Constitutions

Characterised as liberal-democratic constitutions in this way, the post-apartheid Constitutions introduced two major innovations potentially at odds with the crude positivist view of law that had prevailed before 1994: a change to the governing constitutional system from parliamentary sovereignty to constitutional supremacy, and a requirement that the validity of all legal rules should depend on a test for moral conformance with the Bill of Rights.

The first change necessarily entailed an adjustment to the prevailing doctrine of judicial responsibility. At least, if Dyzenhaus is correct that judges in apartheid South Africa mostly justified their role by professions of fidelity to the intentions of Parliament, the transition to a system of supreme-law judicial review conclusively undermined that stance. In its stead, South African judges were required to work out a new doctrine of judicial responsibility, one that reconciled the supremacy of the Constitution with the ongoing importance of Parliament as the primary law-giver.

The required adjustment was clearest in matters involving facial challenges to legislation for contravention of the Bill of Rights. As Dyzenhaus noted at the start of the constitutional negotiations process, the plain fact approach is not well-suited to this kind of inquiry.[64] At least, it is much harder to give precise content to constitutional rights on the basis of assertions about facts in the public record than it is to interpret statutes in the same way. For one, constitutional rights are deliberately formulated in fairly abstract terms. Recourse to the plain fact approach in deciding a facial challenge to a statute must therefore often result in the conclusion that the constitutional legislature had no particular view about how the challenge ought to be resolved, other than that the courts should resolve it.

---

[63] Note that this argument does not imply that the Court could not give effect to the Constitution's transformatory purposes. See Roux, 'Transformative Constitutionalism and the Best Interpretation of the Constitution'.

[64] Dyzenhaus, 'The Disappearance of Law?' 248 n 63.

This example also illustrates the significance of the second change. By subjecting legislation to a foundational test for conformance to the Bill of Rights, the post-apartheid Constitutions necessarily required the courts to abandon the formalist reasoning methods that had prevailed before the transition. To be given any content at all, the rights in the Bill of Rights needed to be treated as principles of political morality, the implications of which for the validity of statutory rules could only be worked out through some or other process of substantive reasoning.

The 1996 Constitution's injunction that constitutional rights should serve as guides to the development of the common law was similarly inhospitable to the formalist reasoning methods that had characterised common-law adjudication in the pre-democratic era. However plausible it might have been under the previous system of parliamentary sovereignty to sustain the idea of the common law as a gapless system of unchanging rules, the explicit injunction in s 39(2) that the judiciary, when developing the common law, should 'promote the spirit, purport and objects of the Bill of Rights' set the 1996 Constitution firmly against this notion. From the enactment of this Constitution onwards, it was clear, judges would need to acknowledge the creativity of their function in developing the common law, and justify their decisions by reference to the values underlying the new constitutional order.

For all these reasons, the post-apartheid Constitutions necessarily entailed a shift away from the crude positivist view of law that had prevailed before 1994. It does not follow from this argument, however, that the post-apartheid Constitutions were incompatible with the more sophisticated account of positivism developed by H.L.A. Hart and others from the 1950s onwards. Though many issues are still in dispute, both modern variants of positivism have shown themselves to be at least plausibly capable of accommodating the practice of rights-based judicial review: inclusive legal positivism through its contention that the subjection of legal rules to a foundational test for moral conformance is nothing more than a contingent fact about certain legal systems,[65] and exclusive positivism through Joseph Raz's distinction, discussed in Chapter 1, between reasoning 'about' and reasoning 'according to' law. Which of the two versions has the better of the argument need not concern us here. It is also irrelevant for our purposes that these attempts to reconcile positivism with the practice of rights-based judicial review have been

---

[65] See Coleman, *The Practice of Principle*; Waluchow, *Inclusive Legal Positivism*.

called into question by Ronald Dworkin and others.[66] It is enough that there are plausible arguments at a theoretical level to suggest that the introduction of the post-apartheid Constitutions might have been accommodated, not by a wholesale rejection of positivism, but through a more incremental adjustment from low to high positivism.

As a matter of legal-professional practice, it is not hard to imagine how this sort of adjustment might have occurred. The subjection of all law to a foundational test for conformance with the Bill of Rights might thus have been absorbed as a change to the South African legal system's secondary rule of recognition. To be sure, the post-apartheid Constitutions required legal professionals to engage in moral reasoning in the interpretation of the Bill of Rights and, in the case of the 1996 Constitution, the development of the common law as well, but this practice was enjoined by the Constitutions, the history and provenance of which was identifiable as a matter of social fact. While some other view of law might in theory have provided a more persuasive account of the forms of legal reasoning required, and in this sense 'invited' those forms of reasoning,[67] the tendency of a legal-professional culture to make only those adjustments that are required to give plausible effect to a new constitution cannot be underestimated. As Chapter 2 argued, there might be something like a legal-cultural lag effect in terms of which pre-existing attitudes to law exert an inertial force on the capacity of a legal-professional culture to adjust to the forms of legal reasoning suggested, but not necessarily entailed, by a new constitution.

5.2.3 The contingent impact: internal factors

The only change *necessarily entailed* by the adoption of the post-apartheid Constitutions, therefore, was a rejection of the crude positivist view of law that had prevailed before 1994. It was in this sense that South African legal-professional culture was thrown into flux. The formalist reasoning methods that had characterised both statutory interpretation and common-law adjudication before the transition to democracy clearly had to change. Beyond this, however, the post-apartheid Constitutions did not dictate a particular view of law. Rather, the trajectory followed by

---

[66] See Dworkin, *Justice in Robes* 140–86 (first published as Dworkin, 'Hart's Postscript and the Character of Political Philosophy').

[67] The term 'invited' in this context derives from Klare, 'Legal Culture and Transformative Constitutionalism' 156.

South African legal-professional culture after 1994 was contingent on other factors, including both external factors of the kind considered by Chanock and Meierhenrich in their accounts of the early development of South African legal-professional culture, and also factors internal to the law itself – to legal-professional views of how the transition to a system of rights-based judicial review might best be accommodated.

From the perspective of this study, the internal factor that is of most interest is the potential usefulness to the Chaskalson Court of promoting a particular view of law. Given the political constraints under which the Court was operating, was there a particular conception of the law/politics distinction that the judges would have been wise to adopt? Or, to put the question slightly differently: over and above the necessarily entailed rejection of the crude form of positivism that had prevailed before 1994, did the transition to a system of rights-based judicial review present any opportunities to the Court to refashion the law/politics distinction in a way that would have assisted it in performing its institutional role?

This question is intriguingly reminiscent of the debate between Ell-mann and Dyzenhaus about the strategies open to liberal judges under apartheid. The question there, it will be recalled, was whether a positivist conception of the egalitarian values running through the common law was preferable to a natural-law conception. Just as Ellmann had seen the better strategy as being to remain within the boundaries of acceptable legal argument set by positivism, so too might it be argued that the Chaskalson Court would have been best advised to refashion the law/politics distinction within an essentially positivistic framework. Similarly, Dyzenhaus's reasons for preferring the common law approach might be thought to support the contrary view, i.e. that the Court ought to have seized the opportunity presented by the constitutional transition to drive a more fundamental transformation of South African legal-professional culture towards a natural-law conception of adjudication and legal-professional practice.

Each of these possible strategies would have had a certain appeal. By refashioning the law/politics distinction within the basic framework of positivism, the Court would have been able to facilitate a process that the legal-cultural-lag-effect argument suggests might in any case have been occurring. From the Court's perspective, its judicial review function would need to have been presented as having been mandated by the Constitution, something which was ascertainable as a matter of social fact. From there it would have been a simple enough matter to claim that, as long as what the Court was doing was rights enforcement, the law/politics distinction was preserved. To be sure, the reasoning methods required to give effect to rights were necessarily substantive and, on the positivist view, no different from the policy-based, consequentialist methods used by the political branches. But this was something that the constitutional drafters had clearly contemplated. The Court's mandate in this respect was therefore legitimate unless and until withdrawn by way of constitutional amendment.

A decision to refashion the law/politics distinction along natural-law lines, by contrast, would have required the Court to drive a much more fundamental transformation of the dominant mode of legal reasoning. On this view, the system-contingent subjection of statutory law (and, after 1996, common law as well) to a test for moral conformance with the Bill of Rights should have been seized on as an opportunity to promote the idea that moral reasoning is an ineluctable fact about *all* adjudication. All that had changed was that judges' duty of fidelity to law, having previously been directed at elaborating the moral principles embedded in the common law, now needed to be directed at elaborating the political morality underlying the Bill of Rights. What distinguishes law from politics on this view is not that judges' decisions do not have implications for policy, but that the reasoning methods used by judges are fundamentally different from the sorts of methods used by the political branches. On both a Dworkinian and Fullerian approach,[68] judges are concerned with elaborating the moral framework subject to which the outputs of democratic politics may legitimately lay claim to citizens' obedience.

The advantage of such a transformation, it may be thought, is that it would have provided, not only a basis for refashioning the law/politics distinction, but also a sophisticated defence of the legitimacy of judicial review. By assimilating the judiciary's mandate under a rights-based constitution to its conception of every judge's duty to give a morally defensible account of law, natural-law theory endeavours to show how the controversial questions of political morality presented by a Bill of Rights may be resolved by reasoning methods that are distinctly legal. Neither of the two modern variants of positivism, by contrast, seeks to draw so sharp a distinction between law and politics. Both accept that, in hard cases at least, judges engage in policy-based, consequentialist reasoning.[69] For some positivists, it follows that judicial review cannot

---

[68] See Lon L. Fuller, *The Morality of Law* (New Haven, CT: Yale University Press, 1964); Dworkin, *Freedom's Law*.

[69] See Raz, *Ethics in the Public Domain* 310–24.

be justified.[70] For others, the acceptance of this fact may be remedied by a supplementary theory of judicial review that seeks to justify a constitutional court's entry into policy as a form of inter-branch dialogue.[71] In theories of this sort, the law/politics distinction is presented as a matter of institutional competence, with the judiciary thought to be better suited to seeing the concrete impact of policies on individual rights, and the political branches better at utilitarian calculations of the public good. By promoting dialogue between the judiciary and the political branches, a system of rights-based judicial review ensures a rough proportionality between ends and means – between the pursuit of welfare-maximising policy goals and the individual interests that are inevitably affected.

Whether a supplementary theory of judicial review of this sort does enough to overcome contemporary positivism's denial of the distinctiveness of legal reasoning is contested.[72] Much will depend on the actual practices of judicial review adopted. All that can be said in the abstract, therefore, is that a dialogical understanding of the Court's institutional role at least presented the Court with a plausible way of refashioning the law/politics distinction within the basic framework of positivism. It is not obvious, however, whether this understanding would have been preferable to the natural-law conception.

There was the possibility of a third strategy, of course, which was forcefully advocated by Klare in the article to which reference has already been made.[73] As we have seen, Klare's argument is premised on a CLS view of law and politics as inseparably intertwined – a view that he contended was strongly suggested, if not necessarily entailed, by the 1996 Constitution. On this basis, Klare argued that the preferable approach for the Court would have been to behave like the ideal CLS judge and openly declare the political nature of its function. By taking the South African public into its trust in this way, the Court would have been able not so much to manage the law/politics tension as to explode it. Such a strategy, Klare acknowledged, would have required the Court to abandon the interpretive methods and substantive political commitments of

---

[70] See, for example, Jeremy Waldron, *Law and Disagreement* (Oxford University Press, 1999).

[71] See, for example, Peter W. Hogg and Allison A. Bushell, 'The Charter Dialogue Between Courts and Legislatures (or Perhaps the Charter of Rights Isn't Such a Bad Thing after All)' (1997) 35 *Osgood Hall Law Journal* 76; Michael C. Dorf and Charles F. Sabel, 'A Constitution of Democratic Experimentalism' (1998) 98 *Columbia Law Review* 267.

[72] See Dworkin, *Justice in Robes* 140–86.

[73] Klare, 'Legal Culture and Transformative Constitutionalism'.

liberal legalism, but then, on his view, that understanding of the South African constitutional project was in any event to be rejected. Rather, the constitutional project had to be seen as a 'postliberal' project of fundamental political and social transformation.

The difficulty with this argument, as noted earlier, is that it overlooks the fact that the institutional form of the 1996 Constitution is essentially liberal-democratic. Had the Court embarked on such a strategy, therefore, it would have had little chance of carrying the legal profession and the broader political community with it. Klare's proposed strategy in effect amounted to the Court-driven transformation of South African legal-professional culture from the top to the bottom half of the two-dimensional matrix considered in Chapter 2. Although the US Supreme Court has been able to defend its independence from that half of the matrix for some time, the chances that the South African Constitutional Court, given the very different political context in which it was operating, would have been able to do so were slim. Indeed, with the exception of a single throwaway line,[74] Klare entirely ignores this factor. When the political context is factored in, the most likely result of the strategy he advocates would have been a precipitous descent into the bottom right-hand sector, with the Court condemned to engaging in ever more desperate strategies to defend itself from political attack.

For all these reasons, Klare's suggested strategy of wholesale legal-cultural transformation never constituted a realistic option for the Court. It would therefore be very surprising if we encountered any traces of it in the Court's record. The other two strategies were at least in theory available. Both were plausibly supported by the post-apartheid Constitutions and both were capable of providing the Court with the intellectual resources it required to refashion the law/politics distinction. The difficulty in this instance, however, was that neither strategy was more obviously preferable to the other. If the legal-cultural lag-effect argument has some force, the most likely trajectory followed by South African legal-professional culture was an incremental adjustment from low to high positivism, in which case the Court might have been better advised to work in support of that trajectory than against it. But there was no compelling argument either way, and thus the most likely scenario is that

---

[74] Ibid. 166 (reporting conversations with 'several distinguished South African lawyers' in which it was put to him that '[t]he fictions of politically and morally neutral adjudication and of the impersonal rule of law may be essential ideological underpinnings of forward progress toward democratic transition').

the Court did not develop any uniform strategy of wholesale legal-cultural transformation. Such a strategy, after all, would have required the judges to agree on the preferred approach. Absent a compelling strategic argument in favour of either a positivist or a natural-law conception of its institutional role, there is no reason to suspect that Justice Chaskalson or any of the other judges would have attempted to drive such an agreement. As elsewhere, conventions of judicial collegiality in South Africa generally leave such matters as a judge's jurisprudential philosophy to individual choice.

If this analysis is correct, our investigation of the Chaskalson Court's adjudicative practices in Part III is likely to reveal no uniform, Court-driven strategy of wholesale legal-cultural transformation. Rather, what we should expect to see are various passages in which either a high positivist or a natural-law conception of the Court's institutional role may be detected, together with sporadic appeals to the importance of the law/politics distinction. In the case of some judges, these appeals might pursue a consistent theme, making it possible to deduce the judge's particular view of law. In other instances, the appeals might be more ad hoc – driven more by the circumstances of the case than any apparent jurisprudential theory. In all cases, we should not expect to see any great philosophical sophistication. Rather, in keeping with the judges' backgrounds as practising lawyers and the reluctance of judges more or less everywhere to engage in grand theorising, we are likely to encounter at best the outlines of a possible defence of the Court's institutional role.

This does not mean, however, that we should not expect to detect other strategies aimed at managing the law/politics tension. From within whatever view of law each of them adopted, all of the judges would still have needed to respond to the post-apartheid Constitutions' injunction to engage in substantive reasoning, and to do so in a way that, on the one hand, would be accepted by the legal profession and, on the other, respected the constraints of the political environment in which the Court was operating. It is therefore reasonable to assume that the judges would have tried to develop a series of strategies for doing this – strategies that Chapter 2 suggested should be called 'adjudicative strategies' in order to capture the sense that they would have been pursued within and through the constraints imposed by law.

In some instances, we might imagine, these strategies would have been peculiar to particular rights in the Bill of Rights as individual judges and, over time, the Court as a collectivity developed an understanding of how best to give effect to the right. In cases like this, the strategy would be

indistinguishable from a doctrinal approach offered by the Court in the ordinary course of things as a legally legitimate interpretation of the Constitution. In other instances, the strategies would have been more cross-cutting – not confined to a particular right in the Bill of Rights but detectable across different areas of law as a recurrent device for managing the law/politics tension. In both instances, we should expect, the Court's attempt to put the law/politics distinction on a more secure footing would have drawn on resources already present in South African legal-professional culture, and particularly the oppositional tradition that had developed under apartheid. We should not discount the possibility, however, that, the Court might also have drawn on nominally external resources. Though paradoxical in some ways, the advantage of this kind of strategy is that it would have enabled the Court to refashion the law/politics distinction by appealing to hitherto untapped sources of authority. It is to this possibility that the next section turns.

5.2.4   The contingent impact: external factors

In just the same way as the development of South African legal-professional culture before 1994 had been shaped by broader social, political and economic processes, so would that culture's post-1994 trajectory have been influenced by factors nominally external to the legal system. For one, as we have seen, the Court was constrained politically. It therefore had to maintain some version of the law/politics distinction as a necessary condition of its independence. There were also other external factors, however, which – far from acting as constraints – may actually have assisted the Court in defining its institutional role. Two such factors in particular are worth exploring: (1) the increasing exposure of South African legal professionals to the global debate over human rights and constitutionalism; and (2) the simultaneous opening up of South African legal-professional culture to indigenous African attitudes to law. The significance of these factors is that they would have challenged South African legal-professional culture's sense of its own boundaries: the first because it involved the redefinition of the legal-professional community to include transnational actors, and the second because it promised to provide a way in which South African legal-professional culture could re-invigorate itself by incorporating the concerns of a section of the population that had hitherto been ignored.

As noted in Chapter 1, the Chaskalson Court's jurisprudence, particularly on socio-economic rights, is widely admired in the comparative constitutional law community. The very fact that we were able to use this community's views of the Court as an indicator of its success, however, suggests that the legal-professional community to which the Court was responding, and within which the legal legitimacy of its adjudicative practices was being assessed, was not restricted to South Africa. Whether or not it is sensible nowadays to talk about a national legal-professional culture in any setting,[75] the Court's judgments were read by a wide range of non-South Africans, including legal academics, judges, practitioners and human rights workers. The Court's legal-professional audience was a global one in this sense, and the views of these foreign commentators played an important role, not only in acculturating the judges to the sorts of reasoning methods that were required to give effect to the post-apartheid Constitutions, but also as a sounding board for the Court's initial attempts to work out its institutional role. Indeed, in many respects, foreign commentators, especially from North America, were a more influential audience than the local South African one. Many of them had played a role as advisors to one or the other of the political parties during the constitution-making process. Others had been frequent visitors to the country, including especially the participants in the series of Judges' Conferences organised by the Centre for Applied Legal Studies in the early 1990s. In turn, South African judges themselves travelled abroad, often drawing on connections and friendships that had been made years before.[76]

The precise influence of these interactions on the judges' understanding of their mandate is a matter of speculation. As we have seen in relation to Klare's intervention, not all the advice the Court received would, or should, have been followed. The point is simply that the globalisation of the Court's legal-professional audience would have emboldened the judges to challenge settled norms and practices while at the same time providing them with the intellectual resources they needed to translate South Africa's oppositional human rights tradition into adjudicative practice. In this sense, the exposure of South African legal-professional culture to global influence after 1994 must be seen as an opportunity. At the same time, however, the judges would have been eager to establish their legal-professional credentials in this broader community. If the capacity of law to limit the exercise of judicial discretion ultimately stems from judges' duty to give principled reasons for

[75] Cotterrell, 'Law and Culture – Inside and Beyond the Nation State'.
[76] See Section 5.3.

their decisions,[77] the judges' exposure to a foreign audience would also have operated as a constraint.

More or less in parallel with this process, the transition to democracy triggered rapid (although for some, not rapid enough) changes to the racial composition of the legal profession and the judiciary. From 1990 onwards, black South Africans increasingly took up senior positions in law firms, professional bodies, legal academe and the Bench. While subject in their turn to the powerful socialising effects of the existing mode of legal reasoning, it is reasonable to suppose that this new breed of legal professional would have brought a distinct set of attitudes to the practice of law, one more in keeping with traditional African notions of restorative justice, non-adversarialism and value syncretism. Understanding the process through which these culturally specific attitudes might have infiltrated and shaped existing legal-professional norms and practices would require a separate study of its own. The limited point for the moment is that this process would once again have presented the Court with an opportunity to challenge the dominant mode of legal reasoning and put the law/politics distinction on a more secure footing. The much debated concept of *ubuntu* would have been particularly important here, providing as it did a philosophical basis for the Court to respond to the post-apartheid Constitution's injunction to engage in substantive reasoning in a way that was authentically African.[78]

The impact on the Chaskalson Court's adjudicative practices of these two nominally external factors – its exposure, on the one hand, to global human rights discourse and, on the other, to indigenous attitudes to law – may be illustrated by means of two examples. Both take the form of possible cross-cutting strategies that the Chaskalson Court might have adopted to assist it in managing the law/politics tension.

The first such strategy would have been to place heavy reliance on foreign decisions, not just as guides to the interpretation of rights, but as forms of quasi-authority. The 1996 Constitution, of course, authorises reference to foreign law in the interpretation of the Bill of Rights.[79] In the comparative constitutional law literature, considerable effort has been devoted to justifying this practice as a form mutual learning, or

---

[77] See Chapter 1.
[78] For a collection of materials on this issue, see Drucilla Cornell and Nyoko Muvangua, *uBuntu and the Law: African Ideals and Postapartheid Jurisprudence* (Oxford University Press, 2012).
[79] Section 39(1)(c).

cross-pollination, between constitutional systems.[80] Much of this debate has taken place against the backdrop of the political backlash against reference to foreign law by the US Supreme Court.[81] In the case of a new constitutional democracy, however, reference to foreign law has the distinct advantage of injecting a familiar sense of the weight of past authority into otherwise alarmingly open-ended moral inquiries. In the South African case, in particular, it might have been advantageous for the Chaskalson Court to blur the distinction between reference to foreign law as a form of authority and the use of foreign law as a mere guide to interpretation. In the absence of a fully developed theory of judicial review, especially early on in a Court's life, extensive reference to foreign authority in this way would have provided the Court with the means to shore up the law/politics distinction until such time as the legal profession adjusted to the more substantive forms of reasoning required.

The second strategy relates to the possible use of *ubuntu* as a device to manage the transition to substantive reasoning. As noted earlier, judges the world over are loath to engage in grand theorising. Both their legal-professional socialisation and also a certain cautiousness about deciding more issues than need to be decided lies behind this.[82] The dialogical approach to judicial review also lends itself to provisional rather than all-encompassing statements of rights.[83] In South Africa, the added reason to eschew such all-encompassing statements is a cultural one. The harmony-seeking spirit of indigenous African philosophy, as exemplified in the central concept of *ubuntu*, tends to disfavour seeing such fundamental values as dignity, freedom and equality as incommensurable.[84] The Court's sensitivity to this issue may provide part of the explanation for its inclination, in its first year of decisions, to engage in what Alfred Cockrell memorably described as 'rainbow jurisprudence' – a tendency to downplay the hard choices between competing values that constitutional

---

[80] Cheryl Saunders, 'The Use and Misuse of Comparative Constitutional Law' (2006) 13 *Indiana Journal of Global Legal Studies* 37; Vicki C. Jackson *Constitutional Engagement in a Transnational Era* (Oxford University Press, 2010).

[81] See Sujit Choudhry, 'Migration as a New Metaphor in Comparative Constitutional Law' in Sujit Choudhry (ed.), *The Migration of Constitutional Ideas* (Cambridge University Press, 2006) 1.

[82] On this phenomenon in the United States, see Cass R. Sunstein, *One Case at a Time: Judicial Minimalism on the Supreme Court* (Cambridge, MA: Harvard University Press 1999).

[83] See references in note 71.   [84] See Cornell and Muvangua, *uBuntu and the Law*.

adjudication is typically thought, at least by those trained in Western analytic philosophy, to require.[85] Cockrell's argument was intended to highlight the Court's failure at that stage to make the necessary transition from formal to substantive reasoning, but there might have been more to the Court's approach than was initially apparent. At least, Cockrell's analysis suggests that it might be worth investigating whether the Court persisted in this mode of reasoning as a way of reconceptualising the law/politics distinction in non-Western terms.

5.3   The Chaskalson Court's judicial ethic

The transition to a system of rights-based judicial review, the previous section has argued, necessarily required the Court to reject the crude positivist view of law that had prevailed before 1994. But the Court could not entirely abandon the law/politics distinction that had for so long underpinned South African legal-professional culture. The liberal-democratic form of the post-apartheid Constitutions and the constraints of the political environment required the Court instead to refashion that distinction and put it on a more secure footing. There were several ways in which the Court might have done this, some of which would have found support from processes internal to the law itself and others from nominally extra-legal factors. In combination, these two sets of factors presented the Court with a range of options, none of which was legally preordained.

It would be wrong, however, to think of the judges as unconstrained by law when they began their work. Though the transition must inevitably have had a destabilising impact on settled norms and practices, the ideal of adjudication according to law in South African legal-professional culture remained intact. Indeed, if anything, that ideal had been strengthened by the role played by law in the transition. Both the contribution made by human rights lawyers to the demise of apartheid and the nature of the negotiated transition itself had demonstrated the worth of the oppositional tradition that had developed before 1994. According to that tradition, as we have seen, law has the capacity to act as a bulwark against the worst excesses of politics, either because it contains an inner morality that those seeking to use it for malign purposes must in the end respect, or because, in South Africa's case,

---

[85] Cockrell, 'Rainbow Jurisprudence'.

the equivalent moral principles happened to have been incorporated into the law as a matter of contingent social fact.

As human rights lawyers under apartheid, this section argues, the judges of the Court would have been influenced by this oppositional tradition. Indeed, the Court included some of its leading exponents. It is therefore reasonable to suppose that the judges would have been inclined to regard the transition to liberal constitutionalism as the triumph of the oppositional tradition over its discredited opponent. Conscious that apartheid had been overthrown by a range of forces, the judges would nevertheless have seen the adoption of the post-apartheid Constitutions as a conclusive vindication of their view of law. Their appointment to the Court would in turn have inclined them to regard the Court's mandate as an invitation of sorts to promote that view. As argued in Section 5.2.3, no particular choice between the natural-law or high positivist take on the oppositional tradition was required, nor a conscious strategy of wholesale legal-cultural transformation. Central to the judges' understanding of their mandate, however, would have been a determination to maintain some version of the law/politics distinction as a necessary condition of the Court's independence.

In pursuit of this argument, this section begins by describing the original composition of the Court and the legal-professional backgrounds and attitudes to law of the judges. In the case of the six judges interviewed by Judicial Service Commission ('JSC'), this task is greatly facilitated by the availability of the interview transcripts. The lengthy and sometimes quite testing interviews reveal much about how these six judges envisaged their role on the Court.[86] In the case of the five judges directly appointed to the Court by the President,[87] a range of other material, including the judges' published writings, is used. From among the particularity of the judges' individual views, the section then tries to build a picture of the common features of their legal-professional socialisation that might be said to have contributed to the Chaskalson Court's judicial ethic: a core set of attitudes about the nature of law and the judicial function that it is plausible to assume were shared by all the judges and which would consequently have informed the Court's adjudicative practices.

Of the eleven judges originally appointed to the Court, seven would have been classified 'white' under apartheid. Of these, two were

---

[86] The interviews are available on the Constitutional Court's website www.constitutional-court.org.za/site/judges/formerjudges.htm.

[87] The judicial appointments process was explained in Chapter 4.

Afrikaans-speaking (Laurie Ackermann and Johann Kriegler) and five English-speaking (Arthur Chaskalson, John Didcott, Richard Goldstone, Kate O'Regan, and Albie Sachs). Only three African judges were appointed: Pius Langa (later to become Deputy President of the Court and Chaskalson's successor as Chief Justice), Tholie Madala and Yvonne Mokgoro. The remaining judge, Deputy President Ismail Mahomed, was a third-generation Indian South African.[88]

These are remarkable figures. Barely six months after the transition to democracy, an ANC-controlled selection process saw the appointment of a majority of judges from the previously dominant white minority group to one of the most powerful institutions in the country. The political imperatives that drove this choice have already been discussed.[89] Here our concern is with the impact that the composition of the Court would have had on the judges' understanding of their role. On the one hand, we may suppose, the appointment of a majority of white judges to the Court would have strengthened all the judges' sense that they had been appointed on the basis of their backgrounds as human rights lawyers rather than on the grounds of race. This would have reinforced any inclination that they might have had to view law as a technical discipline separate from politics. On the other hand, all of the judges would have been painfully aware that the Court was not demographically representative, and that this would make their task of winning the public's confidence that much more difficult. As noted in Chapter 4, the possibility that a white-dominated Court would be seen as an institution dedicated to the preservation of minority-group privilege was real and had to be guarded against. It is reasonable to suppose that this would have made the judges highly sensitive to the need to respect the political branches' primary responsibility for the development of policy, which would once again have reinforced their sense of themselves as lawyers with a distinctly different function.

Chaskalson in particular would have been sensitive to these issues. In his thirty-eight years at the Johannesburg Bar he had built a formidable reputation as a human rights advocate, capable of persuading even the most hostile bench of the justice of his client's case. His method as an advocate was a combination of patient argument and absolute moral conviction. Undergirding this approach was a strong sense of the practice

---

[88] See Kenneth S. Broun, *Black Lawyers, White Courts: The Soul of South African Law* (Athens, OH: Ohio University Press, 2000) 39.
[89] See Chapter 4.

of law, and particularly advocacy, as an ethical calling requiring the highest standards of professionalism and integrity. Though implacably opposed to apartheid, he was not particularly politically active, and never joined the ANC, even after its unbanning in 1990.[90] Rather, Chaskalson sublimated his political views into his identity as a human rights lawyer. In 1978, this commitment was formalised with the foundation of the Legal Resources Centre ('LRC'), which he headed until 1993. In this capacity, Chaskalson was able to use his considerable leadership skills, not only to build a powerful public impact litigation firm, but also to make a difference to the way many South African lawyers conceived of their legal-professional calling and role in society.

As Chaskalson himself later remarked, the LRC was 'established at a propitious time ... [when] the ideology of apartheid was beginning to crumble' and the legal profession was searching for a new vision of law capable of carrying the country through the transition.[91] That vision, as Chaskalson saw it, was the idea of the common law as a repository of 'principles of freedom and justice' that could be used by activist lawyers to protect individual rights against encroachment by the state.[92] Of the two rival understandings of this idea, Chaskalson's own position was probably closer to the natural-law insistence on the inseparable link between law and morality. 'Implicit in modern attitudes to the rule of law', Chaskalson wrote, 'is that law should have a moral content that gives recognition to fundamental rights and freedoms. And it is through the enforcement of these fundamental rights and freedoms by the courts that the rule of law protects individuals and groups against abuses of power.'[93] But Chaskalson was no legal philosopher, and his published writings are less concerned about the jurisprudential classification of his views than they are with propounding an idea of law as an instrument for the protection of individual liberty and the advancement of social justice.[94]

The manner in which Chaskalson went about translating this idea into practice is one of the issues addressed in Part III. But we can get some sense of the challenges Chaskalson thought he was likely to confront from the JSC interviews. As one of the five judges directly appointed to the Court, Chaskalson was not himself interviewed. He was, however, a member of the JSC when it interviewed the applicants for the six

---

[90] Chaskalson was a member of the ANC Constitutional Committee, but served in an advisory capacity rather than as a member of the ANC.
[91] Chaskalson, 'The Past Ten Years'.   [92] Ibid. 295.   [93] Ibid. 297–8.   [94] Ibid. 300.

remaining places. Some of the questions Chaskalson asked the applicants are quite revealing about the concerns he had about the Court's future role. He asked Johann Kriegler, for example, whether he thought his background put him in a position to address the 'political' role of the court, 'not in the party political sense, but in the sense that it has to relate to society, to power struggles between different sectors of the government, between the relationship of powers and the balance of powers'. John Didcott was asked whether there were 'any ... objective values or objective standards one can extract from the Constitution ... or is there somewhere a building towards that which would avoid [the] dilemma [of the possible intrusion of judges' middle class values into the process of constitutional interpretation]?' Among a range of other questions about the role of the Human Rights Commission and the interpretation of the language clause in the Constitution, Chaskalson asked Pius Langa what he thought 'the public perception might be if a Constitutional Court overrules the decisions of a democratically elected Legislature'.

From these and other questions it is apparent that Chaskalson had a keen understanding of the challenges the Court would face. At the centre of this understanding was a concern that the Court might be perceived to be a political court, not just because its decisions would inevitably impact on policy, but also because its reasoning methods would be open to the charge of political bias. As interviewer rather than interviewee, Chaskalson was not required to offer his own answer to these questions, but there are indications, particularly in his exchange with Didcott, that he thought that the answer lay in the Constitution's express provision for the separation of powers and in the judges' capacity to develop reasoning methods that were sufficiently 'objective'. There is certainly no hint that Chaskalson was at all susceptible to the call Klare would later make for the Court to conceive of its mandate as an essentially political project to be pursued through essentially political means.

Chaskalson's Deputy, Ismail Mahomed, had had a similarly long and illustrious career at the Johannesburg Bar before going on, in 1991, after Mandela's release, to become the first non-white judge appointed to the Supreme Court. In Mahomed's case, his time at the Bar, at least initially, was characterised by a daily struggle against racial discrimination. For the first twelve years of his career as an advocate Mahomed thus did not have an office in the chambers in which he worked, his racial classification as an Indian preventing him from owning or even leasing land in the area in which the chambers were situated. Instead, Mahomed would move from borrowed office to borrowed office as his white colleagues went to and from court.[95] Despite this inconvenience, Mahomed built a thriving practice, including many cases under the very Group Areas Act that prevented him from occupying an office of his own. He was also actively involved in representing opponents of the apartheid regime, including one particularly prominent prosecution of the leadership of the United Democratic Front (the ANC's *de facto* internal wing) in 1985.[96]

As one of the four sitting judges directly appointed to the Court under s 99 of the 1993 Constitution, Mahomed was not interviewed by the JSC. His approach to legal practice, however, is apparent from the transcript of an in-depth interview conducted with him in the 1980s.[97] The transcript reveals Mahomed's frustrations with the limits of human rights lawyering in the face of determined repression, but also his delight on those occasions when he was able to exploit the equitable principles of Roman-Dutch common law to win his client's case. The particular case he mentions involved the prosecution of Ebrahim Ismail Ebrahim for various offences related to his former role as an ANC operative. Mahomed was able successfully to argue that the fact that Ebrahim had been seized outside of the country against his will triggered the 'clean hands' doctrine, making both his detention and his prosecution unlawful.[98]

Of the four other members of the Court who had served on the Bench before 1994, Laurie Ackermann stood out as the only apartheid-era judge to have resigned. At first blush, this might seem to suggest that Ackermann was given to grand political gestures. Careful analysis of his resignation letter, however, reveals a deeply principled man who was at pains to emphasise the highly personal nature of his choice.[99] Stressing his excitement about the possibilities of the chair in Human Rights Law that he had been offered by the University of Stellenbosch rather than any dilemmas he may have experienced as a judge under apartheid, Ackermann's letter is a masterful exercise in judicial tact. For Ackermann, it is clear, it was important not to use his resignation as a device to pressurise his fellow judges into doing something that might have gone against their own assessment of their duty. Subsequently, in his submission to the Truth and Reconciliation Commission's Legal Hearing, Ackermann indicated that he could not recall any judgment he had given whilst on the Bench 'the result of which would have been substantially

---

[95] Broun, *Black Lawyers, White Courts* 162–3.   [96] Ibid. 183.
[97] Ibid. 39–40, 61–4, 161–6, 182–91.   [98] Ibid. 189.
[99] The text of the letter is reprinted in Dyzenhaus, *Judging the Judges* 79.

different had [he] applied to it the deeper insights [he] now [had] regarding human rights and their implementation'.[100] Ackermann was thus not one of those liberal judges who saw his duty as being to exploit gaps in the law to keep open the space for human rights lawyering. Rather, he had a profound sense of the determinacy of law as a professional discipline, and therefore of the need to step outside the practice of law to make a contribution to the transition to a new constitutional order.

The other Afrikaner on the Court, Johann Kriegler, was in many ways Ackermann's polar opposite. Describing himself in his JSC interview as a 'maverick', Kriegler qualified several of his answers by distinguishing between those parts in which he was speaking as a lawyer and those parts in which he was speaking as a 'political animal'. When pressed by legal academic Etienne Mureinik to indicate whether he thought the Court's decisions would be political, not only in the sense of impacting on policy but also in the reasoning methods used, Kriegler replied:

> No, quite clearly it could never do its job if it thinks like a politician and frankly I have not come across a single really qualified judicial officer who has the ability to see round corners like politicians do. I have learnt, and I say this in all humility, I have learnt the extreme limitations of our logical process over the last ten months. We are babes in the wood in some respects and I would never like to double think politicians. The judicial role on this court must be a judicial role alert to political realities.

The reference in this extract to Kriegler's experience 'over the last ten months' was to his role as Chairman of the Independent Electoral Commission ('IEC'), which had managed South Africa's first democratic elections in 1994. Much of Kriegler's interview was taken up by strictly irrelevant questions about whether the Commission had been right to condone certain irregularities in the running of the elections, especially in KwaZulu-Natal. Mureinik once again asked the pertinent question, which was whether the global approach the IEC had taken to certifying the elections was an appropriate model for the Constitutional Court's approach to the certification of the final Constitution. Given that it would by definition enjoy the support of at least two thirds of the Constitutional Assembly, Mureinik wondered, 'how bad would . . . the final Constitution have to be to warrant non-certification?' Kriegler's answer demonstrated his confidence in his capacity as a lawyer to exercise an independent judgment, although his

---

[100] Laurie Ackermann, 'Submission to TRC Legal Hearing' (October 1997) 3 (quoted in Dyzenhaus, *Judging the Judges* 79).

combative personality also comes through. After giving due weight to the opinion of the people's representatives, Kriegler said, 'if ... I in my own conscience were satisfied that it was bad, it wouldn't have to be very bad, if it is bad I would say so and let the heavens fall.'

The remaining old-order judges, John Didcott and Richard Goldstone, had both been renowned exponents of the common-law approach to statutory interpretation. In Didcott's case, this had comprised twenty years as a judge on the Natal Provincial Division in which he had perfected the art of interpreting repressive statutes in favour of liberty. He was also famous for not once having handed down the death penalty, although at his JSC interview he was careful to say that this was merely because he had never been presented with a case in which the law conclusively required him to impose such a sentence. Goldstone's best-known decision as a judge of the Transvaal Provincial Division was that in *S v. Govender*,[101] where his ruling that magistrates were required to consider the availability of suitable alternative accommodation in Group Areas Act cases rendered the Act practically unenforceable. Goldstone was later appointed to head a commission to investigate allegations of 'third force' involvement in the violent clashes that had been occurring between ANC and IFP supporters in KwaZulu-Natal. His November 1992 report famously led to the dismissal by President F. W. De Klerk's of six senior military personnel.[102]

Tholie Madala had been appointed to the Eastern Cape Division of the Supreme Court after the transition to democracy in 1994, making him eligible for direct appointment to the Constitutional Court. A quiet and humble man, Madala was a reluctant judge, accepting his role on the Court as a required service to the nation, but never embracing it wholeheartedly. He wrote comparatively few judgments and was not an active participant in argument before the Court. He did, however, broadly share his colleagues' view of law, his most important career contribution having been the establishment of both the University of Natal (Pietermaritzburg) Law Clinic and the Umtata Law Clinic. Before that, he had been an articled clerk in an all-white, liberal law firm. His abiding memory of his time at the firm was the discomfort shown by white clients when learning that their case would be taken by a black man, but also the support he received from the white partners in turning these clients' around.[103]

---

[101] 1986 (3) SA 969 (T).   [102] See Sampson, *Mandela* 444.
[103] Broun, *Black Lawyers, White Courts* 148–9.

Pius Langa had probably had the most varied professional experience of all the judges appointed to the Court, having spent the first seventeen years of his career as a court interpreter/messenger and then magistrate. He joined the Durban Bar in 1977 and became Senior Counsel in 1994, just before his appointment. Langa's practice involved mostly human rights and labour law work, including political trials. In this capacity he had worked closely with attorneys Griffiths and Victoria Mxenge, who were later brutally murdered in separate incidents four years apart.[104] Langa was a founder member of the National Association of Democratic Lawyers and served in various UDF structures in the 1980s and early 1990s. He went on to become a member of the ANC Constitutional Committee and worked on its draft Bill of Rights. Langa's JSC interview concentrated on court administration matters, perhaps prefiguring his later appointment as Deputy President in August 1997 after Ismail Mahomed's departure. Asked whether his past involvement in the ANC would affect his judgment in cases involving the Government, Langa replied: 'I am a lawyer, it causes me no problems at all.'

The three remaining members of the Court had all had a mix of practical and academic experience. Yvonne Mokgoro, like Langa, had worked in the magistrates' court system, in her case as a public prosecutor in Mmbabatho. She had then moved on to a career as a law teacher at the University of Bophuthatswana, the University of the Western Cape and the University of Pretoria. Her decision to study law had been prompted by her unlawful arrest in 1974 after she had attempted to stop the police from detaining an innocent man.[105] Mokgoro's JSC interview focused on a paper she had written on lay participation in the judiciary as a means of re-legitimising it. She was also asked about her views on the relationship between the Constitution and customary law, including the practice of polygamy.

Kate O'Regan, after a brief spell as a labour law and land rights attorney in Johannesburg, had taught law at the University of Cape Town. Just thirty-seven when appointed to the Court, O'Regan's capacity for clear analytic thinking, for which she later became well known, were already apparent in her interview. Indeed, O'Regan was one of the few applicants interviewed who was able to articulate a workable theory of judicial review. In answer to a question by Chaskalson about the Court's counter-majoritarian function, O'Regan answered:

[104] Ibid. 169–71.   [105] Ibid. 132–5.

> Yes. I think that the function of judges in this context . . . is to try and seek
> to find the values that underlie the Constitution and to ensure that they
> structurally are committed or become part of the process and become an
> institution which ensures that the values and purposes which underlie the
> Constitution are brought to fruition rather than a body which should be
> seen immediately as in conflict directly with the legislature.

O'Regan's comparative-law knowledge was apparent in her discussion of the Canadian Supreme Court's watering down of the limitations test in *R v. Oakes*,[106] which O'Regan thought was 'unfortunate'. When Mureinik put to her the same question he had put to Kriegler about the Court's certification role, O'Regan was initially driven to answer that there might need to be two standards of review, one for detailed and another for more general constitutional principles. She then perceptively noted, however, that the real function of the certification process was to constrain the process of negotiations in the Constitutional Assembly itself. This led her to offer a more general comment about the nature of the power that constitutional courts wield in setting the boundaries for political contestation.

Albie Sachs's career as an advocate, legal academic and ANC political activist is well known. After ten years at the Cape Bar he was imprisoned and then exiled to London, where he completed a PhD and taught at the University of Southampton. In total, Sachs spent twenty-three years in exile, much of this in Mozambique, where he assisted the new democratic Government in rebuilding the legal system after 1975. Sachs' co-authored book on this experience reveals a predominantly socialistic approach to law,[107] but he later became central to the development of the ANC's hybrid human rights tradition, as described in Chapter 4. Two years before the Maputo bomb blast in which Sachs lost an arm and the use of one eye, he had joined Kader Asmal as one of the key members of the ANC's Constitutional Committee. His conversion to constitutionalism, Sachs explained at his JSC interview, had occurred during several trips to the United States, including a period of four months at Columbia Law School with Professor Jack Greenberg in the 1970s. Sachs's various books on human rights[108] reflect his developing understanding of the possibility

---

[106] [1986] 1 SCR 103.
[107] Albie Sachs and Gita Honwana Welsh, *Liberating the Law: Creating Popular Justice in Mozambique* (London: Zed Books, 1990).
[108] See Albie Sachs, *Protecting Human Rights in a New South Africa* (Oxford University Press, 1990); Albie Sachs, *Advancing Human Rights in South Africa* (Oxford University Press, 1992).

of a grand synthesis of the liberal and socialist human rights traditions, with the American Constitution as the 'great prototype', as he put it at his interview, but not the 'ideal model'. In his thinking in this respect, Sachs was influenced by Africanist notions of communitarianism, but at the same time disturbed by his experience of the foundering of Mozambique's revolutionary idealism on the rock of weak institutions.

As the most active and prominent member of the ANC applying for a position on the Court,[109] Sachs's JSC interview inevitably included some questions about whether his appointment would be vulnerable to the charge of partisanship. Wim Trengove and Etienne Mureinik, in particular, subjected Sachs to a searching interrogation in relation to his role in a four-member ANC commission of inquiry into the death of Thami Zulu, an MK commander who had died shortly after his release from detention by the ANC.[110] The questions focused on the fact that Sachs had not submitted a minority report, even though he had had certain misgivings about the rather mild criticisms made in the main report. For Trengove and Mureinik, this suggested a lack of independence of mind and a tendency to favour the interests of the ANC over points of principle. What could be expected of Sachs, they asked, when similar issues arose before the Court? Although Sachs clearly struggled with this line of questioning, the overall impression that comes through the transcript is that of a man who was politically committed to the liberation struggle for all the right reasons, who was prepared to make great sacrifices for a cause in which he believed, and who was flexible enough to develop his thinking when faced with contradictory facts. His detailed knowledge of a number of different constitutional systems and the intricate relationship between law and politics in those systems is also apparent. It was not unusual, Sachs correctly argued, for judges who had had high-profile political careers to be appointed to a constitutional court, and indeed there were certain advantages, both from a practical and from an institutional legitimacy point of view. The only issue in the end was whether the judge was capable of forming an independent opinion, free of partisan political bias.[111]

---

[109] Sachs was a member of the ANC's National Executive Committee.

[110] MK (Umkhonto we Sizwe) was the ANC's armed wing.

[111] Like the other judges who were members of the ANC at the time of their interview (Mokgoro, O'Regan and Langa), Sachs undertook to resign his membership of the ANC in the event of his appointment.

The most obvious common denominator between the judges, then, was a profound commitment to the value of human rights and constitutionalism. All of the judges, with the possible exception of Ackermann, had been adherents of the oppositional tradition identified by Ellmann and Dyzenhaus. Some of them (Didcott, Kriegler and Goldstone) had been among its leading exponents on the Bench, while others (Chaskalson, Langa, Madala, and Mahomed) had sustained the tradition through their practice at the Bar. Those who had been in legal academe (O'Regan, Sachs and Mokgoro) had focused on human rights and labour law issues. In Sachs's case, his commitment to human rights had resulted in his imprisonment, exile and attempted assassination. The black judges, as one would expect, had all had first-hand experience of law's instrumental deployment in the service of apartheid, but all had also committed themselves in their practice as lawyers to a nobler vision of law as a force for human emancipation and the advancement of social justice.

The underlying ideological basis for this commitment was fairly uniform. Most of the judges could thus be described as welfare liberals, with several holding deeply religious views that supported this political philosophy. Only Sachs could be described as a socialist, but his revolutionary idealism had been tempered somewhat by his experience in Mozambique. Sachs was also an outlier in terms of the level of his involvement in the struggle against apartheid. He was the only one of the judges who had been a high-ranking member of the ANC. The others had mostly lived out their opposition to apartheid through their practice as lawyers, although a few had been politically active in civil society organisations as well. In basic political outlook, then, the judges were clustered on the centre-left of the political spectrum, more or less in sync with the political ideology informing the 1996 Constitution's Bill of Rights. It follows that, to the external observer, there would have been no real distinction between the judges' personal political views and the values underlying the Constitution.

The judges themselves, however, would have vigorously resisted any suggestion that enforcing their personal political views is what they were required to do. All of them had been socialised in a legal-professional culture in which the distinction between law and politics was highly valued. More than this, they had been socialised in the oppositional tradition within that culture, which had rejected the crude positivist take on the law/politics distinction and substituted in its place a view of law as a form of anti-politics – as capable of acting both as a shield against repression and as an instrument of social justice. In the nature of things, very few of the judges had developed this view into a full-blown theory of adjudication by the time they were appointed. All were very conscious, however, that the deployment of human rights norms against an illegitimate Government was a very different matter from their enforcement in a democracy. They were aware, too, that the perceived legitimacy of their institutional role depended on their being able to sustain the public's faith in the impartiality of their adjudicative practices.

The approach that we should expect from a Court thus composed is a cautious one. In the absence of a uniform view of law underlying the oppositional human rights tradition, we should not expect the judges to have attempted a wholesale transformation of South African legal-professional culture. Klare's call for the judges to conceive of the 1996 Constitution as a post-liberal project of fundamental political and social transformation would have been particularly unappealing – not because the judges would not have viewed the 1996 Constitution as being committed to fundamental political and social transformation, but because they would have thought that the main drivers of this process should be the political branches. If the 1996 Constitution represented a political project at all, it would have appeared to the judges to be a project of liberal constitutionalism in which they had a vital, but in the end, only supporting role to play. Drawing on the oppositional tradition in which they had been socialised, the judges would have seen their role as being to nurture the development of a political culture of respect for judicial independence and the rule of law. The best approach to this task, they would likely have thought, would have been to sustain some version of the law/politics distinction, suitably stripped of the formalist reasoning methods to which they had been opposed as practising lawyers and which the post-apartheid Constitutions in any case plainly rejected. Just how the judges would have gone about this task could not have been predicted. All that might have been expected of a group of judges who had been so deeply involved in the opposition to apartheid was that they would try to develop an understanding of their mandate in a way that was open, on the one hand, to comparative-law influence and, on the other, to indigenous African attitudes to law.

PART III

Thematic Case Studies

Death, desire and discrimination: the Chaskalson Court between constitutional and positive morality

A rights-based constitution embodies a moral vision of society that judges must elaborate using methods acceptable to the legal profession and the broader political community. Although there is considerable disagreement about what this task entails,[1] it is clear that the constitution's morality is not the same thing as 'positive morality',[2] either in the form of traditional social values or public opinion. To be sure, positive morality will influence the choice of constitutional values at the time of the constitution's making. These constitutionalised moral values may thereafter inform public discussion about the desirability of particular legislative measures or executive conduct. In the end, however, the content of the constitution's morality in a system of supreme-law judicial review falls to be determined by the courts. Whatever the degree of popular control over the judicial appointments process, and however much professionally accepted methods of interpretation allow judges to give effect to the framers' intentions and widely held social views, there is likely to be some degree of divergence between the morality the judges impute to the constitution and positive morality in either form.[3]

In South Africa, where the Constitution was the product of a negotiated settlement between political parties whose bargaining power was

---

[1] See text accompanying notes 5–10.

[2] In the sense defined in H. L. A. Hart, *Law, Liberty and Morality* (Oxford University Press, 1962) 17–24.

[3] In cases where professionally accepted methods of constitutional interpretation stress the need to give effect to the framers' intentions (or the original meaning of the constitution), this type of divergence is an inevitable consequence of changing positive morality. In cases where professionally accepted interpretive methods allow judges to keep track of changing positive morality, divergence between constitutional and positive morality is a consequence of the lag-effect of precedent on the adjustment of constitutional morality to positive morality. Even those studies that stress the convergence of constitutional and positive morality over time (e.g. Dahl, 'Policy-making in a Democracy'; Friedman, *The Will of the People*) accept the fact of divergence in the short term.

disproportional to the extent of their public support,[4] the possibility of this kind of divergence was particularly real. As we have seen,[5] the political ideology informing the Bill of Rights in the 1996 Constitution, and to a lesser extent the 1993 Constitution as well, is extremely progressive. In part, this is attributable to the ANC's human rights tradition and its ability, as the dominant force in South African politics, to ensure that its views, particularly on socio-economic rights, were reflected. The progressivism of the post-apartheid Constitutions is also attributable, however, to the exiled ANC's involvement in the international human rights movement and the consequent global interest in South Africa's transition.[6] This aspect of the constitution-making process exposed it to influence, not just by Western liberal values, but by a particularly progressive conception of those values that few Western liberal democracies themselves have chosen constitutionally to endorse, and which was certainly to the left of prevailing public opinion in South Africa. The inclusion in the 1996 Constitution of a right to non-discrimination on the grounds of sexual orientation, for example, was probably not something that the gay and lesbian community in South Africa could have achieved had the constitution-making process not been open to external influence in this way. On other social issues as well, including the right to reproductive freedom and gender equality, the 1996 Constitution was significantly to the left of public opinion.

The progressivism of the post-apartheid Constitutions, and the (not altogether unfounded) attribution of this fact in the public mind to the influence of Western liberal values, posed significant problems for the Chaskalson Court. Over and above the regular challenge of enforcing constitutional morality against countervailing positive morality, the Court had to convince South Africans that the post-apartheid Constitutions' moral values were also *their* moral values: not some alien, neo-colonial imposition that had been the necessary price of an expedited transition, but values which South Africans themselves had freely chosen, or at least would have chosen even if the constitution-making process had not been fettered by the terms of the political agreement struck between the National Party and the ANC.

---

[4] This is true of both the 1993 and 1996 Constitutions: the 1993 Constitution because it was the product of the political agreement struck between the major parties involved in the MPNP, and the 1996 Constitution because its content was subject to conformance to the constitutional principles agreed to during the MPNP.
[5] Chapter 5.   [6] See Klug, *Constituting Democracy*.

In normative constitutional theory, there are three main views about how a constitutional court ought to go about enforcing the constitution's morality. On the first view, the court's proper role is to give effect to the intentions of the constitution's drafters – to remain faithful to their moral vision, however outdated and repugnant this may appear to be from the perspective of the present.[7] On the second view, associated with Ronald Dworkin's theory of 'constructive interpretation', the role of the court should be to interpret the constitution in a way that puts the text, past judicial decisions and the political community's practices in their 'best light'.[8] As Dworkin concedes, this view calls for Herculean judges capable of providing ever more complex theorisations of their community's constitutional tradition. The 'constructive interpretation' approach is therefore vulnerable to the charge of elitism – to the complaint that it promotes the rule of philosopher kings at the expense of the people's foundational right to self-government.[9] To overcome this objection, Wil Waluchow has recently offered a third view, one in which the court's role is conceived as being to vindicate constitutional morality using familiar common-law methods. In place of grand theorisations, Waluchow argues, constitutional courts need to work out their community's constitutional morality by the usual process of analogy drawing, distinction and the statement of general principles.[10]

In its case law on questions of conflicting constitutional and positive morality, this chapter argues, the Chaskalson Court did not do any of these things. Rather, the thread running through its three major decisions in this area is an attempt to draw a link between the post-apartheid Constitutions' moral vision and an idealised conception of positive morality, and in this way to enforce constitutional values as the embodiment of South Africans' higher moral aspirations. In S v. Makwanyane,[11] on the constitutionality of the death penalty, this approach was reflected

---

[7] There are three variants of this view depending on the extent to which the framers' subjective as opposed to objective or hypothetical intentions are emphasised. See Waluchow, *A Common Law Theory of Judicial Review* 56–65. For a defence of the original intent version of this view, see Antonin Scalia, 'Originalism: The Lesser Evil' (1989) 57 *University of Cincinnati Law Review* 849; Antonin Scalia, *A Matter of Interpretation* (Princeton University Press, 1996).

[8] See, for example, Dworkin, 'Law's Ambitions for Itself' 178; Dworkin, *Law's Empire* 52–3.

[9] Waldron, *Law and Disagreement*.

[10] Waluchow, *A Common Law Theory of Judicial Review*. But see Larry Alexander, 'Waluchow's Living Tree Constitutionalism' (2010) 29 *Law and Philosophy* 93, 98 (arguing that 'Waluchow's "constitutional morality" looks very much like Dworkin's legal principles').

[11] 1995 (3) SA 391 (CC), 1995 (6) BCLR 665 (CC) ('*Makwanyane*').

in the Court's creative use of the traditional African value of *ubuntu* as a way of indigenising the moral values at stake. *Makwanyane* also saw the Court confidently rejecting the content of public opinion as a determinant of constitutional meaning – an approach that the chapter argues was aimed at asserting its institutional role as a veto player in national politics, but which was at the same time crucially dependent on the ANC's capacity as a dominant political party to insulate the Court from political attack. In *Bhe* v. *Khayelitsha Magistrate*,[12] on the conformance of the rule of male primogeniture in African customary law to the right to gender equality, the Court vindicated constitutional values by suggesting that they were representative of the true egalitarian spirit of African customary law when stripped of the influence of colonialism. In the third case, *Minister of Home Affairs v. Fourie*,[13] on same-sex marriage, the Court was careful to vindicate the rights at issue in a way that gave the legislature a role in specifying the legal form that the Constitution's moral vision should take.

6.1   Abolishing the death penalty: *S.* v. *Makwanyane*

In 1995, shortly after the *Makwanyane* case was decided, nearly 75 per-cent of South Africans favoured the reintroduction of the death penalty.[14] Despite its use against opponents of the apartheid regime and clear evidence that it had been arbitrarily applied in ordinary criminal law matters, a significant majority of all population groups thought that the death penalty provided both a credible deterrent against violent crime and a fitting punishment for those convicted. These views were not, however, reflected in the 1993 Constitution. On the contrary, the 1993 Constitution contained a series of provisions that suggested that the continued imposition of the death penalty would run counter to its moral vision. Section 8 thus provided that 'every person shall have the right to equality before the law and to equal protection of the law' and s 9 that 'every person shall have the right to life'. Section 10 provided that 'every person shall have the right to respect for and protection of his or

---

[12] 2005 (1) SA 580 (CC), 2005 (1) BCLR 1 (CC).

[13] 2006 (3) BCLR 355 (CC), 2006 (1) SA 524 (CC). As noted in Chapter 3, this case falls just outside the time period of this study, but is included here because it demonstrates a general trend.

[14] Max du Plessis, 'Between Apology and Utopia – the Constitutional Court and Public Opinion' (2002) 18 *South African Journal on Human Rights* 1, 5–6.

her dignity', while s 11(2) prohibited 'cruel, inhuman or degrading punishment or treatment'.

Just how a constitution drafted in a country where the overwhelming majority of citizens supported the retention of the death penalty came to contain so many provisions that pointed the other way is an interesting question. As Justice Chaskalson's judgment in *Makwanyane* notes,[15] an attempt had been made during the constitutional negotiations process to leave the matter to democratic determination. The Sixth Report of the Technical Committee on Fundamental Rights thus reveals that an exception to the right to life was proposed that would have given the Constitutional Assembly the power to decide whether or not to abolish the death penalty.[16] The Seventh Report, however, rejected this idea and recommended instead that the right to life should be included in an unqualified form, thus leaving the matter open for decision by the Constitutional Court.[17]

Why did the ANC and the National Party not give their constituents what they so obviously wanted? The answer, it seems, lies in the ANC leadership's strong opposition to the death penalty and its capacity to withstand any pressure there might have been, either from the National Party or from within the ANC itself, to tilt the constitutional balance the other way. Mandela was central to this capacity. His biographer, Anthony Sampson, records that, during his speech at the opening of the Constitutional Court in February 1995, Mandela reminded his audience 'that the last time he had been in court he was finding out whether he would be sentenced to death'.[18] The symbolism was 'poignant' and Mandela's implication – that he personally was opposed to the death penalty – clear. Mandela himself, Sampson notes, would have preferred the question to have been decided by Parliament, but in the end 'Cabinet decided to send the question to the court'.[19] This is not entirely accurate. The *Makwanyane* case was referred to the Constitutional Court by the Appellate Division, seeking clarification on two issues then exclusively in the former's jurisdiction.[20] But the thrust of Sampson's point – that the ANC leadership had at some stage during the constitutional negotiations process decided to leave the abolition of the death penalty to the Constitutional Court – must surely be right. Only such a decision

[15] *Makwanyane* para 25.   [16] Ibid. n 33.   [17] Ibid.
[18] Sampson, *Mandela* 513.   [19] Ibid.   [20] *Makwanyane* para 3.

could explain the ANC's acquiescence in the unqualified formulation of the right to life.[21]

Whatever its position during the constitutional negotiations, by the time *Makwanyane* came to be decided the ANC's preference for abolition was openly expressed. The South African Government's counsel in the case, George Bizos, thus relayed to the Court that his instructions were to concede that the death penalty was 'a cruel, inhuman and degrading punishment' and therefore that it should be declared unconstitutional.[22] This concession would have been the end of any opposition to the order requested but for the fact that the state's interest in the case was represented, not by the Government, but by the Attorney General of the Witwatersrand, an independent official, who took a different view. Seizing on the 1993 Constitution's failure expressly to address the death penalty question, the Attorney General argued that the constitutional drafters' silence should be understood as an 'intention to leave the issue open to be dealt with by Parliament in the ordinary way'.[23] Given South Africans' well-known support for the retention of the death penalty, this argument implied, it was not for the Court to interpret the open-ended formulations in the Bill of Rights to the opposite effect.

What Chapter 3 referred to as the 'the micro-politics' of the *Makwanyane* case were thus clear. A decision against retention of the death penalty posed no immediate threat to the Court's independence in light of the ANC's stated support for this outcome. On the other hand, such a decision ran the risk of damaging the Court's public support at an early and therefore critical stage of its institutional life. In purely political terms, the choice facing the Court was one between founding its institutional independence on demonstrating its usefulness to the ANC, particularly to those leaders who had made their support for abolition clear, and founding its independence on building broad public support for its role. The success of the former strategy depended on the ANC leadership's capacity to insulate the Court from any adverse public reaction to its decision, and the success of the latter on the extent to which any increase in the Court's public support consequent on a decision to uphold the death penalty raised the costs to the ANC of attacking it.[24]

---

[21] See also Spitz with Chaskalson, *The Politics of Transition* 331 (noting that '[t]he ANC's wish for capital punishment to be abolished was well known, and is clearly stated in its draft Bill of Rights').

[22] *Makwanyane* para 11.   [23] Ibid.

[24] Whether a decision to retain the death penalty would have increased the Court's public support is a moot point. Given the 1993 Constitution's textual support for abolition, it is conceivable that such a decision, however much aligned with popular views, would have

The judges themselves, of course, would not have seen the case this way. Socialised as they were in the oppositional human rights tradition that had developed under apartheid, the judges would have seen their primary duty as being to render a principled decision that extrapolated the meaning of the 1993 Constitution through methods that could be defended as sufficiently objective and apolitical. At the same time, however, the judges would not have been insensitive to the politics of the case, and to the need to frame their decision in a way that promoted the Court's capacity to perform its institutional function over the long run. To some of them, this might have seemed no different from the sensitivity that liberal judges under apartheid had shown to the need to keep open the space for human rights lawyering. To others, the need to frame their decision in a way that promoted the Court's long-term institutional independence might have seemed like a logically entailed meta-principle of constitutional interpretation, one that the Court could legitimately take into account without abandoning its commitment to the ideal of adjudication according to law.

We cannot be sure precisely what considerations of this kind the judges took into account. By closely analysing their written opinions, however, we can get a fairly good idea of their conception of the Court's institutional role (or at least of the conception that they thought it prudent to promote), the justificatory standards they thought they were required to meet, the forms of authority to which they appealed, and ultimately the arguments they deployed to render a decision that responded to the demands of principle while yet remaining sensitive to the politics of the case.

The leading judgment in the case was delivered by Chaskalson himself and occupies just under half of the published record. Like the other judgments, it is structured around three main themes: (1) reference to foreign law as a substitute for substantive elaboration of the Constitution's moral value system; (2) rejection of the relevance of public opinion to the case as a way of asserting the Court's institutional role;

engendered scepticism in the public mind about the Court's commitment to law-governed decision-making, with knock-on effects for its institutional legitimacy. Equally, the causal link between the Court's decision in *Makwanyane* and its low public support has not been conclusively established. As pointed out in Section 6.4, the first survey of the Court's institutional legitimacy was conducted after the *Makwanyane* decision was handed down. While it is reasonable to suppose that this decision had some impact on the comparatively law public support rating found in that survey, there is no way of telling for certain in the absence of a pre-*Makwanyane* survey.

and (3) the use of *ubuntu* as a way of forging a link between constitutional and positive morality.

The judgment begins by addressing the legislative history behind the case. The significance of this issue, as we have seen, was that the multi-party negotiations process had not produced a clear agreement on whether or not to abolish the death penalty. In the absence of agreement, the Attorney General had argued, the Constitution should be understood to have left the abolition of the death penalty to Parliament to decide.[25] On the contrary, Justice Chaskalson held, the legislative history showed that it was the Court and not Parliament that had been mandated to decide this question.[26] In particular, what the Court was required to do was to interpret the most relevant constitutional provision, the prohibition against 'cruel, inhuman or degrading treatment or punishment', together with the rights to life, dignity and equality, in such a way as to give 'expression to the underlying values of the Constitution'.[27]

And thus, one might think, was the stage set for a substantive examination of the implications of the Constitution's moral vision for the question at hand. But this is not what happened. Instead, what follows in Justice Chaskalson's judgment is a very long, and largely question-begging, survey of death penalty decisions in international and foreign law.[28] The textual basis for this part of the judgment was the stipulation in s 35(1) of the 1993 Constitution, the predecessor to s 39(1) of the 1996 Constitution, that:

> In interpreting the provisions of [the Bill of Rights] a court of law shall promote the values which underlie an open and democratic society based on freedom and equality and shall, where applicable, have regard to public international law ... and may have regard to comparable foreign case law.

Though on the face of things a clear invitation to engage in substantive reasoning, Justice Chaskalson interprets this provision to mean something else – that the way to understand the values underlying the 1993 Constitution is to look at the case law of other open and democratic societies. Not just that, but in choosing which open and democratic societies to draw from, Justice Chaskalson does not, as one might expect, first develop a value-laden understanding of what an open and democratic society should look like. Rather, we are led without pause into

---

[25] *Makwanyane* para 11.   [26] Ibid. para 25.   [27] Ibid. para 9.
[28] Ibid. paras 33–86.

an examination of death penalty jurisprudence in the United States, Canada, Germany, Hungary, Europe as a whole, and India. Uncontroversial as this list of jurisdictions is, this way of proceeding entirely freed the Court of the need to engage in substantive reasoning, either directly, in considering what the values of freedom and equality might mean for the retention of the death penalty, or indirectly, in developing a normative standard to determine the choice of open and democratic societies for comparison. Instead, the arguments Justice Chaskalson proffers in his foreign-law survey are all of a strictly technical sort, such as what the effect on the relevance of a particular foreign decision might be of the fact that the right to life in the constitution concerned is qualified in some way,[29] and what judges in different jurisdictions have said about the inevitable arbitrariness of the procedures according to which some convicted persons are sentenced to death and others not.[30]

Justice Kriegler is at least typically forthright in his judgment, stating that, in interpreting what the Constitution says about the death penalty, 'the methods to be used are essentially legal, not moral or philosophical'.[31] In Justice Chaskalson's judgment there is no such admission. Instead, his foreign-law survey is explicitly offered as a response to the injunction to engage in substantive reasoning without ever actually doing so. After fifty or so paragraphs of exhaustive commentary, the survey ends with an aside about the European Court of Human Rights' decision in *Soering*.[32] No attempt is made to summarise the findings of the survey or to draw out any general principles. We are simply left to guess what the relevance of all of this comparative-law learning might be. When it eventually comes, several paragraphs later, the conclusion to this part of the judgment is asserted rather than reasoned through. Taking

---

[29] At paras 38 and 83 of his judgment, for example, Justice Chaskalson points out that the Hungarian Constitutional Court found the death penalty to be unconstitutional notwithstanding the fact that the rights to life and to human dignity in s 54 of the Hungarian Constitution are qualified by the stipulation that 'no one shall be arbitrarily deprived of these rights'.

[30] *Makwanyane* at paras 43–56.

[31] Ibid. para 207. Justice Kriegler goes on to say: 'To be true the judicial process cannot operate in an ethical vacuum. After all, concepts like "good faith", "unconscionable" or "reasonable" import value judgments into the daily grind of courts of law. And it would be foolish to deny that the judicial process, especially in the field of constitutional adjudication, calls for value judgments in which extra-legal considerations may loom large. Nevertheless, the starting point, the framework and the outcome of the exercise must be legal.'

[32] *Soering* v. *United Kingdom* (1989) 11 EHRR 439 (cited in *Makwanyane* para 86).

into account, Justice Chaskalson writes, the fact that 'the death sentence destroys life', 'annihilates human dignity', is prone to arbitrary enforcement and is 'irremediable', the 'death penalty is indeed a cruel, inhuman and degrading punishment'.[33] Of these four propositions, the first two and the last are tritely true, and the third is the only real point made in the foreign-law survey.

Justice Chaskalson's limitations clause analysis is similarly devoid of substantive moral reasoning, notwithstanding his recognition that 'the weighing up of competing values' is integral to the inquiry.[34] Foreign law is once again extensively relied on – not, however, to show what *values* courts in open and democratic societies have taken into account when assessing whether the death penalty might be justified, but to understand the *structure* of the limitations clause analysis.[35] When he finally arrives at the substance of the matter – the Attorney General's argument that the death penalty was justified for purposes of deterrence, prevention and retribution – Justice Chaskalson's approach is closer to that of an advocate in rebuttal than a moral philosopher.[36] Instead of an analysis of whether the death penalty is reasonable and justifiable in an open and democratic society based on freedom and equality, what we get is a series of logical refutations and case-not-proved arguments, as though it were sufficient to meet the Attorney General's argument on its own terms.[37]

These observations are not meant to suggest that Justice Chaskalson's judgment was legally incorrect. The purpose is rather to demonstrate that, despite the unambiguous invitation in the 1993 Constitution to consider moral values, and Justice Chaskalson's repeated assertion that substantive moral reasoning was what was required to resolve the case, he did not in fact engage in any. Just why this was so is a question worth answering, both for purposes of understanding the Chaskalson Court's achievement

---

[33] *Makwanyane* para 95.   [34] Ibid. para 104.

[35] Ibid. paras 105–9. The one exception, a reference to the Tanzanian Court of Appeal's judgment in *Mbushuu* v. *The Republic* (Tanzanian Court of Appeal, 30 January 1995), simply notes that the violation of the prohibition against cruel and degrading punishment in the Tanzanian Constitution was in that case found to be reasonable and necessary' (*Makwanyane* para 114).

[36] *Makwanyane* paras 116–31.

[37] Justice Chaskalson's response to the argument about the death penalty's role in the prevention of crime, for example, is a short paragraph arguing that life imprisonment is an adequate alternative for this purpose. Ibid. para 128.

and for what the answer might tell us about the capacity of constitutional courts in other parts of the world to enforce moral values.

Given his reputation as a judge, it is fair to assume that Justice Chaskalson's failure to engage in substantive reasoning was deliberate, and that his repeated assertions that the constitutional question could be answered only by considering the 1993 Constitution's underlying values were not inadvertent slip-ups but part of a conscious rhetorical strategy to assert the normative superiority of the constitutional value system. Indeed, one could go so far as to say that the normative superiority of the constitutional value system is the central premise of the judgment. It is just that the *content* of this value system is either taken to be obvious or asserted without argument. At crucial points in the judgment Justice Chaskalson thus simply assumes that we know what an open and democratic society based on freedom and equality looks like, what the appropriate inferences to be drawn from his foreign-law survey are, and what the moral arguments against the deterrence, prevention and retribution rationales for the death penalty must be.

That being so, the purpose of Justice Chaskalson's judgment, apart from the need to settle a pressing constitutional question, seems to have been to signal the significance of the transition from parliamentary supremacy to liberal constitutionalism. For this purpose, it was not necessary (and, in fact, potentially quite dangerous) for the Court actually to engage in substantive moral reasoning. Rather, the important thing was for the Court forcefully to make the point that henceforth controversial moral choices, like the decision whether or not to abolish the death penalty, would be settled by reference to the constitutional value system.

The key passage is one omitted from the discussion until now: Justice Chaskalson's treatment of the relevance of public opinion to the case. Interposed between his first foreign-law survey and the preliminary finding that the death penalty amounts to a cruel and inhuman punishment, the section in Justice Chaskalson's judgment about the relevance of 'contemporary attitudes within society'[38] is the fulcrum on which his entire judgment turns. 'Public opinion,' Justice Chaskalson writes, 'may have some relevance to the inquiry, but in itself, it is no substitute for the duty vested in the Courts to interpret the Constitution and to uphold its provisions without fear or favour.' He continues:

---

[38] Ibid. para 87.

If public opinion were to be decisive there would be no need for constitutional adjudication. The protection of rights could then be left to
Parliament, which has a mandate from the public, and is answerable to
the public for the way its mandate is exercised, but this would be a return
to parliamentary sovereignty, and a retreat from the new legal order
established by the 1993 Constitution.[39]

The distinction Justice Chaskalson is at pains to draw in this passage is
that between constitutional morality and positive morality in the form of
public opinion. Just as the Court would later do more explicitly in its
decision in *Carmichele*,[40] what Justice Chaskalson does in this part of his
judgment is to associate the constitutionally unmediated consideration of
social values with the discarded system of parliamentary sovereignty.
That will no longer do, Justice Chaskalson says. The very purpose of
having a supreme-law Constitution is to elevate constitutional values to a
position of normative superiority. Were that not so, there would be no
point in having a supreme-law Constitution and, more importantly, no
point in having a Constitutional Court.

What is really going on in *Makwanyane*, then, is not a failed exercise
in moral philosophy, but a largely successful exercise in judicial politics.
As far as the Court was concerned, the principled answer to the constitutional question was never in doubt. What was in doubt was the South
African public's willingness to accept it. To deal with that challenge, the
last thing the Court needed to do was to engage in abstract philosophis-
ing. Rather, the Court needed to legitimate its decision by using familiar
legal reasoning methods. And the best way of doing that, in turn, was to
bulk up the decision with foreign case citations, giving it the appearance
of a precedent-bound legal opinion when in fact the outcome was
determined by the Court's underlying premise.

A related strategy can be discerned in the third theme running through
the *Makwanyane* decision: the importance to the case of the indigenous
value of *ubuntu*. *Ubuntu*, as Justice Mokgoro points out, '[g]enerally . . .

---

[39] Ibid. para 88. For academic commentary on this passage, *see* Du Plessis, 'Between
Apology and Utopia' 2 (citing this passage in the context of an article explaining how
the Court has sought to educate the public through the use of critical morality); Myron
Zlotnick, 'The Death Penalty and Public Opinion' (1996) 12 *South African Journal on
Human Rights* 70, 73 (noting that Justice Chaskalson does concede that public opinion
might have 'some relevance to the inquiry', but pointing out that he does not in the end
indicate 'what weight is to be given to public opinion').

[40] *Carmichele* v. *Minister of Safety and Security* 2001 (4) SA 938 (CC), 2001 (10) BCLR
995 (CC).

translates as *humaneness*'.[41] It connotes the essentially communitarian value of experiencing and expressing one's humanity in relation to others, and includes such values as compassion, human dignity, and group solidarity. It was therefore clear that *ubuntu* was a potentially powerful value that could be enlisted in support of the abolition of the death penalty. The difficulty for the Court, however, was that the term *ubuntu* was used in a very specific context in the 1993 Constitution, viz., in the epilogue, which dealt with the need for national reconciliation and authorised the creation of what later became known as the Truth and Reconciliation Commission. *Ubuntu* was not listed as a founding value or expressly mentioned in the Bill of Rights.[42] The further difficulty was that *ubuntu* is both a living social value, in the sense that it is part of many indigenous South Africans' personal moral code, and also an idealised social value, in as much as it is talked and written about in African moral philosophy.[43]

One of the truly remarkable things about the *Makwanyane* decision is the skill with which the Court turned these two difficulties to its advantage. Having rejected the relevance of public opinion to the case, the Court needed somehow to make its decision more acceptable to the South African public by forging another kind of link between constitutional values and social values, one more compatible with its institutional function. *Ubuntu* was ideally suited to this task. The fact that it was listed in the epilogue meant that there was at least a textual basis, however precarious, to suggest that *ubuntu* was a cross-cutting constitutional value relevant to the interpretation of the entire Bill of Rights.[44] With *ubuntu* absorbed into the heart of the constitutional value system in this way, the remaining step for the Court was to connect *ubuntu* to social values without contradicting its arguments about public opinion. Here, the dual nature of *ubuntu* as a living social value and as an idealised social value made things relatively easy for the Court. What all six of the judgments that mention *ubuntu* do is to characterise it as an aspirational

---

[41] *Makwanyane* para 308.

[42] It is also not mentioned anywhere in the 1996 Constitution.

[43] See Drucilla Cornell, 'A Call for a More Nuanced Constitutional Jurisprudence: Ubuntu, Dignity and Reconciliation' (2004) 19 *SA Publiekreg/Public Law* 661.

[44] See *Makwanyane* para 224 (per Justice Langa, asserting without argument that *ubuntu* 'is of some relevance to the values we need to uphold'), para 237 (per Justice Madala, arguing that the concept of *ubuntu* 'permeates the Constitution generally'), para 303 (per Justice Mokgoro, arguing that *ubuntu* and its associated values 'underlie . . . the whole idea of adopting a Bill of Fundamental Rights and freedoms in a new legal order').

value – a value residing in South Africans' higher moral selves, whether or not lived out in practice.[45] In this way the *Makwanyane* judgments draw a clear line between the fact of South Africans' preference for the death penalty and the constitutionally required abolition of this form of punishment. 'This is what you would choose to do,' the Court in effect says, 'if you were truly living out the value of *ubuntu*. And it is our duty as constitutional judges to help you to see that.'

In this way, the Court – without doing any substantive reasoning – succeeds in justifying its decision by reference to the moral superiority of the Constitution. The thinnest of legal pretexts, the single mention of *ubuntu* in the epilogue, is used to associate the constitutional value system with a set of ideas whose incompatibility with the death penalty the Court could simply assert. The beauty of this solution was that the Court was able to do this without contradicting its earlier rejection of public opinion. As an indigenous value, *ubuntu* also provided the Court with an important opportunity to legitimate the constitutional value system as authentically South African.

In the next case to be discussed, *Bhe*, the constitutional value system and indigenous social values in the form of customary law were in direct conflict, and the tactic used in *Makwanyane* was therefore unavailable. Nevertheless, as we shall see, the Court found a way of enforcing the constitutional value system against indigenous social values without simply asserting the moral superiority of Western liberal values. The common feature of the two decisions is the Court's ability to give indigenous social values an ideal inflection, and thereby to associate the constitutional value system with South Africans' higher moral aspirations.

6.2   Customary law and the right to equality: *Bhe*

The *Bhe* case[46] concerned a combined challenge to s 23 of the Black Administration Act 38 of 1927 and the principle of male primogeniture in the African customary law of succession. As its name suggests, the

---

[45] See, for example, Justice Langa's statement that *ubuntu* has 'always been mentioned in the context of it being something to be desired, a commendable attribute which the nation should strive for' (para 227), and Justice Mokgoro's notion that *ubuntu* is a 'shared social value' that cuts 'across cultural lines' and is therefore capable of healing social divisions (para 307).

[46] 2005 (1) SA 580 (CC).

Black Administration Act was part of the elaborate apartheid legal framework in terms of which Africans were subjected to separate, unequal and largely administrative rule. Section 23 provided that 'movable property belonging to a Black . . . shall upon his death devolve and be administered under Black law and custom', and that immovable property should devolve 'upon one male person' as determined by regulation. This provision, establishing as it did a separate and unequal legal regime for the administration of African estates, was clearly incompatible with the 1996 Constitution. The fact that, ten years after the transition to democracy, the provision was still on the statute books was attributable to the administrative difficulties involved in unifying the system for intestate succession.[47] That it came to be challenged at all had less to do with the racially discriminatory nature of s 23 than with the fact that this provision kept alive a system of customary law succession that was alleged to be both sexist and discriminatory against illegitimate children.

Understood in this way, the awkwardness of the *Bhe* case for the Court was that it pitched the constitutional value of equality squarely against the cultural traditions and underlying social values of the majority of South Africa's population. Although battered by years of colonial manipulation and more recently by the forces of modernisation, African customary law is still adhered to by more than half of South Africa's population, either formally as the governing system of private law in the former Bantustans, or informally, as a social value system influencing such issues as the payment of a bride price (*lobolo*) and the choice of burial place for a deceased relative. By challenging aspects of these rules as sexist and discriminatory, the applicants in the *Bhe* case were essentially asking the Court to enforce the constitutional value system against the moral guidelines according to which most South Africans still make important life decisions.

Though less elaborate than the strategy used in *Makwanyane*, the Court's response to this challenge is equally instructive about its capacity to enforce constitutional values against countervailing positive morality. Instead of using *ubuntu*, what the Court in *Bhe* does is to distinguish between an ossified, discredited version of African customary law and a more vibrant, living customary law, and then to use the constitutional value system to vindicate the latter at the expense of the former. To

---

[47] The issues are discussed in *Moseneke* v. *Master of the High Court* 2001 (2) SA 18 (CC), in which the Court struck down part of s 23 but not all of it. The Black Administration Act was finally repealed in 2005.

explain this point properly it is necessary first to explain the constitutional status of African customary law, and how the system operates in practice.

Section 39(2) of the 1992 Constitution, as we have seen,[48] provides that, when interpreting legislation and when developing the common law, courts must 'promote the spirit, purport and object of the Bill of Rights'. This provision applies equally to the development of customary law, and thus subjects the content of evolving customary-law practices to the normative superiority of the Constitution.[49] The difficulty, however, is how exactly to understand the trumping role of the Constitution in relation to customary-law practices. It is one thing for a Court, through a system of precedent, to declare a particular rule no longer to be part of the written law, and another for a Court to declare cultural practices, constitutionally recognised as customary law, to be incompatible with the Constitution. In the first case, the Court's order has immediate social effect, since no judge, lawyer or administrative official would likely ignore the decision for fear of damaging their professional reputation. In the case of a customary law rule, however, the decision is unlikely to be as well communicated to the traditional leaders whose responsibility it is to enforce the law. Since the content of customary law is whatever the lived cultural practices amount to, this means that the Court's capacity to influence customary law is much diminished.

Adding further complexity to the *Bhe* case was the fact that, in addition to being a living system of law, customary law in South Africa is also partly codified and partly contained in the decisions of the former Native Courts – a separate court system set up under colonial rule to settle disputes emanating from the 'tribal areas', where customary law was the main system of private law. Although the Native Court system is about to be comprehensively overhauled,[50] there is still a residual tension between *living* customary law, the content of which is determined by reference to social practices, and *official* customary law, the content of which is determined by statute and past judicial decisions. The challenge in *Bhe* to s 23 of the Black Administration Act brought this tension to a head because, as noted, this provision makes the devolution of *movable*

---

[48] Chapter 5.

[49] Section 211 of the 1996 Constitution further provides that '[t]he institution, status and role of traditional leadership, according to customary law, are recognised, subject to the Constitution'.

[50] See the Traditional Courts Bill (B15–2008).

property dependent on custom, but the devolution of *immovable* property dependent on an order of succession prescribed by regulation.

In much the same way as it used the ambiguous constitutional status of *ubuntu* in *Makwanyane*, the Court in *Bhe* exploits this tension to resolve the case. Having played up 'the positive aspects of customary law' earlier on in its judgment,[51] the Court quickly strikes down s 23 as being obviously unconstitutional against the equality clause.[52] It then moves on to the more awkward attack on the principle of male primogeniture in the customary law of succession.[53] Noting that the male heir does not so much succeed to the assets of the deceased head of household as step into his shoes, the Court stresses that the heir's inheritance rights are subject to a 'duty to maintain and support all the members of the family'.[54] In its pre-colonial setting, the Court observes, this system was therefore not obviously disrespectful of women, because they could at least be assured that their needs would be provided for. It was nevertheless patriarchal because women were prevented from becoming heirs and regarded as 'perpetual minors under the tutelage of [their] fathers, husbands, or the head of the extended family'.[55]

Significantly, the Court does not stop at this point to express a view on whether the pre-colonial system of customary law succession would have been found to be unconstitutional against the equality clause, had it survived. Instead, the Court presses on to describe how the pre-colonial system has been 'distorted'[56] by the twin forces of colonialism and modernisation. The former, the Court says, has resulted in the ossification of customary law in statutes and decisions of the Native Courts.[57] The latter has caused the break-up of the extended family system in which the male heir's duty to maintain and support a wide array of dependants at least off-set some of the harsher consequences of the patriarchal system.[58] In the meantime, living customary law, unrecognised until the advent of the new constitutional order, has been developing, sometimes so as to recognise the widow's right to inherit.[59] The constitutional problem, the Court therefore concludes, is not that living customary law is insensitive to changed social circumstances, but that official customary law is still being enforced by magistrates under the Black Administration Act.[60]

---

[51] *Bhe* para 45.   [52] Ibid. paras 60–74.   [53] Ibid. para 75ff.   [54] Ibid. para 76.
[55] Ibid. para 78.   [56] Ibid. para 89.   [57] Ibid. paras 72 and 86.
[58] Ibid. para 80.   [59] Ibid. para 85.   [60] Ibid. para 97.

It should by now be clear what the Court's strategy in *Bhe* was: to associate the constitutional value of equality with the modernising tendency of living customary law, and in this way to reserve constitutional censure for the already discredited colonial system of customary law. As a social fact, of course, customary practices in South Africa were at the time of the judgment still gender-based, and the examples the Court offers of widows inheriting property tended to be more common in urban than rural areas. Nevertheless, there was just enough evidence on the record for the Court to be able to say that the trajectory of living customary law was in the direction of the constitutionally required position, and therefore what it was declaring to be unconstitutional was not South Africans' actual social values but the ossified system of customary law that had been foisted on them by colonial rule.

6.3   Same-sex marriage: *Fourie*

The *Fourie* case came to the Constitutional Court by means of a convoluted route that need not be explained, save to say that the case as argued before the Court combined two questions: (1) whether the common-law definition of marriage should be developed so as to include same-sex couples; and (2) whether the standard marriage vow in s 30(1) of the Marriage Act 25 of 1961 unfairly discriminated against same-sex couples through its use of the words 'husband' and 'wife'.

In the seven years preceding *Fourie*, the Court had heard an impressive array of sexual orientation cases under the 1996 Constitution's equality clause, on topics ranging from the criminalisation of sodomy,[61] immigration rights of same-sex partners,[62] judicial pension benefits,[63] and adoption rights.[64] All of these cases had been decided in favour of the gay and lesbian constitutional complainants. There was thus very little doubt about where the weight of constitutional authority lay in *Fourie*. In any case, in papers before the Court, the state had conceded that the legal framework for the regulation of marriage was constitutionally

---

[61] *National Coalition for Gay and Lesbian Equality* v. *Minister of Justice* 1999 (1) SA 6 (CC), 1998 (12) BCLR 1517 (CC).

[62] *National Coalition for Gay and Lesbian Equality* v. *Minister of Home Affairs* 2000 (2) SA 1 (CC), 2000 (1) BCLR 39 (CC).

[63] *Satchwell* v. *President of the Republic of South Africa* 2002 (6) SA 1 (CC), 2002 (9) BCLR 986 (CC).

[64] *Du Toit* v. *Minister of Welfare and Population Development* 2003 (2) SA 198 (CC), 2002 (10) BCLR 1006 (CC).

indefensible. The only real issue of substance before the Court was whether the constitutional problem lay in the exclusion of gays and lesbians from the institution of marriage, or in the fact that the law denied them the legal benefits of marriage through other means. The further, remedial question was whether the Court, if it found the legal framework for the regulation of marriage to be unconstitutional, should attempt to cure the constitutional defect itself, or instead issue a declaratory order, leaving the amendment of the marriage laws to Parliament.

These two issues brought constitutional morality into conflict with public morality in two different ways. The first type of conflict was between constitutional morality and religious beliefs about the sanctity of heterosexual marriage, which are constitutionally protected in s 15 of the 1996 Constitution.[65] The second type of conflict was more akin to that in *Makwanyane* between a constitutional value – in this case, the value of equality – and public opinion. Despite its now very affirming legal framework for gay and lesbian people, South Africa is a deeply homophobic place, with the President, Jacob Zuma, having openly expressed his disdain for homosexuals,[66] and lesbian women in the townships frighteningly vulnerable to being gang-raped and murdered.[67]

Justice Sachs, writing for all but one of the members of the *Fourie* Court, moved very quickly to a finding that the legal framework for marriage in South Africa was unconstitutional against the equality clause, and therefore that the constitutional claimants were entitled, at the very least, to a declaratory order that their rights had been violated.[68] This did not mean, however, that the institution of heterosexual marriage was unconstitutional. To answer that question, Justice Sachs held, attention had to be paid to the state's argument that the constitutional defect could be cured by developing an alternative institution – either for same-sex couples alone, or for same-sex couples and heterosexual couples – that would confer the same legal benefits as heterosexual marriage.[69]

---

[65] Section 15(1) reads: 'Everyone has the right to freedom of conscience, religion, thought, belief and opinion.'

[66] At a public rally in KwaZulu-Natal in September 2006, Zuma was reported as saying: 'When I was growing up an *ungqingili* [a gay person] would not have stood in front of me. I would knock him out.' He was also quoted as saying that same-sex marriages were 'a disgrace to the nation and to God.' He later apologised for these remarks.

[67] In one of the more prominent such cases, a former member of the South African women's football team was gang-raped and murdered in Johannesburg.

[68] *Fourie* paras 75–9.   [69] Ibid. para 80.

The main argument in support of the alternative option was that this was the only solution that would respect both gay and lesbian people's equality rights and the right to religious freedom.[70] Opening up the institution of heterosexual marriage to same-sex partners, it was contended, would violate religious believers' views that heterosexual marriage was a sacred institution endowed by God for purposes of procreation.[71]

Justice Sachs began his response to this argument by carefully distinguishing religious opposition to same-sex marriage from mere 'bigotry'.[72] As Justice Ackermann had done in an earlier decision on gay and lesbian rights,[73] Justice Sachs stressed that the constitutional question had to be decided on the assumption that it was possible sincerely to believe that same-sex marriage was morally wrong. Nevertheless, he held, there is a crucial difference between recognising the sincerity of religious views about the morality of same-sex marriage and equating the constitutional value system with a particular religious value system. 'It is one thing,' Justice Sachs wrote, 'for the Court to acknowledge the important role that religion plays in our public life. It is quite another to use religious doctrine as a source for interpreting the Constitution. It would be out of order to employ the religious sentiments of some as a guide to the constitutional rights of others.'[74] Section 31 of the Marriage Act, Justice Sachs continued, already provided that marriage officers who were ministers of religion did not have to solemnise marriages that did not conform to the tenets of their religion.[75] This was a constitutionally acceptable way of resolving the conflict between the constitutional value of equality and religious freedom rights.[76]

Justice Sachs's judgment in this way follows the approach taken to same-sex marriage in the Netherlands, Belgium, Spain and Canada, viz. that respect for difference requires the state to refrain from denying, not just the legal benefits of marriage, but also the symbolically important institution of marriage, to same-sex couples.[77] In so doing, Justice Sachs's judgment illustrates an important distinction between constitutional values and religious values, at least in secular states. Where the

---

[70] Ibid. paras 88–98.   [71] Ibid.   [72] Ibid. para 91.

[73] *National Coalition for Gay and Lesbian Equality* v. *Minister of Justice* 1999 (1) SA 6 (CC), 1998 (12) BCLR 1517 (CC).

[74] *Fourie* para 92.   [75] Ibid. para 97.   [76] Ibid. para 98.

[77] See David Bilchitz and Melanie Judge 'For Whom Does the Bell Toll? The Challenges and Possibilities of the Civil Union Act for Family Law in South Africa' (2007) 23 *South African Journal on Human Rights* 466, 467 n 3.

Constitution is not itself understood to be the expression of a particular religious value system,[78] the role of the Constitution is to mediate between competing religious and non-religious value systems. Although certain constitutional values, such as respect for human dignity, may correspond with the values underlying a number of different religions and world views – indeed may be the common denominator between these religions and world views – a constitution of this type, in protecting the freedom of religion, does not necessarily endorse all the values in the religions it protects. Rather, what a secular liberal constitution does is to allow a number of different religious value systems and non-religious value systems to co-exist. This does not mean, however, that the constitution is value-neutral. If there is an overarching value in secular liberal constitutions, it is the value of tolerance and respect for difference. In effect this means that the constitutional value system trumps religious value systems to the extent that those systems would impose their values on others.

The second issue in *Fourie*, it will be recalled, was the question whether, having found the institution of heterosexual marriage to be incompatible with the constitutional value of equality, the Court should itself move to amend the marriage laws, or whether this should be left to Parliament to do. In relation to this issue, what concerned the Court was not respect for religious freedom but respect for the separation of powers. Whether sincerely held or simply the product of prejudice,[79] the Court accepted for purposes of its decision that South Africans' views on same-sex marriage were not consonant with the Constitution's moral vision. Was it then advisable for the Court simply to trump those views, as it clearly had the power to do, or should it defer to Parliament in some way? And if it deferred to Parliament, would that amount to an impermissible abdication of its role in enforcing constitutional morality?

Once again, Justice Sachs finds an ingenious solution to this problem. Recognising that the Court had the power to read the word 'spouse' into the marriage vow in the Marriage Act to bring it 'into line with constitutional values',[80] Justice Sachs nevertheless counsels caution, arguing that the 'precise circumstances of each case' must be looked at before 'determining how best the values of the Constitution can be promoted by

---

[78] As, for example, is the case in the Republic of Ireland.

[79] The Court used the word 'prejudice' to describe social attitudes to same-sex marriage in South Africa on several occasions. See, for example, *Fourie* paras 74 and 113.

[80] Ibid. para 123.

an order that is just and equitable'.[81] In cases of this nature, he continues, where the public is deeply divided over an issue of 'status', it is important that the constitutional remedy be 'secure'.[82] Although the complainants had won their case, and were therefore entitled to immediate relief, any such order would be vulnerable to the charge that it represented the Court's views and not the people's. In the long run, this would not secure the complainants' rights and the rights of other gays and lesbians who wanted to marry. The better solution, therefore, was to enlist the support of the legislature, which was equally responsible for promoting the Constitution's moral vision,[83] in effecting the change to the marriage laws. So as to ensure that the complainants' rights were indeed properly vindicated, and lest the Court be seen to be abdicating its function as primary constitutional interpreter, Justice Sachs added, the Court should provide guidelines about what the constitutionally permissible options for amending the marriage laws were, as well as a deadline for the completion of the legislature's work, failing which the default solution of reading the words 'or spouse' into the Marriage Act would take effect.

The genius of Justice Sachs's solution lies in the way it balances the Court's duty to enforce the constitutional value system against the danger of political backlash.[84] Indeed, Justice Sachs's judgment in *Fourie* is openly strategic about the need to weigh the advantages and disadvantages of immediate enforcement of the complainants' rights. Against Justice O'Regan's argument in dissent that the Court's legitimacy depends on its being seen to be a forum of principle, and thus that there is no choice but to amend the Marriage Act with immediate effect,[85] Justice Sachs considers the likely consequences of such a decision, and concludes that the complainants' interests will be better protected if the constitutionally required change to the marriage laws were made democratically, albeit within the confines of the Court's constitutional guidelines. The Constitution's moral vision, on this approach, is not something that can simply be imposed on the public by an assertion of judicial authority, but something that has to be strategically inserted into the political process – the ultimate goal being to embed the constitutionally required outcome in some kind of democratic consensus.

---

[81] Ibid. para 135.　　[82] Ibid. para 136.　　[83] Ibid. para 138.

[84] For a similar use of this term in this context, see Post and Siegel 'Roe Rage: Democratic Constitutionalism and Backlash'.

[85] *Fourie* para 170.

6.4 Identifying the strategy

All three cases discussed in this chapter required the Chaskalson Court to mediate between conflicting constitutional and social norms: in *Makwanyane*, the 1993 Constitution's commitment to a range of rights that favoured the abolition of the death penalty put it at odds with prevailing public opinion; in *Bhe*, African customary law's denial of women's right to succeed to a deceased estate was inconsistent with the 1996 Constitution's commitment to gender equality, but nevertheless represented a social value system to which many South Africans still owe their allegiance; and in *Fourie*, the 1996 Constitution's right not to be discriminated against on the grounds of sexual orientation conflicted both with sincerely held religious beliefs and also with prejudicial social attitudes. In all three cases, the constitutionally required outcome was not seriously in dispute. The real challenge facing the Court was how to enforce the Constitution's moral vision without alienating a significant section of the South African public.

The Court responded to this challenge in a slightly different way in each case: in *Makwanyane* by elevating *ubuntu* to the status of an overarching constitutional value; in *Bhe* by equating the 1996 Constitution's moral vision with the position towards which African customary law would in any case have developed had its progress not been interrupted by colonial rule; and in *Fourie* by elaborating the point of constitutional principle but leaving the precise legal form of the Constitution's moral vision to democratic determination. Over and above these differences, however, it is possible to discern certain common features of the Court's handling of these cases that collectively amount to what earlier chapters have referred to as an adjudicative strategy: an approach to the fulfilment of the Court's mandate that attempted to reconcile the judges' commitment to the ideal of adjudication according to law with the need to take account of the long-term impact of the decision on the Court's independence.

The adjudicative strategy the Court pursued in these cases does not conform exactly to any of the three main prescriptions in normative constitutional theory about how a constitutional court ought to go about enforcing the constitution's morality. Instead of appealing to the framers' intentions or developing a political theory of the constitution's morality, the Court's approach in all three cases was to forge a link between the constitution's morality and an idealised conception of positive morality, and in this way to suggest that its decision corresponded to the outcome that South Africans themselves would have chosen had they been acting in accordance with their highest moral aspirations. While the conception of positive morality thus invoked is similar to Waluchow's notion of the community's constitutional morality ('its *true* moral commitments in reflective equilibrium'[86]), the Court vindicated this conception, not by using conventional common-law methods, but by creatively using the transition to a new constitutional order to redefine the boundaries of permissible legal argument.

Thus, in *Makwanyane*, the Court deployed *ubuntu* as an overarching constitutional value, even though the plain meaning of the constitutional text suggested that the legal relevance of this term was restricted to the national reconciliation process; and in *Bhe*, the Court made extensive use of an historical narrative in a way that would probably not have been regarded as legitimate before 1994. In *Fourie*, the majority's decision invoked constitutional principle directly, and made greater use of substantive moral reasoning than in the other two cases. Here, the link between constitutional morality and an idealised conception of positive morality was drawn, not through the argument on the merits, but through the trust that the majority's remedial order placed in South Africans' ability, through the democratic process, to bring the Marriage Act into line with the Constitution. We are confident, Justice Sachs's judgment in effect says, that, when the people's representatives reflect on this matter in Parliament, armed with the guidance we have given them, they will arrive at the position required by constitutional principle.

While consistent in this way with the strategy deployed in *Makwanyune* and *Bhe*, the majority's approach to the remedial question in *Fourie* is also not inconsistent with the sort of approach that Dworkin would countenance as being available to a court committed to principled decision-making. As Dworkin argues in *Law's Empire*, a Court's decision on remedy is no less a decision of law and thus the one type of consequence such a decision may legitimately take into account is a consequence that threatens the interests of those whose rights are being vindicated.[87] Rather than being understood as a decision that adjusted constitutional principle in order to make its acceptance by the

---

[86] Ibid. para 226.

[87] Dworkin, *Law's Empire* 391. Justice O'Regan's dissenting judgment in this case took a different view on this question, but her disagreement with the majority may be seen as a disagreement about the requirements of constitutional principle rather than an indication that the majority's decision was purely strategic.

community more likely, in other words, *Fourie* may be seen as a fully principled decision aimed at securing the constitutional claimants' interest in the effective enforcement of their rights.

While *Fourie* is explicable as a fully principled decision in this way, both *Makwanyane* and *Bhe* provide evidence of the Court's preparedness to adjust constitutional principle to mitigate the impact of the decision on its long-term capacity to carry out its institutional function. In these two cases, the constitutionally required outcome was at odds with positive morality and could not be withheld pending democratic discussion. To be sure, the principled answer put the Court in no immediate danger of political attack since the moderate faction in control of the ANC at the time was in a position to shield it from the adverse public reaction to its decision. To this extent, the Court was politically unconstrained. As argued in Chapter 4, however, the moderate faction's capacity to continue to shield the Court in this way depended on its continued control of the ANC, which in turn depended on public perceptions of the extent to which the implementation of the ANC's social transformation project was being hindered by the negotiated settlement. From this perspective, the divergence between constitutional and positive morality in these two cases presented the Court with a strategic choice between, on the one hand, uncompromising commitment to principled decision-making, in the hope that its reputation as a forum of principle would be established by the time the moderate faction ceased to be able to shield it from political attack, and, on the other, building broad public support for its role, in which case some attempt to adjust the principled answer to make it more acceptable to the South African public was required.

In both *Makwanyane* and *Bhe*, the manner in which the judges chose to justify their decision suggests that they were aware of this strategic choice, and that they chose the latter option. Despite the seemingly bold rejection of the relevance of public opinion in the former case, and the preparedness of the Court in *Bhe* to enforce an essentially Western conception of gender equality, both decisions draw back from giving a robustly reasoned account of constitutional morality. In *Makwanyane*, this is evidenced in Justice Chaskalson's frequent references to the need to engage in substantive reasoning while in fact doing just the opposite. In *Bhe*, the Court likewise adjusted the principled answer by withholding constitutional censure of pre-colonial customary practices and contending, without any real sociological support, that such practices would likely have developed in conformity with the 1996 Constitution's egalitarian ethos.

Whether the attempt in these two cases to frame the principled answer in a way that was easier for the South African public to accept succeeded is hard to say. The available survey data suggests that the *Makwanyane* decision did nothing to enhance the Court's public support, and may indeed have been one of the reasons behind the Court's comparatively low institutional legitimacy rating of 27.9 per cent in 1997.[88] Later surveys indicate that the extent of the Court's public support did not significantly increase between 1997 and 2004.[89] Although these figures may have something to do with the newness of the Court as an institution, they also indicate that the Court was unable for the duration of Chaskalson's tenure as Chief Justice to distinguish itself from Parliament.[90] If that is correct, the Court's continued low institutional legitimacy rating reveals the limitations (at least in a country like South Africa) of an adjudicative strategy focused on the language in which a constitutional court's opinions are written. While such a strategy may be quite effective in managing elite responses to the court's decisions, it is not well-suited to driving more thoroughgoing changes in public perceptions of the court. Some recognition of this point may have been behind the Court's decision in *Fourie* to switch to an alternative version of the strategy based on forcing South Africans actively to engage with the requirements of constitutional principle. As much as this approach might have appeared to delay the vindication of the claimants' constitutional rights, it had the advantage of prompting a broader public debate than an order for immediate enforcement would have triggered, and moreover a debate that the Court was to a very large extent able to control.

This last point raises a broader question about the judges' capacity to control the institutional consequences of their decisions. Whatever the extent of the judges' awareness of the impact of *Makwanyane*, *Bhe* and *Fourie* on the Court's institutional independence, there were certain absolute constraints on their room for manoeuvre in these cases. In all of them, the constitutionally required answer was clear enough, and thus

---

[88] See Gibson and Caldeira, 'Defenders of Democracy?' 7 (reporting on the results of an opinion survey conducted in 1996 and 1997 (after the *Makwanyane* case was decided) and citing Heinz Klug, 'Participating in the Design': Constitution-Making in South Africa' (1996) 3 *Review of Constitutional Studies* 18, 54 and Hugh Corder, 'Establishing Legitimacy for Administrative Justice in South Africa' (1995) 2 *Stellenbosch Law Review* 202 as scholars who warned that the decision on capital punishment threatened the Court's legitimacy).

[89] Gibson, 'The Evolving Legitimacy of the South African Constitutional Court' 229, 247–50.

[90] Ibid. 261.

the judges could not have decided these cases in line with positive morality without risking damage to the Court's reputation for principled decision-making. In any case, their socialised aversion to populist decision-making would have precluded them from doing so. The judges therefore had no real option but to give the constitutionally required answer and concentrate their efforts instead on the way they communicated their reasons for that answer.

In this respect, as we have seen, the Court's options were essentially limited to giving a fully reasoned account of constitutional morality or a more restrained account that adjusted principle to make the decision more acceptable to the South African community. Even this probably overstates the Court's room for manoeuvre. Given the origins of the post-apartheid Constitutions in a less-than-fully-democratic political compromise, the judges could not seek refuge in a simple 'original intent' defence of the Court's institutional function. Grand theorisations of the political morality informing the Bill of Rights and Waluchow's common-law strategy were also for various reasons unavailable to them. Nor could the Court simply declare the political nature of its function. As argued in Chapter 5, such an approach, while admirable in many ways, ran the risk of exposing the Court to the charge of imposing its own ideological views on the South African public before it had built the capacity to withstand such an accusation.

In place of all these various possibilities, this chapter has argued, the judges opted to enforce constitutional values by framing them as values that South Africans would themselves have chosen even if their choice had not been fettered by the terms of the negotiated settlement. Imaginative as it was, this was always going to be a difficult strategy for the Court to pursue, since its success depended on attitudinal changes in society that the Court could not wholly control, and certainly not without the assistance of the political branches. It should come as no surprise, then, that, in other areas of law, including the Court's social rights jurisprudence, the judges focused their energies on managing the Court's relationship with the ANC, perhaps realising that the Court's institutional fate was in the end bound up with the ANC's capacity to deliver on the social welfare dimensions of the constitutional project.

Social rights

There is a curious divergence of opinion in the academic literature on the Chaskalson Court's social rights jurisprudence. For almost all foreign commentators, this aspect of the Court's record represents the summit of its achievement – the area of its work where the Court distinguished itself as one of the most technically accomplished and innovative of the constitutional courts established after 1989. For most South African commentators, by contrast, the Court's decisions on social rights constitute the one respect in which it clearly failed to deliver on the promise of the 1996 Constitution.

As we saw in Chapter 1, Dworkin and Sunstein's appreciation of the Chaskalson Court's record is based on what they regard to be its creative and institutionally self-aware decisions in *Grootboom* and *Treatment Action Campaign*.[1] To this may be added the largely positive accounts of these decisions given by Frank Michelman,[2] Mark Tushnet,[3] Rosalind Dixon,[4] Ran Hirschl,[5] Katharine Young,[6] and

---

[1] *Government of the Republic of South Africa and Others* v. *Grootboom and Others* 2001 (1) SA 46 (CC), 2000 (11) BCLR 1169 (CC); *Minister of Health and Others* v. *Treatment Action Campaign and Others (No 2)* 2002 (5) SA 721 (CC), 2002 (10) BCLR 1033 (CC) (discussed in Section 1.4).

[2] Frank Michelman, 'The Constitution, Social Rights and Reason: A Tribute to Etienne Mureinik' (1998) 14 *South African Journal on Human Rights* 499 (largely endorsing the reasoning in *Soobramoney* although criticising the Court's decision to offer unnecessary dicta in relation to s 27(1) and (2)).

[3] Tushnet, *Weak Courts, Strong Rights* 242–4 (referring to *Grootboom* as a 'celebrated' decision and analysing *this* decision as an example of a constitutional court's capacity successfully to enforce ostensibly strong social welfare rights by means of weak remedies).

[4] Rosalind Dixon, 'Creating Dialogue about Socioeconomic Rights: Strong-form versus Weak-form Judicial Review Revisited' (2007) 5 *International Journal of Constitutional Law* 391.

[5] Hirschl, *Towards Juristocracy* 130–34 (a less effusive appreciation than the other commentators listed here, in keeping with the argument of the book).

[6] Katharine G. Young, 'A Typology of Economic and Social Rights Adjudication: Exploring the Catalytic Function of Judicial Review' (2010) 8 *International Journal of Constitutional Law* 385.

Mark Kende.[7] For all of these commentators, the Court's approach to its social rights mandate was both astute in its handling of the separation of powers issues at stake and also instructive about the sort of role constitutional courts may play in relation to these rights.

The response of South African commentators has been very different. Although a few voices have been raised in defence of the Court,[8] the preponderance of academic opinion has been severely critical, with the Court's disinclination to adopt the so-called 'minimum core' approach receiving most attention.[9] Starting with the lukewarm reaction to *Grootboom*,[10] and then intensifying when the minimum core approach was again rejected in *Treatment Action Campaign*,[11] the main thrust of the criticism has been that the Court's failure to attribute any substantive content to social rights has proceduralised them,[12] to the point where there is now little incentive to litigate these rights.[13] The strongest version of this critique has been articulated by David Bilchitz, who, in a forcefully argued book, has set out both the philosophical case for treating social rights on a par with civil and political rights and also the doctrinal case for a more robust approach to their enforcement.[14] In what, at the level

---

[7] Mark S. Kende, *Constitutional Rights in Two Worlds: South Africa and the United States* (Cambridge University Press, 2009) 245–9 (calling *Grootboom* 'seminal' and praising the Court for its pragmatic approach to the interpretation of social rights).

[8] Carol Steinberg, 'Can Reasonableness Protect the Poor? A Review of South Africa's Socio-economic Rights Jurisprudence' (2006) 123 *South African Law Journal* 264; Murray Wesson, '*Grootboom* and Reassessing the Socio-economic Jurisprudence of the South African Constitutional Court' (2004) 20 *South African Journal on Human Rights* 284.

[9] See, for example, Marius Pieterse, 'Coming to Terms with Judicial Enforcement of Socio-economic rights' (2004) 20 *South African Journal on Human Rights* 383; Dennis Davis, 'Adjudicating the Socio-economic Rights in the Constitution: Towards "Deference Lite"' (2006) 22 *South African Journal on Human Rights* 301.

[10] See my own initial reaction to this case: Theunis Roux, 'Understanding *Grootboom*: A Response to Cass R. Sunstein' (2002) 12 *Constitutional Forum* 41.

[11] See, for example, Marius Pieterse, 'Resuscitating Socio-economic Rights: Constitutional Entitlements to Health Care Services' (2006) 22 *South African Journal on Human Rights* 473; Davis, 'Adjudicating the Socio-economic Rights'.

[12] Danie Brand, 'The Proceduralisation of South African Socio-economic Rights Jurisprudence, or "What are Socio-economic Rights For?"' in Henk Botha, André van der Walt and Johan van der Walt (eds.), *Rights and Democracy in a Transformative Constitution* (Stellenbosch University Press, 2003) 33.

[13] Davis, 'Adjudicating the Socio-economic Rights' 314 ('[a] failure by successful litigants to benefit from constitutional litigation of this kind can only contribute to the long term [sic] illegitimacy of the... constitutional enterprise').

[14] David Bilchitz, *Poverty and Fundamental Rights: The Justification and Enforcement of Socio-Economic Rights* (Oxford University Press, 2007).

of constitutional principle, is a very persuasive argument, Bilchitz demonstrates how the Court might have developed an understanding of the
substantive content of social rights that would have required the state to
prioritise its efforts to meet basic needs, without breaching the separation
of powers.

All scholars tend to be more critical of their own country's institutions,
of course. But the divergence of opinion over the Court's social rights
jurisprudence is stark enough to indicate that there may be something
else going on as well. At root, it is suggested, the disagreement in the
academic literature is attributable to legal-cultural factors that predispose
foreign commentators to appreciate the Court's approach and local
commentators to undervalue it. In the United States, in particular, where
normative constitutional theory has long been aware of the sorts of
concerns raised by judicial politics scholars, most commentators are
willing to accept the strategic compromises that constitutional courts
may be required to make. In South Africa, on the other hand, the political
constraints under which constitutional courts operate are either not
seen at all or, if seen, are considered to be irrelevant to legal-academic
criticism.

The interdisciplinary approach adopted in this study means that this
chapter's assessment of the Court's record on social rights inevitably
comes closer to the view held by foreign commentators. From the Court's
perspective, the inherent danger in the minimum core approach was that
it threatened to tie the Court down to a standard of review that was both
too interventionist and too inflexible. Given the political sensitivity of its
role, this was something the Court understandably wanted to avoid. As
we shall see, its overarching strategy depended on managing its relationship with the ANC in a context in which there was no real prospect of
any other political party winning power. In the case of social rights, this
meant that the Court needed to develop a review standard that would
allow it, on the one hand, to signal its deference to the political branches
and, on the other, to intervene where the micro-politics of the particular
case allowed for this. However conceptually flawed and philosophically
unsatisfying, the Court's rejection of the minimum core approach must
be understood in this light.

The chapter begins by considering the history behind the inclusion of
social rights in the 1996 Constitution and shows how it was the ANC
rather than the white minority parties that had consistently favoured this
option. The judges' knowledge of this fact, and their familiarity with and
(in some cases) participation in the early academic debates, influenced

their developing conception of the Court's institutional role. Even so, when the Court came to decide its first social rights case, there were still two main approaches between which the judges had to choose: the minimum core approach, which had exerted a clear influence on the text of the 1996 Constitution, and a more deferential, rational justification approach, which had first been suggested in an academic essay.

The story of the Court's social rights jurisprudence is essentially the story of how it came to favour the second of these two approaches. The rest of the chapter tells that story by analysing the Court's major social rights decisions in turn,[15] describing how the judges' sense of their legal-professional duty and concerns over the Court's institutional independence pulled them in a particular direction. Although the flexible, reasonableness review standard the Court eventually adopted in *Grootboom* had its drawbacks, it was not without certain advantages. Most obviously, in *Treatment Action Campaign*, the Court was able to exploit President Mbeki's political isolation to heighten the level of review and hand down a forceful decision.

7.1 Background to the inclusion of social rights in the 1996 Constitution

It is an obvious point, but one that bears repeating, that social rights were not included in the 1996 Constitution as minority protection rights, but as rights that were expected both to legitimise the Constitution in the eyes of black South Africans and to provide programmatic guidance to the political branches on how to overcome the social and economic legacy of apartheid. Before the transition, the South African Law Commission, in its *Interim Report on Group and Human Rights*,[16] had opposed the inclusion of social rights on the grounds that they did not give rise to enforceable legal obligations.[17] Against this, the ANC had argued that social rights were required to counterbalance the ideological effect of civil and political rights, which – though necessary to guarantee the transition – should not be allowed to brand the Constitution as a

---

[15] The chapter does not discuss the Court's decision in *Khosa and Others* v. *Minister of Social Development and Others; Mahlaule and Others* v. *Minister of Social Development and Others* (2004) 6 SA 505 (CC), 2004 (6) BCLR 569 (CC).

[16] South African Law Commission, *Project 58 – Group and Human Rights: Interim Report* (1991).

[17] See Nicholas Haysom, 'Constitutionalism, Majoritarian Democracy and Socio-economic Rights' (1992) 8 *South African Journal on Human Rights* 451, 454–6.

neo-liberal economic charter.[18] Several of the judges of the Chaskalson Court, most notably Albie Sachs, were central participants in these debates, and may thus be taken to have been familiar with them. Indeed, it is fair to say that, when the Court eventually came to carry out its social rights mandate, the judges were not so much interpreting these rights for the first time as continuing a process of thinking and deliberation that had begun some years before.

Although it is possible to trace the decision to include social rights to the demands made in the 1955 Freedom Charter, the real story begins in 1988 with the publication of the ANC's Constitutional Guidelines for a Democratic South Africa.[19] Before that time, the ANC's views on social rights had developed without regard to the possibility of a justiciable bill of rights.[20] It was only in October 1987, when the ANC first acknowledged that such an instrument could be part of a transitional pact,[21] that serious thinking about how social rights might be judicially enforced began. The Constitutional Guidelines themselves are not particularly detailed, and show how inchoate the ANC's views were at this stage. Nevertheless, the general thrust is clear. In a section entitled 'The Bill of Rights and Affirmative Action', the Guidelines provide that '[t]he state and all social institutions shall be under a constitutional duty to take active steps to eradicate, speedily, the economic and social inequalities produced by racial discrimination'.[22] The Guidelines then go on to say that 'the state shall have the duty to protect the right to work, and guarantee education and social security'.[23]

It is clear from these provisions that the original idea behind the inclusion of social rights was to ensure that a future South African state could never again ignore the welfare needs of the majority of its population. Not just that, but the ANC thought that the state should be put under a positive constitutional duty to redress the social and economic

---

[18] This example illustrates the weakness in Ran Hirschl's otherwise interesting take on the transition to democracy in South Africa (Hirschl, *Towards Juristocracy* (arguing that the South African case supports an understanding of the global expansion of judicial power as being driven by the desire on the part of outgoing political and judicial elites to preserve their hegemony)).

[19] See African National Congress, Constitutional Guidelines for a Democratic South Africa, 1988 (reprinted in (1989) 21 *Columbia Human Rights Law Review* 235).

[20] See Klug, *Constituting Democracy* 74.

[21] See African National Congress, 'Statement on Negotiations' (Press Release, 9 October 1987) www.anc.org.za/show.php?id=3844, cited in Klug, *Constituting Democracy* 79.

[22] ANC, 'Statement on Negotiations' para (j).   [23] Ibid. para (l).

legacy of apartheid. Just how this duty was to be policed, however, was not spelled out. All that the Guidelines say in this respect is that the Bill of Rights 'shall provide appropriate mechanisms for their enforcement'.[24]

The development of the ANC's thinking on the enforcement issue can be seen in the changing views of Albie Sachs, who was a member of the Constitutional Committee that drafted the Guidelines and the ANC's most prominent spokesman on a future Bill of Rights. Sachs's initial position was that the interpretation of the Bill of Rights in general could not be entrusted to 'a body of highly trained and elderly judges, applying traditional wisdom in what is considered a neutral and objective manner'.[25] Although South Africa might eventually move to such a model, Sachs thought, the Bill of Rights should initially be implemented by 'institutions that are democratic in their composition, functioning and perspective, and that operate under the overall supervision of the people's representatives in Parliament'.[26] Social rights, for their part, were an aspect of affirmative action, the 'application' of which should be overseen by a 'Social and Economic Rights Commission'.[27] Earlier in the same essay, Sachs had clearly implied that he thought social rights were not justiciable when arguing that 'attention needs to be given to breaking out of the confines of the Anglo-Saxon legal tradition whereby basically rights are restricted to what is justiciable, to interests that can be protected by recourse to a court of law'.[28]

These views, originally expressed in 1986 in an in-house ANC paper, had already begun to change by the time the Constitutional Guidelines were issued. In a 1989 paper published in the *Columbia Human Rights Law Review*, Sachs supported the idea of a constitutional court, but hedged his bets on whether such a body should be given the power to enforce social rights.[29] A year later, after Arthur Chaskalson and George

---

[24] Ibid. para (h). The fact that the term 'Bill of Rights' was used suggests that a court-based model might have been contemplated, but, if so, none of the difficulties of adapting that model to social rights enforcement was addressed.

[25] See Albie Sachs, 'Towards a Bill of Rights for a Democratic South Africa' (1990) 6 *South African Journal on Human Rights* 1, 15. Although published in 1990, the essay on which this article was based was first presented in March 1986 to an ANC in-house seminar on the Constitutional Guidelines. The shift became complete by the time of the publication of Sachs, *Advancing Human Rights in South Africa*. Sachs himself tells the story of his changing views in Albie Sachs, *The Strange Alchemy of Life and Law* (Oxford University Press, 2009) 165–73.

[26] Sachs, 'Towards a Bill of Rights' 16–17.   [27] Ibid. 16.   [28] Ibid. 14.

[29] See Albie Sachs, 'A Bill of Rights for South Africa: Areas of Agreement and Disagreement' (1989) 21 *Columbia Human Rights Law Review* 13, 25 ('The institution for dealing with

Bizos had joined the Constitutional Committee,[30] Sachs helped to formulate the ANC's Draft Bill of Rights,[31] which called for the establishment of a constitutional court and included a long article on 'social,
educational, economic, and welfare rights'.[32] Significantly, the enforcement provision in this document made no distinction between first- and
second-generation rights.[33] Instead, the article on social rights contained
language drawn from the International Covenant on Economic, Cultural
and Social Rights.[34] At this stage, therefore, it would appear that both
Sachs and Chaskalson were of the view that the international law
approach, as developed by the UN Committee on Economic, Social and
Cultural Rights in its General Comments on the ICESCR, provided the
best framework for the interpretation of social rights, and that this
framework could simply be incorporated into a future South African
Constitution.

By 1992, legal academics in South Africa and abroad were becoming
interested in the issue. Canadian scholars, in particular, after the failure
to have social rights included in the 1982 Charter, were keen to win the
battle on foreign shores.[35] In South Africa, the preponderance of

---

social and economic questions must be Parliament ... The courts should not have the
burden imposed upon them of considering the desirability of legislation dealing with
social and economic questions, *unless such legislation raises issues with a constitutional
dimension*' (emphasis added)).

[30] Klug, *Constituting Democracy* 83. Klug notes that Chaskalson and Bizos joined the
Committee to provide independent advice, and did not become members of the ANC
at this time.

[31] Published in (1991) 7 *South African Journal on Human Rights* 110.

[32] See articles 16(2) and 10, respectively.

[33] See article 16. Article 16(6) did contain a statement saying that 'Parliament shall have a
special responsibility for ensuring that the basic social, educational, economic, and
welfare rights set out in this Bill of Rights are respected'.

[34] Opened for signature 16 December 1966, 993 UNTS 3 (entered into force 3 January 1976)
('ICESCR'). See, particularly, article 10(2) of the Draft Bill: 'The state, [sic] shall, to the
maximum of its available resources, undertake appropriate legislative and executive
action in order to achieve the progressive realisation of basic social, educational, economic and welfare rights for the whole population.' Article 2(1) of the ICESCR provides:
'Each State Party to the present Covenant undertakes to take steps, individually and
through international assistance and co-operation, especially economic and technical, to
the maximum of its available resources, with a view to achieving progressively the full
realization of the rights recognized in the present Covenant by all appropriate means,
including particularly the adoption of legislative measures.'

[35] See Craig Scott and Patrick Macklem, 'Ropes of Sand or Justiciable Guarantees: Social
Rights in a New South African Constitution' (1992) 141 *University of Pennsylvania Law
Review* 1.

academic and legal-professional opinion quickly swung behind inclusion, with Dennis Davis the sole dissenter.[36] Fink Haysom, who, with Halton Cheadle and Clive Thompson, had helped to develop South Africa's labour rights regime, made the telling point that that United States experience, far from providing conclusive proof of social rights' non-justiciability, demonstrated all that could go wrong with a constitution that did not include such rights.[37] The most forceful argument of all, however, was provided by Wits University legal academic Etienne Mureinik, who went on to advise the Democratic Party in the constitutional negotiations process.[38] Mureinik's important insight was to see that social rights were really no different from civil and political rights when it came to their enforcement. In both cases, he argued, a future constitutional court would need to give considerable leeway to the state in choosing the appropriate method to realise rights. Nevertheless, in relation to social rights, as with other rights, the court could play a vital role in requiring the state rationally to justify whatever policies it adopted. Thus, if the state were to decide to build a nuclear submarine rather than schools, the court would be entitled to ask whether this policy decision was justified. Likewise, if the Constitution included a right to nutrition, the court would have the power, not to dictate a market-led or statist developmental model, but to ask what the state was doing to 'eradicate starvation'.[39] Even if this form of review did not result in the striking down of a single programme, 'the procedural benefits would be immense'.[40]

When the interim Constitution came to be drafted in 1993, these arguments, together with the ANC's ongoing insistence that the Constitution needed to deal with the social and economic legacy of apartheid, supported the inclusion of a modest range of social rights.[41] For the most part, however, the interim Constitution focused on rights that were

---

[36] Dennis Davis, 'The Case against the Inclusion of Socio-economic Demands in a Bill of Rights Except as Directive Principles' (1992) 8 *South African Journal on Human Rights* 475.

[37] Haysom, 'Constitutionalism, Majoritarian Democracy and Socio-economic Rights'.

[38] See Etienne Mureinik, 'Beyond a Charter of Luxuries: Economic Rights in the Constitution' (1992) 8 *South African Journal on Human Rights* 464. Mureinik was later to die in tragic circumstances. His role in the constitutional negotiations process is celebrated in a special edition of the *South African Journal on Human Rights* published in 1998.

[39] Ibid. 471.   [40] Ibid. 472.

[41] See, for example, s 30(1)(c) (on children's right to 'security, basic nutrition and basic health and social services'); and s 32 (on the right to basic education).

thought to be vital to the transition.[42] It was not until the final constitution-making process that the full force of the ANC's commitment to social rights came to be reflected in the constitutional text. In its submission to Theme Committee 4 of the Constitutional Assembly, the ANC argued that the inclusion of social rights in the Constitution would reflect South Africa's 'vision and aspirations for the future'.[43] While recognising that these rights posed certain 'difficulties in enforcement', the ANC argued that these difficulties could be overcome, and that the important point was to put the state under a positive duty to 'redress the imbalances of the past'.[44]

At the same time, the Technical Committee responsible for advising the Constitutional Assembly on social rights took the view that there were certain advantages to be had in following the ICESCR formulation. On the one hand, adopting this formulation would help to harmonise South Africa's international and domestic obligations. On the other, the UN Committee's General Comments would provide a ready source of guidance on how social rights ought to be interpreted.[45] This advice squared with the position that the ANC had taken in its 1990 Draft Bill of Rights. In the result, there is a close resemblance between the text of ss 26 and 27 of the 1996 Constitution and Articles 2.1 and 11.1 of the ICESCR. 'Close' but not complete. As others have observed,[46] and as the Constitutional Court was later to remark in *Grootboom*,[47] ss 26 and 27 depart from the ICESCR formulation in several respects. First, the rights themselves are qualified by the addition of the words 'have access to'. Secondly, the state's duties in respect of the rights are qualified by the omission of the word 'maximum' from the phrase 'to the maximum of its available resources' and by the rephrasing of the formulation 'all appropriate means' to read 'reasonable legislative and other measures'. These changes were not present in the ANC's Draft Bill of Rights and thus suggest that, when faced with the imminent prospect of social rights

---

[42] See du Plessis and Corder, *Understanding South Africa's Transitional Bill of Rights* 22–35.

[43] 'Preliminary ANC Submission: Theme Committee 4 – Further Socio-Economic Rights' 1 (quoted in Kirsty McLean, *Constitutional Deference, Courts and Socio-Economic Rights in South Africa* (Pretoria University Law Press, 2009) 15).

[44] Ibid.

[45] Sandra Liebenberg, 'Interpretation of Socio-economic Rights' in Matthew Chaskalson, Janet Kentridge, Jonathan Klaaren and Gilbert Marcus (eds.), *Constitutional Law of South Africa* (Cape Town: Juta, 1999) ch 33, 41–4.

[46] McLean, *Constitutional Deference* 17.   [47] See the discussion in Section 8.3.

review, the Constitutional Assembly had some last-minute misgivings about the appropriateness of the international law model.

Sections 26 and 27 were supported by all the major political parties in the Constitutional Assembly, reflecting a remarkable degree of consensus over the inclusion of a category of rights that has proved controversial elsewhere.[48] This must partly have had to do, as Heinz Klug has observed,[49] with the ANC's resounding electoral victory in 1994, which allowed it to shape the content of the 1996 Constitution to suit its social transformation agenda. But the absence of any meaningful opposition to social rights, even though the other political parties retained a weak veto power,[50] suggests that all the political parties were by this time reconciled to the idea of justiciable social rights. Given the level of state intervention in the construction of apartheid, the imposition on the post-apartheid state of a constitutional duty to redress the social and economic legacy of that system was hardly revolutionary.

When the text of the draft 1996 Constitution came to be reviewed in the Constitutional Court, only three organisations challenged the social rights provisions, in what must have seemed to them, even at the time, as a vain attempt to stave off the inevitable.[51] The first objection raised was that social rights were not universally accepted, as required by Constitutional Principle II. The Court easily dismissed this argument. As it had already ruled in relation to property rights, the test mandated by Constitutional Principle II was not that all rights included in the Constitution should be universally accepted, but that all universally accepted rights should be included.[52] On this basis, the Constitutional Assembly was free to include any 'supplementary' rights it deemed warranted.[53] The second objection, that the enforcement of social rights would inevitably infringe the separation of powers, was likewise easily dismissed. As forceful as this objection had seemed when articulated by the Law Commission ten years

---

[48] See, for example, the Brennan Commission report on the since abandoned proposal for a statutory bill of rights at the federal level in Australia National Human Rights Consultation, *Report* (2009) www.humanrightsconsultation.gov.au/Report/Documents/NHRCReport.pdf.

[49] Klug, *Constituting Democracy* 115.   [50] See the discussion in Chapter 5.

[51] The three organisation were the South African Institute of Race Relations (a well-known conservative think-tank), the Free Market Foundation and the Gauteng Association of Chambers of Commerce and Industry (see annexure 3 to *Ex parte Chairperson of the Constitutional Assembly: In re Certification of the Constitution of the Republic of South Africa, 1996* (1997) 2 SA 97 (CC), 1996 (10) BCLR1253 (CC) (*First Certification Judgment*) ('Summary of Objections and Submissions').

[52] Ibid.   [53] Ibid. para 76.

before, the Court in 1996 was able to assert the emerging academic consensus that there was really no difference between first- and second-generation rights in this respect. The enforcement of both sets of rights would have budgetary implications. There was thus no basis to object to social rights once the Court's power to review civil and political rights had been conceded.[54] The final objection, that social rights were not justiciable, was dismissed on the ground that the requirement of justiciability applied only to those rights that had been included by reason of their universality. 'Nevertheless,' the Court added, 'we are of the view that these rights are, at least to some extent, justiciable ... At the very minimum, socio-economic rights can be negatively protected from improper invasion.'[55]

With that somewhat enigmatic phrase, ten years of deliberation over the wisdom of including social rights in a future South African Constitution ended. From this point on, the debate shifted to the form social rights enforcement would take. In this respect there was, as there still is, less unanimity. On the one hand, the UN Committee's minimum core approach seemed to provide a useful model that had been tested in the international arena. In addition, there was the practical point that South Africa had signed, and was expected soon to ratify, the ICESCR.[56] If South Africa's efforts to realise social rights were to be subject to the minimum core standard at the international level, it made sense for the Court to impose a similar standard at the domestic level, or at least a standard that was not incompatible with it. On the other hand, the Court was plainly in a different institutional position to the UN Committee. As a municipal tribunal, it was susceptible to the vagaries of political support for its role, including the ever-present threat that its powers would be curtailed should its decisions prove inconvenient. These considerations counselled against enforcing social rights too forcefully. If social rights adjudication was to become a permanent feature of South African constitutionalism, the Court would need to proceed cautiously, tailoring its decisions to the micro-politics of each case and gradually inserting itself into the democratic process by which social and economic policy is determined.

With hindsight, it is possible to see that there were essentially two strategic paths open to the Court, corresponding to the two available doctrinal models. The first strategy required the Court to risk its

---

[54] Ibid. para 77.   [55] Ibid. para 78.
[56] South Africa signed the ICESCR in 1994 but has still not ratified it.

institutional independence on the gamble that enforcing social rights early on and aggressively would win it the support of the ANC's urban poor and rural landless constituency. The minimum core approach was well suited to this strategy, since it would enable the Court to insist that all available resources be diverted to meeting basic needs as a matter of urgency. However inconvenient this way of proceeding proved to the ANC, the Court's role would ultimately be defensible in majoritarian terms as one aimed at giving effect to the Constitution's vision of social and economic transformation.

Alternatively, the Court could proceed more cautiously, signalling its deference to the political branches in matters of social and economic policy and enforcing social rights only when it was sure that there would be no adverse consequences for it as an institution. Mureinik's rational justification approach was well suited to this second type of strategy. Since it did not depend on giving content to social rights, the Court could avoid the troublesome possibility of becoming bogged down in its own precedents, forced in controversial cases to choose between fidelity to law and triggering a political conflict it could not contain. This strategy, too, could be defended in majoritarian terms as one ultimately aimed at promoting dialogue between the Court and the political branches over the best method of enforcing social rights. The only downside was that the Court would thereby tie its institutional independence to the success of that dialogue, and to the success more generally of the ANC's social and economic transformation project. Any setbacks in that project, or change to the coalition of groups within the ANC that favoured it, would expose the Court to political attack.

7.2   An 'agonising' start: *Soobramoney*

The first social rights case decided by the Court under the 1996 Constitution, *Soobramoney v. Minister of Health (KwaZulu-Natal)*,[57] was not a particularly hard case, legally or politically speaking. But it was emotionally hard, presenting as it did a tragic set of facts that illustrated the limits of justiciable social rights in the face of scarce resources. Perhaps because of the difficulty of the case in this respect, the Court was drawn into a fairly expansive judgment that traversed issues that were not strictly speaking up for decision. Another reading of the case, however – or so this section will

---

[57] 1998 (1) SA 765 (CC), 1997 (12) BCLR 1696 (CC) ('*Soobramoney*'). The word 'agonising' in this context was first used in *R. v. Cambridge Health Authority; Ex parte B* [1995] 2 All ER 129, 137 (CA) and is used twice in *Soobramoney* at paras 24 and 58.

argue – is that the judges were entirely conscious of what they were doing, and that their decision deliberately set the parameters for future social rights litigation in a case in which the outcome was never in doubt. If so, *Soobramoney* provides support for one of this study's central claims, viz. that the Chaskalson Court shaped the law in politically uncontroversial cases so as to put itself in a position to manage the law/politics tension in other, more politically charged cases.

Soobramoney came to the Court as an appeal from a decision of the Durban High Court refusing the appellant's application for an order mandating that he be provided with renal dialysis treatment at a public hospital. The appellant's request that he be placed on dialysis had earlier been denied by the hospital on the grounds that he fell outside its treatment protocol.[58] Although in its legal form a challenge to the fairness and rationality of the protocol, the case was easily construable in the public mind as a demand for an expensive medical treatment, the provision of which would divert scarce resources away from more pressing needs, such as primary healthcare. The appellant was also litigating on his own, unsupported by any public interest group. In political terms, it was thus an easy case.

The case was also relatively straightforward in legal terms. As presented to the Constitutional Court, it concerned an alleged violation of s 27(3) (right to emergency medical treatment) and s 11 (right to life) of the 1996 Constitution. Neither of these allegations was particularly strong in law. Indeed, *Soobramoney* was the sort of case that, had it been presented to an established constitutional court with a busy docket, would likely not have been heard. Even on the Chaskalson Court's fairly expansive approach to its appellate jurisdiction,[59] the case might have been dismissed without reasons. Nevertheless, the Court took it on, perhaps wanting to enter the social rights arena by delivering what it knew would be a safe decision.

The s 27(3) leg of the case, which was based on an allegation that the appellant's renal condition constituted an 'emergency' within the meaning of that provision,[60] barely got off the ground. Section 27(3), the Court held, was not designed for the sort of situation in which the appellant

---

[58] The protocol stated that a patient's condition should either be curable through dialysis or, if chronic, that the patient be suitable for a kidney transplant. Because the appellant, in addition to his renal condition, also suffered from ischaemic heart disease and cerebro-vascular disease, he was deemed not to be entitled to treatment.

[59] See Sebastian Seedorf, 'Jurisdiction' in Woolman et al. (eds.), *Constitutional Law of South Africa* ch 4.

[60] Section 27(3) provides: 'No one may be refused emergency medical treatment.'

found himself. His condition was chronic, whereas s 27(3) had clearly been intended to cover 'sudden' emergencies such as that presented in the Indian case of *Samity*,[61] where the plaintiff had fallen off a train.[62] If s 27(3) were to be given the broad construction for which the appellant contended, available resources would be drawn away from the fulfilment of the state's 'primary obligations' under s 27(1) and (2).[63]

The s 11 leg of the appellant's case was given even shorter shrift. Although the *Samity* case had been based on the right to life in the Indian Constitution,[64] the structure of the 1996 Constitution was different. Containing as it did a justiciable right to health care services, there was no need to infer this right from s 11.[65] In any case, as had already been decided in relation to s 27(3), the facts of the *Soobramoney* case were distinguishable. In *Samity*, the claimant had suffered 'a sudden catastrophe' calling for 'immediate medical attention'.[66] The appellant, by contrast, was asking the state to provide him with life-prolonging treatment for a long-standing medical condition.[67]

Had the *Soobramoney* decision ended at this point, it would have been legally unremarkable. The precise meaning of s 27(3) arguably needed to be determined, and thus the Court's decision to take the case – despite the obviousness of the answer – would likely not have been called into question. But the *Soobramoney* judgment did not end at this point, and thus invites speculation about why the Court continued. After dismissing the appellant's case under s 27(3) and s 11, the Court took upon itself the task of considering the claim under s 27(1) and (2).[68] This was an unusual move that cannot be said to have been dictated by law. On the contrary, the Court's decision to proceed is criticisable on legal grounds, both for its inconsistency with decisions in other cases,[69] and for its violation of the Court's more general principle against deciding difficult legal questions in the absence of full argument.[70] Perhaps the judges, having decided to take the case in order to clarify the meaning of s 27(3), felt that the tragic circumstances in which the appellant found himself

---

[61] *Paschim Banga Khet Mazdoor Samity and Others* v. *State of West Bengal and Another* (1996) AIR SC 2426.

[62] *Soobramoney* para 13, read with para 18.   [63] Ibid. para 19.   [64] Article 21.

[65] *Soobramoney* para 19.   [66] Ibid. para 20.   [67] Ibid. para 21.   [68] Ibid. para 22.

[69] See, for example, *Minister of Public Works* v. *Kyalami Ridge Environmental Association* 2001 (3) SA 1151 (CC), 2001 (7) BCLR 652 (CC) (cited in Tushnet, *Weak Courts, Strong Rights*, 239 n 32).

[70] Cf. Michelman, 'The Constitution, Social Rights and Reason' 503 n 14 (criticising the Court for its lack of caution in this respect).

required them to give a more fulsome legal answer. Or, as noted earlier, the judges might have been motivated to stake out their general approach to social rights in what they took to be a politically uncontroversial case.

Approached as a case based on s 27(1) and (2), the Court held, the appellant's claim implicated at least two levels of policy decision – the hospital's decision to devote its available renal dialysis machines to particular categories of patient, and the provincial Government's decision on the distribution of its healthcare budget. In respect of both of these levels of decision, the test to be applied was whether the officials in question had acted 'rational[ly]' and 'in good faith'.[71] On the facts, there was no basis to question either of the decisions on this ground. The hospital's treatment protocol, for its part, had clearly been designed in such a way as to maximise the healthcare benefits of the available renal dialysis machines, taking into account such factors as the need to service the machines to prolong their working life and the chances that the patients treated would eventually be able to survive without renal dialysis.[72] Likewise, there was no reason to doubt that the size and distribution of the provincial Government's healthcare budget had been determined with due regard to other pressing demands, both on the funds set aside for health and also on the overall provincial budget.[73]

Although the Court did not say so, the standard of review it adopted in coming to this conclusion appears to have been inspired by Mureinik's article, to which reference was made earlier.[74] Mureinik, it will be recalled, had argued that the value of including social rights in the Constitution would be that it would force Government decision-makers to show that they had made 'a sincere and rational effort' to realise the right in question.[75] This standard is virtually identical to *Soobramoney*'s standard of 'rational decisions taken in good faith'. In both cases, the emphasis is shifted away from defining the content of the right and onto the rationality of the state's conduct.

Given the later debate over the Court's rejection of the minimum core approach, it is worth asking whether the adoption of Mureinik's standard in *Soobramoney* was a calculated move on the part of the Court to introduce its preferred approach to social rights in a politically uncontroversial case. There is no way of knowing for sure, of course, but the circumstantial evidence is strong. Exhibit A is the fact that the Court took the *Soobramoney* case when it might have turned it down as lacking

---

[71] *Soobramoney* para 29.   [72] Ibid. paras 25–8.   [73] Ibid. para 29.
[74] See Section 7.1.   [75] Mureinik, 'Beyond a Charter of Luxuries' 472.

prospects of success. Exhibit B is the Court's decision to proceed to the s 27(1) and (2) issue when this decision was not required by law, and in fact ran contrary to the Court's usual practice. Finally, there is the fact that the Court did indeed later move in the direction prefigured in *Soobramoney*, and that it relied on various (strictly speaking obiter) statements in that decision to give these later decisions credibility.[76]

Against this, it might be argued that both the Court's decision to take the *Soobramoney* case and its decision to raise the s 27(1) and (2) issue were primarily driven by the tragic circumstances in which the appellant found himself. Any refusal to hear the case, however legally justified, would have attracted adverse publicity. The Court therefore had to take the case. Having taken it, the Court could not afford to hand down what would have been perceived as a harshly technical decision to dismiss the appellant's claim without considering the s 27(1) and (2) issue. To the extent that the Court made various statements in *Soobramoney* on which it later relied in other decisions, this was inevitable. As the first decision on social rights, it was always likely that the Court would refer back to *Soobramoney*, and thus the inference that the Court was acting strategically is unfounded. The Court was merely doing what all common-law courts do, viz. responding to the facts before it and slowly edging its way towards a preferred interpretation.

As forceful as this reply is, two further aspects of the *Soobramoney* decision add further weight to the inference that the Court was acting strategically. The first was the Court's failure to review (or even consider reviewing) certain higher-level policy decisions affecting the overall size of the provincial healthcare budget. The second took the form of an introductory (and seemingly throwaway) remark about the relationship between s 27(1) and (2) that presaged an understanding of these two provisions that was later to prove crucial to the Court's rejection of the minimum core approach.

Having raised the possible application of s 27(1) and (2) itself, the Court had no argument before it that its mandate in respect of social rights might conceivably give it the power to review, not just the hospital's decision on its treatment protocol and the provincial Government's decision on the distribution of its healthcare budget, but also the national Government's decisions on the allocation of funds to its various social welfare programmes and on the overall size of the national

---

[76] See the discussion of *Treatment Action Campaign* in Section 7.4.

budget.[77] That the Court's social rights mandate does not extend to these levels of policy decision is not obvious as a matter of constitutional interpretation. On their face, ss 26 and 27 provide that the state must take 'reasonable legislative and other measures within its available resources to achieve the progressive realisation' of the right. Nothing in this formulation precludes the Court from deciding that the realisation of a particular right requires that the distribution of funds between the various social welfare programmes ought to be adjusted, or that the overall size of the national budget should be increased to finance the fulfilment of the state's constitutional obligations.[78] What militates against such a decision, of course, is the Court's need to respect the separation of powers, and to interpret its social rights mandate in a way that is morally justifiable as a matter of democratic theory and rationally defensible as a matter of institutional capacity.

A principled treatment of this question in *Soobramoney* accordingly required the Court to spell out the extent to which its decisions on social rights might interfere with the national Government's budgetary allocations and macro-economic policy more generally. On the one hand, the Court might have decided that the Constitution expressly gave it the power to review legislative and executive action for consistency with social rights, and accordingly that its mandate extended to the performance of this function, whatever the budgetary consequences. On the other hand, it was open to the Court to infer from the structure of the Constitution as a whole an implied limitation on its power to interfere with budgetary allocations, either at all or beyond a certain level.[79] Both approaches would have been plausible as a matter of constitutional interpretation, and either one would have established a clear rule to which the Court might have adhered in future cases.

From the point of view of principle, it would not have mattered which of these two approaches the Court took, provided that it stuck to it. As a matter of adjudicative strategy, on the other hand, consistently committing itself to either one of these two approaches would have come close to institutional suicide. A generally declared rule that the Court's power to enforce social rights was unlimited by budgetary concerns would have given the Court no room for manoeuvre in cases

---

[77] Darrel Moellendorf, 'Reasoning about Resources: *Soobramoney* and the Future of Socio-economic Rights' (1998) 14 *South African Journal on Human Rights* 327.

[78] See Bilchitz, *Poverty and Fundamental Rights* 227–34.

[79] Cf. Tushnet, *Weak Courts, Strong Rights* 234.

where concerns about its institutional independence militated against the application of such a rule. Conversely, a consistent application of the inherent limitation rule would have been tantamount to an abdication of the Court's role in relation to social rights, with knock-on consequences for its legal-professional reputation and ultimately its institutional independence as well. It is not surprising, therefore, that the Court avoided making this choice, and that it continued to vacillate between these two understandings of its social rights mandate in later cases.[80]

The second aspect of the *Soobramoney* decision that strengthens the inference that it raised the s 27(1) and (2) issue for strategic reasons has to do with a potentially far-reaching statement made in what appeared to be a purely introductory passage on the Constitution's commitment to social rights. After setting out ss 26 and 27 in full, the Court remarked, in paragraph 11 of its judgment:

> What is apparent from these provisions is that the obligations imposed on the state by sections 26 and 27 in regard to access to housing, health care, food, water and social security are dependent upon the resources available for such purposes, *and that the corresponding rights themselves are limited by reason of the lack of resources.* (Emphasis added.)

As Frank Michelman pointed out in his comment on the case, this statement was 'not necessary' to the Court's decision.[81] Even conceding the need to address s 27(1) and (2) at all, the Court certainly did not need to say anything so specific about the relationship between these two subsections. Once again, therefore, we are entitled to inquire what the Court might have been up to. Was it simply, as Michelman asked at the time, a case of the Court's falling into in some rather 'loose language',[82] or was the Court consciously outlining an approach to the interpretation of social rights that it intended to use in later cases?[83]

The effect of the above passage is to collapse the obligation correlative to the subsection (1) right into the qualified obligation in subsection (2). As we shall see when discussing *Grootboom* and *Treatment Action Campaign*, this interpretive move later proved crucial to the Court's rejection of the minimum core approach. But it was by no means

---

[80] As more fully argued in Chapter 10, the indeterminacy of the Court's separation of powers doctrine in this respect was an important part of its overarching strategy.

[81] Michelman, 'The Constitution, Social Rights and Reason' 502.   [82] Ibid.

[83] Cf. Scott and Alston, 'Adjudicating Constitutional Priorities in a Transnational Context' 206, 242 n 90.

compelled by the constitutional text, and entails two consequences that the Court might have wanted to avoid. First, if s 27(1) means no more than that the state is bound by the obligations in s 27(2), the possibility of negative infringement of s 27(1), which the Court expressly kept alive in the *First Certification Judgment*,[84] becomes rather remote.[85] Secondly, the collapsing of the obligations in subsection (1) and (2) also seems to preclude the horizontal application of the subsection (1) right.[86]

Given these consequences, the *Soobramoney* Court was either being extremely careless or taking a calculated risk that the strategic advantages of its broad ruling in paragraph 11 would outweigh any adverse side-effects. A full assessment of this issue must await discussion of *Grootboom* and *Treatment Action Campaign*, but note for the moment that the first awkward consequence of the collapsing of the obligations in subsection (1) and (2) may be contained by restricting the ruling to positive obligations, leaving the possibility of negative infringement of the subsection (1) right open. If that is indeed what the *Soobramoney* Court had in mind, then the risks attendant on issuing so broad a ruling might have seemed to it to be worth taking. The important point was to assert the qualified nature of the subsection (1) right. Any adverse side-effects of this ruling could be dealt with at a later stage. One plausible interpretation of what the Court was doing in this passage, at least, is that it was laying the doctrinal groundwork for its later rejection of the minimum core approach. The case for this interpretation will be strengthened if we can find evidence in *Grootboom* or *Treatment Action Campaign* that paragraph 11 of *Soobramoney* was indeed used in this way.

7.3   Choosing the strategy: *Grootboom*

Grootboom is to South African constitutional lawyers what *Brown* v. *Board of Education*[87] is to their American counterparts. Any attempt to analyse the Chaskalson Court's record must take a view on the merits of

---

[84] See discussion of the *First Certification Judgment* in Section 7.1.

[85] Michelman, 'The Constitution, Social Rights and Reason' 504 (giving example of municipal zoning law that makes building of low-cost housing in municipal borders impossible).

[86] Ibid. (giving example of a 'common-law controversy over whether a particular water source is to be tapped for industrial use or rather left for domestic consumption by those who lack a good alternative supply of water').

[87] *Brown* v. *Board of Education* 347 US 483 (1954) and *Brown* v. *Board of Education* 349 US 294 (1955).

this decision. Was it, as some commentators have said about *Brown*, a legally flawed or even flatly unprincipled decision that was nevertheless, in some broader sense, constitutionally required?[88] Or did the Court in *Grootboom* simply get the law wrong, with potentially far-reaching consequences for the future trajectory of South African constitutional law and the realisation of human rights in South Africa?

The answer to this question depends, as noted earlier, on one's view of the considerations that ought to be taken into account when assessing a decision of this magnitude. Judged in purely doctrinal terms, as a statement of constitutional principle, there is much in the decision that can be criticised. When *Grootboom* is assessed from the broader interdisciplinary perspective adopted in this study, however, it emerges as a largely successful attempt on the part of the Court to fashion a sustainable institutional role for itself.

To be clear: this is not simply a matter of siding with those who think that the Court's decision was justified by reason of the separation of powers concerns raised by the case. As indicated below,[89] the proponents of a more interventionist, priority-setting role for the Court probably have the better of the argument on that score. Rather, the assessment offered here depends on factoring in the real-world political constraints impacting on the Court when it took the decision. When the merits of the *Grootboom* decision are assessed from this broader perspective, the outcome must be overwhelmingly positive. As we shall see, the Court was at pains to reconcile its legal-professional duty with the institutional-independence concerns raised by the case, and chose an adjudicative strategy that was well-suited to the overarching strategy it was pursuing. The only reason to qualify this assessment is that the merits of *Grootboom* cannot be assessed on the basis of this decision alone. In the final analysis, the assessment depends on an analysis of the long-term consequences of the decision, both for the Court as an institution and for South Africa as a whole.[90]

---

[88] See the discussion of Herbert Wechsler's famous critique of *Brown* (Wechsler, 'Toward Neutral Principles of Constitutional Law') in Chapter 2. Responses to Wechsler's critique have ranged from those that accept that the decision was less than fully principled, to those that contend that Wechsler misunderstood the point of principle in *Brown*, to those that hold that *Brown* illustrates the fatuousness of any talk of constitutional principle.

[89] See text accompanying note 104.

[90] It is also important, as the conclusion to this chapter argues, not to answer this question anachronistically. The wisdom of the *Grootboom* decision must be assessed on the basis of the considerations the Court might reasonably have taken into account at the time – not on the basis of what we now know about the changed political context for judicial review.

The events that gave rise to the *Grootboom* case are sufficiently well known not to require lengthy recitation. For purposes of this study, what needs to be emphasised are the political dynamics of the case, and the way these dynamics became intertwined with the legal issues for decision. The most useful assessment of the case from this perspective may be found, not in any scholarly account, but in a consultancy report on public interest litigation written for a foreign donor. The report reveals that the applicants in the *Grootboom* case – an indigent squatter community of about 900 people – only brought the case after their plight had come to the attention of a 'prominent provincial ANC politician'.[91] It was this politician's desire to embarrass his political opponents, rather than any planned public litigation strategy, that initially drove the case.

Briefly, what happened was that the applicants had been evicted from land on the outskirts of Cape Town. With nowhere else to go, they took refuge on a nearby sports field. Hearing of their situation, the prominent politician met with the applicants and their court-appointed attorney, who had previously sought a negotiated solution to their plight. The politician's intervention changed the nature of the case, turning it from an all-too-everyday quest for shelter into the first major case on the Government's positive obligations in respect of social rights. That the case reached those proportions, however, seems to be attributable to a miscalculation on the politician's part. The meeting with the applicants and their attorney took place on the eve of the 1999 national and provincial Government elections. At the time, both the local municipality responsible for the land and the Western Cape provincial government were controlled by the New National Party ('NNP'), the ANC's then major political rival.[92] In an apparent attempt to highlight the NNP's inattention to the needs of the poor, the politician advised the applicants to bring legal proceedings against these two organs of state. The applicants' attorney duly wrote a letter to the municipality demanding that it provide his clients with temporary shelter. When the municipality replied that it could do no more than it was already doing, the applicants launched an urgent application in the Cape High Court for mandatory relief.

As it turned out, the named respondents in the application, presumably on the advice of counsel, included not just the local municipality and the provincial government, but also the Cape Metropolitan Council, the

[91] See Gilbert Marcus and Steven Budlender, *A Strategic Evaluation of Public Interest Litigation in South Africa* (Johannesburg: Atlantic Philanthropies, 2008) 51–2.
[92] Ibid.

national housing board and the national Government itself. By the time it was launched, therefore, the *Grootboom* case had already started to take on a wider dimension that was not entirely of the applicants' choosing. This feature of the case continued as it progressed through the High Court, so that when the Constitutional Court came to hear it, what had started as a little bit of local Western Cape politics had broadened into a challenge to the entire housing programme, at all levels of government.

On its face, the application – relying on both s 26 (right to have access to adequate housing) and s 28 (children's rights) of the 1996 Constitution – sought an order directing the municipality, 'alternatively one or more of the other respondents', to provide the applicants and their children with 'adequate and sufficient temporary basic shelter and/or housing ... in such premises, and/or on such land, as is/may be owned and/or leased by one or more of the respondents, pending applicants and their children obtaining permanent accommodation.' The application further sought an order directing that the applicants' children be provided with 'adequate and sufficient basic nutrition, shelter, health and care services and social services'.

Within a few days of the launch of the application, the judge initially responsible for the case visited the sports field where the applicants were staying and made an interim order mandating the respondents to provide temporary accommodation to the applicants' children at the local community hall. Three weeks later, two other judges of the Cape High Court heard the case, and decided it in the applicants' favour. On the s 26 question, the High Court held that paragraph 11 of *Soobramoney* should indeed be understood to mean that the state's positive obligation correlative to the right in s 26(1) was entirely qualified by the obligation in subsection (2).[93] Section 28(1)(*c*), on the other hand, was not so qualified, and accordingly gave rise, not just to an immediately enforceable children's right to shelter, but also a 'derivative' right (when read with the right to family or parental care in s 28(1)(b)) on the part of their parents to accompany them. Applying these two very different standards, the Court found a violation of s 28(1)(*c*) and ordered that the applicants' children and their parents be provided with shelter 'by the appropriate organ or department of state'.[94]

---

[93] *Grootboom and Others v. Oostenberg Municipality and Others* 2000 (3) BCLR 277 (C) paras 13–14 ('*Grootboom* (HC)').
[94] Ibid. 26.

The logic of the Cape High Court's judgment was thus to infer from the textual differences between s 26 and s 28 a distinction between a weak general right to a rational housing programme and a strong children's right to shelter. Though supported in certain respects by the reasoning in *Soobramoney*, this interpretation read more into that decision than was really there. As we have seen, the *Soobramoney* Court's statement that the rights in subsection (1) of ss 26 and 27 are limited 'by reason of the lack of resources'[95] was made in relation to a claim for an expensive medical treatment. It was in that context that the Constitutional Court warned against reading s 27(3) in such a way as to negate the carefully qualified nature of the s 27(1) right.[96] This line of reasoning had no obvious application to the situation in *Grootboom*, where what was being claimed was a good (shelter) that fell within the very core of the right to adequate housing. In glossing over this difference,[97] the High Court's judgment set up a stark opposition between the qualified right to adequate housing in s 26 and children's rights in s 28. As far as the High Court was concerned, the only shelter right the Constitutional Assembly had seen fit to include was that of children. Adults could partake in this right to the extent that they were responsible for children, but beyond this they had no right to demand that the state prioritise the meeting of their urgent shelter needs.

This feature of the High Court's judgment structured the course of the appeal, threatening to reduce it to a narrow issue. For the appellants, the important point became to overturn the ruling in relation to s 28(1)(c), particularly that part of it relating to parents' derivative right to shelter. For the applicants (now respondents on appeal), there was little reason to challenge the High Court's dismissal of the s 26 leg of their claim when the Court's s 28(1)(c) ruling gave them most of what they had asked for.

---

[95] *Soobramoney* para 11.   [96] Ibid. para 19.

[97] See especially the last part of the High Court's treatment of the s 26 leg of the case. In response to the applicants' contention that s 26(1) and (2) should be interpreted, in accordance with international law, as requiring the state to prioritise the provision of basic shelter, the High Court accepted the respondents' contention that 'such an obligation would create impediments towards the implementation of their housing programme because it would dilute scarce resources' (*Grootboom* (HC) 14). Although the Court did not say so, it is clearly here relying on the dictum in *Soobramoney* para 19 about the danger of upsetting the balance of s 27(1) and (2). But, as we have seen, the context is quite different. It is no argument, in response to a claim that the state's efforts to realise a right should be prioritised in accordance with the core content of the right, to say that such an interpretation would 'dilute scarce resources'. That is precisely the point of such an interpretation. (See further Scott and Alston, 'Adjudicating Constitutional Priorities in a Transnational Context' 265.)

Fortunately – for those interested in the Chaskalson Court's social rights jurisprudence, though not necessarily for the respondents[98] – the *Grootboom* case was joined at the appellate stage by the South African Human Rights Commission and the Community Law Centre, intervening as *amici curiae*. By re-opening the s 26 leg of the claim, the *amici* turned what might have been a fairly technical argument over the meaning of s 28(1)*(c)* into a comprehensive re-examination of the state's positive obligations in relation to the right to adequate housing. From the perspective of this study, the *amici*'s intervention also had the further effect of forcing the Chaskalson Court's hand. If *Soobramoney* had been about laying the groundwork for the Court's preferred approach in a case in which the political stakes were fairly low, the *amici*'s intervention turned *Grootboom* into the real deal: a direct assault by a sophisticated public interest litigant on a major plank in the ANC's housing programme.

In outer form, the *amici*'s argument was essentially the same as the argument that had been made by the applicants in the High Court. There, as before the Constitutional Court, the thrust of the s 26 leg of the claim had been that the similarity in wording between s 26 and Articles 2.1 and 11.1 of the ICESCR suggested that the Constitutional Assembly had intended to constitutionalise something like the international law model. According to this view, s 26 had to be understood as imposing on the state in the first instance a minimum core obligation to meet basic shelter needs, and thereafter an obligation progressively to realise the full extent of the right as resources allowed.[99] What the *amici* added to this argument was a detailed examination of the state's housing programme, showing how – despite the tremendous effort that had been made to overcome the apartheid-era backlog – there was still no functioning emergency shelter component. However rational a use of scarce resources the programme as a whole might constitute, the *amici* insisted, the absence of an emergency shelter component meant that that the state had failed to meet its minimum core obligation under s 26.[100]

The Chaskalson Court's response to this argument is instructive, not only about its strategy in relation to social rights, but also about its

[98] See Marcus and Budlender, *A Strategic Evaluation of Public Interest Litigation in South Africa* 58 (raising, but in the end dismissing, the possibility that the *amici*'s intervention might have been 'damaging to the case because it took the focus away from the individual plaintiffs').

[99] See *Grootboom* (HC) 10–12.

[100] See Marcus and Budlender, *A Strategic Evaluation of Public Interest Litigation in South Africa* 60.

overarching approach to its mandate. As we have seen, Sachs and
Chaskalson both participated in the formulation of the ANC's 1990 Draft
Bill of Rights. They had chosen at that time to follow the wording of the
ICESCR quite closely, apparently thinking that the international law
model provided the best guide to the future constitutional court's role.
The Technical Committee advising the Constitutional Assembly on the
drafting of the 1996 Constitution had taken the same view. At some
point, however, subtle changes had been introduced to the wording of ss
26 and 27, glossing the rights in such a way as to suggest that the
international law model might not be entirely appropriate.[101] In *Grootboom*, the Court seized on these changes to cast doubt on the legal
credibility of the minimum core approach and to adopt something like
Mureinik's rational justification approach instead.

Two issues in the main were emphasised. First, the Court noted that
the UN Committee on Economic, Social and Cultural Rights had
developed its understanding of the minimum core after many years of
considering reports from the various States Parties to the Covenant.
There was no 'comparable information' before it.[102] Secondly, among
the changes to the wording of the constitutional provision, the Court
stressed that the right in s 26 was a right 'to have access to' adequate
housing, rather than a right to adequate housing *tout court*. Since access
was conditioned by varying 'needs and opportunities', about which the
Court had little knowledge, it was not in a position to offer a definition of
the minimum core.[103]

This aspect of the *Grootboom* judgment has been extensively criticised,
most forcefully by Bilchitz, who has argued that the Court misunderstood
what its role in defining the minimum core required. Instead of considering the 'needs and opportunities' for enjoyment of the right, the Court
simply needed to state in general terms what the 'invariant, universal
standard' for satisfaction of the state's minimum core obligation was.[104]
This the Court might have done in one of two ways, neither of which
required it to gather any information itself. First, the Court might have
relied on the UN Committee's definition of the minimum core in General
Comment 4 on the Right to Adequate Housing. After all, as the Court
itself said,[105] the concept of the minimum core had been developed on
the back of 'extensive experience' and in such a way as to accommodate

---

[101] See the discussion in Section 7.1.   [102] *Grootboom* para 32.
[103] Ibid. para 33.   [104] Bilchitz, *Poverty and Fundamental Rights* 197.
[105] *Grootboom* para 31.

the varying circumstances in which the States Parties to the Covenant found themselves.[106] Alternatively, the Court might have developed its own understanding of the minimum core, based on the Constitution's underlying values and a purposive interpretation of the reasons behind the inclusion of social rights. Contrary to the Court's protestations, such an approach would not have required detailed information about individual shelter needs or the best methods for providing shelter. It would simply have required a basic understanding of the conditions necessary for human survival, the evidentiary basis for which could have been established by judicial notice.[107]

In the face of this critique, there are really only two explanations for the Court's refusal to adopt the minimum core approach: either the judges sincerely (though mistakenly) believed that the international law model required them to do something that they were not institutionally equipped to do, or they felt that the international law model, though legally plausible, was not legally compelled, and should therefore be discarded in favour of a review standard more in keeping with the overarching strategy they were pursuing

The first explanation is supported by the Court's repeated references to the need for more information on the 'needs and opportunities for the enjoyment of [the] right'.[108] Though conceptually confused in the way Bilchitz demonstrates, the Court does seem to have been convinced that defining the minimum core required it to do something that it was not well equipped to do. The subtext of the Court's description of the role played by the UN Committee was thus that the Committee performed a very different function from that of a municipal constitutional court. The Committee's General Comment 3, the Court emphasised, is 'largely descriptive of how the states have complied with their obligations under the Covenant.'[109] Although the general comment also provided 'a prescriptive definition' of the minimum core, the aim of this definition was to develop 'a common understanding of the norms'.[110]

---

[106] Although South Africa had not yet ratified the Covenant, the Department of Housing had endorsed the UN Committee's approach in its definition of adequate housing in the National Housing Code (McLean, *Constitutional Deference* 140).

[107] Bilchitz, *Poverty and Fundamental Rights* 188 (defining this minimal interest as comprising 'access to accommodation that offers protection from the elements, sanitary conditions, and access to basic services such as sanitation and running water').

[108] *Grootboom* para 32.   [109] Ibid. para 31.

[110] Ibid. para 31, quoting Matthew Craven, *The International Covenant on Economic, Social and Cultural Rights* (Oxford: Clarendon, 1995) 91.

It is apparent from these remarks that the Court thought that the main reason why the minimum core approach could not be followed was that the UN Committee's relationship with the States Parties to the Covenant was very different to its own relationship with the ANC. Whereas the UN Committee largely performed a coordinating function, collecting information from a number of different countries and issuing what were in effect best practice statements, the Court's power of judicial review would inevitably give the minimum core approach a more confrontational edge, potentially bringing it into conflict with the political branches, when what it really required was their support. Although the Court could no doubt have been clearer about this, its real objection to the minimum core approach had more to do with the long-term institutional consequences of adopting this understanding of its mandate than the absence of adequate information in the particular case before it.

The second explanation for the Court's refusal to adopt the minimum core approach is not necessarily exclusive of the first, but places greater emphasis on the political constraints under which the Court was operating. According to this explanation, the Court had certain misgivings about the international law model from the perspective of the overarching strategy it was pursuing. That strategy, as we have seen, depended on managing its relationship with the ANC in a political context in which the ANC was set to govern for some time. In relation to social rights, this meant that the Court needed to proceed fairly cautiously. On the one hand, the ANC's political dominance meant that the realisation of social rights was effectively tied to the success of its social and economic transformation project. On the other, the ANC's political dominance put it in a position to undermine the Court's independence should the Court's interpretation of social rights prove inconvenient. The problem with the minimum core approach from this perspective was that it was both too interventionist and too inflexible: too interventionist because it required the Court to set the Government's priorities for it, and too inflexible because, having set those priorities, the Court would be bound by respect for its own precedents to continue insisting that those priorities be met.[111]

---

[111] The Court was arguably mistaken in both these respects. A broad, interests-based definition of the minimum core of the kind suggested by Bilchitz would not have been noticeably more inflexible than the approach the Court ultimately adopted, especially when combined with a more context-sensitive review standard in respect of the state's efforts to satisfy the minimum core. Such a definition would also arguably have helped to focus the ANC's social welfare programmes, ensuring that, even when the methods by which the ANC sought to achieve its transformation goals changed, the objective would

In light of these misgivings, the Court's main concern was to ascertain the extent to which the minimum core approach was legally compelled. The more legally compelled this approach, the heavier the reputational losses attendant on rejecting it would have been, detracting from the benefits of adopting another approach more in keeping with the Court's overarching strategy. Here, the textual differences between s 26 and Articles 2.1 and 11.1 of the ICESCR became crucial. There was just enough in these differences, when coupled with the different institutional function performed by UN Committee, to suggest that the international law model was not legally compelled, or at least that whatever reputational losses the Court might suffer in consequence of rejecting this approach would be more than off-set by gains in institutional independence – gains that would allow it cautiously to assert its social rights mandate over the short term and perhaps provide a platform for a more interventionist role at some later date.

Having come to that conclusion, the Court set about devising an alternative approach, one sufficiently rooted in the constitutional text to be legally defensible, but at the same time better aligned with its overarching strategy. The rational justification approach suggested by Mureinik was ideally suited to this purpose. Whether because of Mureinik's influence or not,[112] the reference in s 26(2) to the state's obligation to take 'reasonable legislative and other measures' provided a textual hook for this approach that could be used to reinforce the differences between the rest of s 26 and the ICESCR. By emphasising the role of the political branches as the primary drivers of social and economic policy, the rational justification approach was moreover squarely in line with the historical reasons behind the inclusion of social rights in the Constitution.[113] These two considerations were enough to satisfy the requirement of legal defensibility. As to the strategic question, the rational justification approach had certain obvious advantages. Unlike the minimum core approach, it did not require the Court to define the substantive content of social rights or otherwise engage in priority-setting. On the contrary, it left both the goals and the methods of the state's social welfare programmes to the legislature and the executive to define. This

---

have remained the same. Recognising this, however, does not undermine the power of the second explanation, which depends, not on whether the Court was correct in its assessment of the dangers attendant on adoption of the minimum core approach, but on whether these kinds of misgivings may plausibly be said to have influenced it.

[112] Cf. Michelman, 'The Constitution, Social Rights and Reason' 500.

[113] See Section 7.1.

approach was more in keeping with the Court's overarching strategy. As the dominant political party, the ANC had both the power to deliver on the Constitution's promise of social and economic transformation and also the power to sideline the Court from playing any meaningful role in relation to social rights. In those circumstances, what the Court needed to do was to enlist the ANC as a partner, knowing that the realisation of social rights ultimately lay in its hands.

Mureinik's rational justification approach did suffer from one significant drawback, however. In curing the minimum core approach's problem of inflexible interventionism, it was itself in turn inflexibly deferential. This ran contrary to one of the main requirements of the Court's overarching strategy: that it should be able to enforce constitutional rights where the micro-politics of the case allowed for this and where the rights violation was so glaring as to threaten the Court's legal-professional reputation should it fail to intervene. It was therefore important that the rational justification approach should be framed in such a way as to allow the Court to heighten the level of scrutiny when required. The Constitution, after all, clearly mandated the Court to enforce social rights. If the Court never struck down a single programme, then, whatever the enduring *procedural* benefits of the rational justification approach on Mureinik's view,[114] the *strategic* benefits would be lost.

The reasonableness review standard the Court famously devised in *Grootboom* bears all the hallmarks of these considerations. The key feature of the standard is its flexibility. Rather than imposing on the state a minimum core obligation to prioritise the meeting of urgent shelter needs, the standard makes the state's obligation to cater to people in 'desperate need'[115] and otherwise not to exclude 'a significant segment of society'[116] an essential requirement of reasonableness. The shift in emphasis is subtle but nevertheless important. Instead of defining the core content of the right, the Court defines an open-ended category of people ('in desperate need') whom no reasonable social welfare programme may constitutionally ignore. To this it adds another, even more open-ended category ('a significant segment of society') whose omission from any social welfare programme would constitute a further basis for intervention.

When coupled with the requirement that the state must take at least some 'legislative and other measures',[117] this standard comes close to that applied in the Court's equality jurisprudence. As in that area of its work,

---

[114] Cf. Mureinik, 'Beyond a Charter of Luxuries' 472.
[115] *Grootboom* para 63.   [116] Ibid. para 43.   [117] Section 26(2).

the Court's primary concern is for the equal treatment of people according to their relative social and economic vulnerability.[118] In the case of social rights, the presence of a particular right in the Constitution triggers the state's obligation to take positive steps, in the first instance, to enable people to meet their basic needs themselves, and, where this is not possible, to meet their basic needs for them.[119] Without specifying the overall level of resources that must be deployed, or even the minimum levels of provision that need to be met, the reasonableness review standard requires that the steps the state takes must be meaningful, in the sense that they should at least hold out the possibility of realising the right in question. Apart from this difference, however, the assessment of the state's conduct collapses back into something like the Court's approach to allegations of unfair discrimination.[120] In both instances, the Court's attention is drawn to the rationality and fairness of the impugned governmental programme, judged by whether the claimant belongs to a group that has an equal or better claim to inclusion than groups which have in fact been included.[121]

As Bilchitz has argued, this equality-based approach to social rights is conceptually flawed in as much as it is impossible to know whether a particular set of 'legislative and other measures' holds out the possibility of realising a right without knowing what the content of the right is. It is also impossible to compare the treatment of different groups without knowing in what respect they are being compared. By studiously avoiding attributing any content to the right to adequate housing, the *Grootboom* Court devised a standard that was highly discretionary at best, and logically confused at worst.[122]

All of these criticisms are justified. On the approach adopted in this study, however, the merits of the *Grootboom* decision must be assessed with some appreciation for the political context in which the Court found

---

[118] For an extended version of this reading, see Wesson '*Grootboom* and Reassessing the Socio-economic Jurisprudence of the South African Constitutional Court'.

[119] *Grootboom* para 36.

[120] This feature of the Court's approach is generally taken to have been confirmed by its decision in *Khosa and Others* v. *Minister of Social Development and Others; Mahlaule and Others* v. *Minister of Social Development and Others* (2004) 6 SA 505 (CC), 2004 (6) BCLR 569 (CC), where the social rights and equality clause aspects of the constitutional inquiry were effectively fused.

[121] For a more extended version of this reading, see Theunis Roux, 'Legitimating Transformation: Political Resource Allocation in the South African Constitutional Court' (2003) 10 *Democratization* 92.

[122] Bilchitz, *Poverty and Fundamental Rights* 167–70.

itself. In late 2000, when the decision was delivered, the ANC had been in power a mere five years. The national housing programme, while not without flaws, represented a massive undertaking, the seriousness and overall sophistication of which needed to be acknowledged. The adoption of the minimum core approach would have forced a fundamental reorientation in this programme, bringing the Court into direct conflict with the political branches, at a time when it was still vulnerable to political attack. In those circumstances, the Court not unreasonably appears to have decided to compromise on principle, choosing a standard of review that required at least some resources to be diverted to meeting urgent shelter needs, while leaving the scale and timing of any such adjustment to the democratic process.[123]

Though compromised in this way, the reasonableness review standard is not entirely toothless. Its distinct advantage, as noted already, is its flexibility. Both the characterisation of the vulnerable group and the sorts of issues to which the Court may have regard are context-sensitive. In this way, the reasonableness review approach constitutes a shrewd development of the approach Mureinik had suggested. Rather than being confined to simple rationality review, the approach allows the level of scrutiny to be adjusted to the micro-politics of particular cases. Indeed, the very features of the reasonableness review approach that South African scholars have decried constitute its peculiar strength from this perspective. The open-endedness of the Court's categorisation of vulnerable groups, for example, allows the approach to be tailored to the character of a particular claimant group. The contentlessness of the standard, while detracting from its usefulness as a programmatic guide, nevertheless enables the Court to enforce significant changes to social and economic policy, without appearing to set Government's priorities for it. All of these features were well demonstrated by the Court's next social rights case.

7.4   Exploiting the micro-politics: *Treatment Action Campaign*

By any kind of measure, *Treatment Action Campaign* was a politically charged case. It concerned a policy issue that, together with the ANC's failure to condemn the suppression of democracy in Zimbabwe, was one of the most criticised aspects of Mbeki's presidency. The case also

---

[123] See Sunstein, *Designing Democracy* 221–37.

triggered an infamous attack on the Court that constituted the only instance of open defiance of its authority during Chaskalson's term as Chief Justice. And yet, by the time the Court came to decide it, most of the political heat generated by the case had already dissipated. That this was so was largely attributable to the skilful way the constitutional claimant ran it. But the Court's flexible review standard, which this chapter has argued was the product of a conscious adjudicative strategy, undoubtedly also influenced the claimant's approach to the case and the Court's capacity in turn to respond to the way it was framed.[124]

The issue in *Treatment Action Campaign* could not have been more explosive: an allegation by the constitutional claimant – a well-connected and politically credible social movement – that the Department of Health's refusal to support the distribution of a drug capable of preventing the mother-to-child-transmission ('MTCT') of HIV was causing hundreds of preventable infant deaths every month. Not just that, but the subtext of the case was that this policy decision – rather than a function of mistaken priorities – was the direct result of President Mbeki's own misguided views on the toxicity of anti-retroviral drugs. If true, these charges would clearly be devastating to the President's personal reputation. But they would also be virtually impossible for the Court to ignore. *Treatment Action Campaign*, in short, seemed destined to present the Court with an irreconcilable choice between principle and politics.

That the case did not come to this was largely attributable, as noted already, to the way the claimant ran it. Led by Zachie Achmat, the gay-rights activist who had masterminded the two *National Coalition* cases,[125] the Treatment Action Campaign ('TAC') pursued a multi-pronged litigation strategy in which the merits of its demand for a comprehensive MTCT prevention programme were determined in the

---

[124] This is a slightly different interpretation of the case from the one offered by William Forbath, 'Cultural Transformation, Deep Institutional Reform, and ESR Practice: South Africa's Treatment Action Campaign' in Lucie E. White and Jeremy Perelman, *Stones of Hope: How African Activists Reclaim Human Rights to Challenge Global Poverty* (Stanford University Press, 2011) 51 (arguing that the Court's approach in *Treatment Action Campaign* 'favored a more polity-based, less juristocratic or court-centred conception of the realization of social and economic rights' that 'reflect[ed] and [drew] on' the claimant's litigation strategy).

[125] *National Coalition for Gay and Lesbian Equality and Another* v. *Minister of Justice and Others* 1999 (1) SA (CC), 1998 (12) BCLR 1517 (CC) and *National Coalition for Gay and Lesbian Equality and Others* v. *Minister of Home Affairs and Others* 2000 (2) SA 1 (CC), 2000 (1) BCLR 39 (CC).

public domain long before the Court came to decide the constitutional issues.[126] Starting in December 1998, when the TAC was founded, the strategy concentrated, on the one hand, on pressurising the manufacturers of anti-retroviral drugs to reduce their prices and, on the other, on persuading the Department of Health to improve its policies. After an initial period of co-operation with the Government, the TAC met its first obstacle in 1999 when President Mbeki began publicly questioning the safety of AZT, the main anti-retroviral drug then used in the prevention of MTCT.[127] From this point, the development of a comprehensive programme faltered, forcing the TAC to shift its focus from the pharmaceutical companies to the Government.

In mid-2000, the preliminary results of a local South African trial of a new anti-retroviral drug, Nevirapine, were released, indicating that a single dose of this drug, administered to the mother just before giving birth, was highly effective.[128] Shortly thereafter, Nevirapine's manufacturer, Boehringer Ingelheim, offered to supply the drug to the Government free of charge for five years. These two events shifted the policy debate decisively in the TAC's favour. The launch of legal proceedings, however, was delayed to give the Medicines Control Council ('MCC') an opportunity to approve the package insert for the drug, the absence of which was thought to pose a barrier to an immediately enforceable order.[129] In the meantime, the Government decided, in August 2000, to trial Nevirapine at two pilot sites in each of the nine provinces, ostensibly to test for side-effects (something that had already been ruled out by the earlier trial) and to ascertain the demands that would be made on the state to ensure the proper administration of a comprehensive programme. The eighteen pilot sites catered to a mere 10 per cent of the population,[130] and were in any case not opened until May 2001, after political pressure had been placed on the MCC to delay approval of the package insert.[131]

Deeming the coverage of the pilot sites inadequate, the TAC wrote a letter in July 2001 to the national Department of Health and to all nine provincial health departments demanding reasons for the Government's

---

[126] In addition to Forbath, 'Cultural Transformation, Deep Institutional Reform, and ESR Practice', see Heywood, 'Preventing Mother-to-Child HIV Transmission in South Africa'.

[127] Heywood, 'Preventing Mother-to-Child HIV Transmission in South Africa' 282.

[128] Ibid.   [129] Ibid. 285.

[130] *Treatment Action Campaign* para 62.

[131] Heywood, 'Preventing Mother-to-Child HIV Transmission in South Africa' 289.

failure to distribute Nevirapine more widely and requesting an undertaking that a comprehensive MTCT prevention programme would be put in place.[132] By addressing all ten responsible departments in this way, the letter not only complied with procedural requirements, but also sought to drive a wedge between the national Government and the provinces, several of which were keen to expand their programmes.[133] Under threat of litigation, the Western Cape provincial government was the first to breaks ranks, writing separately to the TAC's attorney to inform it of its plan to reach 90 per cent of HIV-positive women by July 2002.[134] As the litigation progressed, several other provincial governments also announced plans to increase the number of test sites, leaving the national Government, and President Mbeki in particular, increasingly isolated.

Legal proceedings formally commenced in the Pretoria High Court in August 2001, one year after the decision to establish the pilot sites had been taken. From this point on, the political aspect of the case fed off the legal aspect and vice versa, with each intermediate legal victory increasing the political pressure on President Mbeki to change course, and each chink in the armour of the Government's unified response to the case emboldening the courts to enforce the claimant's rights more forcefully.

Relying on the review standard set in *Grootboom*, the High Court application alleged that the Government's refusal to allow public-sector doctors who were not working in one of the pilot sites to prescribe Nevirapine and its failure to set a time frame for the rolling out of a comprehensive MTCT prevention programme were unreasonable under ss 27(1)(*a*) and (2) of the 1996 Constitution (right to health care). The cleverness of this framing of the issue lay in the fact that the case was essentially about the TAC's demand for wider access to a named antiretroviral drug. Given the Court's reluctance to involve itself in the technicalities of housing policy in *Grootboom*, this was no easy matter. The case needed to be set up in such a way that the Court could order the distribution of Nevirapine, and all of the support services required to administer it, without appearing to be taking these complex medical and budgetary decisions itself. It was in this respect that the TAC's patient litigation strategy paid off. By waiting for Nevirapine to be registered, and for the Department of Health to start its pilot programme, the TAC was able to depict the Government's policy as a simple case of unequal treatment. Here was a drug, the TAC in effect argued, which the

---

[132] Ibid. 290–91.   [133] Ibid.   [134] Ibid. 292.

responsible regulator had authorised for general use, which was available in the private sector, and which could be accessed in the public sector by those lucky enough to live within reach of one of the pilot sites, and yet the Government was making it practically impossible for other public-sector doctors to prescribe it.

Framed in this way, the policy and budgetary issues raised by the case were amenable to judicial review. Rather than addressing the complicated question of which drug to choose, the claim was focused on the distribution of a drug that the Government itself had already decided was the best treatment available. On the budgetary question, Boehringer Ingelheim's offer to make Nevirapine available free of charge was obviously crucial. This gesture, a consequence of the first prong of the TAC's strategy, meant that the financial implications of broadening access were essentially reduced to the cost of testing for the presence of HIV, training counsellors, and providing formula feed and other support. *Treatment Action Campaign* was in this sense exactly the converse of *Soobramoney*. Whereas *Soobramoney* had been about an individual claim for an expensive medical treatment with far-reaching budgetary implications, *Treatment Action Campaign* was in the nature of a class action for an inexpensive medical treatment whose budgetary implications were relatively minor and predictable.[135]

After the initial hearing in the High Court, the TAC continued to raise public awareness of the case, stressing the urgency of the required policy change and using the deadly consequences of the Government's failure to act as the justified pretext for mass demonstrations.[136] Whether in response to this part of the TAC's strategy or simply recognising the urgency of the matter on its own merits, the High Court handed down a relatively expeditious judgment, in December 2001. Picking up on the claimant's framing of the case, the High Court held that 'the policy [of] ... prohibiting the use of Nevirapine outside the pilot sites in the public health sector is a breach of [government's] negative obligation ... to desist from impairing the right to health care.'[137] As William Forbath has observed, this was pushing things a little.[138] The state's positive

---

[135] See further Forbath, 'Cultural Transformation, Deep Institutional Reform, and ESR Practice' 22.

[136] Heywood, 'Preventing Mother-to-Child HIV Transmission in South Africa' 300–301.

[137] *Treatment Action Campaign v. Minister of Health* 2002 (4) BCLR 356 (T) ('*Treatment Action Campaign* (HC)').

[138] Forbath, 'Cultural Transformation, Deep Institutional Reform, and ESR Practice' 23.

obligation to establish a comprehensive MTCT prevention programme could not be entirely subsumed under the negative obligation not to impair access to a particular drug. But the TAC's strategy had undeniably worked, and prompted the High Court to hand down a wide-ranging supervisory order that mandated the Government forthwith to supply Nevirapine or other suitable drugs in the public sector where medically indicated.[139]

As emphatic as this victory was, it was not a foregone conclusion that the Constitutional Court would follow suit. As in other jurisdictions, intermediate court judges in South Africa enjoy a certain amount of latitude when deciding novel claims. In constitutional cases, particularly, this is a natural consequence of the fact that their decisions are not binding until confirmed by the Constitutional Court.[140] Given its different institutional position, it was clear that the Constitutional Court would be more exposed than the High Court had been to any political backlash from the case. Nevertheless, the boldness of the High Court's decision set in motion a series of events that ultimately made it easier for the Constitutional Court to vindicate the claimant's rights. First, in immediate response to the High Court decision, the Premier of Gauteng, South Africa's wealthiest province, announced that his Government would implement a comprehensive MTCT prevention programme. President Mbeki's Health Minister immediately criticised this announcement, and forced the Premier to give 'the appearance of backing down'.[141] But the implementation of an expanded MTCT prevention programme in Gauteng continued, reaching 70 per cent of public hospitals by October 2002.[142] Together with similar expansions in the Western Cape and KwaZulu-Natal,[143] this development had the effect of disproving the Government's main argument that the TAC's challenge called for an order that it was not capable of fulfilling.

Secondly, on 11 March 2002, the High Court granted an application by the TAC for the execution of its supervisory order pending an application by the government to the Constitutional Court for leave to appeal.[144] In response to this decision, the Government made the crucial tactical error of applying to the Constitutional Court, not just for an order overturning

---

[139] *Treatment Action Campaign* (HC).   [140] See Chapter 5.
[141] Heywood, 'Preventing Mother-to-Child HIV Transmission in South Africa' 304.
[142] Ibid.   [143] Ibid. 292–4.
[144] Ordinarily, the lodging of an appeal in South Africa automatically suspends the execution of the lower court's order.

the High Court's main decision, but also for an order overturning the High Court's decision to grant immediate execution. This pre-hearing appeal, on an issue that would in any case have been superseded had the main appeal been successful, gave the Constitutional Court a crucial opportunity to signal the direction it was likely to go.

The precise chain of events is important to convey. On 24 March, President's Mbeki's Health Minister, Manto Tshabalala-Msimang, was interviewed on national television. In response to a question about whether she would be prepared to 'stand by' the Constitutional Court's decision were it to go the same way as the High Court's decision, she replied that she would not.[145] Although she was immediately forced to retract this remark,[146] the impression of an intransigent Government willing to defy the Constitution if necessary could not have been stronger. At this point, the Government's appeal against the High Court's immediate execution decision played into the Constitutional Court's hands. Heard on 3 April, and decided the next day, the pre-hearing appeal allowed the Court to enter the political fray over the distribution of Nevirapine on a relatively minor point, which had no direct bearing on the outcome of the main appeal.[147] By rapidly dealing with this part of the case, the Court was able to communicate where its sympathies lay.

At the same time, Mbeki was coming under intense international pressure to change his stance. According to R. W. Johnson, the crucial development in this respect was a visit to South Africa by Jean Chrétien, the Canadian Prime Minister, who was due to host a meeting of the G8 in June. Mbeki had been courting Chrétien to support his New Economic Plan for African Development, and was due to attend the G8 meeting. Seeing an opportunity to exert some influence, Chrétien and the Canadian journalists accompanying him 'grilled' Mbeki on his views on HIV/AIDS, making it clear that they were endangering his ambitions of becoming a regional statesman.[148] Whether in response to this experience, or the Constitutional Court's decision on the execution issue, Mbeki finally buckled. On 17 April, two weeks before the main Constitutional Court hearing, the Cabinet issued a statement

---

[145] Heywood, 'Preventing Mother-to-Child HIV Transmission in South Africa' 308.

[146] Ibid. 309.

[147] The outcome of the appeal on this point was not, of course, inconsequential in human terms, given the lives at stake.

[148] Johnson, *South Africa's Brave New World* 201.

recognising the efficacy of anti-retroviral drugs and announcing a universal roll-out plan.[149]

The Cabinet's statement effectively ended the Government's political opposition to the case. Indeed, from this point on, the politics of the case were neatly inverted. From being a case in which a decision against the Government had threatened to expose the Court to significant political backlash, *Treatment Action Campaign* became a case in which the handing down of a principled decision in favour of the TAC was President Mbeki's best hope of political salvation. Completely isolated, both domestically and internationally, the Mbeki's only chance of saving face lay in the issuing of a court order that would force him to do what he was in any case politically compelled to do.

The collapsing of the Government's opposition to the case still left the Court with a challenging judgment to write. Having carefully constructed its reasonableness review standard in *Grootboom* so as to leave the detailed policy choices informing the national housing programme to the political branches to make, the Court was now being asked to interrogate quite closely the arguments the Minister of Health had offered in defence of her department's limited pilot site programme. Unlike the policy choices in *Grootboom*, these arguments could not be left to stand unchallenged. For both legal and political reasons, the Court needed to expose the obfuscatory way in which the Government had conducted its case. At the same time, however, the Court could not afford to ratchet up the level of review too much, lest it be required to repeat this performance in a case in which the micro-politics were less propitious.

To meet this challenge, the Court did several things. First, it relied on the technique Chaskalson had used to such good effect in *Makwanyane*.[150] Rather than giving its own account of the policy arguments in support of Nevirapine, the Court addressed the Government's stated concerns about the expansion of its pilot programme and showed them all to be baseless. The Government's concern that the efficacy of Nevirapine would in some cases be undermined by breast-feeding, for example, was dismissed on the ground that it was better to save some lives than none at all.[151] Likewise, the Government's concern over the possibility that the administration of a single dose of Nevirapine might

---

[149] Ibid. 200.
[150] *S v. Makwanyane and Another* 1995 (3) SA 391 (CC), 1995 (6) BCLR 665 (CC). See the discussion in Chapter 6.
[151] *Treatment Action Campaign* paras 57 and 58.

lead to drug resistance was found to be overstated and in any case outweighed by the proven benefits of this treatment.[152] Proceeding in this way, the Court was able to rebut the Government's arguments against the expansion of its pilot programme without offering a rival policy of its own.

Next, the Court moved on to apply the reasonableness review standard it had developed in *Grootboom*. From among the various criteria it had mentioned in that decision, the Court stressed the need for the Government's response to the AIDS crisis to be 'flexible'.[153] The use of this word in the context of the *Treatment Action Campaign* case was clearly a coded reference to the Department of Health's intransigence in the face of mounting evidence that Nevirapine worked. The fact that the word had already been used in *Grootboom*, however, gave it a fairly neutral tone, and allowed the Court to decide the case against the Government without expressly confirming what everyone thought: that the pilot programme was simply a tactic to delay the progress of the TAC's case. In the neutral language of 'flexibility', the problem with the pilot programme was that the Government's legitimate need to assess the demands that would be made on it by a comprehensive programme was being used as a justification for refusing to supply Nevirapine outside the research and training sites in the meantime. This was clearly unreasonable in circumstances where Nevirapine was medically indicated and where the hospital or clinic in question in fact had the capacity to provide the testing, counselling and support services required.[154]

As regards the main point on which the High Court decision had turned, the Constitutional Court was somewhat ambivalent. In paragraph 46 of its decision, the Court referred to its holding in *Grootboom* that social rights impose on the Government, at the very least, a 'negative obligation' not to impair the given right.[155] The Court failed to develop this point, however, saying simply that it was 'relevant to the challenges to the measures adopted by government for the provision of medical services to combat mother-to-child transmission of HIV'. As Bilchitz has observed, the Court's reluctance to make a ruling on this issue may have been because the evidence did not show that the Government was actively prohibiting the prescription of Nevirapine by public-sector

---

[152] Ibid. para 59.
[153] Ibid. para 68 (quoting *Grootboom* para 43). See also *Treatment Action Campaign* paras 78, 80 and 114.
[154] Ibid.   [155] Citing *Grootboom* para 34.

doctors working outside the research and training sites; it simply did nothing to facilitate access to the drug.[156] There is a fine line, however, between the failure to make a drug available and prohibiting access to it. For all intents and purposes, by refusing to provide public hospitals and clinics with the resources to acquire Nevirapine, the Government imposed a ban on its distribution. Another reading of the Court's decision in *Treatment Action Campaign*, therefore, is that it consciously exploited the slippage between the negative and positive dimension of social rights – first by repeating its earlier dictum in *Grootboom*, and then by deliberately not exploring it so that the negative obligation point could hover in the background as an additional ground for the decision.

The equality dimension of the case was dealt with in a similar way. As we saw in *Grootboom*, the Court's contentless review standard relies on the Government to take at least some action to realise a social right, and then examines whether the action taken treats all similarly placed persons equally. In *Treatment Action Campaign*, the claimant exploited this aspect of the review standard by waiting until the Department of Health had started its pilot programme. It then framed its case as one in which the unreasonableness of the Government's action consisted in the arbitrariness of the choice of the eighteen research and training sites. Although the Constitutional Court did not expressly respond to this argument, it did acknowledge that, '[t]o the extent that government limits the supply of nevirapine to its research sites, it is the poor outside the catchment areas of these sites who will suffer'.[157] In effect, the Court was saying, once the Department of Health decided to make Nevirapine available to 10 per cent of the population, the only basis on which it could deny the rest of the population access to the drug was to argue that the cost of expanding the number of research and training sites was prohibitive.[158]

The Government did in fact make precisely this argument.[159] The problem it encountered, however, was Boehringer Ingelheim's offer to make Nevirapine available free of charge for five years. This gesture effectively nullified its defence to the charge of unequal treatment. With

---

[156] Bilchitz, *Poverty and Fundamental Rights* 158.

[157] *Treatment Action Campaign*, para 70.

[158] This does not mean that the TAC could not have won its case had the government taken no action at all. But it does suggest that, tactically, social rights claimants would be well advised to wait for government to take some initial steps to implement a social welfare programme before launching their case.

[159] *Treatment Action Campaign* para 49.

the major cost associated with the establishment of a comprehensive programme taken out of the equation, it was clear that granting the order requested by the TAC would have only a minimal budgetary impact. The remaining costs associated with developing a comprehensive programme concerned such issues as testing and counselling services, both of which could be absorbed within the Department of Health's existing budget, which was in any case being under spent.[160]

Although much has been made of the Court's conclusive rejection of the minimum core approach in *Treatment Action Campaign*, it is important to note that the claimant did not raise this issue. All the legal resources it required for its case were contained in the reasonableness review approach. The question whether the Government was required to supply Nevirapine as part of its minimum core obligation under the right to health care was raised by the first and second *amici curiae*.[161] The significance of the Court's rejection of the *amici's* argument for purposes of this study is that it confirmed what was already apparent in *Grootboom*, viz. that the Court's disinclination to apply the minimum core approach was not really attributable to the fact that it lacked the requisite information. Rather, it had to do with a far more thoroughgoing concern about the institutional consequences for the Court of defining the minimum core. Significantly, too, the Court's final rejection of the minimum core approach in *Treatment Action Campaign* depended heavily on its statement in paragraph 11 of *Soobramoney*,[162] suggesting that this passage may indeed have been a deliberate attempt on the part of the Court to lay the doctrinal groundwork for its preferred strategy.

Though by no means perfect, the Court's decision in *Treatment Action Campaign* vindicated the cautious approach it had taken in *Grootboom* and its decision there to adopt a flexible standard of review. The reasonableness review approach not only facilitated the TAC's multi-pronged litigation strategy, but also allowed the Court to respond to the eventual collapse in the Government's political opposition to the case. Using the same analytic framework it had devised in *Grootboom*, the Court was able subtly to heighten the level of review, taking a closer look at the Government's detailed policy arguments than it had done in its earlier

---

[160] To make sure of this point, the TAC had strategically limited its suggested order for the expansion of the research and training sites to those public hospitals and clinics where the capacity to administer Nevirapine already existed (*Treatment Action Campaign* para 71).

[161] Ibid. paras 26–39.   [162] Ibid. para 31.

decision. Particularly noteworthy here was the Court's preparedness to take a position on the 'science' of HIV/AIDS, in marked contrast to its reluctance to involve itself in the details of housing policy. The Court was undoubtedly assisted in this regard by the fact that the TAC had already won the public policy argument over the efficiency and effectiveness of a comprehensive MTCT prevention programme. But it was the flexibility of the Court's review standard that both made the TAC's strategy possible and allowed the Court to respond to it.

Not every future social rights case would resolve itself so easily, of course. The TAC had been a particularly astute litigant, with the intellectual and material resources to take advantage of the Court's preferred approach. Despite the collapse of the government's political opposition to the case, therefore, the Court took great care not to ratchet up the level of review too far.

A similar caution was evident in its approach to the question of remedy. Although the Government's foot-dragging on the establishment of a comprehensive MTCT prevention programme was plain to see, the Constitutional Court chose not to follow the High Court's supervisory order, but instead to issue a mandamus ordering the removal of restrictions on the prescription of Nevirapine by public sector doctors outside the research and training sites and the taking of steps to facilitate the provision of Nevirapine throughout the public sector. Critics of this toned down order appeared to be vindicated when the TAC was required to follow up the implementation of the Court's order in the most recalcitrant of the nine provinces.[163] But the Court was here evidently thinking of its longer-term relationship with the ANC and the need, even in this most pressing of cases, to engage the political branches as partners in the constitutional project.

---

[163] See Bilchitz, *Poverty and Fundamental Rights* 163.

8

Property rights

Far from representing a 'victory' for the National Party,[1] the property clause in the 1996 Constitution is best understood as embodying the ANC's hybrid human rights tradition. As we saw in Chapter 4, the ANC had long mediated socialist calls for nationalisation of the means of production and African nationalist demands for full inclusion in the economy. These competing concerns are reflected in the text of the property clause, s 25, which attempts to strike a balance between protecting the institution of private property and allowing significant state intervention to redress past injustices and meet present welfare needs. While it is also possible to see these provisions as the product of an 'insurance swap' between the ANC and the National Party,[2] the better explanation is that the property clause gave expression to the ANC's long-standing preference for a democratically managed market economy.[3]

Whatever its precise political origins, the inclusion of a property clause in the 1996 Constitution clearly gave the Chaskalson Court a central role in overseeing the procedural fairness and moral justifiability of reforms to the existing property rights order. On the one hand, the clause required the Court to guarantee the stability of that order by ensuring that whatever measures were taken to redress past injustices and meet present welfare needs were pursued in an orderly, rule-of-law-respecting fashion. On the other, the clause required the Court to develop the normative framework within which the remoralisation of the existing property rights order should occur. On the face of it, this promised to be one of the most challenging aspects of the Court's work, with the judges

---

[1] Hirschl, *Towards Juristocracy* 94 (using this term and arguing that '[t]he NP won out conclusively on the property rights front').

[2] See Rosalind Dixon and Tom Ginsburg, 'The South African Constitutional Court and Socio-Economic Rights as "Insurance Swaps"' (2012) 4 *Constitutional Court Review* 1.

[3] See further Section 8.1.1.

required to steer between the Scylla of status-quo-protectionism and the Charybdis of redistributive populism.

As it turned out, neither of these fates befell the Court. Instead, the Court was able in its decisions to demonstrate how competing property interests might be reconciled and in this way to give concrete expression to the balance struck in the 1996 Constitution. As in other areas, the explanation for the Court's success lies partly in fortuitous political circumstances and partly in the wisdom and creativity of its doctrinal choices. In the former category, two factors were critical: (1) the ANC's ability during the final constitution-making process to transform a clause that in 1993 had appeared to be a major concession to the National Party into a clause that reflected its conception of the role of property rights in economic development and social transformation; and (2) the ANC's relatively cautious approach to land reform, which spared the Court from having to decide the politically awkward challenge from the commercial farming lobby that many commentators had feared. As to the Court's doctrinal choices, this chapter once again argues that they are best understood as having been driven, not by purely legal or purely political considerations, but by the judges' determination to shape the law in support of the Court's institutional independence. This is true both of the Court's major decision on the structure of the constitutional property clause inquiry, in which it chose a context-sensitive review standard not unlike the standard it had developed in relation to social rights, and also of a series of decisions in which the Court was required to reconcile the right to property in s 25 with the right to housing in s 26.

8.1   Political parameters

8.1.1   The political origins of s 25

The inclusion of a property clause in the interim South African Consti-tution was a predictable consequence of the National Party's relatively strong bargaining position at the MPNP.[4] More remarkable is the fact that the National Party did not insist on a cast-iron property rights guarantee in the schedule of principles governing the drafting of the final Constitution.[5] Instead, those principles simply provided that the final

---

[4] See Spitz with Chaskalson, *The Politics of Transition*. See also Matthew Chaskalson, 'Stumbling towards Section 28: Negotiations over the Protection of Property Rights in the Interim Constitution' (1995) 11 *South African Journal on Human Rights* 222.

[5] See Schedule 6 to the 1993 Constitution.

Constitution should contain all 'universally accepted fundamental rights'.[6] As the Constitutional Court held in its *First Certification Judgment*,[7] this formulation, given contemporary international and state practice, did not mandate the adoption of a property clause – a ruling that would not have come as a surprise to the major political parties in the Constitutional Assembly. The fact that a property clause was nevertheless included in the final Constitution must therefore be attributable to something else: either the ANC's calculation that the political costs of forcing through a property-clause-less Constitution were too high,[8] or the fact that the ANC itself favoured the qualified constitutionalisation of property rights.

The second is the more likely explanation. As we have seen,[9] the ANC's human rights tradition was a complex amalgam of liberal and socialist elements dating back to the deliberately vague Freedom Charter. Although the ANC had at periods in its history veered quite far leftwards in its economic pronouncements,[10] its political centre of gravity was social-democratic in orientation and, as such, not averse to limited constitutional protection for property rights, especially if such protection could be used to communicate its intention to engage in responsible management of the economy. The ANC's need to provide such assurances had already resulted, as we shall see in the next section, in the adoption of a fairly conservative macro-economic strategy, to which the protection of property rights was a logical counterpart. To be sure, the inclusion of a property clause cut across the ANC's commitment to social rights. But it had plenty of experience in mediating these competing concerns, and was able to use its political dominance of the Constitutional Assembly to ensure that property rights were protected in a way that could be reconciled with rights to land restitution, tenure

---

[6] Constitutional Principle II.

[7] *Ex Parte Chairperson of the Constitutional Assembly: In re Certification of the Constitution of the Republic of South Africa, 1996* 1996 (4) SA 744 (CC), 1996 (10) BCLR 1253 (CC) para 72.

[8] As pointed out in Chapter 4, the ANC's failure to win a two-thirds majority in the 1994 elections meant that it was dependent on the co-operation of minority political parties to have the final Constitution adopted by the Constitutional Assembly. To this extent, it might be argued, the National Party still had the power to insist on the inclusion of a property rights guarantee. Had the ANC been determined to exclude property rights from the final Constitution, however, it was open to it either to seek the support of a different minority party coalition, or to use the procedure provided in s 73 of the 1993 Constitution to have the final Constitution adopted by way of referendum.

[9] Section 4.2.   [10] See Alan Hirsch, *Season of Hope* 34–8.

security, housing and healthcare. Whereas the property clause in the interim Constitution, in other words, is attributable to the National Party's capacity to insist on this form of guarantee, the protection given to property rights by the 1996 Constitution had more to do with the ANC's capacity to give full and balanced expression to the two component parts of its human rights tradition.

The different political rationales underlying the two property clauses are reflected in the different formulations used in the constitutional text. Whereas the property rights provisions in the 1993 Constitution bear all the hallmarks of a hard-fought political compromise,[11] the 1996 Constitution contains a much more integrated conception of the link between the wealth-creating and welfare-providing dimensions of property. Instead of appearing in a separate section, as they do in the 1993 Constitution, the various provisions on land reform in the 1996 Constitution are worked into the property clause itself, making it clear that the protection extended to existing property rights is conditioned on the satisfaction of legitimate claims to land restitution, redistribution and tenure security.[12] Section 25(1) thus provides that 'no one may be deprived of property except by law of general application' and that 'no law may provide for arbitrary deprivation of property'. Section 25(2) reinforces these prohibitions by guaranteeing the payment of compensation in the event of the expropriation of property and conditioning the validity of any expropriation on the existence of a 'public purpose' or 'public interest' rationale. Section 25(3), on the other hand, provides that compensation for expropriated property need not amount to market value,[13] while ss 25(4)–(9) make it clear that the state may not be constitutionally barred from engaging in 'reasonable and justifiable' land reform measures.[14]

In combination with the right to housing in s 26, these provisions express an identifiable property rights morality premised on two main principles: (1) recognition that all existing property rights in South Africa are to a certain extent founded on past injustices, and therefore that these rights are held subject to the need to correct these injustices; and

---

[11] See, for example, the detailed provisions on land restitution in ss 121–3 of the 1993 Constitution, which nevertheless fail to define the crucial concept of 'land rights'.

[12] See s 25(5), (6) and (7).

[13] Market value is just one of a number of factors listed in s 25(3) that courts may take into account when assessing the fairness of compensation.

[14] 'Reasonable and justifiable' because the rights in s 25 are subject to the general limitations clause in s 36.

(2) concern for the basic needs of the propertyless, and a corresponding requirement that property rights should not be enforced in a way that denies the human dignity of those who do not have secure access to the property rights system.[15]

In setting out the moral parameters of property rights enforcement in this way, the 1996 Constitution gave the Chaskalson Court a considerable amount of textual guidance on the role it was expected to play. Clearly, it was not required strictly to enforce property rights in the manner of a court interpreting a classic liberal constitution. Rather, the Court was expected to play a mediating role, trading off property rights holders' interest in the sanctity of their holdings, and society's interest in wealth creation and productive investment, against the need, for welfarist but also for restitutionary justice and participatory democratic reasons, to broaden access to the property rights system. From the point of view of government policy, this standard was determinate enough to mean that a neo-liberal approach to economic growth and redistribution, in terms of which those currently excluded from the property rights system are expected to wait for wealth created by others to trickle down to them, would not have passed constitutional muster. Beyond this, however, the property rights provisions in the 1996 Constitution did not prescribe a particular economic policy. That task was left to the political branches.

8.1.2   ANC economic policy after 1994

As noted in Chapter 4,[16] ANC economic policy after 1994 was originally encapsulated in the Reconstruction and Development Programme ('RDP'), which served both as the ANC's 1994 election manifesto and as the intended blueprint for social and economic reform in its first five years in office.[17] The RDP had been endorsed by the Congress of South Africa Trade Unions ('COSATU') and was politically progressive in character, although even at this stage a note of fiscal conservatism was sounded.[18] The main idea informing the RDP was that state-led pro-grammes aimed at generating growth and meeting basic needs would

---

[15] See particularly s 26(3) (prohibiting evictions except on an order of court 'made after considering all the relevant circumstances'). The adoption of provisions of this kind casts considerable doubt on whether the South African case can be explained by the 'hege-monic preservation' thesis of judicial empowerment developed in Hirschl, *Towards Juristocracy*.

[16] See Section 4.4.1.   [17] Hirsch, *Season of Hope* 59.   [18] Ibid. 60.

unlock South Africa's human potential, leading to a 'virtuous circle' in which rising domestic demand would drive growth in local manufacturing capacity.[19] Land reform and housing provision were seen as integral parts of this strategy, with ambitious land redistribution and housing provision targets set for the first five years.[20] Within two years of the ANC's coming to power, however, it became clear that the RDP Office, which had been set up under former COSATU general secretary Jay Naidoo, was more of a hindrance than a help, interfering as it did with the capacity of the line departments to plan and budget for their role in the programme.[21] At the same time, the appointment of the first ANC Minister of Finance, Trevor Manuel, in March 1996, meant that economic policy could be driven in the ordinary way by the Department of Finance.[22] The RDP Office was accordingly dismantled and its functions transferred to the line departments.

The dismantling of the RDP Office and Manuel's appointment as Finance Minister set in train a series of events that were eventually to have a profound impact, as we saw in Chapter 4, on the political context for judicial review. To start with, Manuel's appointment caused a rapid depreciation in the value of the Rand, as overseas investors reacted to what they (wrongly) thought was a move towards less disciplined management of the economy. Although an adjustment in policy had been under discussion for some time, the need to arrest the Rand's slide brought forward the announcement of a more detailed statement of the ANC's macro-economic policy than had been contained in the RDP document, the Growth Employment and Redistribution ('GEAR') strategy, which was released in June 1996. In objective terms, the GEAR strategy was only marginally more conservative than the ANC's existing policy, with the fiscal deficit target for 1999–2000 reduced from the 4.5 per cent of GDP originally set in 1994 to 3 per cent.[23] In combination with the dismantling of the RDP Office, however, and the rushed way in which the new strategy was announced, this was enough to tarnish GEAR

[19] Ibid.
[20] See African National Congress, *The Reconstruction and Development Programme* paras 2.4.14 and 2.5.2.
[21] Hirsch, *Season of Hope* 60.
[22] Before Trevor Manuel's appointment, the ANC had first retained the National Party's Minister of Finance, Derek Keys, and then appointed Chris Liebenberg, a politically non-aligned banker. See Hirsch, *Season of Hope* 66–7.
[23] Hirsch, *Season of Hope* 98.

with the charge of neo-liberalism and to cause a rift between the ANC and COSATU that has never properly healed.

Rather than being seen as a sop to placate COSATU for is disappointment over GEAR, the adoption of a series of social rights in the 1996 Constitution must be seen, as argued in Section 8.1.1, as the authentic expression of the socialist element in the ANC's hybrid human rights tradition. The two processes, the adoption of GEAR and the drafting of the 1996 Constitution, were only coincidentally related in time,[24] and both may be explained in a way that is compatible with the ANC's long-term political commitments.[25] Nevertheless, the adoption of GEAR did give rise to a certain tension between ANC economic policy and the property rights morality in the 1996 Constitution. Whereas the RDP was fully consistent with that morality, the GEAR strategy mainly emphasised the classic liberal, property-rights-respecting element of the ANC's human rights tradition. To this extent it appeared to be out of kilter with the balance struck in the 1996 Constitution between the need to safeguard the stability of the system and the need to reform the system to take account of past injustices and current welfare needs.

The more conservative fiscal deficit reduction targets set in GEAR also arguably placed a restriction on the funds available for land reform and other social welfare measures. Too much should not be made of this, however. For one, the Department of Land Affairs' decision to pursue a willing buyer/willing seller approach to land reform had more to do with the ANC's desire to reassure local and foreign investors than with the fact that GEAR reduced the overall sums available for compensation. The slow progress made in achieving the RDP's 30 per cent land redistribution target was also at least partly attributable to the lack of managerial capacity in the public service. Whatever the actual reason, the point was that ANC land reform policy during the first ten years of democracy never really tested the outer limits of the property clause. Although a swathe of statutes was enacted, they were all careful to respect the terms of the constitutional settlement around land restitution and the balance struck in the 1996 Constitution's property clause.[26]

---

[24] GEAR was approved by Cabinet sometime in May 1996 and the Constitutional Assembly adopted the pre-certification text of the 1996 Constitution on 8 May 1996.

[25] The analysis offered here differs to this extent from that provided in Dixon and Ginsburg, 'The South African Constitutional Court and Socio-Economic Rights as "Insurance Swaps"'.

[26] See Chapter 4 for a list of these statutes.

The ANC's fairly cautious approach to land reform was initially quite a convenient development for the Chaskalson Court. Instead of the anticipated property clause challenge from organised agriculture, the Court was mostly confronted with retail-level disputes between particular property owners and particular land claimants, often in the context of urban evictions. While these cases did require the Court, as we shall see, to give concrete expression to the property rights morality informing the 1996 Constitution, none of them could be described as politically controversial. The remainder of the Court's property rights cases had to do with routine regulatory issues of a sort that might have arisen in any constitutional democracy. To date, there has still been no direct challenge to land reform legislation in the Constitutional Court. Under the interim Constitution, the Transvaal Agricultural Union, a lobby group representing the interests of mostly white farmers, brought an application for direct access to challenge certain provisions of the Restitution of Land Rights Act.[27] This application was refused, however, and the challenge was not reinstituted, arguably because the Court sent a fairly strong signal in its direct access decision that the main challenge was unlikely to prove successful.[28] The compensation provision in s 25(3) of the 1996 Constitution did not come up for review until after Justice Chaskalson's retirement and even then in a case that did not have to do with land reform.[29]

At least as an initial matter, therefore, the Court was sheltered from the political effects of the constitutionalisation of property rights by the ANC's macro-economic strategy and its cautious approach to land reform. The downside of this development, however, as argued in Chapter 4, was that the constitutional project came increasingly to be associated with the more-conservative-than-constitutionally-required policies that the ANC was pursuing. This was particularly true of its willing buyer/willing seller approach to land reform, which came to be attributed in the public mind to the property clause rather than to the ANC's own

---

[27] Act 22 of 1994.

[28] See *Transvaal Agricultural Union* v. *Minister of Land Affairs and Another* 1997 (2) SA 621 (CC), 1996 (12) BCLR 1573 (CC). For a full discussion of the political signalling in this case, see Theunis Roux, 'Turning a Deaf Ear: The Right to be Heard by the Constitutional Court' (1997) 13 *South African Journal on Human Rights* 216.

[29] *Du Toit* v. *Minister of Transport* 2006 (1) SA 297 (CC), 2005 (11) BCLR 1053 (CC) (challenge to compensation awarded under s 8 of the National Roads Act 54 of 1971 read with s 12 of the Expropriation Act 63 of 1975).

freely chosen economic policy.[30] To the extent that both GEAR and the ANC's land reform programme failed to deliver on their targets (typically for reasons that had very little to do with the Court or the constraints of the constitutional settlement), the Court became increasingly vulnerable to political attack.

8.2   The cases

Given this background – a dominant political party pursuing a cautious approach to economic policy and land reform, and a constitutional settlement over property rights that appeared, at least after 1996, to have that dominant political party's support – what ought the Chaskalson Court's approach to the interpretation of the property clause have been?

As in other areas of its work, there were several ways the Court might have proceeded conformably to the ideal of adjudication according to law. One option would thus have been to try to resolve competing property interests by giving a fully theorised account of the political morality informing the 1996 Constitution's qualified protection of property rights: to read off from the history behind the enactment of the property clause and the ANC's human rights tradition a theory of property according to which the competing interests of property owners in the enforceability of their holdings and of the propertyless in the restitution of unjustly acquired property rights, or at least a fairer distribution of such rights, might be reconciled. Both the constitutional text and the history leading up to its enactment were fairly clear, after all, that some combination of the classic liberal concern for the role of property rights in promoting labour and investment and the socialist concern for meeting basic needs was intended. It would not have been too difficult, as the discussion in the previous section has shown, to deduce from all of this certain broad principles of political morality to which all 'law or conduct' needed to conform, and then to use these principles to resolve concrete cases.[31]

Another option would have been to offer no grand theory of property, but simply to go about the business of reconciling competing property interests on a case-by-case basis, generating 'mid-level' principles and

---

[30] As a former consultant to the Department of Land Affairs, I can bear personal witness to a number of occasions on which this charge was made by frustrated officials and land claimants.

[31] This phrase is taken from the supremacy clause, s 2, of the 1996 Constitution.

rules along the way.[32] By following this path, the 1996 Constitution's moral vision would slowly have been revealed, with each new decision rendering the Constitution's abstract language that much more determinate. The downside of this approach, of course, would have been that, at a certain point, these judge-made principles and rules would have become quite determinate, thereby reducing the Court's capacity to adjust its decisions to the sensitivities of controversial cases. But this is exactly what the ideal of adjudication according to law, on one view at least,[33] requires, and therefore nothing to regret from this perspective. In any case, filling out the Constitution's moral vision in this way would have taken some time, and thus the Court might have been able to build the requisite degree of respect for its independence by the time the first irreconcilable conflict between law and politics came along.

A third and final option open to the Court would have been to develop context-sensitive review standards, both in relation to facial challenges to legislation under the property clause and in reconciling competing property interests in the interpretation and application of statutes. On this approach, the Court would have been required to be clear about the principles it was applying, but not so as to offer any attempted reconciliation of these principles in advance of the facts. If its review standards were specified as being context-sensitive in this way, none of the Court's decisions would have stood for anything more than the specific set of considerations required to resolve each particular case.[34] The Court would thus have been vulnerable to the charge of acting like a court of equity, deciding each case on its merits. But this final approach would have had the virtue of flexibility and, philosophically speaking, would have been defensible as respecting the necessary contingency of complex moral judgments on detailed, context-specific information.

What the Chaskalson Court actually did in response to its property rights mandate, the rest of this section argues, came closest to the last option. After a cautious start in its first (and only) property clause challenge under the 1993 Constitution, the Court surprised almost every academic commentator with the novelty of the approach taken in its first case under s 25 of the 1996 Constitution. In this case, the Court devised a test for alleged violations of the property clause that synthesised all the

---

[32] In the sense used in Sunstein, *Legal Reasoning and Political Conflict*.

[33] See the discussion in Chapter 1.

[34] See Michelman, 'Foreword: Traces of Self-Government' 34 (commenting on the tendency of balancing tests to decide no more than the issue presented).

various points of distinction and opportunities for balancing suggested by the constitutional text into a single, highly context-sensitive review standard – one that deprived the right to property of almost all substantive content (as the Court had done in relation to social rights) and made the level of review itself depend on contextual factors. In three other decisions in which both the property clause and the right to housing were implicated, the Court recognised that it was required to find an optimal balance between competing principles, but did not try to strike this balance by theorising the 1996 Constitution's property rights morality. Rather, the Court gave expression to the moral mood or sensibility of the Constitution, in one case by again using *ubuntu* as an overarching value according to which competing property interests might be harmonised to produce a just outcome.

8.2.1 Constructing the constitutional property clause inquiry

The Chaskalson Court decided only two property rights cases under the 1993 Constitution: *Transvaal Agricultural Union*, in which, as noted earlier, it sent out a strong signal about its disinclination to entertain a facial challenge to the Restitution of Land Rights Act,[35] and *Harksen*,[36] which involved a challenge to the Insolvency Act,[37] and in particular those sections that provide for the vesting of property belonging to the spouse of a sequestrated person in the Master of the Supreme Court. The majority judgment in the latter case, written by Justice Goldstone, considered the 'substance' of the sections in question,[38] and found that they provided for the temporary transfer of property only, subject to reasonable safeguards, and therefore that they could not be construed as permitting the unjustifiable expropriation of property.[39] The decision is workmanlike and efficient in style, and moves fairly rapidly through the provisions challenged. No attempt is made to set out the structure of the property clause inquiry or to decide anything more than the narrow question presented. Although the decision may be criticised for not really coming to grips with the potential seriousness of the economic impact of the impugned sections,[40] it is generally

---

[35] Act 22 of 1994.
[36] *Harksen* v. *Lane NO and Others* 1997 (11) BCLR 1489; 1998 (1) SA 300 ('*Harksen*').
[37] Act 24 of 1936.   [38] *Harksen* para 35.   [39] Ibid. para 36.
[40] See Theunis Roux, 'Property' in Woolman et al. (eds.), *Constitutional Law of South Africa* ch 46.

unremarkable.[41] When the date of the decision is considered –
7 October 1997, well after the 1996 Constitution had come into effect –
the overall impression created is that of a Court that was waiting for a
better opportunity to announce its approach to property rights.

That opportunity finally came in *First National Bank*.[42] Decided on 16
May 2002, seven years into Chaskalson's term, when the threat of a major
challenge to the ANC's land reform programme had already subsided,
FNB nevertheless reveals an intention on the part of the Court once and
for all to take the political 'heat' out of its property clause mandate.
Although the style of the comparative-law-rich judgment is very typical
of its author, Justice Ackermann, the fact that it was unanimously
approved without even a separate concurrence suggests that it had more
than the other judges' token support.

Like *Harksen*, *FNB* involved the sort of issue that might have arisen in
any constitutional democracy: a challenge to customs and excise legislation that provided for the forfeiture of property belonging to a third party
in satisfaction of a customs debt. The constitutional claimant was a
financial institution that sold and leased motor vehicles. Under s 114 of
the Customs and Excise Act 91 of 1964, the Commissioner of the South
Africa Revenue Service had detained some of its vehicles as security for
the payment of various customs debts. FNB had no connection to the
debts other than the fact that it had sold or leased the motor vehicles
to the customs debtors. Section 114 nevertheless empowered the Commissioner, not only to detain FNB's vehicles, but also to sell them in
execution of the customs debt, without the need for a court order. In the
circumstances, FNB impugned s 114 as providing for the uncompensated
expropriation of property contrary to s 25(1) and s 25(2)(*b*) of the 1996
Constitution.

After setting out the facts, the legislative provisions and the lower
court's decision at some length, Justice Ackermann broached the property clause inquiry by typifying the primary function of s 25 as being to
strike 'a proportionate balance' between the 'public interest' and 'protecting existing private property rights'.[43] Although the land reform

---

[41] The equality clause aspect of the case, by contrast, was more contested and resulted in
significant standard-setting.

[42] *First National Bank of SA Ltd t/a Wesbank* v. *Commissioner for the South African
Revenue Services and Another; First National Bank of SA Ltd t/a Wesbank* v. *Minister
of Finance* 2002 (4) SA 768 (CC), 2002 (7) BCLR 702 (CC) ('*FNB*').

[43] Ibid. para 50.

provisions in that section were not presently relevant, he remarked, they nevertheless had to be taken into account in understanding the 'societal considerations' to which the protection of individual property rights was subject.[44] Without going into detail on what these considerations were, Justice Ackermann suggested that they had something to do with the 1996 Constitution's commitment to 'social justice' and in particular the fulfilment of 'various social and economic rights'.[45]

The key word in this passage is 'proportionate'. As we have seen, the history behind the adoption of the property clause and the text of the clause itself indicate that the Court's role in relation to property rights is to mediate competing property interests. Neither the drafting history nor the text, however, conclusively suggests that this should be done through an overarching test for proportionality. The threshold distinction between constitutionally protected property interests and other economic interests, for example, is one that could in theory be drawn, and in other jurisdictions has been drawn,[46] conceptually. Such conceptual tests strike a balance between competing property interests, not through a test for proportionality, but by defining a zone of constitutionally unprotected economic interests that the state may freely regulate. The same could be said of the term 'deprivation of property', which may be defined in such a way as to put beyond constitutional protection certain types of regulatory activity. To suggest that in the South African case the balance between competing property interests was one that needed be struck in a 'proportionate' way was therefore to make a doctrinal choice from among competing alternatives. By examining the authority that Justice Ackermann adduced for this approach and also the doctrinal possibilities it pushed aside, we will get a clearer view of the way in which the *FNB* Court constructed the property clause inquiry. In turn, this should assist us in assessing whether there is any correspondence between the approach the Court took in this case and some of the other adjudicative strategies we have seen it pursuing.

As to the question of authority, Justice Ackermann's judgment was in the first instance reliant on a reading of the property clause suggested by South African legal academic, A. J. van der Walt. In a detailed commentary, Van der Walt had argued that the test for violations of the property

---

[44] Ibid. para 49.   [45] Ibid. para 50.

[46] See, for example, *Government of Malaysia* v. *Selangor Pilot Association* [1978] AC 337 (PC); *Societé United Docks* v. *Government of Mauritius* (1985) LRC (Const) 801 (PC); *Penn Central Transportation Co* v. *City of New York* 438 US 104 (1978).

clause and the test imposed by the general limitations clause in s 36 of the 1996 Constitution could be collapsed into a single inquiry.[47] While rejecting aspects of Van der Walt's analysis,[48] Justice Ackermann endorsed the central idea that the balance required was a proportionate one.[49] He then proceeded to bolster this holding by means of a comparative-law survey in which he characterised the approach taken to the deprivation of property in various other jurisdictions as being premised on 'some concept of proportionality'.[50] The survey is necessarily quite selective and in some cases overlooks broader developments in the jurisdiction concerned that might have suggested a different emphasis.[51] It is also arguable that another survey might have been conducted in which the surprising persistence of conceptualist approaches to such issues as the definition of constitutionally protected property and the distinction between the expropriation and deprivation of property might have been highlighted.[52] Nevertheless, Justice Ackermann's survey does enough to suggest that the overarching trend in foreign jurisdictions is towards assessing alleged deprivations of property according to some sort of proportionality test.

Having established this point, Justice Ackermann turns to setting out the test for arbitrary deprivation of property in s 25(1) of the 1996 Constitution. Here, the creativity and expansiveness of his judgment becomes apparent. On the strength of his comparative-law survey, he holds that 'a deprivation of property is "arbitrary" as meant by s 25 when the "law" referred to in s 25(1) does not provide sufficient reason for the particular deprivation in question or is procedurally unfair'.[53] Justice Ackermann then elaborates a detailed test for the establishment of 'sufficient reason' that goes beyond anything that could be said to have been necessarily entailed (as opposed to persuasively suggested) by

---

[47] A. J. van der Walt *The Constitutional Property Clause: A Comparative Analysis of Section 25 of the South African Constitution of 1996* (Cape Town: Juta, 1997) 92–100.

[48] *FNB* para 70.   [49] Ibid. para 50.   [50] Ibid. para 71.

[51] The extracts cited from various Australian decisions, for example, are all premised on the peculiar nature of the property clause guarantee in that country, which occurs in a section of the Australian Constitution allocating powers to the federal legislature (s 51(xxxi)). Justice Ackermann recognises this, and is careful to put the extracts in their proper doctrinal setting. He omits to mention, however, that the more recent trend in the Australian High Court has been to reject the use of proportionality language in the characterisation of federal legislation. See *Leask* v. *Commonwealth* (1996) 187 CLR 579.

[52] See the references in note 47.   [53] *FNB* para 100.

his analysis of the drafting history, the text and foreign case law. At the same time, his test, which is presented as being relevant to one stage only of a six-stage property clause inquiry,[54] is so expansive in scope that it has the effect of rolling up most of the other stages into a single, context-sensitive review standard. To see why this is so, it is necessary to set out the test in full.

Whether or not a law provides 'sufficient reason' for a deprivation of property, Justice Ackermann says:

(a) ... is to be determined by evaluating the relationship between means employed, namely the deprivation in question, and ends sought to be achieved, namely the purpose of the law in question.

(b) A complexity of relationships has to be considered.

(c) In evaluating the deprivation in question, regard must be had to the relationship between the purpose of the deprivation and the person whose property is affected.

(d) In addition, regard must be had to the relationship between the purpose of the deprivation and the nature of the property as well as the extent of the deprivation in respect of such property.

(e) Generally speaking, when the property in question is ownership of land or a corporeal movable, a more compelling purpose will have to be established in order for the depriving law to constitute sufficient reason for the deprivation than in the case when the property is something different and the property right something less extensive.

(f) Generally speaking, when the deprivation in question embraces all the incidents of ownership, the purpose for the deprivation will have to be more compelling than when the deprivation embraces only some incidents of ownership and those incidents only partially.

(g) Depending on such interplay between variable means and ends, the nature of the property in question and the extent of its deprivation, there may be circumstances when sufficient reason is established by, in effect, no more than a mere rational relationship between means and ends; in others this might only be established by a proportionality evaluation closer to that required by s 36(1) of the Constitution.

(h) Whether there is sufficient reason to warrant the deprivation is a matter to be decided on all the relevant facts of each particular case, always bearing in mind that the enquiry is concerned with 'arbitrary' in relation to the deprivation of property under s 25.[55]

---

[54] Ibid. para 46.   [55] Ibid.

In outward form and jurisprudential effect, this passage resembles certain passages in the *Grootboom* judgment and the equality clause component of Justice Goldstone's judgment in *Harksen*. In both these cases, the Court also attempted something like a canonical formulation of the test mandated by a particular right in the Bill of Rights. In both these cases, too, the Court articulated the test in such a way as to be highly context-sensitive.[56] What is different about Justice Ackermann's test in *FNB* is the fact that it (1) expressly ties, not only the analysis within the review standard, but also the choice of the review standard itself, to a factor-based inquiry; and (2) tends to reduce the significance of what are elsewhere in the judgment held out to be separate and distinct stages of the constitutional inquiry. Paragraph (e), for example, proposes different levels of review according to the nature of the property right affected by the statutory scheme, while paragraph (f) suggests that schemes that interfere with some incidents of ownership only, and then perhaps only 'partially', may yet be treated as providing for the deprivation of property. In combination, what these two paragraphs strongly imply is that the Court will not use the first two stages of the property clause inquiry – the threshold question over whether a constitutional property interest has been affected and the question whether the claimant has actually been deprived of property – to filter out constitutional property claims. Rather, the Court will treat all such cases as instances of property deprivation, and focus its attention instead on the question whether the deprivation is 'arbitrary'.

The test also renders two other stages of the property clause inquiry effectively redundant. The fourth stage, which concerns the distinction between deprivations and expropriations, is rendered redundant by the Court's decision to treat expropriations of property as a special form of deprivation.[57] This approach has the effect of subjecting all laws that provide for the uncompensated expropriation of property first to the test for arbitrary deprivation, with the predictable result, as *FNB* itself illustrates, that such laws will be found to be unconstitutional, not for violation of s 25(2)(*b*), but for violation of s 25(1). The sixth, general limitations stage, is rendered redundant by the fact that it is conceptually impossible for a law that fails the less stringent test prescribed by the Court for violations of s 25(1) to pass the more

---

[56] See *Government of the Republic of South Africa and Others* v. *Grootboom and Others* 2001 (1) SA 46 (CC), 2000 (11) BCLR 1169 (CC) paras 39–44; *Harksen* para 51.

[57] *FNB* para 57.

stringent test prescribed by s 36.[58] As the *Du Toit* decision handed down after *FNB* illustrates,[59] there will still be a role for the fifth stage of the constitutional property clause inquiry in cases where the expropriatory effect of the law is not in dispute and where compensation is offered. In such cases, the courts will skip directly to the fifth stage in order to determine whether just and equitable compensation has been paid. Where no compensation is offered, however, and the stated intention of the legislature is merely regulatory, the state will presumably seek to defend the claim on the basis that the law does not provide for the expropriation of property. On the *FNB* approach, such a defence would require the court first to apply the test for arbitrary deprivation, with all the consequences just illustrated.

Interestingly, the one conceptual distinction that is retained in the test – that between 'ownership of land or a corporeal movable' and other forms of property – seems to run counter to the text of s 25. While land is certainly identified in the property clause as a special form of property, to the point that the constitutional drafters felt obliged, in s 25(4)(b), to provide that 'property is not limited to land', the apparent purpose of this singling out is to make it clear that land rights, of all property rights in South Africa, are inherently subject to extensive regulation in the public interest. Justice Ackermann's test, on the other hand, seems to tilt the balance the other way, by prescribing that regulatory interventions that affect the ownership of land should be subject to a higher level of review than other interventions. Or perhaps, in the case of land reform legislation, the importance attached to the 'purpose of the deprivation' would outweigh the fact that the property affected is land ownership? We cannot be sure, suggesting that the test is not just context-sensitive but also quite open to subjective considerations.

Further support for this reading is provided by the fact that, in the very first set of lower court cases decided after *FNB* was handed down, *Mkontwana*[60]

---

[58] The high end of the *FNB* review standard is thus said to be 'less strict than a full and exacting proportionality examination' of the kind conducted under s 36 (ibid. para 98). Although violations of s 25(2)(b) are also nominally subject to the general limitations clause, there are reasons to think that s 36 will be redundant in this instance as well. See Roux, 'Property' ch 46, 23–5.

[59] *Du Toit v. Minister of Transport* 2006 (1) SA 297 (CC), 2005 (11) BCLR 1053 (CC).

[60] *Mkontwana v. Nelson Mandela Municipality and Others* (SECLD Case No 1238/02) and *Bissett and Others v. Buffalo City Municipality and Others* (SECLD Case No 903/2002), 13 September 2003 (unreported).

and *Geyser*,[61] the South Eastern Cape Local Division of the High Court
and the KwaZulu-Natal High Court applied the *FNB* test in identical
challenges to a local government law to divergent effect, the first Court
holding the provision unconstitutional and the second not. Although the
Constitutional Court quickly resolved the discrepancy,[62] the fact that the
two High Courts came to diametrically opposed conclusions suggests that
the *FNB* test is fairly open to interpretation. Indeed, the Chaskalson
Court's own application of the test in its appeal decision in *Mkontwana*
has been criticised for failing to consider important issues.[63]

What, then, are we to make of the test? Like the reasonableness review
standard in *Grootboom*, the test will not satisfy those for whom judges'
legal-professional duty when interpreting constitutional rights is to give
those rights some minimum content. On this conception of the ideal of
adjudication according to law, *FNB* leant too far in the direction of case-
specific justice at the expense of legal certainty. On the alternative
conception discussed in Chapter 1, however, *FNB* has the virtue of
forcing the court to be transparent about the substantive considerations
influencing its decision, whilst yet allowing it to present its decision as
principled. The requirement imposed by the alternative conception, it
will be recalled, is not that the court should declare the political nature of
its function – to confess, in this case for example, that what lies behind its
choice of a strict review standard is not its sincere view of what the
Constitution requires but its conservative ideology. Rather the test
requires the deciding court to give public, principled reasons for its
decisions – reasons that conform to the standards of analytic rigour
and respect for the constitutional text and past decisions set by the legal
tradition in which the Court is working. On this approach, the fact that
two courts reach divergent conclusions on the same legal question is not
to be regretted, provided that, in order to reach these divergent conclusions, the test forces the judges to be clear about the substantive considerations they are taking into account, which would in turn allow the legal
profession and the broader public to examine the justificatory adequacy
of those considerations.

---

[61] *Geyser and Another* v. *Msunduzi Municipality and Others* 2003 (5) SA 18 (N); 2003 (3)
BCLR 235 (N).

[62] *Mkontwana* v. *Nelson Mandela Metropolitan Municipality and Another; Bisset and Others*
v. *Buffalo Municipality and Others; Transfer Rights Action Campaign and Others* v.
Gauteng MEC for Local Government and Housing and Others 2005 (1) SA 530 (CC),
2005 (2) BCLR 150 (CC).

[63] A. J. van der Walt, *Constitutional Property Law* 3rd edn (Cape Town Juta, 2011) 250–56.

The *FNB* test thus conforms to one conception at least of the ideal of adjudication according to law. Was the judges' preference for that conception all that may be said to have influenced their doctrinal choice? As noted at the beginning of this section, the drafting history and the text made possible two other approaches to the fulfilment of the Court's property rights mandate: (1) an approach that proceeded on the back of a more ambitious theorisation of the 1996 Constitution's property rights morality, and (2) a case-by-case, common-law approach that held out the possibility of generating mid-level principles or rules broader than the specific considerations taken into account to decide a particular case. Either one of these approaches could have been used to strike the necessary balance between competing property interests in a more rule-bound, conceptualist way. Why did the Court, apart from a few passages that were rendered redundant by its context-sensitive balancing test,[64] not use them? Perhaps it was because conceptualism has been tried in other jurisdictions with little success? Although Justice Ackermann did not make anything of this in his comparative-law survey, he might easily have shown how a conceptualist approach to the interpretation of property rights in both the United States and the Commonwealth has generally failed to produce satisfying results.[65] Indeed, his comparative-law survey would have been that much stronger if, instead of ignoring this alternative, he had raised it and demonstrated its shortcomings.

The Court's failure fully to justify its choice of a multi-factor balancing approach in this way suggests that its choice may have been motivated by other factors. In the nature of things, the evidence for these other forms of influence is circumstantial, but suggestive nevertheless. First, there is the fact that the Court's institutional role in relation to the enforcement of property rights, like its role in relation to social rights, was a particularly awkward aspect of its mandate. Although *FNB* was decided seven years into Chaskalson's term, after the initial threat of a challenge to the ANC's land reform programme had subsided, the enforcement of property rights remained a potentially controversial area for the Court. It therefore needed to devise a test that would allow it to negotiate the political sensitivities of future cases without engaging in nakedly outcomes-based decision-making. The context-sensitive balancing test

---

[64] See, for example, *FNB* para 57 (defining the term 'deprivation of property').

[65] See Matthew Chaskalson, 'The Problem with Property: Thoughts on the Constitutional Protection of Property in the United States and the Commonwealth' (1993) 9 *South African Journal on Human Rights* 388.

adopted in *FNB* was well suited to this task. Like the reasonableness review standard in *Grootboom*, it enabled the Court to lower the standard of review where a more deferential approach was required, but also to ratchet up the standard where the micro-politics of the case allowed for this.

The second piece of circumstantial evidence is the fact that the *FNB* case was not politically controversial, thus allowing the court to announce its context-sensitive balancing test in a decision that would not itself be regarded as having been motivated by reasons of political expediency. Against this, it could be said, *FNB* was the Court's first property clause case under the 1996 Constitution, and therefore it had to set out the general framework for the inquiry one way or the other. The author of the judgment, Justice Ackermann, was also well known for writing this kind of expansive, no-stone-unturned judgment.[66] Finally, there is the fact that *Grootboom*, in which a similar context-sensitive test was adopted, *was* politically controversial, suggesting that there is no general rule at work here. Still, there is enough in Justice Ackermann's judgment to suggest that it was written, not just with an eye to future cases, but with an eye to future, more politically controversial cases. The passage quoted earlier, in which the 1996 Constitution's commitment to social justice is mentioned, is one example of this. And then there is the sheer flexibility of the test itself, which is indicative of a Court that wanted to reserve as much discretion to itself as possible.

The third and final piece of circumstantial evidence is the resemblance between the *FNB* test and the Court's reasonableness review standard in *Grootboom*. Both tests, as we have seen, are highly context-sensitive and capable of generating varying levels of review according to the seriousness of the rights violation and the micro-politics of the case. And yet the constitutional provisions on which the two tests are respectively based are very different. That the Court should converge on similar tests from such different starting points suggests that more than a mere doctrinal preference was at work here – that the Court was shaping the law to suit the long-term performance of its institutional role in two inherently controversial areas of its mandate.

---

[66] See, for example, *Ferreira* v. *Levin NO and Others; Vryenhoek and Others* v. *Powell NO and Others* 1996 (1) SA 984 (CC), 1996 (1) BCLR 1 (CC) (applying Isaiah Berlin, Karl Popper and Immanuel Kant's's conception of liberty to understand the scope of the right to freedom and security of the person in s 11(1) of the 1993 Constitution).

8.2.2   Reconciling property rights and the right to housing in s 26

The move to a context-sensitive balancing test in *FNB* was paralleled by the approach taken in three other cases that required the Court to mediate competing property interests. None of these cases involved a facial challenge to legislation under the property clause. Rather, all three cases were about reconciling property rights and the right to housing in s 26.

In *Jaftha*,[67] the Court was confronted by a facial challenge under s 26 to a law that permitted the sale in execution of a person's home in satisfaction of a judgment debt. The two homes in question belonged to beneficiaries of the Government's housing programme, having been purchased with subsidies provided under that programme. In both cases, the constitutional claimants had incurred minor debts that they were nonetheless unable to pay. In such circumstances, ss 66(1)(*a*) and 67 of the Magistrates' Courts Act 32 of 1944 allowed the creditor, after receiving judgment in its favour and exhausting the debtor's movable property, to attach and force the sale of the debtor's immovable property. Crucially, the housing subsidy scheme provided that beneficiaries were entitled to a single subsidy only, meaning that the sale in execution of the constitutional claimants' immovable property rendered them effectively homeless.

What makes *Jaftha* an interesting case is that it brought to a head two contending understandings of the 1996 Constitution's economic philosophy. On one view, the case was an easy case since s 25, when read together with s 26, clearly did not countenance the enforcement of property rights in such a way as to render a person homeless for failing to pay a trivial debt. On another view, ss 25 and 26 could not be read in such a way as to prevent the poor from using their immovable property as collateral for a debt, and therefore as a means to climb the property rights ladder.[68] Instead of deciding between these two contending readings, the Court once again shaped the law so as to allow it to decide this kind of case through context-sensitive balancing.

Writing for a unanimous Court, Justice Mokgoro's first doctrinal move was to take a broad approach to the right to housing, distinguishing

---

[67] *Jaftha* v. *Scholtz and Others; Van Rooyen* v. *Stoltz and Others* 2005 (2) SA 140 (CC), 2005 (1) BCLR 78 (CC).

[68] The classic statement of this view is Hernando de Soto, *The Mystery of Capital: Why Capitalism Triumphs in the West and Fails Everywhere Else* (New York, NY: Basic Books, 2000).

Treatment Action Campaign,[69] and holding that where the negative dimension of the right to housing is implicated, the core s 26(1) right is capable of being construed as a free-standing right independent of the obligations in s 26(2).[70] Any legislative measure that deprives a person of existing access, Justice Mokgoro continued, limits this negative right.[71] The effect of this move was to shift the inquiry onto the general limitations clause analysis, which once again allowed the Court to engage in context-sensitive balancing. Even after this move, however, there was one final opportunity for a more conceptual approach – in respect of the question of remedy. In particular, the Court was invited to rewrite s 66(1)*(b)* and s 67 of the Magistrates' Courts Act to specify the minimum value below which a house could not be sold in execution. The Court declined even this opportunity, deciding instead that the Act should be amended to make curial consideration of the execution order mandatory, and then listing a series of factors that had to be weighed by the court of first instance in considering whether or not to order execution.[72]

The second case, *Port Elizabeth Municipality* v. *Various Occupiers*,[73] concerned an application by a local government body under s 6 of the so-called PIE Act[74] for the eviction of a group of squatters from privately owned land. The unanimous judgment, authored by Justice Sachs, is notable for its extended discussion of the way in which the rights enshrined in ss 25 and 26 might be harmonised. While more philosophically ambitious than the Court's other decisions on this issue, *Port Elizabeth Municipality* does not in the end attempt a thoroughgoing theorisation of the 1996 Constitution's property rights morality. Rather, it invokes a moral sensibility, amounting to an ethic of compassion, which both the courts and state agencies tasked with mediating competing property interests are enjoined to embrace.

Citing *FNB* and *Grootboom*, Justice Sachs begins by setting out what he calls 'the broad constitutional matrix' for the interpretation of the PIE Act.[75] As in *FNB*, this is seen as consisting of two principles: renewed respect for property rights, precisely because such respect was not previously extended to all South Africans, and 'the orderly opening-up or

---

[69] *Minister of Health and Others* v. *Treatment Action Campaign and Others (No 2)* 2002 (5) SA 721 (CC), 2002 (10) BCLR 1075 para 39.
[70] *Jaftha* paras 31–3.   [71] Ibid. para 34.   [72] Ibid. paras 50–64.
[73] 2005 (1) SA 217 (CC), 2004 (12) BCLR 1268 (CC) ('*Port Elizabeth Municipality*').
[74] The Prevention of Illegal Eviction from and Unlawful Occupation of Land Act 19 of 1998.
[75] *Port Elizabeth Municipality* paras 14–23.

restoration of secure property rights for those denied access to or deprived of them in the past'.[76] Turning to s 26(3),[77] Justice Sachs characterises the 1996 Constitution's concern for the sanctity of the home as especially meaningful for poor people, and argues that 'society as a whole is demeaned when state action intensifies rather than mitigates their marginalisation'.[78] Properly construed, he holds, s 26(3) may be said to have created a new form of property right, one that does not provide an absolute barrier against eviction, but which rather requires the courts to treat common-law ownership rights and the right not to arbitrarily be evicted from one's home in a non-hierarchical way.[79]

Justice Sachs then finds precisely this approach to the reconciliation of competing property interests in the PIE Act:

> Rather than envisage the foundational values of the rule of law and the achievement of equality as being distinct from and in tension with each other, PIE treats these values as interactive, complementary and mutually reinforcing. The necessary reconciliation can only be attempted by a close analysis of the actual specifics of each case.[80]

While once again illustrating the Court's preference for context-sensitive balancing, the larger significance of this passage is that it demonstrates the way in which the Court viewed the PIE Act as the logical development of the ANC's hybrid human rights tradition and therefore of the 1996 Constitution's approach to property rights. Since the Constitution expressly calls for the statutory fulfilment of constitutional rights, this might seem like a rather obvious point, but it is worth remembering that, in the first decade of democracy, the Court saw the ANC as the main driver of the constitutional project, and therefore as it natural partner in the realisation of that project. Indeed, Justice Sachs even goes so far as to find aspects of his own jurisprudential philosophy embodied in the PIE Act, noting that it 'expressly requires the court to infuse elements of grace and compassion into the formal structures of the law'.[81]

It is at this point that *ubuntu* is offered as an overarching value supporting the harmonisation of competing property interests.[82] 'The Constitution and PIE', Justice Sachs writes, 'confirm that we are not

---

[76] Ibid. para 15.
[77] Section 26(3) provides that '[n]o one may be evicted from their home, or have their home demolished, without an order of Court made after considering all the circumstances. No legislation may permit arbitrary evictions.'
[78] *Port Elizabeth Municipality* para 18.   [79] Ibid. para 23.   [80] Ibid. para 35.
[81] Ibid. para 37.   [82] Ibid. para 37.

islands unto ourselves. The spirit of ubuntu, part of the deep cultural heritage of the majority of the population, suffuses the whole constitutional order.' As noted in Chapter 6, the strategy behind passages like this appears to have been to indigenise the Constitution – to demonstrate that its values were authentically South African. While perhaps a little forced in relation to the death penalty, this strategy had some real purchase in relation to property rights where the Court could rightly claim that the 1996 Constitution embodied the ANC's hybrid human rights tradition. Integral to that tradition, Justice Sachs says, is a view of property rights as affirming of human dignity, but also as capable of undermining human dignity through the 'marginalisation' of the poor.[83] The Court's role in this situation is to ensure that property rights are never enforced in a manner that denies the interconnectedness, and ultimately, the 'human interdependence',[84] of the propertied and the propertyless.

This conceptualisation of the Court's role in enforcing property rights is coherent and morally attractive. Contrary to what Justice Sachs claims, however, it does not really generate any 'legal principles'.[85] Rather, it prescribes a moral attitude that those charged with enforcing property rights are enjoined to adopt. In the entire judgment, the only hard rule of law laid down is that the eviction of homeless people at the instance of a state agency will ordinarily not be justified where reasonable efforts at mediation have not been attempted.[86] Even this rule, however, is not in the end applied, with Justice Sachs finding on the facts that the time for mediation had already passed.[87] Instead, he summarises his discussion in the form of a series of factors that together indicate that the granting of an eviction order would not be 'just and equitable'.[88] While suggested by the language of the provision the Court was asked to apply,[89] this holding is at the same time consistent with the Court's approach in *FNB* and *Jaftha*, and indicative of its general preference for context-sensitive balancing tests in this area of the law.

The last decision worth considering, *President of the Republic of South Africa* v. *Modderklip*,[90] illustrates both how the Chaskalson Court was

---

[83] Ibid. para 18.   [84] Ibid. para 37.   [85] Ibid. para 48.   [86] Ibid. para 39.

[87] Ibid. para 47 (finding too late for mediation).

[88] Ibid. para 59.   [89] Section 6 of the PIE Act uses this term.

[90] *President of the Republic of South Africa and Another* v. *Modderklip Boerdery (Pty) Ltd (Agri SA and Others intervening as amici curiae)* 2005 (5) SA 3 (CC), 2005 (8) BCLR 786 (CC).

occasionally assisted by creative judgments handed down by the Supreme Court of Appeal and also its capacity to shift the doctrinal basis of a decision to more neutral territory. Like *Port Elizabeth Municipality*, *Modderklip* concerned the unlawful occupation of private land by a group of people who had nowhere else to go. In this instance, however, the group was extremely large, having grown to approximately 18,000 people by the time the litigation began.[91] The constitutional claimant, the owner of the land, had attempted on several occasions to have the group removed, first through the use of the trespass laws and then by obtaining an eviction order under the PIE Act. The sticking point, however, was the very large sum of money the sheriff of the High Court demanded from the owner to cover the costs of the eviction. It was also unclear exactly what would happen to the group once evicted.

Faced with this impasse, the owner brought an application in the Pretoria High Court against a range of government agencies for an order requiring them to enforce the eviction order already granted. The application was based on an alleged violation of the owner's s 25(1) right not to be arbitrarily deprived of property and its right to equality in ss 9(1) and (2) of the 1996 Constitution, together with the unlawful occupiers' right to housing in s 26.[92] After succeeding in the Pretoria High Court, the owner was again successful in the Supreme Court of Appeal ('SCA'), this time winning an order for the payment of constitutional damages equivalent to the amount the state would have been obliged to pay had it sought to acquire the land for purposes of its housing programme. The SCA's ingenious order, managing as it did somehow to reconcile the unlawful occupiers' interest in remaining on the land, the owner's interest in receiving fair value for the land, and the state's interest in acquiring land for low-cost housing, was widely applauded. The state nevertheless appealed against the SCA's judgment to the Constitutional Court, where the main issues were whether the owner and the unlawful occupiers' constitutional rights had indeed been breached, and whether the owner had acted timeously in bringing the original application for eviction.[93]

The property rights aspect of the challenge raised the interesting question of whether the right protected by s 25(1) is capable of horizontal application,[94] and also whether the state, by failing to provide land on which the unlawful occupiers could settle, breached both their right to

---

[91] Ibid. para 8.   [92] Ibid. para 11.   [93] Ibid. para 22.

[94] Ibid. para 23. The Court had earlier touched on this question in *Phoebus Apollo Aviation CC v. Minister of Safety and Security* 2003 (2) SA 34 (CC), 2003 (1) BCLR 14 (CC).

housing under s 26 and the owner's s 25(1) right.[95] An answer to either one of these questions would have had doctrinal consequences reaching far beyond the resolution of the *Modderklip* case: the first, because it required the Court to take a position on whether the property rights morality enshrined in s 25 could be said to underpin, not just public law relations, but also private law relations as well; the second, because it required the Court to decide whether, on each occasion that the unlawful occupation of property could be attributed to the state's failure to meet its positive obligations under s 26, a breach of its negative obligations under s 25(1) was entailed.

Rather than answering these questions, the Constitutional Court, in another unanimous judgment – this time written by Justice Langa – shifted the doctrinal basis for the decision onto s 1(c) (the '[s]upremacy of the constitution and the rule of law') and s 34 (right of access to court). Read together, Justice Langa held, these two provisions imposed an obligation on the state to provide 'mechanisms for the resolution of disputes', including a functioning court system and system for the execution of court orders.[96] The state's obligations also went further than this, however. In addition to maintaining the necessary legislative and institutional framework, the state was:

> obliged to take reasonable steps, where possible, to ensure that large-scale disruptions in the social fabric do not occur in the wake of the execution of court orders, thus undermining the rule of law. The precise nature of the state's obligation in any particular case and in respect of any particular right will depend on what is reasonable, regard being had to the nature of the right or interest that is at risk as well as on [sic] the circumstances of each case.[97]

Considered against this standard, Justice Langa held, the state's failure to assist the owner, either by providing alternative land or by purchasing its property, violated s 34.[98]

As far as can be ascertained from Justice Langa's judgment, neither s 1(c) nor s 34 had been put in issue by the constitutional claimant. Shifting the doctrinal basis for the decision onto these provisions was also not required for purposes of amending the SCA's order, since that order was not in the end substantially changed.[99] The main reason for refocusing the inquiry, therefore, appears to have been to avoid settling the two

---

[95] *Modderklip* para 25.   [96] Ibid. paras 39–41.   [97] Ibid. para 43.
[98] Ibid. paras 44–51.   [99] Ibid. para 68.

doctrinal questions just set out. The explanation for this, in turn, would appear to be that the Chaskalson Court was wary about the impact that settling these questions would have had on its chosen adjudicative strategy. A positive answer to the horizontality question, for its part, would have opened the door to the complete constitutionalisation of the private law of property, not through the indirect route already provided by s 39(2),[100] but through the direct horizontal application of s 25 to common-law property rules. While that might have been a welcome result for a court intent on reforming these rules, it was incompatible with the Court's context-sensitive balancing approach, which, as we have seen, was aimed at case-specific resolution of competing property interests. A positive answer to the second question, likewise, would have invited compensation claims from landowners on each occasion on which the unlawful occupation of land could be attributed to the state's failure to fulfil its s 26 obligations. Under s 34, by contrast, compensation was due only where the payment of constitutional damages could be said to constitute 'appropriate relief' for violation of the owner's rights, and even then only after consideration of a range of factors.[101]

Judicial avoidance of doctrinal questions that have wide-ranging systemic effects is, of course, standard practice for many constitutional courts.[102] In the case of the Chaskalson Court's *Modderklip* decision, however, there are reasons to think that more than the usual judicial caution was at work. The SCA's decision, while providing a Solomonic solution on the question of remedy, had arrived at this result through a doctrinal route that cut across the Chaskalson Court's preferred adjudicative strategy in relation to property rights. To preserve the integrity of that strategy, the Court needed to restrict the precedential impact of its decision to the facts of the *Modderklip* case. Shifting the basis for the decision to s 34 suited this purpose, since the Court was able to construct a test for violations of the right of access to court that was similar to both the reasonableness review standard it had devised in *Grootboom* and also the context-sensitive balancing test in *FNB*. According to the s 34 test, as noted earlier, the Court was required to consider whether, in all the

---

[100] This provision enjoins the courts to promote the spirit of the Bill of Rights when developing the common law.

[101] Further support for this contention is provided by the fact that the test the Court establishes for the breach of this duty is a context-sensitive balancing test (*Modderklip* para 43).

[102] See Sunstein, *Legal Reasoning and Political Conflict*.

circumstances, the state had taken reasonable steps to avoid 'large-scale disruptions in the social fabric'.[103] As with the *Grootboom* and *FNB* tests, this gave the Court considerable scope for adjusting the level of review to the gravity of the rights violation and the micro-politics of the case. Another key advantage was that the remedy for violation of the owner's right of access to court took the form of constitutional damages rather than the payment of just and equitable compensation under s 25(3), with all the politically awkward connotations that would have entailed of landowners 'profiting' from the plight of the poor. Circumstantial as the evidence once again is, these two considerations suggest that the Court's decision to switch the doctrinal basis for the SCA's order was motivated by a desire to put the *Modderklip* judgment on a more secure footing – to choose a doctrinal path that would put it in a better position to manage the law/politics tension further down the track.

8.3   Concluding thoughts

The Chaskalson Court's property rights jurisprudence, this chapter has argued, evinced a clear preference for context-sensitive balancing, both in the main property clause inquiry and in cases where the Court was required to reconcile the right to property with the right to housing in s 26. In this way, the Court's property rights jurisprudence paralleled the approach it took in relation to social rights. Given the close interrelationship between these two sets of rights, this correspondence is not surprising. Indeed, in any situation where contending principles are required to be traded off against each other, context-sensitive balancing may seem like the most appropriate method.[104] Nevertheless, other doctrinal possibilities were open to the Court, and the choice of a context-sensitive balancing approach was by no means dictated by the legal materials. In the circumstances, it is not unreasonable to assume that the Court's choice was influenced by extra-legal considerations, and in particular

---

[103] *Modderklip* para 43.

[104] The classic exposition is Robert Alexy, *A Theory of Constitutional Rights* trans. Julian Rivers (Oxford University Press, 2002) (first published in German in 1986) 47 (defining principles as 'optimization requirements' and arguing that, in case of conflict, the judicial role is to maximise the fulfilment of each principle). See also Aharon Barak, *Proportionality: Constitutional Rights and Their Limitations* trans. Doron Kalir (Cambridge University Press, 2012) 234–8 (discussing Alexy's approach to conflicting principles and agreeing with Alexy that conflicting principles are best reconciled through some sort of balancing approach).

by the fact that context-sensitive balancing was ideally suited to managing the law/politics tension in this particularly awkward area of its mandate.

Further support for this view is provided by the fact that the opinion-writing judges arrived at the same doctrinal position by appeal to different forms of authority, and also by the fact that the judgments were all unanimous. Justice Ackermann thus justified his *FNB* judgment through characteristic resort to foreign law, whereas Justice Sachs arrived at his context-sensitive balancing approach in *Port Elizabeth Municipality* by invoking the ANC's hybrid human rights tradition to which he had been a major contributor. Though bound by these two decisions by the time they came to write their judgments in *Jaftha* and *Modderklip*,[105] Justices Mokgoro and Langa likewise embraced the context-sensitive balancing approach without abandoning their characteristic decision-making methods. In combination with the fact of unanimity, this suggests that the judges were acting as a cohesive unit, marshalling their individual judicial styles in pursuit of a broader institutional objective.

Apart from *Harksen*, the only occasion on which the Court did not deploy a context-sensitive balancing approach was in a case not thus far considered, *Kyalami Ridge*.[106] In this 2001 decision, handed down after *Grootboom* but before *FNB* and *Port Elizabeth Municipality*, the Court was confronted with a challenge by a group of property owners to a presidential committee's decision to settle about 300 people, who had lost their homes in a flood, in a transit camp on nearby land. The land was already in use as a prison, but the neighbouring owners nevertheless objected to the settlement of the flood victims on the ground that it was contrary to applicable town planning and environmental laws. There was little trace of balancing in the Court's judgment on this occasion. Instead, Justice Chaskalson decided the case on the basis that, although there was no legislation specifically authorising the Government to establish the transit camp, it was acting in fulfilment of its *Grootboom* obligations to assist those in desperate need, and that it had the same rights as a common-law landowner to deal with its property as it saw fit within the limits of applicable laws. As to that issue, Justice Chaskalson drew

---

[105] *Jaftha* was decided one week after *Port Elizabeth Municipality* and *Modderklip* some seven months later.

[106] *Minister of Public Works and Others v. Kyalami Ridge Ridge Environmental Association and Another (Mukhwevho Intervening)* 2001 (3) SA 1151 (CC), 2001 (7) BCLR 652 (CC).

a relatively formalistic distinction between the 'validity' of the decision to establish the transit camp, which was what the claimants had unsuccessfully impugned, and the question whether all the steps required to 'implement' the decision had been taken, which he left for another day.[107]

The difference in approach in *Kyalami Ridge* may be attributable to the fact that the Court had not yet announced its context-sensitive balancing test in *FNB*, or to the fact that the judgment was written by Justice Chaskalson, who was perhaps more thoroughly steeped than the other judges in the use of formalist arguments to achieve human-rights-regarding outcomes. In any event, it is an outlier decision – a case in which the Court was for some reason drawn into stating a more concrete rule than it had done in its other decisions. The overwhelming tendency in this area of the law, as we have seen, was for the Court to adopt the role of mediator of competing property interests – not by theorising the 1996 Constitution's property rights morality, or by calling it up one case at a time, but by providing practical examples of how competing property interests might be reconciled, and by itself displaying the moral sensibility required. Indeed, in this way, the Court could be said to have taken over the role formerly played by the ANC's moderate faction in mediating the two divergent elements of its human rights tradition.

---

[107] Ibid. paras 59, 64–5, 83, 89, 117.

9

Political rights

The Chaskalson Court's political rights jurisprudence presents something of a paradox: a group of rights, the enforcement of which even some judicial-review sceptics regard as reconcilable with a foundational commitment to democracy,[1] was the group of rights in respect of which the Court's decisions were least convincing. Can the conceptual framework and broader argument of this book help to resolve this puzzle?

To a large extent, yes, this chapter argues. As we saw in Chapter 4, the political context in which the Court found itself was very different from the sort of well-functioning democracy liberal constitutional theory typically assumes to be a necessary condition for independent judicial review.[2] Although much of this book has been directed at refuting this assumption – at showing how the Chaskalson Court was able to turn the ANC's domination of post-apartheid politics to its advantage – the logic of the Court's exceptionalist trajectory broke down in relation to political rights. However justifiable in democratic theory, the enforcement of rights to political participation posed a direct threat to the ANC's political hegemony. The principled enforcement of these rights was therefore hard to accommodate within the Court's overarching strategy. It was as though the ordinary assumptions of liberal constitutional theory were again turned on their head, only this time to reverse effect: the role

---

[1] See John Hart Ely, *Democracy and Distrust: A Theory of Judicial Review* (Cambridge, MA: Harvard University Press, 1980) (proposing a third theory of judicial review, alternative to the dominant 'interpretivist' and 'non-interpretivist' approaches, in terms of which the US Supreme Court's role in enforcing constitutional rights should be restricted to 'representation-reinforcing' review and to opening the 'channels for political participation'). For a critique of this view, see Jeremy Waldron, *Law and Disagreement* (Oxford University Press, 1999) 295–6 (arguing that a commitment to democracy requires the procedures of democracy, as much as substantive rights, to be left to the people to decide).

[2] Jeremy Waldron, at least, is sensitive to this difference. See Jeremy Waldron, 'The Core of the Case against Judicial Review' (2006) 115 *Yale Law Journal* 1346 (moderating his objection to judicial review in political contexts where the institutions of democracy are not functioning properly).

of constitutional courts in opening up the democratic system to marginalised groups, which is the role that seems most easily justifiable in a mature democracy, is precisely the role that the Chaskalson Court found hardest to perform.

The Court's difficulty is reflected in its case law. Although the Court performed relatively well in cases dealing with prisoners' right to vote, it failed, in the two cases that really mattered, to devise a coherent and morally defensible test for violation of political rights. In the first of these cases, *New National Party*,[3] the Court chose a review standard that reduced the state's obligations correlative to the right to vote to the duty to facilitate reasonable attempts to exercise the right. In the second, *United Democratic Movement*,[4] the Court passed up an important opportunity to define the 1996 Constitution's commitment to democracy in a way that might have checked the centralisation of power in the hands of the ANC. Only after Chaskalson's retirement as Chief Justice were rights to political participation adequately theorised, and even then only in a confined area of the Court's jurisprudence that had little impact on the broader problem.

The Court's political rights jurisprudence thus represents one of the most disappointing aspects of its record, and the Court's inability to adapt its overarching strategy provides part of the explanation. But why did the Court find it so hard to adapt its strategy in this instance? Surely the judges were aware that the Court's long-term capacity to defend its independence was contingent on the opening up of democratic politics to genuine competition? They must have been aware, too, of the risk associated with a strategy so deeply invested in the ANC's continued support for the constitutional project – that the ANC might lose its way and turn against the Constitution it had been so instrumental in adopting. Given this risk, why did the judges not try to devise doctrines that might have counteracted the potentially pernicious effects of the ANC's dominance – doctrines that construed political rights in a way that helped to transform South Africa's democracy into one more closely resembling the liberal constitutionalist ideal?[5] The answer, the chapter

---

[3] *New National Party of South Africa v. Government of the Republic of South Africa and Others* 1999 (3) SA 191 (CC), 1999 (5) BCLR 489 (CC).

[4] *United Democratic Movement v. President of the Republic of South Africa and Others (African Christian Democratic Party and Others Intervening; Institute for Democracy in South Africa and Another as Amici Curiae) (No 1)* 2003 (1) SA 488 (CC), 2002 (11) BCLR 1179 (CC).

[5] For a provocative argument along these lines, see Choudhry, "'He Had a Mandate'".

concludes, must have something to do with the limits on the role constitutional courts are able to play in facilitating political competition in circumstances of entrenched one-party dominance.

9.1   Prisoners' right to vote: *August* and *NICRO*

Criminals are nowhere very popular, and being seen to be 'tough on crime' is correspondingly everywhere a vote-getter. Of all countries, South Africa, with its high crime rate,[6] might be thought to conform to this rule, in which case enforcing the constitutional rights of accused and convicted persons should have been one of the more institutionally awkward aspects of the Chaskalson Court's mandate. But South Africa in the first decade of democracy did not conform, as we saw in the death penalty case, to the ordinary political dynamics of crime. Although crime certainly was, as it still is, an important issue for South Africans, the ANC was hardly about to be voted out of office for its failure to deal with the problem. The Court's enforcement of criminal due process rights therefore posed no immediate threat to its co-operative working relationship with the ANC. Rather, the challenge was to enforce these rights in a way that was sensitive to the constraints on the ANC's capacity to deal with crime, and to the impact that too generous a set of safeguards might have on the allocation of resources to other needs. This was not a trivial matter, and the rights of accused and convicted persons, after almost completely dominating the Court's docket in the first year,[7] remained one of the most active areas of its jurisprudence. Generally speaking, however, these cases were not politically charged and thus this study does not consider them except, as here, where they connect to other themes.

Unlike the 1993 Constitution, which expressly provided that the right to vote could be limited by law,[8] the 1996 Constitution leaves the possibility of legislative limitations on the right to vote to inference from the general limitations clause. Section 19(3) thus provides that '[e]very adult citizen has the right – *(a)* to vote in elections for any legislative body established in terms of the Constitution, and to do so in secret'. Perhaps in response to this amended formulation, the 1998

---

[6] See Anthony Altbeker, *A Country at War with Itself: South Africa's Crisis of Crime* (Johannesburg: Jonathan Ball, 2007).

[7] See Chapter 4.   [8] Sections 1*(c)* and 22(6) of the 1993 Constitution.

Electoral Act,[9] which was intended to regulate South Africa's second democratic election in 1999, removed the qualification on prisoners' right to vote that had been present in the 1993 Act.[10]

Seizing on this change, the Legal Resources Centre brought an application in the Transvaal High Court on behalf of two prisoners, one already convicted and the other awaiting trial, for an order mandating the Electoral Commission to do everything in its power to assist the applicants to register and vote in the upcoming general election. In a decision that provides ample *ex post* justification for the creation of a specialist Constitutional Court, the High Court held that, if there was a limitation on the applicants' right to vote, it was a limitation for which they themselves, by reason of their criminal misconduct, had been responsible. The scarce resources available for assisting law-abiding persons to register and vote should not be diverted to assisting those whose 'predicament' was 'of their own making'.[11]

On appeal to the Constitutional Court in *August*,[12] this reasoning was conclusively rejected. Section 19(3)(a), Justice Sachs held, 'by its very nature imposes positive obligations on the legislature and the executive'.[13] In addition to enacting the necessary statutory framework, these obligations include taking 'reasonable steps to ensure that eligible voters are registered', a duty which, according to the Constitution, falls primarily on the Electoral Commission to perform.[14] The right to vote was particularly significant in a country like South Africa, where it had for so long been denied:

> The universality of the franchise is important not only for nationhood and democracy. The vote of each and every citizen is a badge of dignity and of personhood. Quite literally, it says that everybody counts. In a country of great disparities of wealth and power it declares that whoever we are, whether rich or poor, exalted or disgraced, we all belong to the same democratic South African nation; that our destinies are intertwined in a single interactive polity. Rights may not be limited without justification

---

[9] Act of 1998.

[10] Section 16(d) of Act 202 of 1993 (providing that persons 'detained in a prison after being convicted and sentenced without the option of a fine in respect of … (i) [m]urder, robbery with aggravating circumstances and rape; or (ii) any attempt to commit [such an] offence' were disentitled from voting).

[11] See the extract from the High Court's judgment in the Constitutional Court's judgment reported in *August and Another* v. *Electoral Commission and Others* 1999 (3) SA 1 (CC), 1999 (4) BCLR 363 (CC) para 8 ('*August*').

[12] See immediately preceding note.   [13] *August* para 16.   [14] Ibid.

and legislation dealing with the franchise must be interpreted in favour of
enfranchisement rather than disenfranchisement.[15]

Even under the common law, Justice Sachs – the former political prisoner, who had once unsuccessfully sued to enforce his right to receive
reading material[16] – continued, 'prisoners are entitled to all their personal rights and personal dignity not temporarily taken away by law, or
necessarily inconsistent with the circumstances in which they have been
placed'.[17] How much more then, in the constitutional era, should these
rights be seen to be protected and 'reinforced'.[18]

Turning again to s 19(3)(a), Justice Sachs noted that the right to vote
was given 'in unqualified terms',[19] and therefore the only basis for the
Electoral Commission's case, absent any law of general application
limiting the right, was that the applicants, by their conduct, had taken
themselves outside the ambit of the constitutional guarantee, as the High
Court had decided.[20] But this proposition was plainly unsupportable. As
the US Supreme Court had held in *O'Brien* v. *Skinner*, because the state
'physically prevent[s]' prisoners from voting in the normal way, '[d]enial
of absentee registration and absentee ballots is effectively an absolute
denial of the franchise'.[21] Since there was no law of general application
supporting this limitation, the Commission's conduct could not be justified and was accordingly unconstitutional.[22]

The Court's decision in *August* openly invited Parliament to
re-introduce the previous qualification on prisoners' right to vote, or
some more justifiable version of it, into the Electoral Act. Parliament
dragged its heels, however, and the amended Act was eventually passed
only on 6 November 2003, just five months before the third general
election.[23] Under s 8(2)(f) of the amended Act, persons who were
serving a sentence of imprisonment, of any duration, without the option
of a fine, were precluded from registering to vote. A new s 24B(2)
prohibited the same category of persons from voting in the event that
they had registered before their incarceration. These provisions were

---

[15] Ibid. para 17.

[16] See *Rossouw* v. *Sachs* 1964 (2) SA 551 (A) (overturning an unreported decision of the
Cape Supreme Court that a provision of a 90-day detention law did not deprive prisoners
of their ordinary common-law rights). The case is discussed in Dyzenhaus, *Judging the
Judges Judging Ourselves* 67–70.

[17] *August* para 18.   [18] Ibid. para 19.   [19] Ibid. para 20.   [20] Ibid.

[21] 414 US 524, 532–3 (1973) (per Justice Marshall) (quoted with approval in *August* para 21).

[22] *August* para 23.   [23] The Electoral Laws Amendment Act 34 of 2003.

once again immediately challenged, this time by an NGO representing the interests of convicted prisoners ('NICRO') and two convicted prisoners themselves.[24] In argument, counsel for the Minister of Home Affairs conceded that the amended Act limited the applicants' right to vote,[25] and thus the Court's decision was directed exclusively at the question whether ss 8(2)(f) and 24B(2) could be justified under the general limitations clause.

Writing this time for a partially divided Court,[26] Justice Chaskalson began by explaining the nature of the state's justificatory burden, which he held was not purely evidentiary, but rather a duty of legal showing supported by policy arguments and Brandeis-brief-type evidence. In essence, 'the party relying on justification should place sufficient information before the court as to the policy that is being furthered, the reasons for that policy, and why it is considered reasonable in pursuit of that policy to limit a constitutional right'.[27] Having clarified this issue, Justice Chaskalson engaged in his familiar practice of interrogating all of the justificatory arguments put up by the state in turn.[28] The main problem with the state's argument, he held, was that mobile voting stations were being provided for awaiting trial prisoners and those serving sentences *with* the option of fine. There was therefore no real additional cost or logistical difficulty entailed in extending these amenities to other prisoners.[29] Absent that 'factual underpinning', the part of the state's argument which relied on a lack of resources fell 'at the first hurdle'.[30] The other parts of its argument were equally unconvincing: the claim that assisting prisoners to vote would 'favour' them over others who were prevented by logistical difficulties from voting because the justifiability of any failure to make special arrangements needed to be considered separately in relation to each category;[31] and the justification based on the Government's need to be seen to be tough on crime because a political party's interest in 'enhanc[ing] its image' was no reason 'to disenfranchise prisoners'.[32] None of these were serious policy rationales of the sort that had been

---

[24] *Minister of Home Affairs* v. *National Institute for Crime Prevention and the Rehabilitation of Offenders (NICRO) and Others* 2005 (3) SA 280 (CC), 2004 (5) BCLR 445 (CC) ('*NICRO*').

[25] Ibid. para 32.

[26] Justices Madala and Ngcobo dissented on the ground that the government had satisfied its justificatory burden.

[27] *NICRO* para 36.   [28] Ibid. paras 39–67.   [29] Ibid. para 49.

[30] Ibid. para 51.   [31] Ibid. paras 52–3.   [32] Ibid. para 56.

presented in the Canadian case of *Sauvé*,[33] where the Supreme Court had had the benefit of a report by a Royal Commission, which had in turn been considered by a special committee on electoral reform. Betraying just a hint of longing for the kind of support provided to courts in a first-world democracy, Justice Chaskalson concluded that the Court had 'wholly inadequate information on which to conduct [its] limitation analysis', and therefore that the state could not be said to have discharged its burden.[34]

Two points need to be emphasised about the prisoners' right to vote cases before moving on – one that consolidates what has already been said about the politics of these cases, and another that anticipates the main doctrinal issue in the case about to be discussed. First, note the almost dismissive tone with which Justice Chaskalson in *NICRO* rejected the Government's protestations about its need to be seen to be dealing with the problem of crime. The point is not just that the Government's argument was so self-serving; what Justice Chaskalson's comments also reveal is how low down the ANC's policy agenda crime was during the first ten years of democracy. Had it really been serious about this issue, and about the potential impact that according all categories of prisoners the right to vote had on public perceptions about its determination to fight crime, the ANC would have ensured that the 2003 amendments to the Electoral Act were properly thought through and adequately defended. The only other supposition, given Justice Chaskalson's devastating critique, is that the ANC did not take the trouble to defend legislative provisions it cared about. But that supposition is not borne out by other examples, and thus the better view is that these were fairly low-priority cases for the ANC.

The second point relates to the way the Court reconciled these two cases with the case we are about to discuss, *New National Party*.[35] That case, as we shall see, related to the question whether legislative action taken to facilitate the exercise of the right to vote should be treated any differently from legislation aimed at excluding certain categories of citizen from voting. *August* was decided twelve days before *New National Party* and *NICRO* some five years later. In the circumstances, it is

---

[33] *Sauvé* v. *Canada (Chief Electoral Officer)* [2002] SCR 519 (considered in *NICRO* paras 58–64).

[34] Ibid. para 67.

[35] *New National Party of South Africa* v. *Government of the Republic of South Africa and Others* 1999 (3) SA 191 (CC), 1999 (5) BCLR 489 (CC).

reasonable to expect that there would have been some attempt made in *August* and *NICRO* to spell out how these cases related to the law laid down in *New National Party*. In fact, there is very little of this. *August*, as we have seen, contains a broad and unqualified statement of the importance of the right to vote that goes so far as to say that 'legislation dealing with the franchise must be interpreted in favour of enfranchisement rather than disenfranchisement'.[36] This dictum, which drew on a passage from Justice Cory's judgment in *Haig* v. *Canada*,[37] introduces something like a constitutional presumption in favour of the right to vote. Given that the Court was about to ignore this presumption in *New National Party*, this was a curiously unguarded statement for it to make. A few paragraphs further on in Justice Sachs's judgment in *August*, the Commission's obligations in relation to the right to vote are said to be 'to take reasonable steps to create the opportunity to enable eligible prisoners to register and vote'.[38] This is the review standard that the Court went on to justify in *New National Party*, but it is introduced in *August* without argument or attribution to the companion case.[39] In *NICRO*, too, Justice Chaskalson's treatment of the review standard laid down in *New National Party* is relatively terse, glossing the holding in that case as being that the right to vote 'requires proper arrangements to be made for its effective exercise'.[40] The Court's failure properly to integrate *August* and *NICRO* with its decision in *New National Party* suggests that it wanted to contain the doctrinal impact of the latter case, and in this way limit the reputational damage of what the next section is about to argue was one of its most politically compromised decisions.

9.2 Judicial review of electoral system rules: *New National Party*

New National Party was one of a pair cases[41] brought by minority political parties challenging the requirement in ss 1(xii) and 6(2) (read with s 38(2)) of the 1998 Electoral Act that citizens who wanted to register as voters on the national common voters' roll, and vote in an election, had to be in possession of a particular kind of identity

---

[36] *August* para 17.   [37] [1993] 2 SCR 995, para 104.   [38] *August* para 22.

[39] It would have been a simple enough matter for the Court to refer to its forthcoming judgment in *New National Party*.

[40] *NICRO* para 28.

[41] The other being *Democratic Party* v. *Minister of Home Affairs and Another* 1999 (3) SA 254 (CC), 1999 (6) BCLR 607 (CC) CCT 11/99.

document, either a 'bar-coded ID' issued under s 8 of Identification Act
72 of 1986, or a temporary identity certificate issued under the Identification Act 68 of 1997, or a temporary registration certificate issued under
s 6(2) of the 1998 Electoral Act (this last certificate being sufficient for
registration but not for voting). The provisions prevented two main
categories of citizen from voting: those who were not in possession of
any kind of identity document at all, and those who were in possession of
identity documents issued before 1 July 1986, the cut-off date specified in
s 8 of the 1986 Identification Act.[42] Surveys conducted before the 1998
Electoral Act came into effect revealed that five million otherwise eligible
voters, constituting 20 per cent of the voting population, did not have
one or the other of the specified documents.[43] Roughly half of these
people, who were mostly young Africans living in rural areas,[44] had no
form of documentation at all, and the other half, which included a small
proportion of 'citizens' of the former TBVC states,[45] but who were
predominantly coloured, Indian or white voters,[46] were in possession
of pre-1986 documentation. In its amended application, only the exclusion of the second category of people was challenged,[47] presumably
because the NNP knew that the first category consisted of people likely
to vote for the ANC.

On its face, the applicant's case challenged an apparently race-neutral
electoral rule that it alleged prevented a significant number of citizens
from voting. Underlying the case, however, was the fact that many of the
people who were allegedly prevented from voting by this rule were
members of one of South Africa's three main minority groups, and as
such likely to vote for the applicant or one of the other minority parties.

---

[42] Pre-1986 identity documents were nevertheless valid and the holders of such documents
were not under any legal obligation to apply for the new form of documentation (*New
National Party* para 115).

[43] Ibid. paras 29–30.   [44] Ibid. paras 133, 143.

[45] The nominally independent Bantustans. The proportion of the electorate estimated to be
in possession of this type of identity document was 0.6 per cent (ibid. para 30).

[46] The fact that most of this category of persons were members of minority groups is
nowhere spelled out in the judgment, but it is a reasonable inference from (a) the very low
proportion of former TBVC citizens in this category; (b) the fact that pre-1986 documents were issued under old-order legislation; (c) the fact that the exclusion of just the
TBVC voters was thought by the Electoral Commission to be 'discriminatory' (ibid. paras
131, 151) and (d) the fact that the New National Party brought the case, and that its claim
was initially targeted only at the second category of excluded voters.

[47] Ibid. para 9 (describing the amendment of the order requested by the applicant to target the
non-recognition in the definition of 'identity document' in s 1(xii) of the 1998 Electoral Act
of documents recognised as documents in s 8(3) of the 1986 Identity Act).

Unlike *August* and *NICRO*, therefore, the *New National Party* case directly challenged the ANC's dominant-party position. To be sure, a successful outcome would not have made any difference to the ANC's capacity to win an overall majority, but its capacity to win two thirds of the vote and thus the power unilaterally to amend the Constitution was certainly in play.[48] The fact that the case was brought by the successor party to the National Party obviously also raised the political stakes. Any indication, therefore, that the Court's decision deviated, without proper legal justification, from the approach taken in *August* and *NICRO* raises a concern about the possible influence of these extra-legal factors.

Crucial to the determination of this issue is whether there were any relevant differences between the provisions impugned in *NICRO* and those in *New National Party* that might have justified two distinct doctrinal approaches. Superficially, the provisions challenged were quite similar: *NICRO* concerned a provision that disenfranchised a particular category of prisoner, and *New National Party* a provision that prevented citizens without the required form of identification from voting. The difference, of course, was that in *NICRO* the disenfranchised prisoners were absolutely disqualified from voting, whereas in *New National Party* it was possible for those without the requisite identity documents to obtain them. The applicant alleged, however, that, owing to the slow rate of progress in the issuing of documents, a significant number of those who had applied for the new bar-coded ID would not be issued their documents in time.[49] There were also questions around whether the Electoral Commission had done enough to bring the new identification requirements to the attention of otherwise eligible voters.[50] The alleged regulatory exclusion of those without the required identity documents, in other words, flowed from a combination of the legislative provision itself and the alleged administrative impossibility of issuing the required identity documents to all those who applied for them in time for the election. The other relevant difference was that, in *NICRO*, the regulation was expressly aimed at excluding a specified category of voter, whereas in *New National Party* the exclusion was incidental to a regulatory provision whose primary purpose was to guarantee the integrity of the electoral process.

---

[48] On the requirements for amendment of the Constitution, see Section 9.3.

[49] *New National Party* para 18. The 1998 Electoral Act, as we saw in the discussion of *August*, was promulgated just five months before the 1999 general election.

[50] Ibid. para 18.

That the effect of the provisions impugned in *New National Party* was to erect an administrative hurdle in the way of certain citizens from voting was not disputed. What was disputed was whether citizens who made reasonable efforts to register and vote would be prevented from doing so by the inability of the Department of Home Affairs to issue the necessary documentation in time.[51] The constitutionality of the provisions thus came down to whether the hurdle they erected in the way of these citizens from voting was adequately justified on policy grounds and whether any resultant impairment of the right to vote was attributable to Parliament's failure to foresee the consequences of its rule. This meant, in turn, that the key to the outcome of the case was the standard of review applied by the Court. Two main approaches were available: the Court could either apply the same general limitations clause standard that it would later go on to apply in *NICRO* or some other standard that it read into the right itself. The first approach would be tantamount to a holding that any regulation of the right to vote, even regulation aimed at facilitating the exercise of the right, should be treated as a limitation of the right subject to justification under the general limitations clause. The second approach would allow the Court to distinguish provisions like those in *NICRO*, which were expressly aimed at excluding certain categories of people from voting, from provisions like those in *New National Party*, which were aimed at facilitating the right to vote, but which had the incidental effect of disenfranchising certain categories of voter. If the Court took this second approach, there were two further doctrinal options open to it: to decide either that the standard of review in respect of all such facilitative provisions should be significantly lower than that for express regulatory exclusions (say, a rational basis standard), or that the importance of the right to vote, coupled with the fact that facilitative provisions might have the incidental effect of exclusion, required a higher standard of review, approximating that applied under the general limitations clause.

The consequences of each of these options, in turn, were clear. While choosing a lower standard of review for facilitative provisions would give due recognition to the distinction between facilitative and expressly exclusionary regulation, it would at the same time lower the constitutional standard for those facilitative provisions that had the incidental effect of exclusion. In would be a test, in other words, that targeted the

---

[51] Ibid. paras 42–3.

form of the regulation rather than its substantive impact. Equally clearly, if a lower standard were chosen for facilitative provisions, the general limitations clause would effectively be taken out of the equation, since (as we saw in Chapter 8 when considering the *FNB* case[52]) no law that failed this lower-level test could conceivably be justified under s 36. On the other hand, if the standard of review for provisions aimed at facilitating the right to vote were set higher, approximating reasonableness review, there would be no real difference between the standard applied to purposely exclusionary provisions and the standard applied to facilitative provisions; the second variant of the second approach would effectively collapse back into the first approach. The general limitations clause would also again be rendered redundant, since provisions that failed this higher standard, provided it were not higher than the general limitations clause standard itself, could not conceivably be saved under s 36. The distinct advantage of setting a higher standard of review for threshold violations of the right, however, was its capacity to catch precisely the kind of provision at issue in the *New National Party* case: provisions aimed at facilitating the right to vote, but which had the incidental effect of preventing a significant section of the citizenry from voting. Choosing this doctrinal option would thus have been to choose substance over form. It would also have had the further advantage of according to the right to vote its proper importance – of giving real effect to Justice Sachs's rhetoric in *August* about the particular significance of this right in a country like South Africa.

Writing for a ten-judge majority, Justice Yacoob effectively chose the first variant of the second approach: he distinguished provisions that were expressly aimed at excluding certain categories of citizens from voting from facilitative provisions, and imposed a lower standard of review for the latter type of provision. The first part of his judgment is devoted to establishing the proposition that measures taken to facilitate the exercise of the right to vote are not to be construed as limitations on the right.[53] As one would expect, the rhetorical thrust of these comments is to play down the possibility that the very arrangements taken to facilitate the exercise of the right may actually place significant impediments in the way of its enjoyment, of a kind that would ordinarily be scrutinised under the general limitations clause. After confirming that '[t]he importance of the right to vote is self-evident and can never be

---

[52] See Section 8.2.1.   [53] *New National Party* paras 10–17.

overstated', for example, Justice Yacoob immediately qualifies this remark by saying that '[t]here is no point . . . in belabouring its importance' and that 'the mere existence of the right to vote without proper arrangements for its effective exercise does nothing for a democracy; it is both empty and useless'.[54] Two paragraphs later on, Justice Yacoob remarks that '[t]he Constitution recognises that it is necessary to regulate the exercise of the right to vote so as to give substantive content to the right'.[55] The apparent purpose of these comments is to suggest that, since the right to vote requires positive steps to be taken by the state before it can be exercised, these steps should be subject to a fairly low standard of review. This argument, of course, begs the question as to whether such steps might not be as threatening to the effective exercise of the right to vote as an express curtailment of the right. It also opens the door to disenfranchisement under the guise of formally neutral electoral rules, which was precisely what the applicant in New National Party was alleging had occurred. At its strongest, the argument suggests that there is no 'substantive content to the right' other than the content given to it by legislation, which would of course amount to judicial abdication of any responsibility for the enforcement of the right.

That these comments were indeed intended to justify the choice of a fairly low standard of review is confirmed by the rest of Justice Yacoob's judgment. Recognising that Parliament's discretion to design the electoral system as it sees fit needs to be disciplined by the Bill of Rights, he held that there were essentially two safeguards against the abuse by Parliament of its power in this respect. The first was the general safeguard emanating from the principle of legality that there should be a rational relationship between the means adopted in a legislative scheme and a legitimate government purpose.[56] The second was the safeguard provided by the state's constitutional duty not to violate fundamental rights, including in this case the right to vote.[57] There can be no complaint about this holding as a set of general propositions. In giving content to the right to vote, however, Justice Yacoob's judgment takes a surprising turn. Instead of reverting to his statement about the importance of the right to vote, and applying the constitutional presumption

---

[54] Ibid. para 11.   [55] Ibid. para 13.

[56] Ibid. para 19 (not citing but derived from Fedsure Life Assurance Ltd and Others v. Greater Johannesburg Transitional Metropolitan Council and Others 1999 (1) SA 374 (CC), 1998 (12) BCLR 1458 (CC) para 58).

[57] New National Party para 20.

against disenfranchisement laid down in *August*,[58] he asserts, more or less without justification, that the standard of review in respect of the violation of the right to vote is to be derived from the consequences Parliament should be expected to avoid in regulating the right. In particular, Justice Yacoob holds, the 'consequence' Parliament must avoid is that 'those who wish to vote and who take reasonable steps in pursuit of the right, are unable to do so'. 'More,' he adds, cannot be expected of Parliament.'[59]

On this approach, the right to vote is not something that is guaranteed to citizens – good or bad, responsible or irresponsible – but something that citizens need to earn by acting reasonably. This comes perilously close to the proposition rejected in *August* that prisoners, by their criminal conduct, forfeit the right to vote. The difference, we are asked to accept, is that prisoners, having been incarcerated, are entirely in the hands of the state, whereas law-abiding citizens, being free, are under a duty of active citizenship to play their part in realising the right to vote. On this view, citizens who fail to take reasonable steps to ensure that they are registered to vote and that they do in fact vote, have only themselves to blame, even if, in the end, they are prevented from voting, not because they do not want to vote, or try to vote, but because the state has failed to act reasonably (as opposed to rationally) to facilitate the exercise of their right. The onus to act reasonably, in other words, is shifted onto the citizen, whereas the state's obligation is something more qualified: 'to provide for the machinery, mechanism or process that is reasonably capable of achieving the goal of ensuring that all persons who want to vote, and who take reasonable steps in pursuit of that right, are able to do so'.[60]

A fairer division of constitutional responsibility, Justice O'Regan argued in dissent, would be to expect citizens to 'comply with reasonable regulations made by Parliament and the Commission in order to exercise their right to vote'.[61] Such a test would accord to the right to vote the requisite degree of importance, given both its centrality to the functioning of the democratic system and its historic significance in South Africa.[62] The right to vote, Justice O'Regan had earlier pointed out, was no ordinary right, but one that was buttressed by the inclusion of '[u]niversal adult suffrage, a national common voters roll, regular elections and a multi-party system of democratic government' as one of the specially entrenched founding values in s 1 of the 1996

[58] *August* para 17 (discussed above).   [59] *New National Party* para 21.
[60] Ibid. para 23.   [61] Ibid. para 126.   [62] Ibid. paras 116–17.

Constitution.[63] The right to vote was also unique in being 'preservative of all rights'.[64] As such, alleged violations of the right, including not only express exclusions but also limitations flowing from good-faith attempts on the part of the state to give effect to the right, were deserving of the highest level of scrutiny.[65]

Responding to this argument, Justice Yacoob objected that Justice O'Regan's test would violate the separation of powers by authorising the Court to review legislation for reasonableness – something that he contended may only properly occur after a finding that a right has been violated.[66] Coming from the future author of the *Grootboom* judgment, this was a strange contention indeed. As Justice O'Regan retorted, the Court is frequently called on to apply broad equitable standards when testing whether there has been a violation of a right.[67] Such a degree of scrutiny is called for either where the formulation of the right itself invites it, or where the importance of the right is such that it requires this degree of heightened protection. In this case, since the right to vote was not internally qualified, the Court was required to assess its importance in the constitutional scheme and in light of South Africa's history, and choose a review standard that ensured that the right was adequately protected.

The further flaw in Justice Yacoob's objection, as we have seen, is that, when a right is not conceptually defined, but turned into a right to the application of a particular review standard, the general limitations clause is typically rendered redundant, either because the chosen review standard is equivalent to the standard applied under the general limitations clause, or because, being lower than that standard, it becomes conceptually impossible for the Government to save the law under s 36. To argue, therefore, as Justice Yacoob does,[68] that the only point in the constitutional inquiry where considerations of reasonableness may legitimately be taken into account is the general limitations clause is to consign considerations of reasonableness to a constitutional backwater, where

---

[63] Ibid. para 116.

[64] Ibid. para 122 (quoting *Yick Wo v. Hopkins* 118 US 356, 370 (1886) per Justice Matthews).

[65] *New National Party* para 122.   [66] Ibid. para 24.

[67] Ibid. para 123 (pointing out that there are other rights, apart from the right to vote, 'which contain broad equitable defining characteristics', and that there is therefore no hard-and-fast rule against the 'inclusion of an equitable consideration at the threshold level of the right').

[68] Ibid. para 24.

they are never likely to affect the outcome of a case. At least, as soon as the Court decides to interpret a right as requiring a particular standard of review at the threshold stage of the constitutional inquiry, it must give due consideration to whether the standard it chooses is consistent with the importance of the right in the constitutional scheme.

By the same token, Justice O'Regan's judgment fails fully to consider, or follow through on, its own inexorable logic. Although she dissents from Justice Yacoob's judgment on the ground that the review standard he chooses is too deferential, she goes along with his judgment to the extent that she argues that provisions aimed at facilitating the exercise of the right to vote should not be seen as limitations of the right.[69] As noted earlier, however, when the test for threshold violations of the right to vote is said to be that the state must act reasonably, the distinction between provisions that are expressly aimed at excluding a particular category of citizen from voting, and provisions that are aimed at facilitating the exercise of the right to vote, collapses – not because it cannot be maintained conceptually, but because the standard of review is in each instance the same. This is borne out by the awkwardness of Justice O'Regan's attempt at the end of her judgment to apply the general limitations clause analysis to provisions she has already found to be unreasonable. As she says there, '[g]iven the definition of the right I propose and have applied, the exercise under s 36 in this case is similar to the exercise carried out to determine whether the challenged provisions were reasonable.'[70] In the circumstances, it might have been better for Justice O'Regan simply to argue that the right to vote is of such cardinal importance that any attempt to regulate it, including regulation aimed at facilitating the exercise of the right, should be treated as a limitation subject to review under the general limitations clause.

Despite this problem, Justice O'Regan's judgment, of the two, is the one that is easier to reconcile with *August* and the Court's later decision in *NICRO*. The distinct advantage of her approach is that it translates Justice Sachs's statement in *August* about the importance of the right to vote into a review standard that adequately protects the right against the incidental limiting effects of good-faith attempts to facilitate its exercise. Her judgment is also more consistent with the Court's approach in other cases, including, for example, *Treatment*

---

[69] Ibid. paras 123–4.   [70] Ibid. para 160.

Action Campaign, where the Court was at pains to point out that separation of powers concerns should not be factored into the interpretation of the scope of a right.[71] Finally, Justice O'Regan's approach accords better with the approach taken in foreign law and in normative constitutional theory, where the right to vote, of all the rights, is taken to be one that a constitutional court may legitimately enforce, if need be, through strict scrutiny.

Is it then a reasonable inference to make that Justice Yacoob and the other members of the Court who signed on to his judgment were concerned about the possible impact of the case on the Court's independence? Everything does seem to point that way. What made the *New National Party* case so difficult was that it directly challenged the ANC's electoral dominance. Whereas in other cases the Court was able to exploit this feature of the political context – either by using the ANC's dominance to shelter it from the adverse effects of public opinion or enlisting the ANC as a partner in the implementation of the constitutional project – here the path of constitutional principle ran directly counter to the ANC's pressing interest in maximising its share of the vote in the 1999 general election. The judges were accordingly put in the position of having to prioritise one or the other of the two sets of constraints impacting on them: on the one hand, the pull of the law towards according the right to vote its proper place in the constitutional scheme; and, on the other, the Court's institutional interest in preserving its co-operative working relationship with the ANC. Faced with this choice, the majority in *New National Party* appears to have favoured the latter course. While not wholly implausible, Justice Yacoob's decision is convoluted and grudging, paying lip-service to the importance of the right to vote while all the while working rhetorically to justify a review standard that imposes a more onerous burden on the citizen to access the right than it does on the government to facilitate its exercise. In contrast, Justice O'Regan's judgment is clear and forceful, pointing the way to the path of principle not followed.

---

[71] *Minister of Health and Others* v. *Treatment Action Campaign and Others (No 2)* 2002 (5) SA 721 (CC), 2002 (10) BCLR 1075 (CC) para 99 (holding that 'any intrusion into the domain of the executive' consequent on the enforcement of a right in the Bill of Rights is an intrusion 'mandated by the Constitution itself'). The Court's separation of powers doctrine is discussed in more detail in Chapter 10.

9.3 Floor-crossing: *United Democratic Movement*

The second case that illustrates the Court's inability to reconcile its over-arching strategy with the enforcement of political rights is the so-called 'floor-crossing case', *United Democratic Movement*.[72] The legal and political background to the case was complex but bears setting out in full.[73]

Both the 1993 Constitution and the 1996 Constitution (as originally enacted) imposed a ban on floor-crossing in the national and provincial legislatures.[74] In addition, s 157(3) of the 1996 Constitution provided that the total number of members of a particular party in a Municipal Council should correspond to that party's proportional share of the vote, which effectively prevented local councillors from crossing the floor.[75] At all three levels, the ban on floor-crossing was consequent on the choice of a closed-list proportional representation system. Since voters under such a system vote for a party and not a particular individual, it was argued, parliamentarians needed to be prevented from undermining the result of an election by crossing the floor. The choice of a proportional representation system, in turn, was driven by fears that (1) a constituency-based system would be distorted by apartheid's race-based residential zoning laws; and (2) such a system, given the ANC's electoral dominance, would give little representation to minority parties.

Not everyone agreed with this view. The major threat to the consolidation of democracy, the contrary argument ran, was the absence of a realistic alternative to the ANC. In such a situation, democratic institutions ought to be designed in such a way as to support the emergence of a 'loyal opposition' that could compete for votes and hold the Government to account.[76] The problem with a proportional representation system, on this approach, was that it allowed minority political parties to be represented in Parliament without requiring them to broaden their

---

[72] *United Democratic Movement v. President of the Republic of South Africa and Others (African Christian Democratic Party and Others Intervening; Institute for Democracy in South Africa and Another as Amici Curiae) (No 1)* 2003 (1) SA 488 (CC), 2002 (11) BCLR 1179 (CC).

[73] This paragraph and the next draw on the excellent summary provided in Choudhry, "'He Had a Mandate'" 37–9.

[74] See ss 43(b) and 133(1)(b) of the 1993 Constitution. In the case of the 1996 Constitution, the ban was contained in a transitional provision, item 23A of Annexure A to Schedule 6.

[75] There was also a specific ban on floor-crossing in s 27 of the Municipal Structures Act.

[76] Ian Shapiro and Courtney Jung, 'South Africa's Negotiated Transition: Democracy, Opposition, and the New Constitutional Order' (1995) 23 *Politics and Society* 269 (cited in Choudhry, "'He Had a Mandate'" 38).

constituency. This was particularly worrisome under the 1993 Constitution, where the various provisions relating to the Government of
National Unity had produced a kind of consociationalism in which no
party had an incentive to challenge the status quo. When coupled with
the ban on floor-crossing, it was argued, the likely result would be a
situation where MPs on all sides would be beholden to their political
leaders.[77] This situation, in turn, would inhibit the fragmentation of the
ANC into its left and right factions – a development that was required for
the opening up and full flourishing of South Africa's democracy.[78]

When the 1996 Constitution came up for certification, an argument
very much along these lines was put to the Constitutional Court. The ban
on floor-crossing, it was contended, violated a range of constitutional
principles, including those relating to the need for a multi-party system
of democratic government with 'checks and balances to ensure accountability, responsiveness and openness' and the principle that all 'universally accepted fundamental rights' should be respected.[79] The judges were
not persuaded. Far from violating these principles, they held, the ban on
floor-crossing supported them by ensuring that parliamentarians were
accountable to their parties, which were in turn accountable to the
electorate.[80] The particular value of the ban on floor-crossing was that
it 'prevent[ed] parties in power from enticing members of small parties to
defect from the party on whose list they were elected to join the
governing party'.[81] 'If this were permitted,' the Court warned, 'it could
enable the governing party to obtain a special majority which it might
not otherwise be able to muster and which is not a reflection of the views
of the electorate'.[82]

The political build-up to the floor-crossing case began two and a half
years later, in July 1999, when the two largest minority parties, the New
National Party and the Democratic Party, entered into an agreement with
a smaller minority party to form the Democratic Alliance. The immediate impetus behind the agreement was the need to secure control of the
Western Cape province, which had been won outright by the National
Party in the first democratic election, but which it would have lost to the

---

[77] Shapiro and Jung, 'South Africa's Negotiated Transition' 277.
[78] Ibid. 300–301.
[79] See *Ex Parte Chairperson of the Constitutional Assembly: In re Certification of the
Constitution of the Republic of South Africa, 1996* 1996 (4) SA 744 (CC), 1996 (10) BCLR
1253 (CC) ('*First Certification Judgment*') paras 180–88.
[80] Ibid. paras 185–6.   [81] Ibid. para 187.   [82] Ibid.

ANC in 1999 but for the support of the Democratic Party. Given the ban on floor-crossing, it was not possible for the Democratic Alliance to hold seats in the Western Cape legislature as a separate political party, but it was able to contest the December 2000 local government elections. The new political party did impressively well, winning 53.5 per cent of the vote in the Cape Town metropolitan area, and a majority of all the local government votes cast in the Western Cape.[83] Just over a year later, however, the New National Party fell out with the Democratic Party over the alleged sidelining of the former's members in the governance structures of the Democratic Alliance. On this occasion, the ban on floor-crossing worked the other way, preventing local government councillors who had formerly been members of the New National Party from crossing the floor to align themselves with the ANC.

In a transparent attempt to overcome this hurdle and win control of both the Cape Town municipality and the Western Cape legislature, the ANC entered into a pact with the New National Party to co-operate at all three levels of government. To give effect to this pact, the ANC tabled two constitutional amendments and two supporting statutes that together permitted floor-crossing in the national, provincial and municipal legislatures during two fifteen-day window periods and also during the fifteen days immediately following the commencement of the legislation.[84] In the case of the two recurrent window periods, a 10 per cent threshold was set on the proportion of representatives from a political party that were required to cross the floor before any one representative was permitted to cross. No threshold was set in respect of the first fifteen-day window period.

Despite its origins in the ANC-NNP pact, the Democratic Party supported the legislative package, apparently thinking that it might be able to gain some political advantage out of it. In the result, the package was passed with an 86 per cent majority in the National Assembly.[85] It soon became clear, however, that the amendments threatened the survival of smaller minority parties, which stood to lose many of their best members through precisely the sort of enticements that the Constitutional Court had warned about in its *First Certification Judgment*. In June 2002, the United Democratic Front ('UDM'), a splinter party that had

---

[83] See Tom Lodge, 'The South African Local Government Elections of December 2000' (2001) 28 *Politikon* 21, 40–41.

[84] The legislative package is summarised in *United Democratic Movement* paras 4–7.

[85] Ibid. para 56.

broken away from the ANC, launched a constitutional challenge against the package in the Cape High Court. A Full Bench of this Court suspended the operation of the four statutes pending the Constitutional Court's decision.

The UDM's challenge was multi-faceted.[86] It suffices for our purposes, however, to discuss just that part of it that related to the two constitutional amendments. Section 74 of the 1996 Constitution provides that Bills amending the Constitution should be passed by special majority, the precise level of support required depending on the nature of the amendment. Amendments to the founding values thus require a 75 per cent majority in the National Assembly together with the support of six provinces in the upper house.[87] Amendments to the Bill of Rights, on the other hand, require just two-thirds support in the National Assembly together with the support of six provinces.[88] Finally, amendments to the rest of the Constitution require the same level of support in the National Assembly as amendments to the Bill of Rights, but the support of six provinces only in instances where provincial interests are affected.[89] It was not disputed that the two constitutional amendments, which did not directly alter the text of the founding values or the Bill of Rights, had been properly passed under the third of these procedures. What was disputed was whether the amendments, given their substantive effects, ought to have been passed under one or the other of the first two procedures.[90] It was further contended that the amendments affected the 'basic structure' of the Constitution, and that they should therefore not have been passed at all.[91]

Writing without attribution of the judgment to a particular judge, the Court began by addressing the public controversy surrounding the case:

> This case is not about the merits or demerits of the provisions of the disputed legislation. That is a political question and is of no concern to this Court. What has to be decided is not whether the disputed provisions are appropriate or inappropriate, but whether they are constitutional or

---

[86] Another important aspect of its claim concerned the challenge to the Loss or Retention of Membership of National and Provincial Legislatures Act 22 of 2002 on the ground that it had not been passed within a 'reasonable period' of the adoption of the 1996 Constitution, as required by item 23A of Annexure A to Schedule 6. This part of the case was successful. See *United Democratic Movement* paras 85–113.

[87] Section 74(1).   [88] Section 74(2).   [89] Section 74(3).

[90] *United Democratic Movement* para 13.   [91] Ibid. paras 14–17.

unconstitutional. It ought not to have been necessary to say this for it is true of all cases that come before this Court. We do so only because of some of the submissions made to us in argument, and the tenor of the public debate concerning the case which has taken place both before and since the hearing of the matter.[92]

Together with Justice Chaskalson's discussion of the relevance of public opinion to the death penalty case,[93] this is one of the few occasions on which the Court acknowledged the possibility that there might be external, political constraints on its decision-making processes. As in that instance, the purpose of the exercise is to deny the influence of these constraints and publicly to reaffirm the Court's commitment to constitutional principle; as in that instance, too, the Court protests a little too much and in so doing opens a window onto its concern about the threat posed by the case to its institutional independence.

The problem on this occasion lies in the Court's attempt to set up a strict dichotomy between, on the one hand, the political dimensions of the case, which it associates with the examination of the 'merits' or the 'appropriate[ness]' of the impugned legislation, and, on the other, the purely legal or constitutional aspects. That sharp distinction, as we saw in Chapter 1, is unnecessarily formalistic and does not comport with either of the two main conceptions of the ideal of adjudication according to law. The *United Democratic Movement* case, by its very nature, required the Court to test the floor-crossing legislation against the substantive political values informing the 1996 Constitution. Such an exercise, according to both conceptions of the ideal, need not have drawn the Court into the forbidden zone of politics, provided that it was clear and transparent about the substantive values it was applying. What was forbidden was ideological or outcome-oriented decision-making. Far from putting concern about these possible influences to rest, the Court's retreat into formalism creates exactly the opposite impression: that the Court was intent on justifying an unduly deferential decision by appeal to an overly strict conception of the law/politics distinction.

The Court's treatment of the three legs of the applicant's challenge tends to confirm this view. In respect of each leg, the thrust of the Court's argument is to depict democracy as too ill-defined a concept, either at all or in the 1996 Constitution, to justify robust judicial intervention in

---

[92] Ibid. para. 11.   [93] See Chapter 6.

support of the applicant's claim. Thus, in relation to the basic structure argument, the Court held that:

> The electoral system adopted in our Constitution is one of many that are consistent with democracy, some containing anti-defection clauses, others not; some proportional, others not. It cannot be said that proportional representation, and the anti-defection provisions which support it, are so fundamental to our constitutional order as to preclude any amendment of their provisions.[94]

This passage does not do justice to the substance of the applicant's claim. Fairly construed, the claim was not that the choice of a proportional representation system with a ban on floor-crossing was fundamental to the 1996 Constitution, but that the ban on floor-crossing was a necessary adjunct to a proportional representation system, once such a system had been chosen. It was the combination of the two provisions, in other words, that the applicant was arguing was constitutionally required and whose severance threatened the constitutional order. To meet this argument, the Court needed to consider whether the removal of the ban on floor-crossing, by undermining the position of smaller parties, might facilitate the ANC's goal of winning two-thirds of the vote and control of all nine provinces. If the amendments could indeed be said to facilitate that goal, there was at least a plausible argument that constitutional democracy was threatened, not just by the ANC's ability to amend the Constitution, but also by its ability to prevent any other party from establishing itself through its performance at provincial or local government level as a credible electoral alternative. In its *First Certification Judgment*, as we have seen, the Court had acknowledged precisely this danger when dismissing an objection to the ban on floor-crossing.[95] Its failure to give proper consideration to this danger in the above passage weakens the justificatory force of its decision.[96]

As Sujit Choudhry has pointed out, part of the reason for the Court's reluctance to take over the Indian Supreme Court's 'basic structure' doctrine might have been that, in the 1996 Constitution, the special entrenchment of various founding values in s 1 fulfils a very similar function.[97] The contention that the lifting of the ban on floor-crossing threatened democracy was thus repeated in the second leg of the applicant's case, which dealt with the question whether the legislative package

---

[94] *United Democratic Movement* para 17.   [95] *First Certification Judgment* para 187.
[96] For a similar argument, see Choudhry, '"He Had a Mandate"' 44.   [97] Ibid. 47.

ought to have been passed according to the special procedure required by s 74(1) of the Constitution for amendments to the founding values. In considering this leg, the Court pays more attention to the substance of the applicant's claim and attempts to justify its departure from the approach taken in the *First Certification Judgment*. Once again, however, the force of the applicant's argument is not adequately acknowledged, and the Court's decision is less convincing to that extent.

The first relevant difference that the Court asks us to notice is that, in the case of the 1993 Constitution, proportional representation was specifically mentioned in Constitutional Principle VIII, whereas s 1(d) of the 1996 Constitution is silent about the form of the electoral system required to satisfy its commitment to multi-party democracy. 'If it had been contemplated that proportional representation should be one of the founding values,' the Court argues, 'it is difficult to understand why those words were omitted from section 1(d).' Having been omitted, it could not be said that proportional representation was 'implied as a requirement of multi-party democracy'.[98]

This argument, as others have pointed out,[99] assumes that the constitutional principles included in the 1993 Constitution ceased to constrain the form of the 1996 Constitution as soon as the Court had certified it. Instead, the founding values in s 1 of the 1996 Constitution must be seen to have taken over the role formerly played by the constitutional principles, and to have overridden them to the extent of any inconsistency. This reading clearly has far-reaching consequences for the ongoing relevance of the constitutional principles, which were so fundamental to the National Party's acceptance of the negotiated settlement. Had s 46(1) of the 1996 Constitution not provided for proportional representation in the National Assembly, for example, that would have been a ground for objection on the basis of Constitutional Principle VIII. On the approach taken in *United Democratic Movement* however, as soon as

---

[98] Ibid. para 29.

[99] See Steven Budlender, 'National Legislative Authority' in Woolman et al. (eds.), *Constitutional Law of South Africa* 17–28. Others trace this assumption to the Court's earlier statement in the *First Certification Judgment* para 18 that, once the Court had certified the text of the 1996 Constitution, 'that [was] the end of the matter and compliance or non-compliance thereof with the [constitutional principles] can never be raised again in any court of law'. See Iain Currie and Johann de Waal, *The Bill of Rights Handbook* 5th edn (Cape Town Juta, 2005) 7. This statement, however, is itself very terse and in any case is capable of being read as meaning no more than that the original text of the 1996 Constitution, rather than any amendments to it, could not be subjected to certification again.

the Constitution was certified, this constraint on the form of the electoral system fell away. In effect, the constitutional principles are seen as a stepping-stone measure only, providing a once-off opportunity for contesting the conformance of the 1996 Constitution to the terms of the negotiated settlement but nothing more enduring than that. Such a momentous doctrinal choice at the very least required some justification. But none is provided.

In any case, as noted earlier, the second leg of the applicant's claim did not depend on the contention that a system of proportional representation was constitutionally required, but on the contention that the ban on floor-crossing was needed *in conjunction* with such a system to ensure the accountability of parliamentarians to the electorate, as the Court had apparently decided in its *First Certification Judgment*.[100] The Court's response to this contention was particularly unconvincing. While the link between voter and party may be stronger in a proportional representation system, it reasoned, there was still a link between voter and party in a constituency-based system and thus the decision of a member to cross the floor in such a system 'is equally open to the accusation that he or she has betrayed the voters'.[101] It is not clear what the Court meant by this statement. Generously interpreted, it amounts to an attempted *reductio ad absurdum* argument that, whatever the electoral system, a decision to cross the floor is to some extent a betrayal of the voters' mandate. Since a commitment to democracy implies a commitment not to betray the voters' mandate, every electoral system that does not contain a ban on floor-crossing is to that extent undemocratic. But there are many electoral systems that do not prohibit floor-crossing and it is absurd to say that all of them are undemocratic. The proposition that the absence of a ban on floor-crossing detracts from democracy must therefore be false.

Once again, this does not do justice to the applicant's case. The applicant's contention was not that a ban on floor-crossing is everywhere a necessary condition of democracy, but that in a system of proportional representation a provision of this sort is especially important because voters vote for a particular party and not a particular person. A decision to cross the floor in such a system is a total betrayal of the vote, whereas in the case of a constituency-based system it is only a partial betrayal because voters must be taken to have voted in some measure for the

---

[100] *First Certification Judgment* paras 185–6.
[101] *United Democratic Movement* para 34.

person who crossed the floor. This is a relevant difference, both from the point of view of representation and from the point of view accountability. As to the first issue, a representative who crosses the floor in a constituency-based system still represents all the voters in his or her constituency, and may thus be called on to act in their interests. In a proportional representation system, by contrast, representatives who cross the floor cease to represent that hypothetical proportion of the electorate whose vote secured their seat. As to the second issue, voters in a constituency-based system who are dissatisfied with their representative's decision to cross the floor may hold that particular individual to account at the next election. In a proportional representation system, on the other hand, all that they can do is to vote for the party for which they previously voted. Such a vote may or may not have a disciplining effect on representatives who cross the floor, depending on the outcome of the election and on the floor-crosser's position on his or her new party's list.

The Court's next argument is equally unconvincing:

> We were referred in argument to a number of democratic countries with proportional representation systems in which defection is not allowed. No case was cited to us, however, in which a court in any country has ever held that, absent a constitutional or legislative requirement to that effect, a member of a legislature is obliged to resign if he or she changes party allegiance during the life of a legislature.[102]

The first sentence of this passage appears to be setting up a statement in the next sentence that there are examples of countries with proportional representation systems that do not maintain a ban on floor-crossing. Instead, the second sentence refers to the fact that no court has ever found that, as a matter of democratic principle (rather than by reason of an express constitutional or legislative provision) a representative who crosses the floor is obliged to resign. Why the absence of any foreign authority on this point should be a guide to the interpretation of the 1996 Constitution is not spelled out. This observation is in any case neither here nor there without some indication of the reason for the absence of any foreign authority. Perhaps no case requesting a court to order a floor-crosser to resign has ever been argued? And perhaps the reason for that, in turn, is that no other Constitution has ever provided for proportional representation without a concomitant ban on floor-crossing – exactly the

---

[102] Ibid. para 35.

converse proposition to the proposition that the first sentence of this passage appears to be setting up.

What the Court really means to convey by this passage, it seems, is that striking down legislative choices about the inclusion or removal of a ban on floor-crossing is just not the sort of thing courts do. It thus concludes this part of the judgment by arguing that: 'Where the law prohibits defection, that is a lawful prohibition, which must be enforced by the courts. But where it does not do so, courts cannot prohibit such conduct where the legislature has chosen not to do so.'[103] This argument, however, simply begs the question: does the 'law' in this case (the commitment in s 1(d) of the 1996 Constitution to the value of multi-party democracy) prohibit defection as a necessary adjunct to a proportional representation system? To answer that question, the Court was required to give real meaning and content to the principle of democracy in South African constitutional law – to read off from the text of the Constitution as a whole and the history of its enactment the substantive political commitments that South Africans may be said to have made when adopting the 1996 Constitution.

The gravamen of the applicant's complaint – 'that in the conditions prevailing in South Africa an anti-defection provision is required to promote multi-party democracy' – is finally addressed in paragraph 45 of the judgment. Here, for the first time, the Court gives full expression to the risk posed by the removal of the ban on floor-crossing to South Africa's 'new and fragile democracy'.[104] Using virtually the same language it had used in the First Certification Judgment, the Court summarises the applicant's argument as being that 'the ANC has the ability to attract members from other parties by offering them inducements to cross the floor' and that 'if defections are permitted this is likely to weaken the position of smaller parties and thus to weaken multi-party democracy'.[105] In the First Certification Judgment, this argument was central to the Court's dismissal of the objection to the ban on floor-crossing. In United Democratic Movement, however, the Court depicts it as impermissibly requiring it to protect South Africa's democracy from a risk that emanates from the voter-sanctioned balance of political power. Acknowledging that the threshold requirement of 10 per cent undoubtedly favours the ANC,[106] the Court holds that '[t]he fact that a particular system operates to the disadvantage of particular parties does not mean

---

[103] Ibid.   [104] Ibid. para 49.   [105] Ibid.   [106] Ibid. para 46.

that it is unconstitutional.'[107] This is a remarkable statement. Doctrinally, it means that there is no constitutional barrier to a political party's amending the Constitution with the clear purpose of gaining an electoral advantage, and with the clear effect of achieving that advantage, provided that the resulting electoral system is democratic according to the Court's virtually contentless understanding of that term.[108] A more complete denial of the Court's responsibility for protecting the quality of South Africa's democracy could hardly be imagined.

The third and final leg of this part of the applicant's claim concerned the contention that the constitutional amendments violated the right to vote in s 19 and as such ought to have been passed according to the special procedure provided in s 74(2) of the 1996 Constitution. The Court's response to this argument was once again to deny that it had the power to repair a systemic weakness in South Africa's democracy that the voters themselves theoretically had the power to correct. 'The rights entrenched under section 19', the Court held, 'are directed to elections, to voting and to participation in political activities. Between elections, however, voters have no control over the conduct of their representatives.'[109] The scope of the right to vote, on this approach, is restricted to a once-off expression of approval or disapproval of representatives' past behaviour at election time. It followed that the right could not be said to have been violated by actions undertaken between elections. The heart of the applicant's case, however, was not that *voters* should be able to control their representatives' behaviour, but that the *Court* should protect the integrity of the democratic system in which their votes were cast.[110] To answer that question properly the Court needed to define the scope of the right to vote by reference to its own legitimate role in preventing the

---

[107] Ibid. para 47.

[108] The only content that the Court gives to the term 'multi-party democracy' is that it 'clearly excludes a one-party state, or a system of government in which a limited number of parties are entitled to compete for office' (ibid. para 24) and that it 'contemplates a political order in which it is permissible for different political groups to organise, promote their views through public debate and participate in free and fair elections' (at para 26). On the Court's treatment of the 'purpose' and 'effect' of the amendments, see Choudhry, '"He Had a Mandate"' 43.

[109] *United Democratic Movement* para 49.

[110] As Sujit Choudhry has pointed out, the applicant's claim in *United Democratic Movement* was in this sense a claim about the fairness and openness to competition of the background rules structuring the democratic process (Choudhry, '"He Had a Mandate"' 7 n 16, citing inter alia Samuel Issacharoff and Richard H. Pildes, 'Politics as Markets: Partisan Lockups of the Democratic Process' (1998) 50 *Stanford Law Review* 643).

gerrymandering of the electoral system. It was not enough in response to the applicant's concern about this issue to say that voters assume the 'risk' that 'representatives may act inconsistently with their mandates'.[111] The conduct at issue in *United Democratic Movement* was far more serious than that. It took the form of a transparent attempt to alter the rules of the democratic game so as to favour the ANC and prevent any other political party from presenting itself as a credible electoral alternative.[112] The Court's failure to counteract this threat can only be attributed to its extreme reluctance, for what we must assume were institutional reasons, to pierce the veil of South Africa's dominant-party democracy.

9.4   Resolving the paradox

The Chaskalson Court's decisions in *New National Party* and *United Democratic Movement* stand out from the rest of its record as unusually deferential and unconvincing. In *New National Party*, the Court eviscerated a right that it elsewhere recognised as among the most important in the constitutional scheme, and in *United Democratic Movement* the Court failed to protect the democratic system against an electoral-rule change that it acknowledged would likely entrench the ANC's dominant position. In both cases, the Court placed form over substance: in *New National Party*, by ignoring the possibility that limitations on the right to vote consequent on good faith attempts to facilitate its exercise might be just as serious as limitations flowing from purposely exclusionary provisions, and in *United Democratic Movement* by entrusting the health of South Africa's democracy to provisions for voter censure that it must have known would in practice provide little check on the ANC's attempt to alter the electoral system in its favour.

To judge by its later decisions on the national and provincial legislatures' duty to facilitate public involvement in their processes,[113] the

---

[111] *United Democratic Movement* para 50.

[112] In the wake of the Court's decision in *United Democratic Movement*, the ANC took control of both the Western Cape and KwaZulu-Natal, the two provinces where it had failed to win a majority in the 1999 election. That the Constitutional Court's faith in the robustness of South Africa's democracy was not entirely misplaced is demonstrated by the fact that the Democratic Alliance eventually won back control of the Western Cape. For the duration of the ANC's period in government in this province, however, the Alliance was prevented from building its record as a competent alternative government.

[113] See *Doctors for Life International* v. *Speaker of the National Assembly and Others* 2006 (6) SA 416 (CC), 2006 (12) BCLR 1399 (CC) (striking down several health-related bills

Court's difficulty in these cases did not derive from the paucity of the constitutional text or the poverty of South Africa's democratic tradition. In these other cases, decided shortly after Justice Chaskalson's retirement, the Court was able to invoke a rich history of pre-colonial practice and extra-parliamentary struggle to give content to the 1996 Constitution's commitment to multi-party democracy. Nor were *New National Party* and *United Democratic Movement* alone in being politically controversial. *Grootboom* and *Treatment Action Campaign*, as we have seen, presented at least as great a threat of political backlash and yet the Court was prepared in these cases to speak constitutional truth to political power. What made *New National Party* and *United Democratic Movement* so different?

The answer, it would seem, lies in the particular kind of threat these cases posed to the Court's institutional independence. As we have seen in the preceding chapters, the Court was continually able to defy the ordinary assumptions of liberal constitutional theory by exploiting the ANC's dominance to carve out a role for itself as an independent check on the abuse of political power. For most of Justice Chaskalson's tenure, this strategy made sense. The ANC, as the largest political party and torch-bearer for both South Africa's human rights tradition and also its democratic ideals, was the Court's logical partner in the constitutional project. If the 1996 Constitution's heady promises were to be fulfilled, the ANC clearly had to be kept onside, and its commitment to constitutional democracy carefully nurtured. In relation to political rights, however, this strategy broke down. At least, the Court was confronted with a much more difficult-to-resolve tension between the political conditions for its institutional effectiveness and the requirements of constitutional principle.

What distinguishes the decisions in *New National Party* and *United Democratic Movement* from the rest of the Court's record, in other words, is the extent to which it was forced in these two cases to compromise on constitutional principle to accommodate its institutional concerns. Whereas the decisions discussed in other chapters reveal the Court's capacity to exploit South Africa's dominant-party democracy to build its reputation for decision-making according to law, the Court's

on this ground); and *Matatiele Municipality and Others* v. *President of the Republic of South Africa and Others* 2007 (1) BCLR 47 (CC) (striking down a constitutional amendment for the same reason).

political rights jurisprudence illustrates the limits of this strategy: reliant as it was for its institutional independence on preserving its co-operative working relationship with the ANC, the Court was prevented by the terms of that relationship from developing doctrines that would have allowed it eventually to break free.

10

Cross-cutting strategies

The last three chapters have focused on three different sets of constitutional rights and shown how the Chaskalson Court's case law in each of these areas reflected the judges' concern for the Court's independence. Both the content given to constitutional rights and also the approach taken to standards of review, these chapters have argued, were influenced by the judges' perception of the possible impact of their decisions on the Court's capacity to continue performing its institutional role over the long run.

This chapter changes tack somewhat. Instead of confining itself to a single set of rights, it addresses three cross-cutting strategies that the judges may be seen to have deployed in the cases already studied. The first such strategy concerned the Court's separation of powers doctrine in the narrow sense, i.e. its case law on the nature and limits of its role in enforcing constitutional norms. The importance of this issue lies in the fact that it was this aspect of the Court's case law through which the judges might have attempted to address some of their concerns about the Court's independence in a publicly accessible and consistent way. If the Court's separation of powers doctrine can be shown to have been principled in this sense, many, if not all, of the doctrinal choices that this study has attributed to the extra-legal influence of the political context in which the Court found itself would be re-appropriated for the realm of the legal – absorbed back, that is, into the morally persuasive and coherent account of the post-apartheid Constitutions that the judges all along purported to be giving. On the other hand, if the development of the Court's separation of powers doctrine can itself be shown to have been subject to concerns about the Court's independence, then this aspect of its case law will provide further support for this study's central contention.

The second part of the chapter focuses on the Court's case law on access and jurisdiction. The Court's approach to these questions provided it with an obvious way of controlling the flow of cases to it, and thus with a general device for managing the law/politics tension. Are there any trends in these two areas of the Court's case law that support the main argument of this study? Although seemingly contradictory at first, this section argues, the Court's case law on access and jurisdiction may indeed be read in this way. By stemming the flow of judicially and politically unmediated cases to it, the Court's strict approach to applications for direct access bought the Court time to measure the political temperature of cases, while also enlisting the ordinary courts in the business of constitutional interpretation, thus legalising and politically neutralising an activity that might otherwise have been regarded as alien to adjudication in the ordinary sense. The Court's comparatively more expansive approach to questions of jurisdiction supplemented this strategy by ensuring that the Court retained ultimate control over every case with a constitutional dimension, and thus over the delicate process of maintaining political-branch support for judicial review.

By restricting the flow of cases to it in this way, and forcing them through the ordinary courts, the Chaskalson Court likely reduced the overall size of its docket. It consequently had less opportunity to pick and choose cases. But the distinct advantage of this outcome was that the Court was able to devote much more time and decision-making energy to each individual case that came to it, thus enhancing its capacity to manage the impact of the case on its institutional independence. The final section of the chapter offers a few examples of this aspect of the Court's overall strategy, showing how it was able to package even fairly intrusive decisions in judicious language carefully calculated to enlist the political branches' support for the constitutional project.

10.1   The Court's separation of powers doctrine

Here is the Chaskalson Court justifying its order for mandatory relief in *Treatment Action Campaign*:

> The primary duty of courts is to the Constitution and the law, 'which they must apply impartially and without fear, favour or prejudice'. The Constitution requires the state to 'respect, protect, promote, and fulfil the rights in the Bill of Rights'. Where state policy is challenged as inconsistent with the Constitution, courts have to consider whether in formulating and implementing such policy the state has given effect to its constitutional obligations. If it should hold in any given case that the state has failed to do so, it is obliged by the Constitution to say so. In so far as that

constitutes an intrusion into the domain of the executive, that is an intrusion mandated by the Constitution itself.[1]

The passage recycles the conceit to which all constitutional courts must at some point resort: beyond interpretation and above politics, unmediated even by the judges' concern for their court's independence, the Constitution is just somehow there as the self-executing source of the court's authority. It is not we, the judges, who are holding you to account, the passage intones, but the people, whose wishes we are simply implementing.

But, of course, this is all just rhetoric: the Constitution does not interpret itself, and it mandates no definite 'intrusion into the domain of the executive' other than the degree of intrusion that the judges strive in their decision to justify and, over the long run, to get away with. That the people gave the Court the power to enforce the Constitution in the full knowledge that it would be exercised in this way does not by itself justify each particular exercise of the power. The Court must do the justifying, and in so doing it cannot but violate one of the most sacred principles of the rule of law: that no one should be a judge in their own cause. For some, this is a good reason not to confer the power.[2] For others, if the *nemo judex* principle must be infringed, it is better that an independent judiciary infringe it than an institution prone to populist pressures.[3] Clearly, however, once the power of review *has* been conferred, judges must try to make sense of it, and wield the power in a way that is morally defensible, or at least in a way that is as morally defensible as the undeniable fact of the power's anti-majoritarian operation permits.

The legal norms that a court develops in the course of discharging this justificatory burden form part of its separation of powers doctrine. 'Part' because the doctrine also concerns the extent of permissible legislative and executive intrusion into the *judicial* domain, and between the legislative and executive branch inter se. The system is not, the standard account runs, one of absolute separation, but rather one of checks and balances, in which each branch is permitted some degree of intrusion

---

[1] *Minister of Health and Others* v. *Treatment Action Campaign and Others (No 2)* 2002 (5) SA 721 (CC), 2002 (10) BCLR 1075 (CC) para 99 (footnotes omitted).

[2] Cf. Waldron, *Law and Disagreement* 297 (rejecting Ronald Dworkin's *nemo judex* defence of judicial review on the grounds that '[a]lmost any conceivable decision-rule will eventually involve *someone* deciding in his own case').

[3] Aharon Barak, *Proportionality* 387.

into the others' sphere of operation. But it is the court that oversees the system and the court that ultimately determines, not just the permissible degree of legislative intrusion into the executive domain and vice versa, but also the extent of its *own* power to intrude into the other branches' domains. Typically, this is not done through any kind of comprehensive or systematic theory. Rather, the court develops its separation of powers doctrine case by case, invoking and thus giving content to the doctrine on each occasion that it determines the standard of review in relation to a particular right or the form of the remedy it provides.

That, at least, is the standard account. It has been set out at some length because one possible objection to the argument of this study is that the doctrinal choices that the preceding chapters have attributed to the Chaskalson Court's concern about its institutional independence are really just the product of its separation of powers doctrine – of the judges' attempt to reconcile their duty to enforce constitutional rights with a principled understanding of the Court's institutional capacities and competencies. It is this principled understanding, the objection goes, that the judges all along knew would provide the best defence against attacks on the Court's independence. Even if that were not true – even if it would have been strategically better for the judges to have traded off considerations of constitutional principle against considerations of the Court's long-term institutional independence – that is not what they did. The mere fact that some of the Court's decisions in politically controversial cases have been shown to be less than fully principled does not indicate that the judges were motivated by a concern for their Court's independence. All that it indicates is that they misunderstood the requirements of the separation of powers in those cases, and even then only if the account of those requirements given in this study is to be preferred to the Court's own reasoning.

This would be a devastating critique if it could be substantiated. But it can't. Far from being consistent, this section argues, the Chaskalson Court's separation of powers doctrine took two main and interchangeable forms, and the interchangeability of those forms was central to its capacity to manage the law/politics tension. To make good on this claim it is necessary first to map out what a fully principled approach to the separation of powers would have looked like, and then to show how the Court's decisions in the cases we have discussed not only deviated from this approach, but deviated in ways that reinforce the conclusions drawn in earlier chapters.

A constitutional court's separation of powers doctrine, we have noted, consists of two aspects: norms about the permissible limits of the political branches' intrusion into each other's domains and also the Court's sphere of operation, and norms about the permissible limits of the Court's checking role. It is the latter aspect of the doctrine that concerns us here because it is this aspect that would have allowed the Court to trade off considerations of constitutional principle against considerations of its long-term institutional independence. Constitutional courts work out this second aspect, we have further noted, in the course of justifying their choice of review standard in respect of each right and, if a violation is found, in their choice of remedy. A fully principled approach to the former issue requires a court to develop a morally defensible account of the importance of the right in the constitutional scheme and the circumstances in which it may be limited. A fully principled approach to the second issue requires a court to frame its remedial order with due regard to the seriousness of the rights violation and the actions needed to put an end to it, and then to justify its order by means of a morally defensible account of the respective roles of the different branches in performing this task.

The importance of the right in the constitutional scheme must be considered at both stages of the constitutional inquiry: when the scope of the right is being defined and when the question whether it has been permissibly limited is being decided. At the first stage, the scope of each right must be defined in a way that does justice to the constitutional text and the importance of the right in the country's democratic tradition. The limitations standard set for the right, whether special or general,[4] must likewise give effect to the text, and be tailored to the importance of the right in the Constitution and the respective capacities and competencies of the various branches in making discretionary choices about its fulfilment. If these principles are respected, the fact that curial enforcement of the right strays into areas traditionally reserved for the political branches is irrelevant.

The text of the 1996 South African Constitution refines these general principles in the following way. First, it gives some indication of the importance of certain rights. Although it does not establish a formal hierarchy of rights in the manner, say, of the German Constitution's

---

[4] On the distinction between special and general limitations clauses, see Stu Woolman and Henk Botha, 'Limitations' in Woolman et al. (eds.), *Constitutional Law of South Africa* ch 34; Currie and de Waal, *The Bill of Rights Handbook* 165, 187–8; Barak, *Proportionality* 141–5.

prioritisation of the right to dignity,[5] it does bolster certain rights by committing itself to a range of foundational values, including the value of a 'multi-party system of democratic government' and 'human dignity' and 'the achievement of equality'.[6] Secondly, it expressly divides the inquiry into the scope and permissible limitation of constitutional rights into two stages, with the second stage governed by a general limitations clause that applies equally to all rights.[7] In structural form, this means that the 1996 South African Constitution is closer to the 1982 Canadian Charter than it is to either the American or the German Constitution.[8] For the most part, limitations on constitutional rights are to be determined according to a single analytic framework that must be derived from the text of the general limitations clause. The 1996 Constitution does not exclude the possibility of special limitations on rights, however, and the language of some of the rights – including the socio-economic rights in ss 26 and 27, the right to property in s 25, and the right to equality in s 9 – suggests that courts, in addition to defining the scope of each right, may devise different levels of review in respect of different rights. The 1996 Constitution in this sense adopts a 'hybrid' approach in which consideration of the special limitations accompanying a particular right may render the operation of the general limitations clause redundant, notwithstanding the fact that this clause applies in principle to all rights.[9] Where the general limitations clause *is* applicable, s 36(1)(*a*) confirms that the 'nature of the right' is one of the issues that a court must consider when determining the extent of the right's permissible limitation.

The 1996 Constitution's regulation of the scope of the courts' power to devise remedies for violation of constitutional rights is less detailed, with s 38 simply providing that a range of parties may 'approach a competent court' and that the court may grant 'appropriate relief, including a

---

[5] Article 1(1) of the German Constitution provides that '[h]uman dignity shall be inviolable'. This is the only right that is specified as being illimitable in this way.

[6] Section 1 of the 1996 Constitution.   [7] Ibid. s 36.

[8] The American Constitution, of course, does not formally contain either a general limitations clause or many special limitations clauses. In the course of its interpretation, however, the US Supreme Court has developed three different review standards that it applies to various rights according to a categorisation approach. See Barak, *Proportionality* 509–12. The German Constitution contains numerous special limitations clauses.

[9] See Barak, *Proportionality* 144 (citing Gerhard van der Schyff, *Limitations of Rights: A Study of the European Convention and South African Bills of Rights* (Nijmegen: Wold Legal Publishers, 2005) 128.

declaration of rights'.[10] This formulation left the Chaskalson Court with a very wide discretion to construct its remedial jurisprudence as it saw fit.[11] Whether this aspect of its separation of powers doctrine was fully principled, therefore, depends less on questions of adherence to the constitutional text and South Africa's political tradition and more on questions of rational consistency and morally justifiability. But the underlying question remains the same: was there any correlation between unprincipled variation in the Court's approach and independently verifiable concerns about its institutional independence?

A comprehensive assessment of this issue and the rest of the Chaskalson Court's separation of powers doctrine would require consideration of its entire record.[12] There is enough, however, in the cases we have looked at to establish the main point: that the Court did not adhere to a fully principled doctrine, but instead alternated between two rival understandings of its legitimate role in enforcing constitutional rights depending on the threat posed by the case to its institutional independence. According to the first understanding, separation-of-powers considerations should not be factored into the Court's determination of questions of constitutionality since the determination of such questions falls squarely within the Court's domain. According to the second understanding, separation-of-powers considerations inform the limits of the Court's legitimate role in enforcing the Constitution, and should therefore be factored into the Court's determination of the scope of constitutional rights, their permissible limitation and the remedies through which constitutional violations may be corrected. On the first understanding, in other words, determining questions of constitutionality is simply what constitutional courts do, and any consequences that flow from the performance of this function, including invalidation of choices made by the other branches, must be accepted as a necessary side-effect of the adoption of a supreme-law constitution. On the second understanding, there is no Constitution other than the Constitution that the Court as an institutionally limited actor is empowered to enforce. It follows that the Constitution is violated only to the extent that the alleged violation is one that the Court is competent to identify.

---

[10] Section 172(1)(b) in addition provides that, '[w]hen deciding a constitutional matter within its power, a court ... may make any order that is just and equitable'.

[11] See Currie and De Waal, *The Bill of Rights Handbook* 190–228; Michael Bishop, 'Remedies' in Woolman et al. (eds.), *Constitutional Law of South Africa* ch 9.

[12] For an account of this sort, see Sebastian Seedorf, 'Separation of Powers' in Woolman et al. (eds.), *Constitutional Law of South Africa* ch 12.

The clearest statement of the first understanding occurs in the extract from the *Treatment Action Campaign* decision quoted at the beginning of this section. As we have seen, the rhetorical thrust of these remarks is to suggest that the Constitution is a self-executing document that the Court is duty-bound to enforce. Whatever 'intrusion' into the political branches' sphere of operation follows from the Court's fulfilment of this duty cannot possibly breach the separation of powers because such intrusion is 'mandated by the Constitution itself'.

In *Treatment Action Campaign*, the Court used this understanding to justify a more intrusive order – mandatory relief – than it had handed down in *Grootboom*, where a declaratory order was made. A fully principled defence of this decision would have required the Court to point to some relevant difference in the importance of the right at issue, the severity of its violation, or the capacity of the political branches to remedy the constitutional defect. No such defence was attempted, however. Nor could it have been. The rights implicated in the two cases – the right to housing and the right to health – enjoy an equal constitutional status. The seriousness of the violation of each right was also comparable: while the prospect in *Treatment Action Campaign* of further preventable infant deaths occurring as a result of the state's failure to provide nevirapine outside the research and training sites was certainly grave, it was no graver than the prospect in *Grootboom* of preventable deaths occurring as a result of the exposure of homeless people to the elements. The only real difference between the two cases was the degree of political controversy surrounding them, with *Grootboom* arising as an incidental challenge to the Government's housing policy, and *Treatment Action Campaign* coming to the Court after a two-year-long, bitterly contested public impact litigation campaign. Had the Court chosen to do so, it might have made something of the Minister of Health's threat, in the midst of that campaign, not to implement the Court's order. That, at least, would have provided some principled basis for the more intrusive remedy in the second case. But to do so, the Court would have needed to confront the Government over its threatened disrespect for the Constitution – just the sort of conflict that the Court had for so long been so careful to avoid. Instead of justifying its order in this way, therefore, the Court deployed the first understanding of its separation of powers doctrine so as to present its order for mandatory relief as constitutionally compelled. It then framed this order as a midway point between a declaration of rights and a supervisory interdict, justifying its disinclination to choose the latter form of remedy on the grounds that '[t]he government has always executed and respected orders of this Court'.[13] In this way, the Court was able to dress up what was in fact a fairly intrusive remedy as a restrained and respectful response to the constitutional violation at issue. At the same time, it took care to confirm its confidence in the political branches' willingness and capacity to implement its order, thereby morally obligating them to do what it had held they were constitutionally required to do, and what the Court itself, lacking purse or sword, was incapable of doing.

The absence of any principled separation-of-powers justification for the more intrusive remedy in *Treatment Action Campaign* lends further support to this study's reading of the case as one in which the micro-politics allowed the Court more boldly to assert its checking role. As discussed in Chapter 7, the case had been run by the constitutional claimant in a way that cleverly isolated President Mbeki and his Health Minister from their cabinet colleagues and powerful provincial ANC leaders. In this context, the Court was free to hand down a fairly prescriptive order without any immediate risk to its institutional independence. To be sure, there were other considerations favouring such an order, not least the fact that the Government had already approved nevirapine for distribution in its research and training sites and the fact that the financial costs of extending the drug's availability beyond these sites were not prohibitive. But the decisive factor appears to have been the reduced prospect of any political backlash.

The Court's understanding in *Treatment Action Campaign* of its legitimate role in remedying constitutional violations stands in stark contrast to its approach in *Grootboom*, not just in relation to the remedy chosen but also in regard to the relevance of separation of powers considerations to the Court's role in determining the content of constitutional rights. As we saw in Chapter 7, the *Grootboom* Court justified its refusal to adopt the minimum core approach by reference to the institutional inappropriateness of this form of priority-setting. The weakness of this argument has been exposed by Bilchitz.[14] More recently, Aharon Barak, the former President of the Supreme Court of Israel, has warned against the dangers of overstating constitutional courts' limitations in reviewing the constitutionality of complex policy choices. As he puts it: 'If a member of the legislative or executive branch can reach a decision regarding polycentric issues, a member of the judiciary should be able to

---

[13] *Treatment Action Campaign* para 129.
[14] Bilchitz, *Poverty and Fundamental Rights* 197–207.

examine whether or not those decisions are lawful'.[15] The key to under-standing the Court's legitimate role, as this quote suggests, is to distin-guish between the business of policy formulation and the business of constitutional standard-setting. Provided the Court sticks to the latter task, its intrusion into the political branches' domain is justifiable as the necessary side-effect of its constitutionally mandated function. In *Groot-boom*, this distinction is forgotten (or suppressed), and the Court's limitations in performing a function that it is *not* constitutionally man-dated to perform – designing social and economic policy – are treated as reasons not to perform the function it *is* mandated to perform – deter-mining the content of rights. In this way, the decision in *Grootboom* may be seen to have been premised on the second of the two understandings outlined earlier, one in which separation of powers concerns are allowed to intrude into the Court's primary role as constitutional interpreter.

Once again, this variation in the Court's presentation of its separation of powers doctrine correlates to concerns about its institutional inde-pendence. *Grootboom*, as we have seen, was the first case in which the Court was called on to deal with a direct challenge to a major plank in the ANC's social and economic reform programme. Of the two doctrinal options open to it – the minimum core approach, which would have seen it setting relatively concrete constitutional standards, and Mureinik's more flexible rational justification approach – the latter fitted better with its strategy of managing its relationship with the ANC. To bolster the doctrinal merits of this choice, the Court adopted an understanding of the separation of powers that overstated its institutional limitations in giving content to social rights. By the time *Treatment Action Campaign* came to be decided, this choice was set, and the Court could not afford to backtrack on its rejection of the minimum core approach without risking allegations of inconsistency. But it could exploit the inherent flexibility of its reasonableness review standard by more closely scrutinising the Gov-ernment's conduct.[16] It was also able to exploit the micro-politics of the case at the remedial stage by articulating a more uncompromising ver-sion of its separation of powers doctrine than it had applied at the rights definition stage. By moving between the two rival understandings of its legitimate role in this way, the Court was able to respond to the different political demands of these cases without sustaining any significant damage to its legal-professional reputation.

---

[15] Barak, *Proportionality* 390.   [16] See the discussion of this issue in Section 7.4.

A similar shift to the second version of the Court's separation of powers doctrine is detectable in *New National Party*. In this case, as we saw in Chapter 9, the majority (temporarily) abandoned the idea that the level of review in respect of a constitutional right should be related to its importance in the constitutional scheme, and instead claimed that separation of powers concerns precluded it from reviewing legislative and executive conduct for reasonableness at the rights definition stage. This study is not alone in criticising this aspect of the decision.[17] While the test the majority devised was not unlike the reasonableness review standard it later adopted in *Grootboom*, the right to vote in s 19(3) – unlike the rights to health and housing – is textually unqualified. What the Court in effect did, therefore, was to insert a special limitations clause into s 19(3) in circumstances where positive state action was required to realise the right. While the analogy with the standard adopted in relation to social rights was not wholly inapposite, there is no general reason why positive rights should be subjected to a lower standard of review than negative rights,[18] and no particular reason in this instance why the Court should have overridden the clear textual implication in s 19(3) that any limitation on the right to vote, including limitations consequent on positive state action to give effect to the right, should be subject to justification under the general limitations clause. When coupled with its unwarranted downgrading of the importance of the right in the constitutional scheme, the Court's deployment of the second version of its separation of powers doctrine reinforces the suspicion that its decision was motivated by concerns for its institutional independence – concerns, that is, that the first version of its separation of powers doctrine required it to ignore, but which the Court nevertheless needed to heed and trade off against any resultant reputational damage.

Too little has been said in this study about the Court's remedial jurisprudence to do justice to this aspect of its separation of powers doctrine.[19] Recall, however, the difference of opinion in the same-sex marriage case, *Fourie*. As she had done in *New National Party*, Justice O'Regan there came down in favour of a strict understanding of the Court's institutional role. Acknowledging that '[t]he doctrine of the separation of powers is an important one,' she held that it could

---

[17] See Currie and De Waal, *The Bill of Rights Handbook* 465; Seedorf, 'Separation of Powers' ch 12, 70–71.

[18] Barak, *Proportionality* 422–34.

[19] See the magnificent discussion of this issue in Bishop, 'Remedies'.

nevertheless not 'be used to avoid the obligation of a court to provide appropriate relief that is just and equitable to litigants who successfully raise a constitutional complaint'.[20] 'The power and duty to protect constitutional rights,' Justice O'Regan continued, 'is conferred upon the courts and courts should not shrink from that duty. The legitimacy of an order made by the Court does not flow from the status of the institution itself, but from the fact that it gives effect to the provisions of our Constitution.'[21]

This defence of the Court's remedial powers is very similar to the one provided in *Treatment Action Campaign*: the cardinal issue is whether the Constitution has been violated; if that is established, the Court is under a duty to remedy the violation and separation of powers considerations are irrelevant. Against this defence, the majority in *Fourie*, by signing on to Justice Sachs's judgment, endorsed the alternative understanding of the Court's legitimate role in terms of which separation of powers considerations should be factored into the determination of 'appropriate relief', or at least relief that is 'just and equitable'.[22] Although it is possible to understand the Court's order in this instance as a principled limitation of the applicant's constitutional rights in the interests of ensuring their enforceability,[23] Justice Sachs's remarks display a concern for the Court's institutional independence that goes beyond mere issues of capacity or competence. In *Fourie*, the Court clearly had the *constitutional* power to amend the Marriage Act. The real question was whether it had the *institutional* power to enforce and ultimately survive a decision that ran so obviously contrary to majoritarian wishes.

In contrast to *Makwanyane*, where the Court had used a similar divergence between constitutional and positive morality to assert its institutional role, the Court in *Fourie* was far more cautious, openly recognising the practical limits on its power in a rare display of institutional vulnerability. The difference between the two decisions may be explained by reference to the ANC political leadership's unambiguous support for the outcome in *Makwanyane* as opposed to its more

---

[20] *Minister of Home Affairs and Another* v. *Fourie and Another* 2006 (1) SA 524 (CC), 2006 (3) BCLR 355 (CC) para 170.

[21] Ibid. para 171.

[22] See Bishop, 'Remedies' ch 9, 55–77 (explaining how the provision in s 172(1)(*b*) that the Court may make an order that is 'just and equitable' allows it to balance considerations of the wider effect of its order against its primary duty under s 38 to put the constitutional claimant in the position they would have been in had their rights not been violated).

[23] See the discussion in Section 6.4.

ambivalent attitude towards the policy issue raised in *Fourie*, and also the timing of the two decisions, with *Makwanyane* decided during the period in which the Court was insulated by its impending role in the certification of the 1996 Constitution and *Fourie* decided shortly after Justice Chaskalson's retirement, when several positions on the Court were about to be filled.[24] While it would be wrong to use this single example as conclusive proof of the argument of this study, it does provide powerful support for the central contention that the judges were attuned to the impact of their decisions on the Court's independence and that they sought to manage this impact through their doctrinal choices. It also suggests that the judges' sensitivity to this issue may have increased as the political environment for judicial review deteriorated.

10.2   Access and jurisdiction

One of the main ways constitutional courts manage the law/politics tension, earlier chapters have argued,[25] is by controlling the content of their docket. Constitutional courts thus typically have the discretion to decide not just who may approach them, either directly or on appeal, but also what classes of legal question may be posed, and what the requirements for the framing of a question as a legal question properly within the court's jurisdiction are. Depending on the extent to which these docket-management decisions need to be publicly justified, the court may be able to use them completely to avoid, or at least to control the timing of, politically controversial cases, without damage to its legal-professional reputation.

This aspect of the Chaskalson Court's record has not as yet been emphasised, but there is enough in the cases discussed in previous chapters to suggest the role that the Court's decisions on access and jurisdiction may have played in its overall strategy. Two issues in particular are worth examining: the Court's direct access jurisprudence, which was briefly mentioned in Chapter 8 in relation to the *Transvaal Agricultural Union* case; and the interpretation of the term 'constitutional

---

[24] *Fourie* was decided on 1 December 2005, six months after Jacob Zuma's dismissal as Deputy President and three weeks after the (ultimately unproven) rape charges against him became public. While the *Fourie* decision thus falls into the period where Zuma's political star appeared to have faded, his and his supporters' opposition to gay rights was well known.

[25] See Sections 2.2 and 3.2.

matter' in s 167(3) of the 1996 Constitution, which was the basis on which the Court assumed jurisdiction in most of the cases discussed.

Transvaal Agricultural Union formed part of a larger body of case law in which the Court set relatively strict rules governing the circumstances in which constitutional claimants were entitled to access it directly.[26] There is no suggestion in the literature that the Court's record in this respect was anything but consistent: the Court never declined to take a case that its direct access rules suggest it ought to have taken, and on several occasions it allowed politically controversial cases to come directly to it.[27] Nevertheless, the Court's strict direct access jurisprudence may be read as supporting its overall strategy. In case after case, when asked to weigh the principle, on the one hand, that complex constitutional questions and the factual disputes underpinning them should be properly ventilated in the lower courts, and the principle, on the other, that particularly pressing constitutional cases should be decided on an urgent basis, the Court came down in favour of the former.[28] This discernible tilt in the Court's direct access jurisprudence, particularly given its professed concern elsewhere for the hurdles faced by poor litigants in accessing the Court,[29] is significant. Had the Court's preferred strategy been about building its institutional legitimacy – about becoming a people's court in the manner, say, of the Indian Supreme Court[30] – it is reasonable to assume it would have struck this balance differently, in a way more sympathetic to the difficulties faced by poorly resourced claimants in prosecuting a case through the lower courts.[31] The fact that the Court did not suggests that it saw some additional benefit in its strict approach to questions of direct access, over and above the stated benefit of issue clarification, and more valuable to it even than the benefit foregone of building its popular support.

Just what this benefit might have been is illustrated by *Treatment Action Campaign*. That case, as we saw in Chapter 7, came to the Court

---

[26] See Currie and De Waal, *The Bill of Rights Handbook* 132–5.

[27] Ibid. 134 n 162.   [28] Ibid. 132–5.

[29] See *Ex parte Gauteng Provincial Legislature: In re Dispute Concerning the Constitutionality of Certain Provisions of the Gauteng School Education Bill of 1995* 1996 (3) SA 165 (CC), 1996 (4) BCLR 537 (CC) para 36 (holding that indigent litigants should not be discouraged from litigating by the threat of an adverse costs order).

[30] On the Indian Supreme Court's 'epistolary jurisdiction', see P. N. Bhagwati, 'Judicial Activism and Public Interest Litigation' (1985) 23 *Columbia Journal of Transnational Law* 561, 571–3.

[31] For a more detailed examination of the Court's record in this respect, see Dugard and Roux, 'The Record of the South African Constitutional Court' 107; Dugard, 'Courts and the Poor in South Africa'.

after a public impact litigation campaign in which the constitutional claimant cleverly exploited the flexibility of the Court's reasonableness review standard. While the Court's task was also facilitated by the Minister of Health's ill-conceived decision to demand the suspension of the High Court's order, the airing of the drug-treatment issues in the High Court allowed the constitutional claimant to win the policy argument before the case reached the Constitutional Court. Had the Chaskalson Court's direct access jurisprudence been less strict, the claimant might well have been advised to initiate the litigation in the Constitutional Court as a court of first and last instance. (The constitutional issue was certainly urgent enough, overlayed as it was by the allegation that the Government's refusal to expand the number of research and training sites was causing hundreds of preventable infant deaths every month.) Had that occurred, however, the Constitutional Court would have been presented, not only with a complex set of factual issues to determine, but also with a far more politically intractable case in which the Government's opposition to the order would have been at its zenith.

The Court's strict direct access jurisprudence may be seen in this way to have provided it with a measure of political cover, allowing not only factual and legal questions, but also the political dynamics of cases, to crystallise before coming to the Court. There was a distinct downside to this approach, however. In addition to reducing the Court's chances of becoming a people's court, with its own constituency independent of the ANC, the Court's strict approach to applications for direct access probably contributed to its relatively small case load. As we saw in Chapter 3, the Court decided on average twenty-three cases per year, out of an average of fifty enrolled.[32] By way of comparison, the Russian Constitutional Court received about 15,000 petitions from 1994 to 1995, of which 98 per cent were declined by the Secretariat of the Court. Of the remaining 2 per cent (300 petitions), thirty-nine were decided on their merits.[33] The Colombian Constitutional Court, working in a country with a population roughly comparable to that of South Africa (45 million), decides an average of 1,000 cases per year.[34]

---

[32] See Dugard and Roux, 'The Record of the South African Constitutional Court' 108.

[33] Ibid 120 n 7, citing Epstein, Knight and Shevtsova, 'The Role of Constitutional Courts in the Establishment and Maintenance of Democratic Systems of Government' 122 n 6.

[34] See Rodrigo Uprimny Yepes, 'The Enforcement of Social Rights by the Colombian Constitutional Court: Cases and Debates' in Roberto Gargarella, Pilar Domingo and Theunis Roux (eds.), *Courts and Social Transformation in New Democracies: An Institutional Voice for the Poor?* (Dartmouth: Ashgate, 2006) 127, 131 n 12.

Whether the Court would have received vastly more cases had its approach to direct access been different is a counterfactual and cannot be answered with any certainty. The point remains, however, that the constitutional provision regulating this issue, s 167(6)(a) of the 1996 Constitution,[35] left the Court with considerable discretion and that it used this interpretive freedom to design a strict approach. When considered together with its textually uncompelled endorsement of the principle of avoidance, in terms of which courts must, if possible, decide a case 'without reaching a constitutional issue',[36] it is fair to say that the Chaskalson Court on the whole preferred doctrines that were more likely to reduce than expand its overall caseload.

At first blush, this finding appears to be at odds with another aspect of the Court's record, its approach to questions of jurisdiction. According to s 167(3)(a) and (b) of the 1996 Constitution, the Constitutional Court is the 'highest court in all constitutional matters' and 'may decide only constitutional matters, and issues connected with decisions on constitutional matters'. Section 167(3)(c) further provides that the Constitutional Court 'makes the final decision whether a matter is a constitutional matter or whether an issue is connected with a decision on a constitutional matter'. Once again, these provisions left the Court with a wide discretion to determine the sorts of cases that could come to it. On this occasion, however, the Court adopted a fairly expansive approach, broadening the concept of 'constitutional matter' to the point where virtually any case, with a little effort, could be brought under its jurisdiction.[37] In a 2001 case, the Court thus decided that the term 'constitutional matter' covered six broad types of dispute, including disputes involving a claim that executive or administrative action was inconsistent

---

[35] The paragraph provides: 'National legislation or the rules of the Constitutional Court allow a person, when it is in the interests of justice and with leave of the Constitutional Court – (a) to bring a matter directly to the Constitutional Court.'

[36] *National Coalition for Gay and Lesbian Equality and Others* v. *Minister of Home Affairs and Others* 2000 (2) SA 1 (CC), 2000 (1) BCLR 39 (CC) para 21 (per Justice Ackermann).

[37] See Frank I. Michelman, 'The Rule of Law, Legality and the Supremacy of the Constitution' in Woolman et al. (eds.), *Constitutional Law of South Africa* ch 9–11; Seedorf, 'Jurisdiction' 4–102 ('the Constitutional Court has adopted an understanding of the all-pervasiveness of the Final Constitution in the legal system that effectively renders the distinction between constitutional and non-constitutional matters illusory'); Carole Lewis, 'Reaching the Pinnacle: Principles, Policies and People for a Single Apex Court in South Africa' (2005) 21 *South African Journal on Human Rights* 509, 519 (describing the distinction between constitutional and other matters as 'illusory'). For a less critical account, see Currie and De Waal, *The Bill of Rights Handbook* 103–106.

with the Constitution; disputes involving a claim that a statute either violated the Constitution on its face or should be interpreted conformably to the Constitution; and disputes about the fulfilment of a lower court's duty to interpret a statute or develop the common law so as to promote the 'spirit purport and objects of the Bill of Rights'.[38] In this way, the Court assumed jurisdiction over any exercise of public power and the interpretation and application of all constitutionally mandated legislation, including the Restitution of Land Rights Act 22 of 1994, the Labour Relations Act 66 of 1995, the National Environmental Management Act 107 of 1998, the Broadcasting Act 4 of 1999, and the Promotion of Administrative Justice Act 3 of 2000.

Although the Court's expansive approach to jurisdiction was arguably a logical consequence of its identification of legality as a justiciable constitutional principle, the elevation of legality to this status was not constitutionally compelled.[39] Likewise, while the 1996 Constitution contains several provisions that suggest that it should be read as an 'all-pervasive' normative order,[40] it does not follow from this that the Court should have assumed something close to plenary jurisdiction. In theory, the text of the 1996 Constitution left room for the Chaskalson Court to limit its jurisdiction to matters in which it was required to develop a new constitutional norm (as opposed to matters in which an existing constitutional norm was merely applied).[41] That being so, it is once again reasonable to assume that the Court's choice of a fairly expansive approach to questions of jurisdiction might have been informed by extra-legal considerations of its preferred institutional role. If that is true,

---

[38] *S v. Boesak* 2001 (1) SA 912 (CC), 2001 (1) BCLR 36 (CC) para 14. The six areas are set out in Michelman, 'The Rule of Law, Legality and the Supremacy of the Constitution' 7–8.

[39] See Michelman, 'The Rule of Law, Legality and the Supremacy of the Constitution' (arguing that the Court's decisions in *Fedsure Life Assurance Ltd and Others* v. *Greater Johannesburg Transitional Metropolitan Council and Others* 1999 (1) SA 374 (CC), 1998 (12) BCLR 1458 (CC) and *Ex Parte President of the Republic of South Africa: In re Pharmaceutical Manufacturers Association of South Africa* 2000 (2) SA 674 (CC), 2000 (3) BCLR 241 (CC) were in tension with the Court's attempts elsewhere to define its jurisdiction as a limited jurisdiction in line with s 167. For criticism of Michelman's argument, see Seedorf, 'Jurisdiction' ch 4, 74–7; Kate O'Regan, 'On the Reach of the Constitution and the Nature of Constitutional Jurisdiction: A Response to Frank Michelman' in Stu Woolman and Michael Bishop (eds.), *Constitutional Conversations* (Pretoria University Press, 2008) 63, 75–6.

[40] See Michelman, 'The Rule of Law, Legality and the Supremacy of the Constitution' ch 11, 38–41; Seedorf, 'Jurisdiction'.

[41] Seedorf, 'Jurisdiction' ch 4, 109–25.

however, how might we reconcile this aspect of the Court's record with its strict approach to questions of direct access? What strategic benefit might the Court have seen in requiring the majority of cases to come to it by way of appeal, on the one hand, while expanding its jurisdiction to decide those cases, on the other?

These two aspects of the Court's record make sense if we think about the judges as being concerned about the Court's possible political isolation as the apex court on constitutional matters. Had the Court pursued a more generous approach to applications for direct access, it would have decided a greater proportion of its cases as a court of first and last instance. Apart from the legal-technical benefits of avoiding this situation, there were institutional benefits to forcing the majority of cases to come to it by way of appeal. The discussion of *Treatment Action Campaign* has shown one dimension of this: the capacity for lower-court litigation to diffuse, or at least to crystallise, the politics of cases. The other dimension was the advantage to the Court of enlisting the ordinary courts (the High Courts and the Supreme Court of Appeal) as constitutional interpreters. In addition to the benefits of hearing their views on the questions presented, the involvement of the ordinary courts in constitutional decision-making reinforced the Court's preferred depiction of such activity as a purely legal exercise. On this view, only the matters exclusively within the Court's jurisdiction according to s 167(4) of the 1996 Constitution were 'political',[42] and even then not in any partisan-political sense but in the sense that they required the Court to review a class of cases that implicated the need for comity between the three branches of government at the highest level.[43] Other issues, falling within

---

[42] See *President of the Republic of South Africa and Others* v. *South African Rugby Football Union and Others* 1999 (4) SA 147 (CC), 1999 (7) BCLR 725 (CC) paras 72–3 (describing the issues covered in this subsection as 'crucial political areas' in which the Court's decision 'would inevitably have important political consequences'. Section 167(4) covers a range of issues, including disputes between organs of state about their respective 'powers and functions', abstract review of bills, the constitutionality of constitutional amendments and provincial constitutions, and allegations that the President has failed to fulfil his or her constitutional obligations.

[43] *President of the Republic of South Africa and Others* v. *South African Rugby Football Union and Others* 1999 (2) SA 14 (CC), 1999 (2) BCLR 175 (CC) para 29. The *SARFU* decisions may be distinguished in this way from the stricter approach to the law/politics distinction taken in *United Democratic Movement* v. *President of the Republic of South Africa and Others (African Christian Democratic Party and Others Intervening; Institute for Democracy in South Africa and Another as Amici Curiae) (No 1)* 2003 (1) SA 488 (CC), 2002 (11) BCLR 1179 (CC) ('*United Democratic Movement*'), which, as we saw in

the Court's concurrent jurisdiction, were susceptible to ordinary legal decision-making methods, as evidenced by non-specialist courts' ability to resolve them. But the Court – for reasons related to its efforts to ensure the ANC's continued support for the constitutional project – needed to retain ultimate control over these cases. Its strict approach to direct access was therefore supplemented by an expansive approach to the definition of 'constitutional matter' that enabled it to take more or less any case on appeal that it deemed was in the interests of justice for it to decide.[44]

One final respect in which the Court's approach to questions of access and jurisdiction may be seen to have supported its overall strategy has to do with the way the Court's relatively light case load allowed it to concentrate on the careful wording of its decisions. A strategy that was primarily focused, not on popular acceptance of the Court's role, but on the political branches' continued support for the constitutional project, required the Court to invest a considerable amount of time and energy into crafting its decisions for maximum justificatory effect. The remaining section of this chapter is devoted to this issue.

10.3 Purely rhetorical strategies

On a purely rhetorical level, two broad themes may be detected in the Chaskalson Court's case law: the first concerns the posture the Court adopted in relation to the law/politics distinction; the second, the Court's use of diplomatic language to manage its relationship with the ANC.

Chapters 1 and 5 of this study have already touched on the possible significance of the first issue. It was argued there that the liberal-legalist ideal of adjudication according to law favours maintenance of a strict conception of the law/politics distinction and that the judges of the Chaskalson Court, given their backgrounds as human rights lawyers under apartheid, were predisposed to this way of presenting their decisions. For reasons both of sincere commitment and strategic advantage, the judges would have seen maintenance of the public's faith in the ideal of adjudication according to law as an essential component of their work.

Chapter 9, also concerned an issue within the Court's exclusive jurisdiction (constitutionality of constitutional amendments).

[44] On the Court's interpretation of the 'interests of justice' criterion see Currie and de Waal, *The Bill of Rights Handbook* 126–8; Kate Hofmeyer, 'Rules and Procedure in Constitutional Matters' in Woolman et al. (eds.), *Constitutional Law of South Africa* ch 5, 21–9.

While Karl Klare's lament that the Court should have been more open about the political nature of its function has a certain appeal, this kind of judicial-veil lifting was never really on the cards.[45] Given the political context described in Chapter 4, it was important for the Court to focus its energies on building the public's confidence in the political neutrality of South Africa's new liberal-democratic institutions.

This sense of the constraints impacting on the Court squares with Nonet and Selznick's analysis of the movement of political systems towards 'responsive law'.[46] While setting out a normative conception of the judicial function not dissimilar to Klare's, these authors warn against the danger – the impossibility even – of a court's driving the kind of change they describe before public confidence in the neutrality of liberal-democratic institutions has been properly consolidated. If Chapter 4 established anything, it established that the risk of regression back towards 'repressive' law to which Nonet and Selznick refer was real for most of Chaskalson's tenure as Chief Justice, and certainly in the period after the Court had fulfilled its certification function.

We need not rehearse now all of the instances in which the Court invoked a strict conception of the law/politics distinction. It is enough simply to recall the Court's dismissal of the relevance of public opinion in *S v. Makwanyane*,[47] its overstated invocation of the limits of its institutional role in *Grootboom*,[48] and its admonition in *United Democratic Movement* of those who had dared to suggest that its decision would be influenced by anything other than its sincere desire to give effect to the Constitution.[49] In these decisions and others, the Court maintained a consistent rhetorical stance that a clear line between law and politics could be drawn and that it was intent on drawing it. At times, this posture collapsed back into formalism, but for the most part the Court attempted to distinguish law from politics while at the same time responding to the need to engage in substantive reasoning. It did this, the case discussions revealed, mostly not by elaborate political

---

[45] Klare, 'Legal Culture and Transformative Constitutionalism'.

[46] Nonet and Selznick, *Toward Responsive Law* (first published in 1978).

[47] 1995 (3) SA 391 (CC), 1995 (6) BCLR 665 (CC).

[48] *Government of the Republic of South Africa and Others v. Grootboom and Others* 2001 (1) SA 46 (CC), 2000 (11) BCLR 1169 (CC).

[49] *United Democratic Movement v. President of the Republic of South Africa and Others (African Christian Democratic Party and Others Intervening; Institute for Democracy in South Africa and Another as Amici Curiae) (No 1)* 2003 (1) SA 495 (CC), 2002 (11) BCLR 1213 (CC).

theorising,[50] but by giving expression to the moral sensibility of the Constitution, and on occasion by appealing to the harmonising spirit of *ubuntu*.

The second rhetorical theme concerns the tone of the language in which the Court's decisions were couched. In keeping with its overall strategy, the Court was careful to package its decisions in respectful language that assumed the political branches' ongoing commitment to the constitutional project. At times, and perhaps for some of the judges more than others, this rhetorical style was entirely natural. For a judge like Albie Sachs, who had been so immersed in the development of the ANC's human rights tradition, interpreting the post-apartheid Constitutions must have seemed like the continuation of his life's work, and any suggestion that the ANC was less than fully committed to the Constitutions' moral values would have been hard to take seriously. The ANC, after all, was the driving force behind the constitutional project. Why should it not be addressed in a style that acknowledged its intellectual contribution to the document the Court was enforcing? For others, like Arthur Chaskalson, diplomacy was part of the lawyer's craft. If apartheid-era judges could be persuaded by skilled advocacy to see the injustice of that system, then the same rhetorical skills could be deployed to convince the ANC of the wisdom of the Court's doctrinal choices.

Here, for example, is the opening paragraph of the decision in *Treatment Action Campaign*:

> The HIV/AIDS pandemic in South Africa has been described as 'an incomprehensible calamity' and 'the most important challenge facing South Africa since the birth of our new democracy' and Government's fight against 'this scourge' as 'a top priority'. It 'has claimed millions of lives, inflicting pain and grief, causing fear and uncertainty, and threatening the economy'. These are not the words of alarmists but are taken from a Department of Health publication in 2000 and a ministerial foreword to an earlier publication.[51]

As legal doctrine, this passage is entirely redundant: nothing in this opening paragraph is essential to justifying the decision handed down. As legal rhetoric, however, the passage is masterful, and entirely necessary to the Court's assertion (and protection) of its institutional role. The

---

[50] This study departs, therefore, from the analysis of the Court's case law offered in David Robertson, *The Judge as Political Theorist: Contemporary Constitutional Review* (Princeton University Press, 2010) 226–80.

[51] *Treatment Action Campaign* para 1 (footnotes omitted).

punch-line – the revelation that the quoted words are in fact taken from official Government documents – is cleverly withheld until the last sentence, maximising its effect and setting up at a rhetorical level the doctrinal argument that follows, viz. that where Government has already committed itself to providing a certain type of medical treatment to a section of the population, it is unreasonable to deny other similarly situated sections the same treatment. 'These are your own words, this is your own policy', the opening paragraph intones, 'how can there be any objection to our helping you to implement it properly?' Lest there be any doubt about the effect of these remarks, the fourth paragraph continues the rhetorical assault, calling the Government's MTCT programme 'part of a *formidable* array of responses to the pandemic'.[52] None of this is high-flown political theory. All of it is rhetorical craftsmanship – the careful packaging of a decision so as to make it more palatable to those who must obey it.

In the same decision, as we saw earlier in this chapter,[53] the Court considered the respective merits of a mandatory versus a supervisory order. Remarking that the latter form of remedy might be 'necessary' in some cases to 'secure compliance' with its order, the Court (writing collectively for maximum effect) opted for the less intrusive remedy. 'The government has always respected and executed orders of this Court', the judges noted. 'There is no reason to believe that it will not do so in the present case.'[54] Given the political backdrop to the case, which included a televised statement by the Minister of the Health that the Government would refuse to obey the Court's order if it upheld the High Court's decision, this part of the judgment tests our credulity. Its rhetorical effect, however, was once again masterful. By so openly placing its trust in the executive branch, the Court upped the moral ante, and thereby improved the chances of its decision being enforced.

---

[52] Ibid para 4 (emphasis added).   [53] See Section 10.1.
[54] *Treatment Action Campaign* para 129.

~

Conclusion

Any power a constitutional court has to influence democratic politics depends on its claim to being, if not above politics, then at least a political actor of a particular type: one whose institutional role is limited to holding other political actors to the terms of the Constitution. The plausibility of any such claim is in turn dependent on the court's conformance to societal understandings of the methods judges may legitimately use to determine constitutional meaning, alternatively, its capacity to transform these understandings in the course of performing its institutional function. Law in this sense both constitutes and constrains judicial power: whatever lies within the realm of the legal is the court's legitimate business, and whatever lies without, the forbidden zone of politics. But the boundary between the two is fluid and contested, and there is considerable scope for a court to reposition it in its favour – in the direction, that is, of an understanding that better suits the sustained assertion of its institutional role.

The Chaskalson Court's achievement, this study has argued, is attributable to the judges' understanding of this politico-legal dynamic. While the Court's decision-making record may be criticised for maintaining an overly strict, and at times strained, conception of the law/politics distinction, the judges' commitment to the liberal-legalist ideal underlying this conception was sincere and genuine. As human rights lawyers under apartheid, they had witnessed firsthand the capacity of law to restrain the abuse of political power. Their reading of the post-apartheid Constitutions as being dedicated to this same goal was defensible on historical and textual grounds. Although an alternative reading of these documents – especially the 1996 Constitution – as requiring the Court to demystify the law/politics distinction, and openly declare the political nature of its function, was not implausible as a textual matter, the political context in which the Court found itself militated against this kind of judicial candour. In 1995, when the Court began its work, South Africa's new constitutional institutions were fragile, and the Court was consequently required to do all it could to maintain the public's faith in the objectivity of its decision-making practices. Confronted by the danger of the Court's being seen to be, on the one hand, an extension of the ANC's political power and, on the other, an institution for the protection of minority-group privilege, the judges wisely chose to present their decisions as legally compelled.

In addition to this rhetorical stance, the judges made one other foundational choice that drove much of the Court's decision-making record: that the key to the Court's institutional independence lay in harnessing and retaining the ANC's commitment to the constitutional project. At the time the judges made this choice, it was entirely sensible. The ANC was the central player in South Africa's liberation struggle and its inclusive, non-racist ideology provided the best hope of unifying that country's population. Before its banning in 1961, and thereafter in exile, the ANC had developed a hybrid human rights tradition that was both sophisticated in its harmonisation of the two main currents in international human rights law and authentically South African. Despite their origins in the political agreement struck with the outgoing National Party Government, the post-apartheid Constitutions were strongly influenced by this tradition. The Court was therefore able to depict its institutional role as being tantamount to holding the ANC to its own long-standing commitments. Add to this the ANC's overwhelming electoral dominance, the fact that it was likely to be in office for some time, and the fact that the judges' successors were almost certain to be appointed through a selection process controlled by the ANC, and the wisdom of the Court's overarching strategy is abundantly clear.

There was always a risk associated with this strategy, however. Precisely because the ANC was a 'broad church' that brought together diverse interest groups, the party threatened after 1994 to prevent the emergence of the pluralist democracy on which the long-term health of the constitutional project depended. While the Court was initially able to turn this situation to its advantage, and exploit the ANC's self-interested commitment to judicial review, the political foundations for this strategy began to crumble as the ANC descended into internecine fighting. This development would not have mattered so much had the ANC indeed splintered into its constituent parts, for then the ordinary precondition for independent judicial review would have been satisfied. Instead, however, the ANC remained formally united, at least as a force in electoral politics. Not just that, but the wisdom of the constitutional settlement became one of the main points of contestation within the party, with factions on both the left and the right inclined to attribute South Africa's developmental shortcomings to the constraints imposed by the 1996 Constitution.

The full effects of the ANC's slide into factionalism only became apparent towards the end of Chaskalson's term as Chief Justice. Still, it is arguable that the judges ought to have foreseen the risk associated with their reliance on the ANC, and taken steps to mitigate it. A shift to a more populist strategy, on the model of the Indian Supreme Court, would have been too radical a change in direction, but the Court was presented with several less drastic opportunities to adjust its chosen path. One of these opportunities, at least, was taken. In *Treatment Action Campaign*,[1] the Court demonstrated its capacity to adapt to the changing political context by acting as a forum for the resolution of the ANC's internal policy battles. In two other cases, however, *United Democratic Movement*[2] and *New National Party*,[3] the Court failed to develop doctrines that might have contributed to opening up South Africa's dominant-party democracy. To this extent, the Chaskalson Court may be said to have contributed to some of the difficulties facing the current Court, which (as argued below) is operating in a much tougher political environment – one that is still dominated by the ANC, but where the faction now influential within the party is less committed to the value of judicial independence.

The Chaskalson Court should not, however, be too strongly criticised in this respect. The 1996 Constitution assumed the existence of a well-functioning multi-party democracy; the construction of more politically realist doctrines therefore ran against the grain of the constitutional text. Given the fragility of its institutional situation, the Court's reluctance actively to go in search of these doctrines is understandable. It is doubtful in any event whether such doctrines would have been able to counteract the powerful political forces operating in South Africa between 1995 and 2005. The ANC's electoral dominance was the product of its (not under-served) reputation as South Africa's liberator, and the Court was not in

---

[1] *Minister of Health and Others* v. *Treatment Action Campaign and Others (No 2)* 2002 (5) SA 721 (CC), 2002 (10) BCLR 1075 (CC).

[2] *United Democratic Movement* v. *President of the Republic of South Africa and Others (African Christian Democratic Party and Others Intervening; Institute for Democracy and Another as* Amici Curiae*) (No 1)* 2003 (1) SA 488 (CC), 2002 (11) BCLR 1179 (CC).

[3] *New National Party of South Africa* v. *Government of the Republic of South Africa and Others* 1999 (3) SA 191 (CC), 1999 (5) BCLR 489 (CC).

control of the electorate's assessment of the benefits of repeatedly returning the ANC to office.

What the Court *was* able to control was its doctrinal choices in cases where the ANC's electoral dominance was not itself the issue. As to that, this study has argued that the Court's overarching strategy manifested itself in several different ways. In cases involving questions of positive morality, the Court enforced the Constitution as the embodiment of South Africans' highest moral aspirations. Here, the ANC's dominance insulated the Court from the ordinary political repercussions of its lack of public support. In social rights cases, the Court's managerialist strategy was most clearly on display, with the Court choosing a context-sensitive review standard that allowed it to adjust its enforcement of the Constitution to the micro-politics of each case. In property rights cases, too, the Court's approach was highly context-sensitive, striking a balance between competing interests in the spirit of the ANC's hybrid human rights tradition.

Was the Court's preparedness in this way to shape its doctrines to suit its overarching strategy reconcilable with its duty to do justice according to law? On a strict reading of that duty, a court must attempt to do no more than apply the law to the case at hand. Institutional considerations are relevant only to the extent that they form part of the Court's principled separation of powers doctrine. When that aspect of the Court's record was examined, however, it too was shown to have been influenced by extra-legal concerns for the Court's institutional independence. Indeed, more than this, the Court's ability to switch between two understandings of its legitimate role in enforcing the Constitution was a crucial part of its overarching strategy. To this extent, the Court does appear to have traded off its duty to do justice according to law against the need to manage the impact of its decisions on its institutional independence.

That the Court was driven to this sort of compromise was a function of the legal and political context in which it found itself. According to the two-dimensional matrix developed in Chapter 2, a constitutional court's capacity to negotiate the law/politics tension will be determined by its proximity to one of four ideal types. Chapters 4 and 5 set out the case for locating the Chaskalson Court for the majority of its institutional life in the top right-hand sector of the matrix, where it was strongly constrained by both law and politics. Constitutional judges in this situation face perhaps the most challenging task of all. Lacking the freedom to decide cases exclusively according to law, and denied also the opportunity to indulge their private political ideologies or engage in purely political strategies, they must continually strive to strike an institutionally optimal balance between the legal and political constraints impacting on them.

The key to understanding the Court's achievement lies in the adjudicative strategies it deployed to this end. But what exactly was that achievement? As noted in Chapter 1, the Court never built the kind of public support that is ordinarily taken to be the mark of a successful constitutional court. The required political culture of respect for judicial independence was also still very much under construction by the time Justice Chaskalson left office. In this sense, the Court could not be said to have achieved the degree of institutional independence characteristic of a court in a mature constitutional democracy. Nevertheless, the Court was very successful in another sense – in negotiating the law/politics tension to avoid political attack while performing its constitutionally mandated function. As we have seen, despite the deteriorating political environment for judicial review, the Court continued to be a very effective veto player in South African politics. It was also largely successful in managing South African legal-professional culture's transition to the Bill of Rights era. While its failure to construct a comprehensive political theory of the post-apartheid Constitutions was disappointing to some, it developed an authentically South African style of moral reasoning that was arguably more appropriate.

Despite this achievement, the changes to the external political environment that were apparent at the time of Justice Chaskalson's retirement continue to threaten the Court. Indeed, if anything, the current Court faces even more formidable challenges. The political battle between Thabo Mbeki and Jacob Zuma for the leadership of the ANC has left a divided party with no clear vision for South Africa's future. The Mbeki faction's attempt to build an alternative political party based on the principles of the Freedom Charter has for all intents and purposes failed, taking many talented members of the bureaucracy with it.[4] If South Africa is pursuing a particular economic development strategy, it is one that is hard to discern from among the morass of conflicting policy statements and failed state institutions.[5] So-called Black Economic Empowerment wealth transfers aimed at deracialising the economy have run their course, with little wealth left to spread around. Unsurprisingly,

---

[4] See Klug, *The Constitution of South Africa* 159 (reflecting on the poor showing of the Congress of the People in the 2009 general election).

[5] Johnson's somewhat tendentiously written study, *South Africa's Brave New World*, is nevertheless the best available single treatment of this issue.

poor South Africans have lost patience with the pace of change, and the time for gradualist, rule-of-law-respecting social reform is running out.[6]

What can the current judges do about this situation? Is a wholesale conversion to a more populist strategy, one focused on building the Constitutional Court's institutional legitimacy, now both desirable and possible? Something like this change is required. For as long as the ANC was a strong and united political force, the Court's managerialist strategy made sense. But this condition no longer holds. The Court cannot, as it did before, rely on the ANC to shelter it from the ordinary political effects of its lack of public support. With the nation's continued commitment to the terms of the constitutional settlement now one of the main issues of contention in the party, the Court needs to build its own mass-based constituency.

Fortunately for the Court, the prospects for pursuing this sort of strategy have improved. As much as the ANC's descent into factionalism threatens the Court, it also provides an opportunity for the Court to clearly distinguish itself from the governing party. In 1995, when the Court began its work, the ANC had been voted into office on a tidal wave of emotion and optimistic faith in its capacity to reconstruct the country. While the post-apartheid Constitutions set the moral parameters and goals for this process of reconstruction, they left considerable space for the political branches to fill in the gaps – to make the purely political choices about how best to deliver on the Constitutions' aspirational promises. In this setting, it made sense for the Court to defer to the ANC's primary policy-setting role, even to the point, as demonstrated in its social rights jurisprudence, of downplaying its own legitimate role in constitutional standard-setting. But this approach has outlived its usefulness. The ANC, while still politically dominant, is no longer unambiguously committed to the value of liberal constitutionalism.[7] Its moral

---

[6] This issue is well documented in Fiona Forde, *An Inconvenient Youth: Julius Malema and the 'New' ANC* (Johannesburg: Picador Africa, 2011) (describing the growing influence of the poor and marginalised within the ANC).

[7] On 23 November 2011, the South African Cabinet released a statement announcing a planned assessment of the impact of the decisions of the Constitutional Court on social transformation. The statement was seen by many as the first step in a plan to rein in the Court, either by formally reducing its powers or by intimidating the judges into showing greater deference to the political branches. On 28 February 2012, the Minister of Justice and Constitutional Development, Jeff Radebe, released a Discussion Document on the 'Transformation of the Judicial System and the Role of the Judiciary in the Developmental South African State' (accessible at www.justice.gov.za). The Discussion Document, despite several reassuring statements about the ANC's continued commitment to liberal

stature is at the same time much diminished by proven allegations of widespread corruption and maladministration. Most important of all, the ANC has failed to devise policies that show any realistic promise of lifting the majority of South Africans out of poverty. For all the risks that these developments pose to the constitutional project, they also provide a clear opportunity for the Court to reduce its reliance on the ANC and build its own political support base among South Africa's poor and marginalised – precisely the group that the 1996 Constitution in any case holds up for prioritised attention.

Such a change in strategy would require adjustment to many of the Court's established doctrines. The Court's strict approach to applications for direct access, for example, would need to be relaxed to allow poor litigants to bypass expensive lower-court litigation processes. In making these adjustments, the Court would risk charges of inconsistency. But there are reasons to think that the Court could manage the changes required by exploiting the flexibility already built into some of its most important doctrines. The most obvious case in point is its reasonableness review standard for violation of social rights, which, as we have seen, is amenable to application in this way. The Court's approach to social rights would in any case logically be at the centre of any attempt to expand its public support. If the 1996 Constitution could be interpreted, as it was always intended to be interpreted, as conclusively on the side of the poor, the Court would be well on its way to insulating itself against the effects of the ANC's loss of direction.

By way of example, the rest of this Conclusion explores this question, i.e. how might the Court adapt its existing strategy in relation to social rights to safeguard its institutional independence while continuing to give effect to the 1996 Constitution? It will be helpful to start by revisiting the road not travelled by the Court in *Grootboom*[8]– to see whether there is anything in the approach the Court there rejected that could prove useful to it now. To do this is not to contradict the favourable view taken in Chapter 7 of the Court's chosen strategy. Nor is it to suggest that the Court can somehow reverse itself back up the jurisprudential track to the

---

constitutionalism, failed to clarify the purposes of the proposed assessment, and uncertainty consequently remains over exactly what the government's intentions are. In public discourse, there has been much talk of a 'second transition' in which the yoke of the 1996 Constitution will be thrown off and Parliament restored to a position of unqualified supremacy.

[8] *Government of the Republic of South Africa and Others* v. *Grootboom and Others* 2001 (1) SA 46 (CC), 2000 (11) BCLR 1169 (CC).

crossroads it confronted in *Grootboom*, to take that decision again, only this time with the benefit of hindsight. It is simply to ask whether elements of the approach rejected in *Grootboom* may be recovered or re-tooled in an effort to adapt the reasonableness review approach to the challenges now facing the Court.

The distinct advantage that the minimum core approach all along had, and still has, over the reasonableness review approach is that it takes social rights seriously, treating them, not as 'weak' rights,[9] for whose presence in the Constitution the Court needs to apologise (as though the Constitutional Assembly made some kind of mistake), but as 'strong' rights that were included in the Constitution to complement and counterbalance civil and political rights in a way that is amenable to convincing moral justification.[10] To this may be added the considerable textual and constitutional-historical support for the minimum core approach. The 1996 Constitution, as we have seen, makes no distinction between first and second-generation rights: it does not relegate social rights to a separate chapter on directive principles of state policy, or treat the two sets of rights any differently in the way the Bill of Rights is laid out. To be sure, the realisation of social rights is said to be subject to progressive realisation within the state's available resources. But then that is true as a practical matter of all rights. In any case, the inclusion of these qualifications need not be taken as licence to deprive social rights of all content.

When these textual considerations are combined with the historical reasons behind the inclusion of social rights in the 1996 Constitution, the conclusion is inescapable that the minimum core approach, though not legally compelled, would have been at least legally defensible. The minimum core approach was also not entirely without strategic merit. As noted in the earlier discussion,[11] when the Court began its work, one possible option open to it was to enforce social rights immediately and strongly in the hope that this would win it the support of the ANC's urban-poor and rural-landless constituency. In addition to building a popular support base, such a strategy would have aligned the Court with the ANC's deepest political traditions, dating back to the Freedom Charter and before. In this way, the

---

[9]   This terminology was coined by Tushnet, *Weak Courts, Strong Rights*. For Tushnet, *Grootboom* was an example of a weak social right, and *Treatment Action Campaign* a strong one (242–7). The classification of a right according to the weak/strong binary, in other words, depends on the way the Court enforces it, rather than on any inherent quality of the right. As the terms are used here, it is the inherent quality of the right that counts.

[10]   See particularly the first two chapters of Bilchitz, *Poverty and Fundamental Rights*.

[11]   See Section 7.1.

Court would have been able to position itself as the voice of the ANC's social rights conscience, holding the Constitution up to the party as a mirror of its most enduring commitments.

The political environment for a change to something like the minimum core approach is now propitious. The ANC's loss of political direction and descent into factionalism not only requires the Court to fill the policy gap, but has also created the political space for it to do so. The inherent flexibility of the reasonableness review approach means that the Court should be able to effect this required change in strategy without conclusively rejecting its existing doctrines. What is required is rather an adjustment that exploits the reasonableness review approach's latent capacity to set clear guidelines for social and economic policy. If the reasonableness review approach was in its origins an approach that tried to enlist the political branches as partners in the realisation of social rights, the Court now needs to focus on spelling out the constitutional basis for this partnership. It needs to be more specific, in other words, about the content of social rights and more forthright about the Court's legitimate role in setting standards for legislative and executive conduct.

The social rights cases decided since Justice Chaskalson's departure from office indicate that the judges are aware that a change in direction is required, but that they have yet to adapt the reasonableness review approach to the new political environment. In *Olivia Road*,[12] for example, the Court was confronted with a determined and calculated scheme on the part of the City of Johannesburg to bypass legislation aimed at protecting slum dwellers against arbitrary eviction. Instead of unequivocally condemning the City's scheme, and setting standards for the proper treatment of the constitutional claimants, the Court developed a dictum in *Grootboom* to impose on the state a duty of 'meaningful engagement' in these circumstances.[13] The emptiness of this duty was later illustrated by another case, *Joe Slovo*,[14] in which the Court ordered the relocation of a large and relatively well-settled community of people,

---

[12] *Occupiers of 51 Olivia Road, Berea Township, and 197 Main Street, Johannesburg v. City of Johannesburg and Others* 2008 (3) SA 208 (CC); 2008 (5) BCLR 475 (CC).

[13] Ibid paras 15–17 (referring to *Grootboom* paras 84 and 87). In terms of this duty, government agencies are required, when seeking to evict unlawful occupiers from state-owned land, to consult the occupiers about such issues as the availability of alternative accommodation and the impact of the eviction on their livelihoods.

[14] *Residents of Joe Slovo Community, Western Cape v. Thubelisha Homes and Others (Centre on Housing Rights and Evictions and Another,* Amici Curiae) 2010 (3) SA 454 (CC); 2009 (9) BCLR 847 (CC).

notwithstanding evidence of 'broken promises' made to them by the government agency in question.[15]

In two other cases decided in 2009, the Court overturned a Supreme Court of Appeal decision specifying the minimum amount of free water to which poor urban residents are constitutionally entitled,[16] and then struck down a provision of a provincial slum clearance statute on the ground that it was not capable of being reasonably interpreted in accordance with the Constitution and national legislation.[17] The former case, *Mazibuko*, has been criticised as illustrating the inherent conservatism of the Court's approach.[18] This assessment is too sweeping. The decision illustrates rather the limits of the reasonableness review approach in a context of widespread governmental inefficiency. Where that is the case, a relatively more sophisticated agency can effectively head off a constitutional challenge by continually adjusting its policy to defuse the claim. While this means that social rights may still be used to drive beneficial changes to policy, the Court's role is reduced to that of ad hoc arbiter of reasonableness. The problem with this, in turn, is that every instance of governmental inefficiency needs to be separately litigated – something that is beyond the capacity of both the Court and the public interest litigation sector in South Africa.

To overcome this problem, the Court needs to adapt the reasonableness review approach to allow it to play a role in constitutional

---

[15] The community had initially agreed to the relocation on the basis of an offer that they would be entitled to access affordable rental housing on the redeveloped land. Opposition to the relocation started when the rental housing turned out to be more expensive. The Court's relocation order to land 15km distant included an order for transport to the residents' places of employment and an undertaking that 70 per cent of the units in the new housing development would be set aside for members of the community. The community's preference was nevertheless for a so-called 'in situ' upgrade (i.e. redevelopment without relocation). In a sequel to the case, the Constitutional Court discharged its order because of the government's persistent inability to comply with the conditions precedent to the relocation (*Residents of Joe Slovo Community, Western Cape* v. *Thubelisha Homes and Others (Centre on Housing Rights and Evictions and Another*, Amici Curiae) 2011 (7) BCLR 723 (CC)). It now seems as though the site will after all be subject to in situ upgrading.

[16] *Mazibuko and Others* v. *City of Johannesburg and Others (Centre on Human Rights and Eviction as* Amicus Curiae*)* 2010 (4) SA 1 (CC), 2010 (3) BCLR 239 (CC).

[17] *Abahlali Basemjondolo Movement SA and Another* v. *Premier of the Province of KwaZulu-Natal and Others* 2010 (2) BCLR 99 (CC).

[18] Jackie Dugard, 'Can Human Rights Trump the Commercialization of Water in South Africa? Soweto's Legal Fight for an Equitable Water Policy' (2010) 42 *Review of Radical Political Economics* 175.

standard-setting. As Bilchitz has pointed out,[19] such a role is defensible on separation of powers grounds. Indeed, a review standard according to which the Court spells out the substantive grounds on which it is prepared to overturn governmental policy is more readily justifiable than one in which its power to strike down social welfare programmes is contingent on ad hoc assessments of reasonableness. By clarifying the standards set by social rights, the Court will be able to draw out the 1996 Constitution's implications for concrete policy debates.

Much of the groundwork for reconceptualising the reasonableness review approach in this way has already been laid by South African legal academics.[20] What this study adds to this literature is an argument about the institutional feasibility of the changes required. In response to Sandra Liebenberg's call for the Constitutional Court to play a more active role in developing the normative content of social rights, for example, Bob Hepple expressed scepticism about:

> whether the judiciary, particularly a Constitutional Court which no longer has among its members those who were involved in drafting the Bill of Rights, will be willing to take on this enhanced role or to place greater burdens on the state. Judicial deference to the legislature and the separation of law and politics are deeply embedded in South Africa. There are also reasons that lie at the heart of using law as an instrument for social change. These have to do both with the complexity and multidimensional nature of social disadvantage, and with the inability of law as one social system to penetrate other self-regulating systems. A system of 'responsive' or 'reflexive' enforced self-regulation, backed by the ultimate sanction of judicial enforcement, may in the long run be more effective than direct judicial enforcement.[21]

While sharing the politico-realist premise on which this criticism is founded, this study has attempted to show that constitutional courts possess more than the 'passive virtues' that Alexander Bickel made famous.[22] The political contexts in which constitutional courts operate impose significant constraints on their ability to decide cases according to law. But they also provide opportunities for a constitutional court that is

---

[19] Bilchitz, *Poverty and Fundamental Rights*.

[20] In addition to Bilchitz, *Poverty and Fundamental Rights*, see McLean, *Constitutional Deference* and Sandra Liebenberg, *Socio-Economic Rights: Adjudication under a Transformative Constitution* (Cape Town: Juta, 2010).

[21] Bob Hepple, 'Book Review of Sandra Liebenberg, *Socio-Economic Rights: Adjudication under a Transformative Constitution*' (2011) 70 *Cambridge Law Journal* 669, 671.

[22] Alexander M. Bickel, *The Least Dangerous Branch*.

sensitive to its environment to enhance law's power to influence politics. This was the lesson that liberal judges and human rights lawyers learned under apartheid. It was also the insight on which the Chaskalson Court's largely successful attempt to devise an institutionally sustainable role for itself was based. What is required now is for the current judges to apply this lesson to the changed political circumstances in which the Court finds itself.

In these changed circumstances, this conclusion has argued, discretion may not be the better part of valour. While a more deferential approach was appropriate to the first decade of democracy, when the ANC was more strongly committed to the constitutional project, it is not suited to a situation in which the ANC continues to dominate the popular vote while failing to deliver on its election promises. In this situation, judicial deference simply threatens to confirm the charge that the Court is on the side of those who would use law to resist meaningful social transformation. While the Court cannot drive the required changes itself, it can help to dispel the myth that liberal constitutionalism is necessarily the enemy of politically driven social change. To do that, the Court will need to take some risks: it will need to intrude even further into politics than it has to date, trusting that the public will accept the required expansion of law's domain. Importantly, the redefinition of the boundary between law and politics in this way would not necessarily entail the contraction of democratic politics. As this study has been at pains to point out, law and politics are not locked in a zero-sum game competing for a finite quantity of social and economic power. On the liberal-legalist conception at least, law can be both the moral conscience and the instrument of democratic politics.

BIBLIOGRAPHY

Abel, Richard L., *Politics by Other Means: Law in the Struggle against Apartheid 1980–1994* (New York, NY: Routledge, 1995)

Adam, Heribert, 'Corporatism as Minority Veto under ANC Hegemony in South Africa' in Hermann Giliomee and Charles Simkins (eds.), *The Awkward Embrace: One-Party Domination and Democracy* (Cape Town: Tafelberg, 1999) 261

Adam, Heribert, Frederik van Zyl Slabbert and Kogila Moodley, *Comrades in Business: Post-Liberation Politics in South Africa* (Cape Town: Tafelberg, 1998)

African National Congress, 'Constitutional Guidelines for a Democratic South Africa, 1988' (1989) 21 *Columbia Human Rights Law Review* 235

African National Congress, 'Draft Bill of Rights' (1991) 7 *South African Journal on Human Rights* 110

African National Congress, *The Reconstruction and Development Programme: A Policy Framework* (Johannesburg: Umanyano Publications, 1994)

Albertyn, Cathi, 'Judicial Independence and the Constitution Fourteenth Amendment Bill' (2006) 22 *South African Journal on Human Rights* 126

Albertyn, Cathi and Beth Goldblatt, 'Facing the Challenge of Transformation: Difficulties in the Development of an Indigenous Jurisprudence of Equality' (1998) 14 *South African Journal on Human Rights* 248

Alexander, Larry, 'Waluchow's Living Tree Constitutionalism' (2010) 29 *Law and Philosophy* 93

Alexy, Robert, *A Theory of Constitutional Rights*, trans. Julian Rivers (Oxford University Press, 2002)

Altbeker, Anthony, *A Country at War with Itself: South Africa's Crisis of Crime* (Johannesburg: Jonathan Ball, 2007)

Altman, Andrew, 'Legal Realism, Critical Legal Studies, and Dworkin' (1986) 15 *Philosophy & Public Affairs* 205

Andrews, Penelope and Stephen Ellmann (eds.), *The Post-Apartheid Constitutions: Perspectives on South Africa's Basic Law* (Johannesburg: Witwatersrand University Press, 2001)

Asmal, Kader and Adrian Hadland, *with Moira Levy, Politics in My Blood: A Memoir* (Johannesburg: Jacana, 2011)

Asmal, Kader with David, Chidester and Cassius Lubisi (eds.), *Legacy of Freedom: The ANC's Human Rights Tradition* (Johannesburg: Jonathan Ball, 2005)

Atiyah, P. S. and R. S. Summers, *Form and Substance in Anglo-American Law: A Comparative Study of Legal Reasoning, Legal Theory, and Legal Institutions* (Oxford: Clarendon Press, 1987)

Bailey, Michael A. and Forrest Maltzman, *The Constrained Court: Law, Politics, and the Decisions Justices Make* (Princeton University Press, 2011)

Barak, Aharon, *Proportionality: Constitutional Rights and Their Limitations*, trans. Doron Kalir (Cambridge University Press, 2012)

Bates, Robert H., Rui J. P. de Figueiredo, Jr and Barry Weingast, 'The Politics of Interpretation: Rationality, Culture and Transition' (1998) 26 *Politics & Society* 603

Baum, Lawrence, *The Puzzle of Judicial Behavior* (Ann Arbor, MI: University of Michigan Press, 1997)

Beatty, David M., *Talking Heads and the Supremes: The Canadian Production of Constitutional Law* (Toronto: Carswell, 1990)

Bhagwati, P. N., 'Judicial Activism and Public Interest Litigation' (1985) 23 *Columbia Journal of Transnational Law* 561

Bickel, Alexander M., *The Least Dangerous Branch: The Supreme Court at the Bar of Politics* 2nd edn (New Haven, CT: Yale University Press, 1986)

Bilchitz, David, *Poverty and Fundamental Rights: The Justification and Enforcement of Socio-Economic Rights* (Oxford University Press, 2007)

Bilchitz, David and Melanie Judge 'For Whom Does the Bell Toll? The Challenges and Possibilities of the Civil Union Act for Family Law in South Africa' (2007) 23 *South African Journal on Human Rights* 466

Bishop, Michael, 'Remedies' in Stu Woolman, Theunis Roux and Michael Bishop (eds.), *Constitutional Law of South Africa* 2nd edn (Cape Town: Juta, 2006) ch 9

Black, Jr, Charles L., *The People and the Court: Judicial Review in a Democracy* (New York, NY: Macmillan, 1960)

Blackshield, Tony and George Williams, *Australian Constitutional Law & Theory: Commentary and Materials* 5th edn (Sydney: Federation Press, 2010)

Bond, Patrick, *Elite Transition: From Apartheid to Neo-Liberalism in South Africa* (London: Pluto, 2000)

Brand, Danie, 'The Proceduralisation of South African Socio-economic Rights Jurisprudence, or "What are Socio-economic Rights For?"' in Henk Botha, André van der Walt and Johan van der Walt (eds.), *Rights and Democracy in a Transformative Constitution* (Stellenbosch University Press, 2003) 33

Brenner, Saul and Harold J. Spaeth, 'Issue Specialization in Majority Opinion Assignment on the Burger Court' (1986) 39 *The Western Political Quarterly* 520

Broun, Kenneth S., *Black Lawyers, White Courts: The Soul of South African Law* (Athens, OH: Ohio University Press, 2000)

Budlender, Steven, 'National Legislative Authority' in Stu Woolman, Theunis Roux and Michael Bishop (eds.), *Constitutional Law of South Africa* 2nd edn (Cape Town Juta, 2002)

Butler, Anthony, *Cyril Ramaphosa* (Johannesburg: Jacana, 2007)

Casillas, Christopher J., Peter K. Enns and Patrick C. Wohlfarth, 'How Public Opinion Constrains the U.S. Supreme Court' (2010) 54 *American Journal of Political Science* 1

Caldeira, Gregory A. and James L. Gibson, 'The Etiology of Public Support for the Supreme Court' (1992) 36 *American Journal of Political Science* 635

Calland, Richard, *Anatomy of South Africa: Who Holds the Power?* (Cape Town: Zebra Press, 2006)

Callinicos, Lulu, *Oliver Tambo: Beyond the Engeli Mountains* (Claremont: David Philip, 2004)

Cameron, Edwin, 'Legal Chauvinism, Executive-Mindedness and Justice: L. C. Steyn's Impact on South African Law' (1982) 99 *South African Law Journal* 38

   'Nude Monarchy: The Case of South Africa's Judges (1987) 3 *South African Journal on Human Rights* 338

Chanock, Martin, *The Making of South African Legal Culture 1902–1936: Fear, Favour and Prejudice* (Cambridge University Press, 2001)

Chaskalson, Arthur, 'From Wickedness to Equality: The Moral Transformation of South African Law' (2003) 1 *International Journal of Constitutional Law* 651

   'Human Dignity as a Foundational Value of Our Constitutional Order' (2000) 16 *South African Journal on Human Rights* 193

   'The Past Ten Years: A Balance Sheet and Some Indicators for the Future' (1989) 5 *South African Journal on Human Rights* 293

Chaskalson, Matthew, 'Stumbling towards Section 28: Negotiations over the Protection of Property Rights in the Interim Constitution' (1995) 11 *South African Journal on Human Rights* 222

   'The Problem with Property: Thoughts on the Constitutional Protection of Property in the United States and the Commonwealth' (1993) 9 *South African Journal on Human Rights* 388

Chavez, Rebecca Bill, 'The Rule of Law and Courts in Democratizing Regimes' in Keith E. Whittington, R. Daniel Kelemen and Gregory A. Caldeira (eds.), *The Oxford Handbook of Law and Politics* (Oxford University Press, 2008) 63

Choudhry, Sujit, '"He Had a Mandate": The South African Constitutional Court and the African National Congress in a Dominant Party Democracy' (2009) 2 *Constitutional Court Review* 1

'Migration as a New Metaphor in Comparative Constitutional Law' in Sujit Choudhry (ed.), *The Migration of Constitutional Ideas* (Cambridge University Press, 2006) 1

Clayton, Cornell W. and Howard Gillman (eds.), *Supreme Court Decision-Making: New Institutionalist Approaches* (University of Chicago Press, 1999)

Clingman, Stephen, *Bram Fischer: Afrikaner Revolutionary* (Cape Town: David Philip, 1998)

Cockrell, Alfred, 'Rainbow Jurisprudence' (1995) 11 *South African Journal on Human Rights* 1

Coleman, Jules L., *The Practice of Principle: In Defense of a Pragmatist Approach to Legal Theory* (Oxford University Press, 2001)

Coleman, Jules L. and Brian Leiter, 'Determinacy, Objectivity and Authority' (1993) 142 *University of Pennsylvania Law Review* 549

Corder, Hugh, 'Establishing Legitimacy for Administrative Justice in South Africa' (1995) 2 *Stellenbosch Law Review* 202

   Judges at Work: The Role and Attitudes of the South African Appellate Judiciary, 1910–50 (Cape Town: Juta, 1984)

Cornell, Drucilla, 'A Call for a More Nuanced Constitutional Jurisprudence: Ubuntu, Dignity and Reconciliation' (2004) 19 *SA Publiekreg/Public Law* 661

Cornell, Drucilla and Nyoko Muvangua, *uBuntu and the Law: African Ideals and Postapartheid Jurisprudence* (Oxford University Press, 2012)

Cotterrell, Roger, 'Law and Culture – Inside and Beyond the Nation State' (2008) 31 *Nordisk Jurisdisk Tidsskrift* 23

   'The Concept of Legal Culture' in David Nelken (ed.), *Comparing Legal Cultures* (Aldershot: Dartmouth, 1997) 13

Couper, Scott, *Albert Luthuli: Bound by Faith* (Scottsville: University of KwaZulu-Natal Press, 2010)

Couso, Javier, 'The Transformation of Constitutional Discourse and the Judicialization of Politics in Latin America' in Javier A. Couso, Alexandra Huneeus and Rachel Sieder (eds.), *Cultures of Legality: Judicialization and Political Activism in Latin America* (Cambridge University Press, 2010) 141

Cover, Robert M., *Justice Accused: Antislavery and the Judicial Process* (New Haven, CT: Yale University Press, 1975)

Craven, Matthew, *The International Covenant on Economic, Social and Cultural Rights* (Clarendon: Oxford, 1995)

Cross, Frank B., *Decision Making in the U.S. Courts of Appeals* (Stanford University Press, 2007)

   'Political Science and the New Legal Realism: A Case of Unfortunate Interdisciplinary Ignorance' (1997) 92 *Northwestern University Law Review* 251

Currie, Iain and Johann de Waal, *The Bill of Rights Handbook* 5th edn (Cape Town: Juta, 2005)

Dahl, Robert A., 'Policy-making in a Democracy: The Supreme Court as a National Policy-maker' (1957) 6 *Journal of Public Law* 279

Danelski, David, 'The Influence of the Chief Justice in the Decisional Process of the Supreme Court', in Walter H. Murphy and C. Herman Pritchett (eds.), *Courts, Judges, and Politics* 2nd edn (New York, NY: Random House, 1974) 525

Davis, Dennis, 'Adjudicating the Socio-economic Rights in the Constitution: Towards "Deference Lite"' (2006) 22 *South African Journal on Human Rights* 301

'The Case against the Inclusion of Socio-economic Demands in a Bill of Rights Except as Directive Principles' (1992) 8 *South African Journal on Human Rights* 475

Davis, Dennis M. and Karl Klare, 'Transformative Constitutionalism and the Common and Customary Law' (2010) 26 *South African Journal on Human Rights* 403

Denzau, Arthur T. and Douglass C. North, 'Shared Mental Models: Ideologies and Institutions' (1994) 47 *Kyklos* 3

De Soto, Hernando, *The Mystery of Capital: Why Capitalism Triumphs in the West and Fails Everywhere Else* (New York, NY: Basic Books, 2000)

Dixon, Rosalind, 'Creating Dialogue about Socioeconomic Rights: Strong-form versus Weak-form Judicial Review Revisited' (2007) 5 *International Journal of Constitutional Law* 391

Dixon, Rosalind and Tom Ginsburg, 'The South African Constitutional Court and Socio-Economic Rights as "Insurance Swaps"' (2012) 4 *Constitutional Court Review* 1

Domingo, Pilar, 'Judicial Independence: The Politics of the Supreme Court in Mexico' (2000) 32 *Journal of Latin American Studies* 704

Dorf, Michael C. and Charles F. Sabel, 'A Constitution of Democratic Experimentalism' (1998) 98 *Columbia Law Review* 267

Du Plessis, Lourens M. and Hugh Corder, *Understanding South Africa's Transitional Bill of Rights* (Cape Town: Juta, 1994)

Du Plessis, Max, 'Between Apology and Utopia – the Constitutional Court and Public Opinion' (2002) 18 *South African Journal on Human Rights* 1

Dubeck, Leslie, 'Understanding "Judicial Lockjaw": The Debate over Extrajudicial Activity' (2007) 82 *New York University Law Review* 569

Dubow, Saul, *The African National Congress* (Stroud: Sutton Publishing, 2000)

Dugard, Jackie, 'Can Human Rights Trump the Commercialization of Water in South Africa? Soweto's Legal Fight for an Equitable Water Policy' (2010) 42 *Review of Radical Political Economics* 175

'Courts and the Poor in South Africa: A Critique of Systemic Judicial Failures to Advance Transformative Justice' (2008) 24 *South African Journal on Human Rights* 214

Dugard, Jackie and Theunis Roux, 'The Record of the South African Constitutional Court in Providing an Institutional Voice for the Poor: 1995–2004' in

Roberto Gargarella, Pilar Domingo and Theunis Roux (eds.), *Courts and Social Transformation in New Democracies: An Institutional Voice for the Poor?* (Dartmouth: Ashgate, 2006) 107

Dugard, John, *Human Rights and the South African Legal Order* (Princeton University Press, 1978)

'Should Judges Resign? A Reply to Professor Wacks' (1984) 101 *South African Law Journal* 286

'The Judicial Process, Positivism and Civil Liberty (1971) 88 *South African Law Journal* 181

Duxbury, Neil, *Patterns of American Jurisprudence* (Oxford: Clarendon Press, 1995)

Dworkin, Ronald, *A Matter of Principle* (Oxford: Clarendon Press, 1986)

Freedom's Law: The Moral Reading of the American Constitution (Cambridge, MA: Harvard University Press, 1996)

'Hart's Postscript and the Character of Political Philosophy' (2004) 24 *Oxford Journal of Legal Studies* 1

Justice in Robes (Cambridge, MA: Harvard University Press, 2006)

'Law's Ambitions for Itself' (1985) 71 *Virginia Law Review* 173

Law's Empire (Cambridge, MA: Harvard University Press, 1986)

'Objectivity and Truth: You'd Better Believe It' (1996) 26 *Philosophy & Public Affairs* 87

'Response to Overseas Commentators' (2003) 1 *International Journal of Constitutional Law* 651

Taking Rights Seriously (Cambridge, MA: Harvard University Press, 1977) 14–45

Dyzenhaus, David, *Hard Cases in Wicked Legal Systems: South African Law in the Perspective of Legal Philosophy* (Oxford: Clarendon Press, 1991)

Judging the Judges, Judging Ourselves: Truth, Reconciliation and the Apartheid Legal Order (Oxford: Hart Publishing, 1998)

'Law's Potential' (1992) 7 *Canadian Journal of Law & Society* 237

'The Disappearance of Law?' (1990) 107 *South African Law Journal* 227

Ebrahim, Hassen, *The Soul of a Nation: Constitution-Making in South Africa* (Cape Town: Oxford University Press, 1998)

Ellmann, Stephen, *In a Time of Trouble: Law and Liberty in South Africa's State of Emergency* (Oxford: Clarendon Press, 1992)

'Learning from "The Making of South African Legal Culture"' (2012) 28 *Law in Context* (forthcoming)

Ely, John Hart, *Democracy and Distrust: A Theory of Judicial Review* (Cambridge, MA: Harvard University Press, 1980)

Epstein, Lee and Jack Knight, *The Choices Justices Make* (Washington, DC: Congressional Quarterly, 1998)

'Toward a Strategic Revolution in Judicial Politics: A Look Back, a Look Ahead' (2000) 53 *Political Research Quarterly* 625

Epstein, Lee, Jack Knight and Olga Shevtsova, 'The Role of Constitutional Courts in the Establishment and Maintenance of Democratic Systems of Government' (2001) 35 *Law & Society Review* 117

Epstein, Lee and Jeffrey A. Segal, 'Measuring Issue Salience' (2000) 44 *American Journal of Political Science* 66

Eskridge, William N., 'Overriding Supreme Court Statutory Interpretation Decisions' (1991) 101 *Yale Law Journal* 331

'Reneging on History? Playing the Court/Congress/President Civil Rights Game' (1991) 79 *California Law Review* 613

Eskridge, William N. and Philip P. Frickey, 'Law as Equilibrium' (1994) 108 *Harvard Law Review* 26

Fallon, Jr, Richard H., 'Legitimacy and the Constitution' (2005) 118 *Harvard Law Review* 1787

'Reflections on the Hart and Wechsler Paradigm' (1994) 47 *Vanderbilt Law Review* 953

Feinstein, Andrew, *After the Party: A Personal and Political Journey inside the ANC* (Johannesburg: Jonathan Ball, 2007)

Ferejohn, John and Barry Weingast, 'A Positive Theory of Statutory Interpretation' (1992) 12 *International Review of Law & Economics* 263

Ferejohn, John, Frances Rosenbluth and Charles Shipan, 'Comparative Judicial Politics' in Charles Boix and Susan C. Stokes (eds.), *The Oxford Handbook of Comparative Politics* (Oxford University Press, 2009) 727

Fiss, Owen, 'The Right Degree of Independence' in Irwin P. Stotzky, *Transition to Democracy in Latin America: The Role of the Judiciary* (Boulder, CO: Westview Press, 1993) 55

Forbath, William, 'Cultural Transformation, Deep Institutional Reform, and ESR Practice: South Africa's Treatment Action Campaign' in Lucie E. White and Jeremy Perelman, *Stones of Hope: How African Activists Reclaim Human Rights to Challenge Global Poverty* (Stanford University Press, 2011) 51

Forde, Fiona, *An Inconvenient Youth: Julius Malema and the 'New' ANC* (Johannesburg: Picador Africa, 2011)

Forsyth, C. F., *In Danger for their Talents: A Study of the Appellate Division of the Supreme Court of South Africa 1950–80* (Cape Town, Juta, 1985)

Forsyth, Christopher and Johann Schiller, 'The Judicial Process, Positivism, and Civil Liberty II' (1981) 98 *South African Law Journal* 218

Fraenkel, Ernst, *The Dual State: A Contribution to the Theory of Dictatorship*, trans. E. A. Shils (New York, NY: Oxford University Press, 1941)

Friedman, Barry, 'Taking Law Seriously' (2006) 4 *Perspectives on Politics* 261

'The History of the Countermajoritarian Difficulty, Part Four: Law's Politics' (2000) 148 *University of Pennsylvania Law Review* 971

'The Politics of Judicial Review' (2005) 84 *Texas Law Review* 257

The Will of the People: How Public Opinion Has Influenced the Supreme Court and Shaped the Meaning of the Constitution (New York, NY: Farrar, Straus and Giroux, 2009)

Friedman, Lawrence M., 'The Concept of a Legal Culture: A Reply' in David Nelken (ed.), *Comparing Legal Cultures* (Aldershot: Dartmouth, 1997) 33

The Legal System: A Social Science Perspective (New York, NY: Russell Sage Foundation, 1975)

Fuller, Lon L., 'Positivism and Fidelity to Law: A Reply to Professor Hart' (1958) 71 *Harvard Law Review* 630

'The Forms and Limits of Adjudication' (1978) 92 *Harvard Law Review* 353

The Morality of Law (New Haven, CT: Yale University Press, 1964)

Galligan, Brian, *The Politics of the High Court* (Brisbane: University of Queensland Press, 1987)

Gevisser, Mark, *The Dream Deferred: Thabo Mbeki* (Johannesburg: Jonathan Ball, 2007)

Gibson, James L., 'The Evolving Legitimacy of the South African Constitutional Court' in François du Bois and Antje du Bois-Pedain (eds.), *Justice and Reconciliation in Post-Apartheid South Africa* (Cambridge University Press, 2008) 229

Gibson, James L. and Gregory A. Caldeira, 'Defenders of Democracy? Legitimacy, Popular Acceptance, and the South African Constitutional Court' (2003) 65 *Journal of Politics* 1

Gibson, James L., Gregory A. Caldeira and Vanessa Baird, 'On the Legitimacy of National High Courts' (1998) 92 *American Political Science Review* 340

Gibson, James L., Gregory A. Caldeira and Lester Kenyatta Spence, 'Measuring Attitudes Toward the United States Supreme Court' (2003) 47 *American Journal of Political Science* 354

Giliomee, Hermann, 'South Africa's Emergent Dominant-Party Regime' (1998) 9(4) *Journal of Democracy* 128

The Afrikaners: Biography of a People (Cape Town: Tafelberg, 2003)

Giliomee, Hermann, James Myburgh and Lawrence Schlemmer, 'Dominant Party Rule, Opposition Parties and Minorities in South Africa' (2001) 8 *Democratization* 161

Giliomee, Hermann and Charles Simkins (eds.), *The Awkward Embrace: One-Party Domination and Democracy* (Cape Town: Tafelberg, 1999)

Gillman, Howard, 'The Court as an Idea, Not a Building (or a Game): Interpretive Institutionalism and the Analysis of Supreme Court Decision-making' in Cornell W. Clayton and Howard Gillman (eds.), *Supreme Court Decision-Making: New Institutionalist Approaches* (University of Chicago Press, 1999) 65

The Votes that Counted: How the Court Decided the 2000 Presidential Election (University of Chicago Press, 2001)

Gillman, Howard and Cornell W. Clayton, 'Beyond Judicial Attitudes: Institutional Approaches to Supreme Court Decision-Making' in Cornell W. Clayton and Howard Gillman (eds.), *Supreme Court Decision-Making: New Institutionalist Approaches* (University of Chicago Press, 1999) 1

Gillman, Howard and Cornell W. Clayton (eds.), *The Supreme Court in American Politics: New Institutionalist Interpretations* (Lawrence, KS: University Press of Kansas, 1999)

Ginsburg, Tom, *Judicial Review in New Democracies: Constitutional Courts in Asian Cases* (Cambridge University Press, 2003)

'The Constitutional Court and the Judicialization of Korean Politics' in Andrew Harding and Penelope Nicholson (eds.), *New Courts in Asia* (London: Routledge, 2009) 113

'The Global Spread of Constitutional Review' in Keith E. Whittington, R. Daniel Kelemen and Gregory A. Caldeira (eds.), *The Oxford Handbook of Law and Politics* (Oxford University Press, 2008) 81

Gloppen, Siri, Robero Gargarella and Elin Skaar (eds.), *Democratization and the Judiciary: The Accountability Function of Courts in New Democracies* (London: Frank Cass, 2002)

Godwin, Peter, *The Fear: The Last Days of Robert Mugabe* (London: Picador, 2010)

Gordin, Jeremy, *Zuma: A Biography* (Johannesburg: Jonathan Ball, 2008)

Greenawalt, Kent, 'Discretion and Judicial Decision: The Elusive Quest for the Fetters that Bind Judges' (1975) 75 *Columbia Law Review* 359

Gumede, William Mervin, *Thabo Mbeki and the Battle for the Soul of the ANC* rev. edn (Cape Town: Zebra Press, 2007)

Hadland, Adrian and Jovial Rantao, *The Life and Times of Thabo Mbeki* (Johannesburg: Zebra Press, 1999)

Hahlo, H. R. and Ellison Kahn, *South Africa: The Development of its Laws and Constitution* (London: Stevens & Sons, 1960)

Halmai, Gábor, 'The Hungarian Approach to Constitutional Review: The End of Activism? The First Decade of the Hungarian Constitutional Court' in Wojciech Sadurski (ed.), *Constitutional Justice, East and West: Democratic Legitimacy and Constitutional Courts in Post-Communist Europe in a Comparative Perspective* (The Hague: Kluwer Law International, 2002) 189

Halpin, Andrew, *Reasoning with Law* (Oxford: Hart Publishing, 2001)

Hart, H. L. A., 'American Jurisprudence through English Eyes: The Nightmare and the Noble Dream' (1977) 11 *Georgia Law Review* 969

Law, Liberty and Morality (Oxford University Press, 1962)

'Positivism and the Separation of Law and Morals' (1958) 71 *Harvard Law Review* 593

The Concept of Law (Oxford: Clarendon Press, 1961)

Hart, Jr, Henry M., 'The Supreme Court, 1958 Term – Forward: The Time Chart of the Justices (1959) 73 *Harvard Law Review* 84

Hart, Jr, Henry M. and Albert M. Sacks, *The Legal Process: Basic Problems in the Making and Application of Law*, ed. William N. Eskridge, Jr and Philip P. Frickey (New York, NY: Foundation Press, 1994)

Haysom, Nicholas, 'Constitutionalism, Majoritarian Democracy and Socio-economic Rights' (1992) 8 *South African Journal on Human Rights* 451

Haysom, Nicholas and Clive Plasket, 'The War Against Law: Judicial Activism and the Appellate Division' (1988) 4 *South African Journal on Human Rights* 303

Haynie, Stacia L., *Judging in Black and White: Decision Making in the South African Appellate Division, 1950–1990* (New York, NY: Peter Lang, 2003)

Helmke, Gretchen, *Courts under Constraints: Judges, Generals, and Presidents in Argentina* (Cambridge University Press, 2005)

Hepple, Bob, 'Book Review of Sandra Liebenberg, *Socio-Economic Rights: Adjudication under a Transformative Constitution*' (2011) 70 *Cambridge Law Journal* 669

Heywood, Mark, 'Contempt or Compliance? The TAC Case After the Constitutional Court Judgment' (2003) 4(1) *ESR Review* 7

'Preventing Mother-to-Child HIV Transmission in South Africa: Background, Strategies and Outcomes of the Treatment Action Campaign Case Against the Minister of Health' (2004) 19 *South African Journal on Human Rights* 278

Hirsch, Alan, *Season of Hope: Economic Reform under Mandela and Mbeki* (Scottsville: University of KwaZulu-Natal Press, 2005)

Hirschl, Ran, *Towards Juristocracy: The Origins and Consequences of the New Constitutionalism* (Cambridge, MA: Harvard University Press, 2004)

Hodder-Williams, Richard, 'Is There a Burger Court?' (1979) 9 *British Journal of Political Science* 173

Hofmeyer, Kate, 'Rules and Procedure in Constitutional Matters' in Woolman et al. (eds.), *Constitutional Law of South Africa* ch 5, 21–9

Hogg, Peter W. and Allison A. Bushell, 'The Charter Dialogue Between Courts and Legislatures (or Perhaps the Charter of Rights Isn't Such a Bad Thing after All)' (1997) 35 *Osgood Hall Law Journal* 76

Holden, Paul, *The Arms Deal in Your Pocket* (Johannesburg: Jonathan Ball, 2008)

Holmes, Stephen, 'Judicial Independence as Ambiguous Reality and Insidious Illusion' in Ronald Dworkin (ed.), *From Liberal Values to Democratic Transition: Essays in Honor of János Kis* (Budapest: Central European University Press, 2004) 3

'Lineages of the Rule of Law' in José María Maravall and Adam Przeworski (eds.), *Democracy and the Rule of Law* (Cambridge University Press, 2003) 19

Huneeus, Alexandra, Javier Couso and Rachel Sieder, 'Cultures of Legality: Judicialization and Political Activism in Latin America' in Javier A, Couso, Alexandra Huneeus and Rachel Sieder (eds.), *Cultures of Legality:*

Judicialization and Political Activism in Latin America (Cambridge University Press, 2010) 3

Hunt, Murray, 'The Human Rights Act and Legal Culture: The Judiciary and the Legal Profession' (1999) 26 *Journal of Law and Society* 86

Issacharoff, Samuel and Richard H. Pildes, 'Politics as Markets: Partisan Lockups of the Democratic Process' (1998) 50 *Stanford Law Review* 643

Jackson, Vicki C., *Constitutional Engagement in a Transnational Era* (Oxford University Press, 2010)

Johnson, R. W., *South Africa's Brave New World: The Beloved Country Since the End of Apartheid* (London: Allen Lane, 2009)

Johnson, R. W. and David Welsh (eds.), *Ironic Victory: Liberalism in Post-Liberation South Africa* (Cape Town: Oxford University Press, 1998) 24

Kairys, David (ed.), *The Politics of Law: A Progressive Critique* 3rd edn (New York, NY: Basic Books, 1997)

Kende, Mark S., *Constitutional Rights in Two Worlds: South Africa and the United States* (Cambridge University Press, 2009)

'The Fifth Anniversary of the South African Constitutional Court: In Defense of Judicial Pragmatism' (2002) 26 *Vermont Law Review* 753

Kennedy, Duncan, *A Critique of Adjudication (Fin de Siècle)* (Cambridge, MA: Harvard University Press, 1998)

Kidd, Michael, 'Internal Security and Specialist Judges: A Study of the Composition of the Appellate Division in Internal Security Cases from 1986 to the Present' (1990) 6 *South African Journal on Human Rights* 417

Klare, Karl E., 'Legal Culture and Transformative Constitutionalism' (1998) 12 *South African Journal on Human Rights* 146

Klug, Heinz, *Constituting Democracy: Law, Globalism and South Africa's Political Reconstruction* (Cambridge University Press, 2000)

'Participating in the Design': Constitution-Making in South Africa' (1996) 3 *Review of Constitutional Studies* 18

The Constitution of South Africa: A Contextual Analysis (Oxford: Hart, 2010)

Knight, Jack and Lee Epstein, 'On the Struggle for Judicial Supremacy' (1996) 30 *Law & Society Review* 87

Kommers, Donald P., *The Constitutional Jurisprudence of the Federal Republic of Germany* (Durham, NC: Duke University Press, 1989)

Kress, Ken, 'Legal Indeterminacy' (1989) 77 *California Law Review* 283

Kritzer, Herbert M., 'Martin Shapiro: Anticipating the New Institutionalism' in Nancy Maveety (ed.), *The Pioneers of Judicial Behavior* (Ann Arbor, MI: University of Michigan Press, 2003) 387

Krygier, Martin, 'Institutional Optimism, Cultural Pessimism and the Rule of Law' in Martin Krygier and Adam Czarnota (eds.), *The Rule of Law after Communism* (Aldershot: Ashgate/Dartmouth, 1999) 77

Kurkchiyan, Marina, 'Russian Legal Culture: An Analysis of Adaptive Response to an Institutional Transplant' (2009) 34 *Law & Social Inquiry* 337

Laurence, Patrick, 'Liberalism and Politics' in R. W. Johnson and David Welsh (eds.), *Ironic Victory: Liberalism in Post-Liberation South Africa* (Cape Town: Oxford University Press, 1998) 45

Leiter, Brian, 'Legal Indeterminacy' (1995) 1 *Legal Theory* 481

'Positivism, Formalism, Realism' (1999) 99 *Columbia Law Review* 1138

'The End of Empire: Dworkin and Jurisprudence in the 21st Century' (2004) 36 *Rutgers Law Journal* 165

Leon, Tony, 'Etienne Mureinik's Role in Securing and Constitutionalising the Independence of the Universities and Judicial Selection' (1998) 14 *South African Journal on Human Rights* 190

Lewis, Carole, 'Reaching the Pinnacle: Principles, Policies and People for a Single Apex Court in South Africa' (2005) 21 *South African Journal on Human Rights* 509

Liebenberg, Sandra, 'Interpretation of Socio-economic Rights' in Matthew Chaskalson, Janet Kentridge, Jonathan Klaaren and Gilbert Marcus (eds.), *Constitutional Law of South Africa* (Cape Town: Juta, 1999) ch 33

Socio-Economic Rights: Adjudication under a Transformative Constitution (Cape Town: Juta, 2010)

Lodge, Tom, *Black Politics in South Africa Since 1945* (London: Longman, 1983)

Mandela: A Critical Life (Oxford University Press, 2006)

'The South African Local Government Elections of December 2000' (2001) 28 *Politikon* 21

Llewellyn, Karl, *The Common Law Tradition: Deciding Appeals* (Boston: Little, Brown, 1960)

Mackie, John, 'The Third Theory of Law' in Marshall Cohen (ed.), *Ronald Dworkin and Contemporary Jurisprudence* (Totowa, NJ: Rowman & Allanheld, 1983) 161

Mandela, Nelson, *Long Walk to Freedom: The Autobiography of Nelson Mandela* (London: Abacus, 1995)

Marais, Hein, *South Africa Pushed to the Limit: The Political Economy of Change* (Claremont: University of Cape Town Press, 2011)

March, J. G. and J. P. Olsen, 'The New Institutionalism: Organisational Factors in Political Life' (1984) 78 *American Political Science Review* 734

Marcus, Gilbert and Steven Budlender, *A Strategic Evaluation of Public Interest Litigation in South Africa* (Johannesburg: Atlantic Philanthropies, 2008)

Mather, Lynn, 'Law and Society' in Keith E. Whittington, R. Daniel Kelemen and Gregory A. Caldeira (eds.), *The Oxford Handbook of Law and Politics* (Oxford University Press, 2008) 681

Maveety, Nancy, 'The Study of Judicial Behavior and the Discipline of Political Science' in Nancy Maveety (ed.), *The Pioneers of Judicial Behavior* (Ann Arbor, MI: University of Michigan Press, 2003) 1

McKinley, Dale T., *The ANC and the Liberation Struggle: A Critical Political Biography* (London: Pluto Press, 1997)

McLean, Kirsty, *Constitutional Deference, Courts and Socio-Economic Rights in South Africa* (Pretoria University Law Press, 2009)

Mehta, Pratap Bhanu, 'India's Unlikely Democracy: The Rise of Judicial Sovereignty' (2007) 18 *Journal of Democracy* 70

Meierhenrich, Jens, *The Legacies of Law: Long-Run Consequences of Legal Development in South Africa, 1652–2000* (Cambridge University Press, 2008)

Michelman, Frank I., 'Foreword: Traces of Self-Government' (1986) 100 *Harvard Law Review* 4

  'The Constitution, Social Rights and Reason: A Tribute to Etienne Mureinik' (1998) 14 *South African Journal on Human Rights* 499

  'The Rule of Law, Legality and the Supremacy of the Constitution' in Stu Woolman, Theunis Roux and Michael Bishop (eds.), *Constitutional Law of South Africa* 2nd edn (Cape Town: Juta, 2006) ch 11

Moellendorf, Darrel, 'Reasoning about Resources: *Soobramoney* and the Future of Socio-economic Rights' (1998) 14 *South African Journal on Human Rights* 327

Moseneke, Dikgang, '*Striking a Balance Between the Will of the People and the Supremacy of the Constitution*' (Claude Leon Public Lecture, University of Cape Town, 29 September 2011)

Moustafa, Tamir, 'Law versus the State: The Judicialization of Politics in Egypt' (2003) 28 *Law & Social Inquiry* 883

Mureinik, Etienne, 'Beyond a Charter of Luxuries: Economic Rights in the Constitution' (1992) 8 *South African Journal on Human Rights* 464

  'Dworkin and Apartheid' in Hugh Corder (ed.), *Essays on Law and Social Practice in South Africa* (Cape Town: Juta, 1988) 181

  'Pursuing Principle: The Appellate Division and Review under the State of Emergency' (1989) 5 *South African Journal on Human Rights* 60

Murphy, Walter, *Elements of Judicial Strategy* (University of Chicago Press, 1964)

Nelken, David, 'Using the Concept of Legal Culture' (2004) 29 *Australian Journal of Legal Philosophy* 1

Nonet, Philippe and Philip Selznick, *Toward Responsive Law: Law and Society in Transition* (New Brunswick, NJ: Transaction Publishers, 2001)

O'Malley, Padraig, *Shades of Difference: Mac Maharaj and the Struggle for South Africa* (London: Penguin, 2007)

O'Regan, Kate, 'On the Reach of the Constitution and the Nature of Constitutional Jurisdiction: A Response to Frank Michelman' in Stu Woolman and Michael Bishop (eds.), *Constitutional Conversations* (Pretoria University Press, 2008) 63

Patapan, Haig, 'High Court Review 2001: Politics, Legalism and the Gleeson Court' (2002) 37 *Australian Journal of Political Science* 241

'High Court Review 2002: The Least Dangerous Branch' (2003) 38 *Australian Journal of Political Science* 299

Judging Democracy: The New Politics of the High Court of Australia (Cambridge University Press, 2000)

Peller, Gary, '"Neutral Principles" in the 1950s' (1988) 21 *University of Michigan Journal of Law Reform* 561

Perry, H. W., Jr., *Deciding to Decide: Agenda Setting in the United States Supreme Court* (Cambridge, MA: Harvard University Press, 1991)

Pierce, Jason L., *Inside the Mason Court Revolution: The High Court of Australia Transformed* (Durham, NC: Carolina Academic Press, 2006)

Pieterse, Marius, 'Coming to Terms with Judicial Enforcement of Socio-economic Rights' (2004) 20 *South African Journal on Human Rights* 383

   'Resuscitating Socio-economic Rights: Constitutional Entitlements to Health Care Services' (2006) 22 *South African Journal on Human Rights* 473

Posner, Richard A., *Law, Pragmatism, and Democracy* (Cambridge, MA: Harvard University Press, 2003)

Post, Robert and Reva Siegel 'Roe Rage: Democratic Constitutionalism and Backlash' (2007) 42 *Harvard Civil Rights–Civil Liberties Law Review* 373

Pottinger, Brian, *The Mbeki Legacy* (Cape Town: Zebra Press, 2008)

Pritchett, C. Herman, *The Roosevelt Court: A Study in Judicial Politics and Values, 1937–1947* (New York, NY: Macmillan, 1948)

Ramseyer, J. Mark, 'The Puzzling (In) dependence of Courts: A Comparative Approach' (1994) 23 *Journal of Legal Studies* 721

Ray, Laura Krugman, 'The Road to *Bush v Gore*: The History of the Supreme Court's Use of the Per Curiam Opinion' (2000) 79 *Nebraska Law Review* 517

Raz, Joseph, *Ethics in the Public Domain: Essays in the Morality of Law and Politics* (Oxford: Clarendon Press, 1994)

   'Legal Principles and the Limits of Law' (1972) 81 *Yale Law Journal* 823

   'On the Authority and Interpretation of Constitutions: Some Preliminaries' in Larry Alexander (ed.), *Constitutionalism: Philosophical Foundations* (Cambridge University Press, 1998) 152

   'Postema on Law's Autonomy and Public Practical Reasons: A Critical Comment' (1998) 4 *Legal Theory* 1

Robertson, David, *The Judge as Political Theorist: Contemporary Constitutional Review* (Princeton University Press, 2010) 226–80

Roux, Theunis, 'Democracy' in Stu Woolman, Theunis Roux and Michael Bishop (eds.), *Constitutional Law of South Africa* 2nd edn (Cape Town: Juta, 2006)

   'Legitimating Transformation: Political Resource Allocation in the South African Constitutional Court' (2003) 10 *Democratization* 92

   'Principle and Pragmatism on the Constitutional Court of South Africa' (2009) 7 *International Journal of Constitutional Law* 106

'Property' in Stu Woolman, Theunis Roux and Michael Bishop (eds.), *Constitutional Law of South Africa* 2nd edn (Cape Town: Juta, 2002) ch 46

'The Arbitrariness Vortex: Constitutional Property Law after *FNB*' in Stu Woolman and Michael Bishop (eds.), *Constitutional Conversations* (Pretoria University Press, 2008)

'The Constitutional Value System and Social Values in South Africa' in András Sajó and Renáta Uitz (eds.), *Constitutional Topography: Values and Constitutions* (The Hague: Eleven International Publishing, 2010)

'The South African Constitutional Court and the Hlophe Controversy' paper presented at the Centre for Comparative Studies 21st Anniversary Celebration, *International and Comparative Perspectives on Constitutional Law*, Melbourne (November 2009)

'Transformative Constitutionalism and the Best Interpretation of the South African Constitution: Distinction without a Difference?' (2009) 20 *Stellenbosch Law Review* 258

'Turning a Deaf Ear: The Right to be Heard by the Constitutional Court' (1997) 13 *South African Journal on Human Rights* 216

'Understanding *Grootboom*: A Response to Cass R. Sunstein' (2002) 12 *Constitutional Forum* 41

Sachs, Albie, 'A Bill of Rights for South Africa: Areas of Agreement and Disagreement' (1989) 21 *Columbia Human Rights Law Review* 13

Advancing Human Rights in South Africa (Oxford University Press, 1992)

Justice in South Africa (Berkeley, CA: University of California Press, 1973)

Protecting Human Rights in a New South Africa (Oxford University Press, 1990)

The Strange Alchemy of Life and Law (Oxford University Press, 2009) 165–73

'Towards a Bill of Rights for a Democratic South Africa' (1990) 6 *South African Journal on Human Rights* 1

Sachs, Albie and Gita Honwana Welsh, *Liberating the Law: Creating Popular Justice in Mozambique* (London: Zed Books, 1990)

Sadurski, Wojciech, *Rights Before Courts: A Study of Constitutional Courts in Postcommunist States of Central and Eastern Europe* (Dordrecht: Springer, 2005)

Sajó, András, 'Reading the Invisible Constitution: Judicial Review in Hungary' (1995) 15 *Oxford Journal of Legal Studies* 253

Sampson, Anthony, *Mandela: The Authorised Biography* (London: Harper Collins, 1999) 95

Sarat, Austin, 'Studying American Legal Culture: An Assessment of Survey Evidence' (1977) 11 *Law & Society Review* 427

Saunders, Cheryl, 'The Use and Misuse of Comparative Constitutional Law' (2006) 13 *Indiana Journal of Global Legal Studies* 37

Savage, Katharine, 'Negotiating South Africa's New Constitution: An Overview of the Key Players and the Negotiation Process', in Penelope Andrews and

Stephen Ellmann (eds.), *The Post-Apartheid Constitutions: Perspectives on South Africa's Basic Law* (Johannesburg: Witwatersrand University Press, 2001) 164, 164 n 2

Scalia, Antonin, *A Matter of Interpretation* (Princeton University Press, 1996)
'Originalism: The Lesser Evil' (1989) 57 *University of Cincinnati Law Review* 849

Schauer, Frederick, 'Easy Cases' (1985) 58 *Southern California Law Review* 399
Playing by the Rules: A Philosophical Examination of Rule-Based Decision-Making in Law and Life (Oxford: Clarendon Press, 1991)
Thinking Like a Lawyer (Cambridge, MA: Harvard University Press, 2009)

Scheppele, Kim Lane, 'Guardians of the Constitution: Constitutional Court Presidents and the Struggle for the Rule of Law in Post-Soviet Europe' (2006) 154 *University of Pennsylvania Law Review* 1757

Schubert, Glendon A., *Judicial Policy Making: The Political Role of the Courts* (Glenview, IL: Scott, Foresman, 1974)
'The Dimensions of Decisional Response: Opinion and Voting Behavior of the Australian High Court' in Joel Grossmann and Joseph Tanenhaus (eds.), *The Frontiers of Judicial Research* (New York, NY: Wiley, 1968)
The Judicial Mind: The Attitudes and Ideologies of Supreme Court Justices, 1946–1963 (Evanston, IL: Northwestern University Press, 1965)
'Two Causal Models of Decision-Making by the High Court of Australia' in Glendon Schubert and David J. Danelski (eds.), *Comparative Judicial Behavior: Cross-Cultural Studies of Political Decision-Making in the East and West* (New York, NY: Oxford University Press, 1969) 335

Schwartz, Herman, *The Struggle for Constitutional Justice in Post-Communist Europe* (University of Chicago Press, 2000)

Scott, Craig and Philip Alston, 'Adjudicating Constitutional Priorities in a Transnational Context: A Comment on *Soobramoney*'s Legacy and *Grootboom*'s Promise' (2000) 16 *South African Journal on Human Rights* 206

Scott, Craig and Patrick Macklem, 'Ropes of Sand or Justiciable Guarantees: Social Rights in a New South African Constitution' (1992) 141 *University of Pennsylvania Law Review* 1

Sebok, Anthony, *Legal Positivism in American Jurisprudence* (New York, NY: Cambridge University Press, 1998)

Seedorf, Sebastian, 'Jurisdiction' in Stu Woolman, Theunis Roux and Michael Bishop (eds.), *Constitutional Law of South Africa* 2nd edn (Cape Town: Juta, 2002) ch 12

Segal, Jeffrey A., 'Separation-of-Powers Games in the Positive Theory of Congress and Courts' (1997) 91 *American Political Science Review* 28
'Supreme Court Deference to Congress: An Examination of the Marksist Model' in Cornell W. Clayton and Howard Gillman (eds.), *Supreme Court Decision-Making: New Institutionalist Approaches* (University of Chicago Press, 1999) 237

Segal, Jeffrey A. and Harold J. Spaeth, *The Supreme Court and the Attitudinal Model Revisited* (New York, NY: Cambridge University Press, 2002)

Shapiro, Ian and Courtney Jung, 'South Africa's Negotiated Transition: Democracy, Opposition, and the New Constitutional Order' (1995) 23 *Politics and Society* 269

Shapiro, Martin, *Courts: A Comparative and Political Analysis* (University of Chicago Press, 1981)

'Judicial Review in Developed Democracies' (2003) 10 *Democratization* 7, 8–12

Law and Politics in the Supreme Court: New Approaches to Political Jurisprudence (New York, NY: Free Press, 1964)

'Morality and the Politics of Judging' (1989) 63 *Tulane Law Review* 1555

'Political Jurisprudence' (1964) 52 *Kentucky Law Review* 294

'Some Conditions for the Success of Constitutional Courts: Lessons from the U.S. Experience' in Wojciech Sadurski (ed.), *Constitutional Justice, East and West: Democratic Legitimacy and Constitutional Courts in Post-Communist Europe in a Comparative Perspective* (The Hague: Kluwer Law International, 2002) 37

'Whither Political Jurisprudence: A Symposium' (1984) 36 *Western Political Quarterly* 533

Silbey, Susan S., 'Legal Culture and Legal Consciousness' in Neil J. Smelser and Paul B. Baltes (eds.), *International Encyclopaedia of the Social & Behavioural Sciences* (Amsterdam: Elsevier, 2001) 8623

Slotnick, Elliot E., 'The Chief Justices and Self-assignment of Majority Opinions: A Research Note' (1978) 31 *The Western Political Quarterly* 219

Smith, Rogers M., 'Historical Institutionalism and the Study of Law' in Keith E. Whittington, R. Daniel Kelemen and Gregory A. Caldeira (eds.), *The Oxford Handbook of Law and Politics* (Oxford University Press, 2008) 46

Snyder, Eloise C., 'The Supreme Court as a Small Group' (1958) 36 *Social Forces* 232

Solum, Lawrence B., 'On the Indeterminacy Crisis: Critiquing Critical Dogma' (1987) 54 *University of Chicago Law Review* 462

Sólyom, László and Georg Brunner (eds.), *Constitutional Judiciary in a New Democracy: The Hungarian Constitutional Court* (Ann Arbor, MI: University of Michigan Press, 2000)

South African Law Commission, *Project 58 – Group and Human Rights: Interim Report* (1991)

Southall, Roger, 'Opposition in South Africa: Issues and Problems' (2001) 8 *Democratization* 1

'The Centralization and Fragmentation of South Africa's Dominant Party System' (1998) 97 *African Affairs* 443

Spitz, Richard with Matthew Chaskalson, *The Politics of Transition: A Hidden History of South Africa's Negotiated Settlement* (Oxford: Hart Publishing, 2000)

Spriggs II, James F., Forrest Maltzman and Paul J. Wahlbeck, 'Bargaining on the U.S. Supreme Court: Justices' Responses to Majority Opinion Drafts' (1999) 61 *Journal of Politics* 485

Staton, Jeffrey K., *Judicial Power and Strategic Communication in Mexico* (Cambridge University Press, 2010)

Steinberg, Carol, 'Can Reasonableness Protect the Poor? A Review of South Africa's Socio-economic Rights Jurisprudence' (2006) 123 *South African Law Journal* 264

Stephenson, Matthew C., '"When the Devil Turns": The Political Foundations of Independent Judicial Review' (2003) 32 *Journal of Legal Studies* 59

Stone Sweet, Alec, *Governing with Judges: Constitutional Politics in Europe* (Oxford University Press, 2000)

Stotzky, Irwin P. (ed.), *Transition to Democracy in Latin America: The Role of the Judiciary* (Baltimore, MD: Johns Hopkins University Press, 1993)

Sunstein, Cass R., 'Against Positive Rights' in András Sajó (ed.), *Western Rights? Post-Communist Application* (The Hague: Kluwer Law International, 1996) 225

   Designing Democracy: What Constitutions Do (New York, NY: Oxford University Press, 2001)

   Legal Reasoning and Political Conflict (Cambridge, MA: Harvard University Press, 1995)

   One Case at a Time: Judicial Minimalism on the Supreme Court (Cambridge, MA: Harvard University Press 1999)

   'Social and Economic Rights? Lessons from South Africa' (2000/2011) 11 *Constitutional Forum* 123

Sunstein, Cass R., David Schkade, Lisa M. Ellman and Andres Sawicki, *Are Judges Political? An Empirical Analysis of the Federal Judiciary* (Washington, DC: Brookings Institution Press, 2006)

Suttner, Raymond, 'Party Dominance "Theory": Of What Value?' 2006 (33) *Politikon* 277

Tamanaha, Brian Z., *Beyond the Formalist-Realist Divide: The Role of Politics in Judging* (Princeton University Press, 2010)

   Law as a Means to an End: Threat to the Rule of Law (Cambridge University Press, 2006)

Tate, C. Neal, 'The Literature of Comparative Judicial Politics: A 118 Year Survey' (2002) 12(2) *Law & Courts* 3 and (2002) 12(3) *Law & Courts* 3

Teitel, Ruti, 'Transitional Jurisprudence: The Role of Law in Political Transformation' (1997) 106 *Yale Law Journal* 2009

Thompson, Leonard, *A History of South Africa* rev. edn (New Haven, CT: Yale University Press, 1995)

Tushnet, Mark, *Weak Courts, Strong Rights: Judicial Review and Social Welfare Rights in Comparative Constitutional Law* (Princeton University Press, 2008)

Van der Schyff, Gerhard, *Limitations of Rights: A Study of the European Convention and South African Bills of Rights* (Nijmegen: Wold Legal Publishers, 2005)

Van der Walt, A. J., *The Constitutional Property Clause: A Comparative Analysis of Section 25 of the South African Constitution of 1996* (Cape Town: Juta, 1997)

Constitutional Property Law 3rd edn (Cape Town: Juta, 2011)

Vanberg, Georg, 'Establishing and Maintaining Judicial Independence' in Keith E. Whittington, R. Daniel Kelemen and Gregory A. Caldeira (eds.), *The Oxford Handbook of Law and Politics* (Oxford University Press, 2008) 99

The Politics of Constitutional Review in Germany (Cambridge University Press, 2005)

Vigne, Randolph, *Liberals Against Apartheid: A History of the Liberal Party of South Africa, 1953–68* (Basingstoke: Macmillan, 1997)

Wacks, Raymond, 'Judges and Injustice' (1984) 101 *South African Law Journal* 266

Wahlbeck, Paul J., James F. Spriggs II, Forrest Maltzman, 'The Politics of Dissents and Concurrences on the U.S. Supreme Court' (1999) 27 *American Politics Research* 488

Waldron, Jeremy, *Law and Disagreement* (Oxford University Press, 1999)

'The Core of the Case Against Judicial Review' (2006) 115 *Yale Law Journal* 1346

Waluchow, W. J., *A Common Law Theory of Judicial Review: The Living Tree* (Cambridge University Press, 2007)

Inclusive Legal Positivism (Oxford: Clarendon Press, 1994)

Weber, Max, *Economy and Society: An Outline of Interpretive Sociology*, ed. Guenther Roth and Claus Wittich (Berkeley, CA: University of California Press, 1978)

Wechsler, Herbert, 'Toward Neutral Principles of Constitutional Law' (1959) 73 *Harvard Law Review* 1

Weingast, Barry, 'The Political Foundations of Democracy and the Rule of Law' (1997) 91 *American Political Science Review* 245

Wellman, Vincent A., 'Dworkin and the Legal Process Tradition: The Legacy of Hart & Sacks' (1987) 29 *Arizona Law Review* 413

Wesson, Murray, '*Grootboom* and Reassessing the Socio-economic Jurisprudence of the South African Constitutional Court' (2004) 20 *South African Journal on Human Rights* 284

Whittington, Keith E., 'Constitutionalism' in Keith E. Whittington, R. Daniel Kelemen and Gregory A. Caldeira (eds.), *The Oxford Handbook of Law and Politics* (Oxford University Press, 2008) 281

'Legislative Sanctions and the Strategic Environment of Judicial Review' (2003) 1 *International Journal of Constitutional Law* 446

'Once More unto the Breach: PostBehavioralist Approaches to Judicial Politics' (2000) 25 *Law & Social Inquiry* 601

Political Foundations of Judicial Supremacy: The Presidency, the Supreme Court, and Constitutional Leadership in U.S. History (Princeton University Press, 2007)

Widner, Jennifer, *Building the Rule of Law: Francis Nyalali and the Road to Judicial Independence in Africa* (New York, NY: W. W. Norton, 2001)

'Courts and Democracy in Postconflict Transitions: A Social Scientist's Perspective on the African Case' (2001) 95 *American Journal of International Law* 64

Wilson, Richard A., *The Politics of Truth and Reconciliation in South Africa: Legitimizing the Post-Apartheid State* (Cambridge University Press, 2001)

Woolman, Stu and Henk Botha, *'Limitations' in Stu Woolman*, Theunis Roux and Michael Bishop (eds.), *Constitutional Law of South Africa* 2nd edn (Cape Town: Juta, 2006) ch 34

Yepes, Rodrigo Uprimny, 'The Enforcement of Social Rights by the Colombian Constitutional Court: Cases and Debates' in Roberto Gargarella, Pilar Domingo and Theunis Roux (eds.), *Courts and Social Transformation in New Democracies: An Institutional Voice for the Poor?* (Dartmouth: Ashgate, 2006) 127

Young, Katharine G., 'A Typology of Economic and Social Rights Adjudication: Exploring the Catalytic Function of Judicial Review' (2010) 8 *International Journal of Constitutional Law* 385

Zlotnick, Myron, 'The Death Penalty and Public Opinion' (1996) 12 *South African Journal on Human Rights* 70

INDEX

Note: Chaskalson Court is often shortened to 'Court' in subheading entries.